THE INSIDERS' GUIDE®
TO
Richmond

THE INSIDERS' GUIDE® TO

Richmond

by
Paula Kripaitis Neely
and
Michael Ryan Croxton

The Insiders' Guide®
An imprint of Falcon® Publishing, Inc.
A Landmark Communications Company
P.O. Box 1718
Helena, MT 59624
(800) 582-2665
www.insiders.com

Sales and Marketing: Falcon Publishing, Inc.
P.O. Box 1718
Helena, MT 59624
(800) 582-2665
www.falconguide.com

•

SEVENTH EDITION
First Printing

•

© 1999
by Falcon Publishing, Inc.

•

Printed in the
United States of America

•

Publications from The Insiders' Guide® series are available at special discounts for bulk purchases for sale promotions, premiums or fundraisings. Special editions, including personalized covers, can be created in large quantities for special needs. For more information, please contact Falcon Publishing.

ISBN 1-57380-097-X

Preface

If you're a newcomer or a visitor, we hope this book will help you discover our city with the ease and confidence of an experienced resident. If you've lived here long enough to be an Insider, you may find, as we did, that the guide will give you a more complete understanding of the city and all that it offers. Some chapters may even help put current events in better perspective. This guide is also handy to have when you're entertaining guests from out of town.

As we researched this book, we found that there is far more in this city than we ever imagined, from alternative healers and paint-ball courses to "cyber"-restaurants and inner-city driving ranges. And, having both lived here for more than 20 years, we've learned that you'll never have time to do it all. But it's all here in case you'd care to try.

Although we tried to include everything that we thought should be included in this book, we were quickly overwhelmed by the sheer volume of what there is to mention. So, if you don't see your favorite place or event listed here, it may be because we had to make some tough choices about what to include — or, and we're only human, maybe a few great finds have eluded us. When we publish the next edition, we will undoubtedly include some different places, and we welcome your ideas about what you would like to see in these pages. Just send a letter to Insiders' Guides Inc. P.O. Box 2057 or visit *The Insiders' Guide® to Richmond* online at www.insiders.com. There's a comment response card in the back of this book and at the web site. We'd love to hear from you. Enjoy your time in Richmond.

About the Authors

Paula Kripaitis Neely

Paula Kripaitis Neely is a freelance writer and public relations consultant who has lived in Richmond since 1972. She established Neely Communications in 1989 and assists a variety of clients with publications, media relations and special events. Her work has appeared in numerous regional and national publications, and she's received a string of awards from Press Women International, the International Association of Business Communicators and the Virginia Public Relations Association.

A graduate of Virginia Commonwealth University, she has held marketing and public relations management positions with the Science Museum of Virginia and the Virginia Department of Motor Vehicles. A Delaware native, she enjoys living in the Old Church area of Hanover County with her children — Brian, Laura and Sarah — and her husband Richard, a native Richmonder whose considerable knowledge about the area helped make this book possible.

Michael Ryan Croxton

Born of native-Richmond form-fit mattress tycoons, Michael Ryan Croxton has lived a life of bedded luxury, with little want — especially want of a better hometown. This satisfaction comes not from sheltered ignorance. Throughout his meandering experience, which has led him to the far corners of the world (Mississippi and New York), nothing has yet stolen or even tapped his affection for Richmond, and it seems likely, nothing will.

Upon resettling in Richmond, Michael set to fulfilling some personal aspirations. Upset with the current music trend — the melancholy mantra of grunge and gansta rap — Michael and cofounder Balyan Pounds created Happy Records®, a record label with the charge of placing the musical Zeitgeist on a happy tack. Happy Records® debuted with the Happy Scene release, *Take My Teenage Head*. It was to be followed by the jangly pop rhythms of The Godfathers of Popcorn Punk, in their self-titled release. Currently in the works is the soon to be released Lane Vine's EP *I Got a Car. I Got a Girl*.

A hotel-lounge comic by night and a freelance writer and editor by day, Michael has done work for Richmond ad agencies, local newspapers and the adventure guidebook publishing company Beachway Press.

Editors' Note:

The editors of this book would like to thank Andi Lucas, a Richmond writer and editor, for updating *The Insiders' Guide to Richmond* for this 7th edition.

Acknowledgements

John Albers, City of Richmond
Jadian Altemus
Arts Council of Richmond
Ashland Hanover Chamber of Commerce
Windsor Barnett
Barbara Batson
William H. Baxter, Retail Merchants Association of Greater Richmond
Virginia Tourism Development Group
Chesterfield County Information Office
Chesterfield County Recreation and Parks Department
Chesterfield County Schools
David Clinger
Virginius Dabney's *Richmond: The Story of a City*
George and Teresa Davis
Downtown Presents . . .
Phil DuHamel
Gracie Fauntleroy
Robert Ferrell
Fredericksburg Department of Tourism
Kelly Gravely
Greater Richmond Chamber of Commerce
Greater Richmond Partnership Inc.
Hanover County Economic Development Office
Hanover County Recreation and Parks Department
Hanover County Schools
Herald-Progress Newspaper
Henrico County Industrial Development Authority
Henrico County Recreation and Parks Department
Henrico County Schools
Historic Richmond Foundation
Carolyn and Robert Kripaitis
Barbara Lee Kruger, Capital Area Agency on Aging

Elaine Lidholm
John Markon
Maymont Foundation
Downtown Richmond, Inc.
Metro Richmond Convention and Visitors Bureau
Pamela Michael
Pauline Mitchell
Tyler C. Millner
Pauline Mitchell
Ethel and Richard Neely
Richard, Brian, Laura and Sarah Neely
Ashley Neville
Virginia Wine Marketing Program, Virginia Department of Agriculture and Consumer Services
Margaret Peters, Virginia Department of Historic Resources
Petersburg Visitors Center
George Peyton, Retail Merchants Association of Greater Richmond
Richmond Department of Parks, Recreation and Community Facilities
Richmond Public Schools
Steve Row
Sarah C. Ruffin
James K. Sanford's *Richmond: Her Triumphs, Tragedies & Growth*
David Slonaker
Staff, Richmond Times-Dispatch Library
James K. Schultz's *Richmond: A River City Reborn*
Fritta Spencer
Mat Taylor
Maggi Tinsley and the staff of the Valentine Museum
Harry Ward's *Richmond: An Illustrated History*
Ralph White
And various other trusted friends and confidants.

Table of Contents

Directory of Maps

Richmond

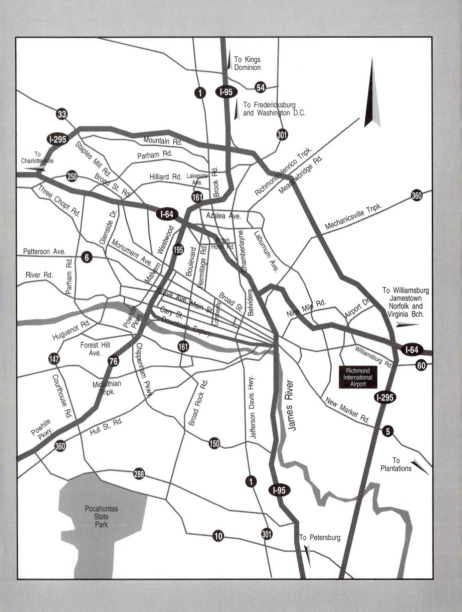

Greater Richmond

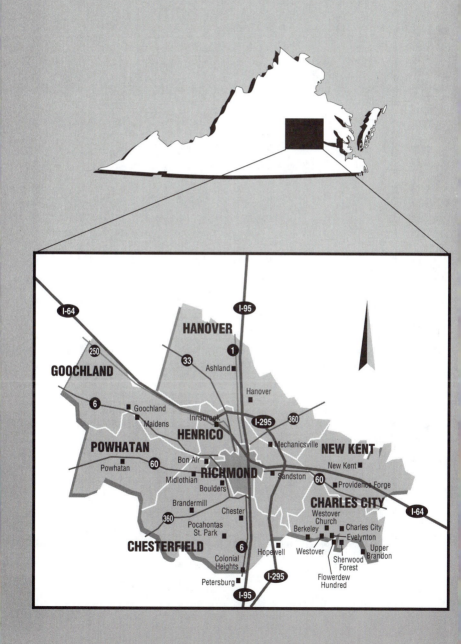

Downtown Richmond

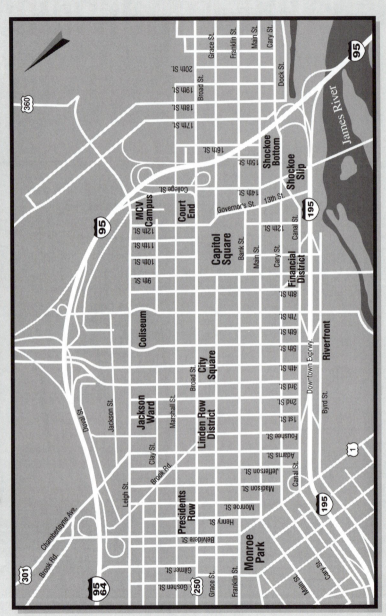

History

It used to be said that Richmond, like Rome, was built on seven hills.

You don't hear this much anymore, maybe because no one could ever agree on what hills were supposed to be part of this comparison with the Eternal City. Among those most frequently mentioned are nine: Church Hill, Gamble's Hill, Oregon Hill, Shockoe Hill, Libby Hill, Chimborazo Hill, Navy Hill, Union Hill and Maddox Hill.

Perhaps the comparison developed because a building of Roman Imperial architecture — the State Capitol — sat atop one of the hills and dominated the skyline in early lithographs. Its architect, Thomas Jefferson, modeled it after Maison Carree, a Roman temple at Nimes, France, which he found to be "one of the most beautiful, if not the most beautiful and precious morsel of architecture left to us by antiquity." His only change from the original was to make the Capitol's columns Ionic instead of Corinthian.

Charles Dickens, when he visited Richmond in 1842, counted neither seven nor nine hills, but eight. "We rode and walked about the town, which is delightfully situated on eight hills, overhanging the James River; a sparkling stream, studded here and there with bright islands, or brawling over rocks," he later wrote in his *American Notes*.

It may be the city's enduring physical beauty, to which Dickens alludes, that has given it such eternal appeal.

The thing that strikes most visitors is the number of trees and parks; indeed, Richmond has an exceedingly large number of them. Then there is the city's human scale and easygoing lifestyle, things it has managed to retain along with an architectural treasure-trove that makes every walking tour a delight. History plays its role at every turn and, like many Richmonders, you soon may find yourself talking about epic events of the past almost as if they happened yesterday.

Triassic Beginnings

Richmond, the historic city, traces its origins to massive rock formations (visible amid rapids in the James River) that once were part of Africa.

Recent discoveries place the Richmond Basin in a geological period called Triassic, about 210 million years ago. Back then, the North American and African continental tectonic plates were welded together but beginning to pull apart, thus creating the Atlantic Ocean. The African plate was pushed and pulled down into the earth's mantle and, as the rock heated from the friction and pressure, sediments of the African crust melted and squeezed upward into the crust of the North American plate through deep faults or cracks.

In cutting across this rock fall zone, the James River drops some 100 feet in 7 miles, reaching sea level at Richmond's 14th Street bridge. It is here that the character of the river changes from rapids, which at times are robust enough for Class V whitewater rafting, to a meandering tidal estuary.

It is this natural geological feature that attracted Native Americans. They built their settlement of Powhatan Village on what today is Fulton Hill.

Settling the City

It was this same feature that attracted the first English explorers in 1607, less than 10 days after they landed at Jamestown. They had sailed up the river looking for a route to the East India Sea. Here, at the falls of the river, they were struck by the potential of the rapids to operate water wheels. Grist and flour mills were vital to the economy of the time, as were sawmills, and the first report by Capt. Christopher Newport to King James emphasized the possibilities of harnessing the power of the rapids. The river also offered a navigable route from the Atlantic Ocean to the interior of the new land and easy transport for goods produced along the river's edge.

Richmond thus became the site of one of the first English settlements in America. It was here that the first hospital in America was established, and plans were laid for a great university although it was never built. The first tobacco, iron and coal produced in America, as well as timber, formed the backbone of the economy.

Great plantation homes, many still standing today, were built along the James, and present-day Richmond was laid out in 1737 — named for Richmond-on-the-Thames in Surrey County, England. French Huguenots had settled in the area earlier, and in the late 1730s there was an effort to attract German immigrants. One, Jacob Ege, a Wurttemberger, built a stone house, the oldest building still standing in Richmond, on Main Street between 19th and 20th streets.

Revolutionary War

It was on Church Hill at St. John's Church, before an assembly that included George Washington and Thomas Jefferson, that Patrick Henry spoke 47 unforgettable words: "Why stand we here idle? Is life so dear and peace so sweet as to be purchased at the price of chains and slavery? Forbid it, Almighty God! I know not what course others may take; but as for me, give me liberty or give me death!"

The shot heard round the world was fired 30 days later at Concord, Massachusetts.

As the Revolutionary War took shape, plans were made to use tobacco in Richmond warehouses as money, and the cannon factory at Westham, 6 miles to the west, was busy turning out guns. Richmond's Chatham Rope Yard was making rigging for ships, and the Rubsamen Works across the river in Chesterfield was manufacturing powder. Public records from the state capital at Williamsburg were brought to Richmond for safekeeping from the British, and the capital was moved to Richmond permanently in 1780.

But the British, nevertheless, were coming. In January 1781, Richmond was occupied and burned by three British armies under Benedict Arnold. Continental Army troops under the Marquis de Lafayette and Baron von Steuben thwarted a second attack. But British forces under Cornwallis occupied the town again in June, burning tobacco and other goods in the streets. En route to Richmond, Cornwallis made his headquarters for 18 days at Hanover Tavern. Local lore says he left without paying his bill.

Lafayette and Col. Anthony Wayne pursued the British down the James, and the British surrendered at Yorktown four months later.

Early Economic Development

As the young United States looked westward for growing room, no one was more aware of the significance of the James River than George Washington. On November 15, 1784, he appeared before the Virginia General Assembly in Richmond to promote the formation of a company "for clearing and extending the navigation of the James River from tidewater up to the highest parts practicable on the main branch thereof."

The first Richmond sections of the canal were completed in 1789 and 1794, and water was let into the Richmond Basin between Eighth, 11th, Canal and Cary streets in 1800. The "Great Waterway to the West," what was to become the James River and Kanawha Canal, helped open up America's heartland for trade to and from points abroad and transformed Richmond into an important commercial center.

As the early 1800s unfolded, Richmond was beginning to realize its great potential for economic development. Tobacco production was firmly established; the Richmond area was a major exporter of American coal; four iron works were in operation; Richmond was a major flour-milling center; and manufacturing plants were busy turning out furniture, glass, books, textiles and refined sugar.

The Richmond, Fredericksburg and Potomac Railroad Company was chartered in 1834, and within the next 20 years Richmond became a major railroad center served by 20 lines. Richmond College, now the University of Richmond, was chartered in 1840, and

Photo: Edgar Allan Poe Museum

The Old Stone House is the oldest standing building in the original boundaries of the city.

Richmond's Medical College of Virginia was incorporated in 1854. Interestingly enough, the city had a German-language newspaper, and 25 percent of the white population in those days was German.

The Civil War

Mounting intersectional animosities and tension over the slavery issue reached a boiling point with abolitionist John Brown's raid on Harpers Ferry in West Virginia.

Virginia overwhelmingly opposed secession and breakup of the Union and even attempted to call all states to a peace conference in Washington. But the die was cast after seven Southern states seceded from the Union, and President Lincoln called for troops from Virginia to help suppress the rebellion in the Deep South. The Virginia Convention, meeting in Richmond, voted almost 2-to-1 in favor of withdrawing from the Union.

Thus Richmond, for the second time, was thrust into a war of secession. The city became the capital of the Confederate States of America and its principal manufacturing, supply and hospital center.

"On to Richmond!" became the battle cry of Federal troops, with the city as their primary objective for four years. Seven military drives were hurled at the city. In one, the Battle of

Cold Harbor, the Union army suffered 7,000 casualties in less than 30 minutes.

During the war years bacon went from 12¢ a pound to $8 a pound and butter from 25¢ to $25 a pound. Lack of meat led Confederate President Jefferson Davis to recommend rats as being "as good as squirrels." Rats sold in some places for $2.50 each, and the superintendent of a local military hospital made available a recipe for cleaning, basting and roasting the rodents.

Word of Petersburg's fall came to Davis on Palm Sunday, 1865, while he was attending services at St. Paul's Church. It was now clear that Richmond could no longer be defended, and warehouses and stores were set afire. Nine hundred buildings were burned during the evacuation fire, including almost everything in the area bounded by Main, Fourth and 15th streets and the James River. With fires raging out of control, the city's surrender took place the next day.

When President Lincoln arrived unexpectedly, and somewhat unceremoniously, on April 4, the smoke from the devastated business and commercial district still lingered. From Rocketts Landing he walked up Main Street and then to the White House of the Confederacy.

It would be five years before Virginia would be readmitted to the Union, during which time it underwent Reconstruction, including two years of military rule. Yet, almost phoenix-like, Richmond's economy rebounded, and the city entered an energetic period of industrialization and urbanization.

To find out much more on Richmond's role in the War Between the States, see this book's chapter on The Civil War, or pick up a copy of *The Insiders Guide® to Civil War Sites in the Eastern Theater*, now in its second edition.

A New Century

By the 1890s and the turn of the century, the economy was booming: iron, tobacco, flour, paper, brick, woolens, locomotives, ships, fertilizer, carriages, soap and spices were being produced. Richmond's Bessemer works was the third largest in the South. Truly, the city exemplified the New South.

In 1903 Maggie L. Walker, the daughter of a former slave, founded what is now Consolidated Bank and Trust Company, making her the nation's first female bank president.

In 1914 Richmond was chosen as the site for the headquarters of the Fifth Federal Reserve District, making it the focal point of finance for much of the Southeast. For this and other reasons, the city came out of World War I with enhanced business prestige. From 1910 to 1920 the population jumped 34.5 percent.

Richmond weathered The Great Depression better than most cities because of the Depression-resistant tobacco base of its economy. It even saw another building boom in the late 1930s. But then, through World War II and for the next two decades, things remained fairly status quo.

The opening of Reynolds Metals Company's new corporate headquarters building in the late 1950s, the founding of the fledgling James River Corporation in 1969, and the completion in 1978 of the downtown riverfront headquarters of the Federal Reserve Bank (designed by Minoru Yamasaki) set the stage for the explosive era of growth that dramatically changed the face of the city.

In the 1980s, with strong regional government cooperation, a massive expansionary period began. Richmond became firmly established as a major corporate center as well as a U.S. beachhead for a large number of Japanese and European companies, and the area grew into a major distribution and financial center.

It was also during this period that local residents raised $8 million in 60 days for The Diamond, a showcase minor-league baseball stadium with skyboxes, a restaurant and all of the amenities (see our Spectator Sports chapter). A $22 million expansion of the Virginia Museum of Fine Arts doubled gallery space and gained the museum international acclaim (see our chapter on The Arts). The first phase of the $450 million James Center was completed. And the $200 million Tobacco Row project — covering 15 contiguous city blocks, the largest historic renovation project in the nation and an important boost for downtown housing — got under way.

Richmond Today

It has been estimated that one out of every five people living in the Richmond area today didn't live here three years ago. Some have come with the avalanche of new companies that now call Richmond home. Some came here to study at colleges and universities and then decided to stay. Others have simply come, often without jobs, seeking a haven that, as an Old World exchange student said, "has a certain continuum about it."

This influx of new blood has generated an energy that is enhanced by Richmond's position as an urban center at the heart of what's described as an emerging Golden Crescent stretching from Baltimore and Washington south to Virginia's bustling ports of Hampton Roads. Add to this Motorola's scheduled de-

INSIDERS' TIP

As you drive by the Country Club of Virginia you are at the spot where Tarleton's British legion, arriving via Three Chopt Road, and Cornwallis' forces, arriving via River Road, linked up for their June 1781 advance on Richmond.

velopment of a $3 billion, 230-acre "anchor site" semiconductor manufacturing complex employing 5,000 people and construction of a $1.5 billion Siemens/Motorola memory chip complex employing 1,500 people, and you have the makings of a 21st-century "Fab City," with everything that designation implies.

Richmond today ranks among the nation's largest Fortune 500 corporate headquarters centers. It is a major financial center, buoyed by the presence of the headquarters of the Fifth Federal Reserve District, big accounting firms and a vast array of securities and investment firms.

Crisscrossed by north-south and east-west interstates and rail lines, with its own deep-water port and perhaps the nation's fastest-growing air cargo facilities, Richmond has become an important distribution center.

Partners for Livable Places named the Richmond area one of the dozen or so "most livable and innovative" metropolitan areas in the nation. *Inc.* magazine picked it as one of the top-30 "Hot Spots" for new and expanding business. *Health* magazine ranked the Richmond area No. 1 among "America's Ten Healthiest Cities." And *City & State* magazine placed Richmond's government among the nation's top 10, based on financial health and management.

Famous sons and daughters include Pocahontas, the Indian princess; Nancy Langhorne, who later became Lady Astor, the first woman elected to the British House of Commons, and her sister, Irene, the famous Gibson Girl of the 1890s; Edgar Allan Poe, the father of the mystery story; other writers such as Mary Johnston, Ellen Glasgow, James Branch Cabell and today's Tom Wolfe and Patricia Cornwell; George W. Goethals, chief engineer of the Panama Canal; former U.S. Supreme Court Justice Lewis F. Powell Jr.; tennis, football and golf greats Arthur Ashe Jr., Willie Lanier, Lanny Wadkins, Bobby Wadkins and Vinny Giles; and entertainers such as Shirley MacLaine, Warren Beatty and the late Bill "Bojangles" Robinson. In addition, professional careers launched here include those of Pulitzer Prize-winning editorial cartoonist Jeff MacNelly and TV commentator Roger Mudd.

Says the meeting planners guide of the Metropolitan Richmond Convention & Visitors Bureau: "Virginia's capital is like no other . . . Its architect was Thomas Jefferson. Its spokesman was Patrick Henry. Its lawmaker, John Marshall. Its poet, Edgar Allan Poe. And its general, Robert E. Lee."

Richmond's Oliver W. Hill, the civil rights lawyer, played a key role in the landmark *Brown vs. the Board of Education* decision. In addition, the city has been blessed with risk-takers and corporate visionaries — the Gottwalds of Ethyl, Brent Halsey and Bob Williams of James River Corporation, Jim Wheat of Wheat First Butcher Singer, the Reynoldses of Reynolds Metals, Claiborne Robins of A.H. Robins, J. Harwood Cochrane of Overnite Transportation and subsequently of Highway Express, the Bryans of Media General, the Wurtzels of Circuit City Stores, and a host of other business and community leaders who have helped make Richmond what it is today.

The beauty of the city's public places is something to enjoy, and Richmonders make the most of it with street festivals, outdoor concerts, baseball at The Diamond, arts in the parks and whitewater rafting on the James (see our Annual Events, Arts, Parks and Recreation and Spectator Sports chapters). This leads into a cultural world that is packed with symphony, ballet, opera, galleries, theater, museums, impromptu performances, food festivals, garden and flower shows, spring and holiday house tours and so many other offerings that *Style Weekly*, the local arts and cultural journal, once was led to headline: "Lordy, Lordy, So Much To Do, So Little Time!"

Modern-day Richmond — something people refuse to believe until they see it — is described by Pulitzer Prize-winning editor and historian Virginius Dabney as an "intriguing blend of the old and the new — of Charleston and Savannah on one hand, and Atlanta and Dallas on the other. While showing the élan and drive in business and industrial realms, the city clings — a bit precariously at times — to its distinctive 18th- and 19th-century heritage."

In trying to describe in a few words what today's Richmond is all about, this is probably the closest we can get.

First Things First

With a colonial history going back to the early 1600s, Richmond has had plenty of opportunity to pioneer a number of "firsts." They include:

First Hospital

America's first hospital, a "guest house for sick people," was built in 1611 at Henricus, the first major English settlement in the Richmond area.

First Tobacco

After observing Native Americans cultivating tobacco, John Rolfe in 1612 followed their example and planted a crop just east of Richmond in the area he named Varina, after a variety of Spanish tobacco. The popularity of the "noxious weed" in England convinced colonists that if money didn't grow on trees, then it most certainly grew on tobacco plants.

First Iron and Coal

America's first ironworks were established in 1619 at Falling Creek in Chesterfield County where there were heavy outcroppings of ore. The first coal mining in the New World began in the Richmond area in the mid-1700s, and by the 1790s accounted for a healthy share of the area's exports.

First Thanksgiving

The first Thanksgiving in America took place at Berkeley Plantation in 1619, a year before the Pilgrims landed at Plymouth Rock.

Oldest Medical College Building in South

The Egyptian Building (1845) of Virginia Commonwealth University's Medical College of Virginia is the oldest medical college building in the South and is considered the finest example of Egyptian Revival architecture in America. The building was remodeled in 1939 with funds given by Bernard Baruch, the New York

Photo: Berkeley Plantation

The first Thanksgiving, 1619.

financier, in honor of his father, Simon Baruch, who was an MCV graduate and the father of modern hydrotherapy.

First Military Aircraft

It was in Civil War military campaigns around Richmond that the first military "aircraft" (tethered balloons) were used for aerial reconnaissance.

First Electric Streetcar

The first commercial streetcar system powered by overhead electric lines from a central station was put into operation in Richmond in 1888 by Julian Frank Sprague after he was unable to persuade New York to accept the idea. Sprague was a former assistant to Thomas A. Edison.

First Female Bank President

The first female bank president in the United States was Maggie L. Walker, daughter of a former slave, who organized St. Luke's Penny Savings Bank in Richmond in 1903. The bank of which she was president is now part of Richmond's Consolidated Bank & Trust Company, the oldest African-American-owned bank in the nation.

First Cellophane

The first cellophane in the United States was produced in Richmond in 1930 by DuPont. Today Kevlar fiber, pound-for-pound rated five times stronger than steel and used in bulletproof vests, is made exclusively in Richmond by DuPont, as are other high-tech fibers tradenamed Nomex, Teflon and Tyvek.

First Canned Beer

The first beer in the United States in tin-plated steel cans — Krueger Ale, produced by the Krueger Brewery of Newark — was test-marketed in Richmond beginning on January 24, 1935. The conservative Richmond market was a favorite for new-product tests — "if it sells in Richmond, it will sell anyplace," was a marketing slogan. The 1935 innovation that made beer packaging history was eclipsed by a better container, the recyclable all-aluminum can, developed in Richmond in 1963 by Reynolds Metals Company.

First Household Foil

Reynolds Wrap household foil, produced by Richmond-based Reynolds Metals Company, was pioneered in test markets in Richmond in 1947.

First Tamari Brewery Outside of Japan

Tamari, the soy seasoning of choice in the elite circles from the tables of shoguns to the Ginza's best restaurants, was brewed exclusively in Japan for centuries — until 1987, when San-Jurushi of Japan chose Richmond as the home of its first international brewery.

First ISDN Phone Service

In the forefront of telecommunications development, C&P Telephone (now Bell Atlantic-Virginia), headquartered in Richmond, pioneered the nation's first commercial (non-trial) Integrated Services Digital Network (ISDN) in 1988.

The equipment of the Greater Richmond Transit Company is modern and comfortable but tragically underutilized.

Getting Around

In Richmond you can get from one side of town to the other in about 15 or 20 minutes, from downtown to the airport in about 10 minutes and move quickly onto major interstates—north, east, south and west—that put you within a daytrip's reach of some of the East Coast's major urban centers and most popular recreation and vacation spots. But if you're driving, or riding for that matter, be sure to "buckle up" —and that's not just our friendly suggestion, it's the law.

Inside the Metro Area

Streets and Expressways

The Richmond area has a very well-designed, well-maintained street and expressway system. Local governments and the Virginia Department of Transportation have done a good job of anticipating urban growth, and new and expanded roads are usually put in place before there is a heavy need for them.

Rush-hour backups do occur at toll booths on the Downtown and Powhite expressways. But these backups are usually relatively short and predictable — usually between 7 to 9 AM and 4 to 6 PM on weekdays. A number of wide, new bridges have been completed across the James River in recent years. This makes river crossings much less problematic than they used to be, save for those drivers who insist on using the Huguenot Bridge to avoid paying the 50¢ expressway tolls.

Before you buy a house, rent an apartment or select an office site, you might want to experiment at rush hour with several alternate routes (and bridges, if you are looking at a home on one side of the river and an office on the other).

If you're used to driving in Los Angeles; Washington, D.C.; Houston; Charlotte; or Atlanta, you'll find driving around Richmond a real breeze. The automobile is the favored mode of transport in Richmond, and highway planners and builders have placed high priority on trying to make driving as much a pleasure as possible.

Traffic Patterns

Unless there is a sign forbidding it, you can turn right on red. The same holds true for left turns from a one-way street onto another one-way street.

Right of way in traffic circles is for the most part as you would expect, with all traffic yielding to cars in the circle. One of the major exceptions is the circle around the Lee Monument on Monument Avenue. Here, through traffic on Monument has the primary right of way, so great care must be taken if you are moving around the circle or if you are crossing it via Allen Avenue.

The system of street numbers and names is generally pretty sane. If someone gives you an address on a numbered street between First and 40th, double-check to see if this is in the East End (Church Hill and Shockoe Bottom) or on the South Side (Forest Hill and Bainbridge); similar street designations exist in both places. Few streets change names, although Malvern does become Westwood as it crosses Broad Street, and Monument Avenue and W. Franklin Street exchange names at Stuart Circle. Boulevard (the proper name of a major thoroughfare) going north flows into Hermitage. Boulevard south takes you onto Westover Hills Boulevard after you cross the river, and Westover Hills Boulevard south flows into Belt Boulevard.

Parking

Observe parking signs and parking meter

regulations carefully. In Richmond they mean what they say. The police department has a good supply of parking tickets that they dole out liberally. Towing has been honed to a science along streets where early morning and late-afternoon rush-hour parking is prohibited.

City law requires that a car be towed if there are three or more delinquent parking tickets on record for that car. If your car is towed from a downtown street, you'll need to call police information at 780-6718 to retrieve it. Property owners also are quick to have vehicles left in private parking places towed.

Parking lots and decks downtown are plentiful, and they are fairly well-dispersed throughout different areas of the center of the city. In fact, for the first time in Richmond's history, there are probably too many parking decks. This has put some pressure on monthly rates, so you'll be wise to shop around. Rates range from $20 a month in peripheral lots to $125 monthly in decks and parking garages in top-line office buildings. Hourly rates range from 50¢ to $2.50, depending on location. Some decks offer special "early bird," all-day rates.

FYI

Unless otherwise noted, the area code for all phone numbers listed in this chapter is 804.

Public Transit

Greater Richmond Transit Company (GRTC)
• 358-GRTC

The equipment of the GRTC is modern and comfortable but tragically underutilized. The GRTC fleet consists of almost 200 buses and eight trolleys. GRTC recently purchased a number of nonpolluting Westinghouse electric buses. The buses run off and on and are said to require less maintenance and can travel for up to 80 miles between charges, reaching speeds of 55 mph.

Richmond's public transit system is undergoing a lot of change these days in an

effort to popularize the public transportation option. A bus transfer plaza has been proposed for Grace Street, between 7th and 8th streets. Patrons will have access to fare and route information. The city has purchased 50 bus shelters which will further designate bus stops while providing patrons with relief from the elements and a place to sit. Perhaps the city's largest project is the redevelopment of the old Main Street Station as a transportation hub, with access to Amtrak, taxis, airport limos, buses and trolleys. Funding has been secured for the restoration, and the date of completion will be sometime in 2001.

The basic GRTC fare is $1.25 (cash only), although 150 outlets carry Super Saver tickets that will save you 25 percent. Transfers cost 15¢, but are just 10¢ with Super Saver tickets and are free for seniors and the disabled. Seniors and disabled can also ride for a reduced fare.

In an experimental program underwritten by Virginia Commonwealth University, VCU students can ride free during the fall and spring semesters simply by showing a student ID. Last year some 225,000 students participated. The success of the program may lead to including University of Richmond and Virginia Union students.

Bus routes cover the city of Richmond and extend into Henrico County. Daily service on most routes begins at 5:30 AM and ends at midnight. For all schedule, route and ticket outlet information, call 358-GRTC.

Park and Ride

GRTC bus service is available at peak hours from lots at Interstate 64 and Airport Drive (305 spaces), Parham and Fordson roads (352 spaces), Glenside Drive and Staples Mill Road (480 spaces) and Gaskins Road at Mayland Drive (399 spaces).

In addition, other types of park-and-ride

facilities are on U.S. Highway 1 at John Tyler Community College (100 spaces); at U.S. Highway 360 and Va. Highway 653 at Rockwood Park (150 spaces); at I-64 and Va. Highway 623 (30 spaces); at I-64 and Va. Highway 617 at Oilville (15 spaces); U.S 360 at Mechanicsville (109 spaces); and on U.S. Highway 60 at Bottoms Bridge (40 spaces).

Ridesharing

The Commuter Center
• **643-RIDE**

This service, operated by Ridefinders, coordinates ridesharing by bus, carpool and vanpool. If you are interested in finding a bus route, carpool partner or a vanpool group to get to and from work, you should first find out if your company has an established relationship with Ridefinders and the Greater Richmond Transit Company. If your company does not have one, contact the Commuter Center directly by phone. If you rideshare at least three days a week, you'll be entitled to Guaranteed Ride Home, a service operated by Ridefinders for regular bus riders and carpoolers. The service provides a ride if you have a midday emergency, miss your bus or unexpectedly have to work late.

Taxis

Taxis can be hailed on the street, but don't expect to snag one. Taxis on the street usually already have a fare or are in the process of responding to a pickup call. The best thing is to call one of the 50 cab companies listed in the Yellow Pages or ask the receptionist at the office or hotel you are visiting to make arrangements for you. Be sure to factor the cab's response time into your planning and make your arrangements early.

Uniform taxi rates are set by the Richmond City Council and by county boards of supervisors. They are $1.50 for the first one-fifth mile, 30¢ for each additional one-fifth mile, and 30¢ for each minute of delay, including traffic delay. There is an extra charge of $1 each for addi-

Cruise the James River in style aboard the *Annabel Lee*.

Photo: Metro Richmond Convention and Visitors Bureau

tional passengers older than 6. A $1 surcharge may be added between 9 PM and 6 AM. All tolls are charged to the passenger. At the driver's discretion, riders 65 years of age and older are eligible for a 20 percent discount off meter fare. Riders may request and receive an estimate of fare before the trip begins and a written receipt upon arrival at the destination. Comments and suggestions about taxi service are welcomed by the Taxicab Services Coordinator, Greater Richmond Transit Company at 358-GRTC.

Links with Other Parts of the World

Easy Access to Recreation Areas

Richmond's location at the intersection of north-south Interstate 95/Interstate 85 and east-west Interstate 64, and at the junction of other major highways, places it within easy reach of resort, vacation and recreation areas. In just an hour or two of east or southeast travel, you can reach the Chesapeake Bay or one of the many rivers that flow into the giant estuary, arrive in the resort area of Virginia Beach or be well on your way to North Carolina's Outer Banks. An hour or so to the west lie the Blue Ridge Mountains with ample opportunities for camping, hiking, backpacking and skiing. Within the same amount of time, in any direction, you'll find history—Colonial Williamsburg, Fredericksburg, Petersburg, Jefferson's Charlottesville — as well as the museums and cultural offerings of Washington, D.C.

Scheduled Intercity Bus and Rail Service

Greyhound Bus Lines
2910 N. Boulevard • 254-5938,
(800) 231-2222; charter service (800) 454-2487
Greyhound is a nationwide bus service offering regularly scheduled as well as char-

ter service. The station is across from The Diamond and just a few blocks off Broad Street.

Winn Transportation/ Winning Tours Inc.
1831 Westwood Ave.
• 358-6666, (800) 296-9466
This travel agency provides scheduled motor coach service to Williamsburg as well as charter and tour services across the nation and into Canada. It makes a weekly scheduled round trip to Williamsburg on Mondays, with stops at the Pottery outlet shopping center, Busch Gardens and in the historic area of Colonial Williamsburg. Service departs the busline office at 1831 Westwood Avenue at 8:10 AM and returns at 6:30 PM in the summer and 4:30 PM November–April.

James River Bus Lines
915 N. Allen Ave. • 321-7661
James River Bus Lines have regularly scheduled round-trip Sunday service to points south, including Petersburg, Suffolk, Portsmouth, Norfolk and Virginia Beach. The service departs from the Greyhound terminal at 8 AM, and returning buses depart Virginia Beach at 7 PM. It also has a regular run to Atlantic City every Wednesday and Saturday and most major holidays, departing from 915 N. Allen Ave. at 6 AM and returning at 3 AM.

Amtrak
7519 Staples Mill Rd. • (800) USA-RAIL;
(800) 368-8725 package express
Amtrak provides passenger rail service on main north-south routes and to the east, as well as connecting service to the west. Northern destinations include Washington, D.C.; Philadelphia, New York and Boston. Southern stops include Raleigh, North Carolina; Columbia, South Carolina; Tampa and Orlando. One train goes to Newport News daily. Richmond is one of the cities included in Amtrak's NortheastDirect service which covers passenger rail travel anywhere from Boston to Newport News. The train station is a modern, one-level structure with barrier-free access for wheelchairs and is open 24 hours a day. It's just a short distance off I-64W.

Charter Bus, Van and Limousine Services

You'll find most of the major bus companies and limo services advertised in the Bell Atlantic Yellow Pages. But there are some who deserve mention.

Tourtime America
5115 Commerce Rd. • 275-0300

Tourtime America has some of the most commodious charter buses in town, equipped with all the amenities to suit any group, of any size. These buses are particularly used by VIP groups.

Virginia Overland Transportation
6020 Midlothian Tnpk. • 233-1152

Serving Virginia for over 50 years, Virginia Overland offers safe and affordable charters (coaches, school buses and trolleys) for anything from weddings to conventions.

Groome Transportation
5500 Lewis Rd., Sandston • 222-7226

Groome handles bus and executive sedan charters.

Historic Richmond Foundation
707 E. Franklin St. • 780-0107

If you have a small group interested in a guided van tour of the city and of Civil War sites, then you might want to check out the daily van tours offered by the Historic Richmond Foundation. Tour prices range from $13–$16 per person.

Airports

Richmond International Airport

Airport Dr., Sandston • 226-3000

Richmond International (RIC) is convenient to downtown and is served by 16 airlines, including seven major airlines and nine regional, low-fare carriers. With about 160 arrivals and departures daily, Richmond International offers nonstop service to and from cities such as New York, Chicago, Boston, Dallas, Toronto, Baltimore, Cleveland, St. Louis, and Atlanta as well as direct service to destinations including the West Coast and Canada. Twice-per-week scheduled charter service is available to Freeport in the Bahamas.

About $70 million in passenger-side enhancements have been completed in recent years or are in progress at Richmond International Airport, making the airport one of the most user-friendly in the nation. It has 15 enclosed boarding bridges, ample parking (with two newly completed parking decks that hold 5,000 vehicles), an international arrivals terminal serving charter carriers, a teleconferencing and meeting center and a fully staffed visitors information center.

The airport operates a general-purpose Foreign Trade Zone with intermodal access, it is a UPS hub, and it is one of the nation's fastest-growing air cargo centers. Greater Richmond's growth as a distribution center and its strategic East Coast location have played an important part in the increase.

Richmond International is also the site of the Virginia Aviation Museum that focuses on the "golden years" of flight between the two world wars. (See our Attractions chapter.)

Parking

Long-term and short-term parking are available immediately adjacent to Richmond International's terminal building, and free shuttle service provides transportation between the terminal and satellite parking lots.

When you are in a rush to make your flight, look for the Valet Parking signs and spaces as you drive up to the terminal. Give the attendant your name, keys and flight information. You'll receive a receipt and be on your way. To save even more time, call the RIC Valet Parking Hotline (226-3089) before your scheduled day of departure so your receipt can be prepared in advance. When you arrive at the airport, just sign the receipt and give the attendant your keys. There is a fee for this service, but payment by credit card can be arranged by calling the Valet Parking Hotline, just in case you're low on cash or in a hurry when you return to Richmond.

Ground Transportation

Richmond International Airport offers a wide array of ground transportation options. These services and ground transportation information are located at the center island of Terminal Drive across from the baggage claim area. Courtesy phones to area hotel shuttles are available, as are pre-arranged limousine and/or executive sedan services. In addition, approximately 30 independent taxi companies serve the airport.

Groome Transportation
• 222-7222

Groome offers limousine service from Richmond International Airport to all parts of the Rich-

RichmondSpeak

If you want to understand and speak the Richmond language, you need to be familiar with these idiosyncrasies:

The River: This is the place where many Richmonders have summer homes and where they go to boat or fish. It can mean any one of the rivers flowing into the Chesapeake Bay: usually the Rappahannock, the Potomac, the York, the Mattaponi or the Piankatank, or any one of the creeks flowing into these rivers, or any bay or inlet attached thereto. It can also be used to refer to locations on the Chesapeake Bay proper.

The word "river" is pronounced so that it sounds like "REV-ah." When Richmonders refer to rivers closer to home, such as the James and the Chickahominy, they usually refer to them by name, but not always, especially in the case of the James.

The Beach: This, for the most part, means Virginia Beach. But, in some cases, it can

Photo: Richmond Times-Dispatch

The James River flows through the center of Richmond.

mean resorts on North Carolina's Outer Banks. Seaside vacations up north are at places called "The Shore" or "The Cape." In Virginia, it's "The Beach."

The Club: This usually means the prestigious Commonwealth Club, but it also can mean the Country Club of Virginia.

The Slip: This is shorthand for Shockoe Slip.

The Bottom: Likewise, shorthand for Shockoe Bottom.

Powhatan: This, among other things, is the name of a famous Indian chief and of a nearby county. It is "POW-a-tan," never "pow-HATAN."

Powhite: This one looks pretty simple, but it's not. Even many Richmonders have a problem pronouncing it properly. It should not be pronounced so that it sounds like a synonym for "white trash." You're supposed to say it — and we think we've got this right — so it comes out "POW-hite," or something reasonably close (with the emphasis on the "POW," as in Powhatan). It's worth working on, because one of the main arteries in the Richmond area is the Powhite Expressway, a route you may find yourself referring to frequently.

Henrico: This is the name of one of the counties in the Richmond area. It is pronounced "Hen-RYE-co," never "HENRY-co."

Staunton: When you pronounce the name of this community in Virginia's Shenandoah Valley, be sure you do not pay any attention to the letter "u" in the middle. It's "Stanton."

Southside/South Side: The part of the state of Virginia to the south of Richmond is the Southside (all one word), or Southside Virginia. The part of the Richmond metro area that lies south of the James River is the South Side (two words).

Vepco: Even though the name of the local electric utility company is Virginia Power, lots of people still can't shake calling it "Vepco," the shorthand name used in the days when the utility was Virginia Electric & Power Company.

Nickel Bridge: This is the Boulevard Bridge. The toll to cross it used to be 5¢. Now it's 25¢, but Quarter Bridge just doesn't have the same ring to it.

---

mond area, with departures from the terminal every 10 minutes or less.

Groome also provides hourly service to Petersburg, Fort Lee and Williamsburg. In addition, approximately 30 independent taxi companies serve the airport.

Chesterfield County Airport

7511 Airfield Dr. • 743-0771

The Chesterfield County Airport serves corporate and general aircraft and is a reliever airport for Richmond International.

Hanover County Airport

11152 Airpark Rd., Ashland • 798-6500

Hanover County Airport is a smaller general-aviation facility specializing in single- and twin-engine planes and freight work.

General Aviation

Services and Charters

Corporate hangars are leased and main-

INSIDERS' TIP

Greater Richmond (Chesterfield, Hanover and Henrico counties and the City of Richmond) covers 1,224 square miles, more than the state of Rhode Island (1,214 square miles).

tained at Richmond International by Richmond-area businesses. In addition, several general charter, air ambulance and aviation service firms are based at the airport. Firms with charter aircraft include:

Aero Industries, 222-7211
Heloair Inc. (helicopters), 226-3400
MartinAir Inc., 222-7401
Million Air, 222-3700.

Air ambulance services include:
AAAS Advanced Aeromedical Air Ambulance Service, (800) 346-3556
Advanced Air Ambulance Service, (800) 633-3590.

In addition, one air charter firm is at Chesterfield County Airport:
Dominion Aviation Services Inc., 271-7793

Sundance Aviation Inc., 798-6500, offers the only air charter service at Hanover County Municipal Airport.

Of the firms mentioned above, aircraft maintenance is offered by Aero Industries, Dominion Aviation, Million Air and Sundance Aviation. The Chesterfield County Airport also operates a repair station with Federal Aviation Administration-certified mechanics. Many aircraft maintenance firms also operate aircraft schools.

Richmond was founded at the falls of the James River.

Washington Airport Shuttle

Groome Transportation
**5500 Lewis Rd., Sandston • 222-7222;
(800) 552-7911; 222-7226 charter service**

Richmonders are fortunate that they can take advantage of air service in and out of Washington, D.C. One convenient way to do this is to utilize ground transportation to and from Ronald Reagan National Airport provided by Groome Transportation. The cost of the minibus shuttle is $30. Weekday departures begin at 6:30 AM at Richmond International Airport with a stop, 30 minutes later, at the Holiday Inn-Crossroads on Staples Mill Road near Broad Street. The last departure from Richmond leaves the airport at 4:30 PM and the Holiday Inn-Crossroads at 5 PM. Reservations are not required. Call for weekend schedules.

Greater Richmond is like a gigantic gastronomic playground when it comes to places to eat.

Restaurants

Greater Richmond is like a gigantic gastronomic playground when it comes to places to eat. The restaurant scene's variety means you will find just about anything that suits your mood. And local restaurant reviewers surely must be gaining weight trying to keep up with the steady flow of new chefs and their concoctions.

One caution: Just as new restaurants open, old ones occasionally close or change hours of operation. So, before you venture forth, a call ahead might be a good idea.

This guide focuses primarily on locally owned restaurants. The chain restaurants are all here in abundance, so we won't waste time counting the countless McDonald's and Hardees. They're not hard to spot.

Price Code

The dollar sign ($) with each restaurant entry is an indication of the probable cost of dinner for two people, without figuring in the addition of alcoholic beverages and tip. Lunch at most places costs about half that of dinner. The code works this way:

Less than $25	$
$25 to $40	$$
$41 to $55	$$$
$56 and more	$$$$

Restaurants accept major credit cards, unless otherwise noted.

Virginia's laws regarding smoking in restaurants are as follows: restaurants with a seating capacity of 50 or more must have a nonsmoking section sufficient to meet customer demand; by law, signs must be posted indicating whether a restaurant has a nonsmoking section. This means a lot of your smaller places aren't required to have nonsmoking sections. If this is going to be a problem for you, call ahead to see what your options are.

What follows is not a complete list of Richmond's good restaurants, but it will get you started.

In order to help you find a specific type of restaurant, we have listed Richmond's restaurants according to the following categories:

Alive with History
Accent on Continental
All-Star Surf and Turf
Awash in Specialities of the Sea
Awesome Steaks and Chops
Bastions of The Fan
Best Virginia (and North Carolina
    and Tennessee) Barbecue
Breweries
British Pubs
Cajun
Caribbean
Carryout
Caterers
Chinese
Coffeehouses and Bagel Shops
Delis
Family Restaurants
Fast Food
Fondue
French
Greek
Indian
Italian
Japanese
Korean
Lunch Places
Mexican and Southwestern
Museum and Garden Cafes
Other Casual Places
Pizza
Soul Food
Southern
Something Different
Street Vendors and Food Courts
24-hour Eats
Vegetarian
Vietnamese

Alive with History

Beauregard's Thai Room
$ • 103 E. Cary St. • 644-2328

A number of old-time Richmond buildings still stand in this historic block of E. Cary Street. At No. 103, you'll find a restaurant with an English-basement cafe/bar, a shady, brick-walled courtyard with a fountain and an upstairs dining room that's stylish without being pretentious. The bar and patio are comfortable, Old South places to enjoy light fare for lunch or dinner. The Thai Room upstairs features Thai dishes from start to finish — green curry chicken, ginger beef, shrimp with baby corn, soups and vegetarian dishes. The Thai chef is the genuine article. The restaurant is open for lunch Monday through Friday and for dinner Monday through Saturday. Reservations are recommended on the weekends.

Coach House Tavern
$$ • 10600 Harrison Landing Rd., Charles City • 829-6003

Berkeley Plantation is part of a land grant awarded by James I in the early 1600s, and President Lincoln visited it twice when it was a base for the Army of the Potomac in 1862. Here, in the Coach House Tavern, you can enjoy a meal worthy of the country's first Thanksgiving, which took place on the grounds of the plantation in 1619. Specialties include pan-roasted oysters with Surry bacon and cream in a warm puff pastry, grilled prime rib of veal and Colonial onion soup in an edible bread bowl. Reservations are required for dinner and are suggested for lunch during the spring, summer and fall and on weekends. The restaurant is open for lunch daily and for dinner Friday and Saturday. A brunch is served on Sundays.

Fox Head Inn
$$$$ • 1840 Manakin Rd. (Rt. 621), Goochland • 784-5126

In Goochland County's horse country, the Fox Head Inn is in an 1880s farm house filled with fox hunting motifs and surrounded by a magnificent grove of trees. It is within easy reach of downtown Richmond via Interstate 64, but it's wise to get directions before you venture forth. The four-course, fixed-price menu features an array of elegant selections. Specialties include homemade desserts, such as Fox Hunter pie and Sally Lunn bread. Dinner is served Wednesday through Sunday. Reservations are required, and coat and tie are requested. Smoking is not allowed in the dining rooms.

Half-Way House
$$$ • 10301 Jefferson Davis Hwy. • 275-1760

Midway between Richmond and Petersburg, this old country tavern, built in 1760, serves dinner in the brick-floored English basement. If you like Colonial Williamsburg, you have to see this place because it's the genuine article. The menu offers a selection of filet mignon, lobster and shrimp plus daily chef's specials. Reservations are suggested. The restaurant serves lunch Monday through Friday and dinner nightly.

Henry Clay Inn
$$ • 114 N. Railroad Ave., Ashland • 798-3100

With a columned portico overlooking the campus of Randolph-Macon College, the Henry Clay Inn captures the comfortable elegance of a bygone era. The dining room is small and homey and specializes in Southern specialties, breads and desserts. Before or after your meal you can browse

---

INSIDERS' TIP

Just because a ham is processed in Virginia, it's not necessarily a "Virginia ham." Virginia hams are specifically peanut- and corn-fed hams cured and smoked in a certain way. And "Smithfield hams" are only from the Smithfield region's peanut-fed hogs, which are cured in hickory, oak, apple and peanut-shell smoke, then aged for about a year.

through the inn's gift shop and art gallery that features the work of local artists and artisans. The inn is next to Ashland's vintage railroad station, and if you are lucky you can enjoy the sights of passing trains. Reservations are suggested. Brunch and dinner are served on the weekends. Private dining is available on request.

Indian Fields Tavern

$$$ • 9920 John Tyler Memorial Hwy., Charles City • 829-5004

Indian Fields Tavern is a great place to enjoy excellent food and casual elegance in the country. The innovative fare blends both traditional and new Southern cuisine and includes entrees such as fresh fish, Crab Cakes

Photo: Hanover County Parks and Recreation

Some area restaurants serve meals inspired by colonial cooking. (See the "Alive with History" section in this chapter.)

Harrison (two crab cakes on grilled Sally Lunn bread with grilled Smithfield ham and hollandaise sauce), and a mixed grill of lamb, Surry sausage and quail with hunter's sauce. The tavern's bread pudding is probably the best you'll ever sample.

The restaurant is just a short distance from the main entrance to Evelynton Plantation on State Route 5, a scenic highway that meanders through the James River plantation country. Evelynton Plantation originally was part of William Byrd's expansive Westover Plantation and has been the home of the Ruffin family since 1847. A member of the family operates the tavern. With a cozy atmosphere inside and with outdoor dining on screened porches in spring, summer and fall, Indian Fields is a popular place, so it's wise to make reservations before you go. The restaurant serves dinner and lunch daily, with a brunch on Sundays.

Linden Row Inn
$$ • 100 E. Franklin St. • 783-7000

Linden Row, which dates to the 1850s, is said to be built on the site of a garden where Edgar Allan Poe played as a child, perhaps the inspiration for the "enchanted garden" of his poem "To Helen." Its restaurant is a unique hideaway in the midst of the city. It also has a nifty brick-paved patio sandwiched between the inn and dependencies, where meals are served in warm weather.

The menu offers seafood, steaks and three specialty items nightly. Diners can wait for their parties in comfortable double parlors filled with period furnishings. The restaurant serves breakfast, lunch and dinner daily and suggests reservations.

Mr. Patrick Henry's Inn
$$$ • 2300 E. Broad St. • 644-1322

This cozy inn on historic Church Hill is one block west of St. John's Church. It offers a gour-

met restaurant on the main floor, a pub in the English basement and a garden patio. The fare is imaginative and innovative and includes fresh seafood, regional cuisine, homemade breads, desserts and soups. The boneless roasted duck with molasses and fresh berries served over wild-rice cakes never fails to please. Mr. Patrick Henry's is open for lunch Monday through Friday and for dinner Monday through Saturday. Reservations are suggested.

None Such Place
$$ • 1721 E. Franklin St. • 644-0832

Situated on the corner of 18th and E. Franklin streets in Richmond's oldest commercial building in Shockoe Bottom, None Such Place features two floors of casual, fine dining specializing in contemporary Virginia cuisine exquisitely prepared by executive chef Michael Hall. All desserts are prepared fresh on premises. The restaurant and bar offers a great atmosphere — old brick, wood beams, flickering candlelight and a blazing fireplace in winter — for after-work, dinner or a late-night rendezvous. Lunch is served Monday through Friday and dinner is served Monday through Saturday. Reservations are recommended.

Accent on Continental

Caffe Gallego
$$ • 100 S. 12th St. • 344-7000

In the James Center II, this restaurant has some seating in the atrium, providing the atmosphere of outdoor dining. Dinner offerings include shrimp scampi, steak à la Pizzaiola, shrimp and scallops in a sun-dried tomato sauce and the chef's seasonal appetizer and entree specials. A lunch buffet features hot entrees, soup, 16 salads and more. The restaurant serves breakfast, lunch and dinner seven days a week. Reservations are suggested for lunch and dinner.

FYI
Unless otherwise noted, the area code for all phone numbers listed in this chapter is 804.

None Such Place resides in Richmond's oldest commercial dwelling in Shockoe Bottom.

Photo: Michael Ryan Croxton

The diners and restaurants in downtown Richmond are sure to make your tastebuds tango.

Davis & Main
$$ • 2501 W. Main St. • 353-6641

A popular place, Davis & Main offers a full dinner menu until 12 AM. Specialties include fresh grilled poultry, seafood, beef and pork, grilled garden vegetables and fruit, dinner salads, pizzas, pasta of the day and excellent sandwiches. The menu offers a suggested wine to try with each of the grilled entrees.

The atmosphere is casual, yet pleasantly and unpretentiously sophisticated. Don't be discouraged if there's a waiting line during the normal dinner hour; it usually moves quickly. If you're looking for a late-night place where the music doesn't get too loud, this is it. (See our Nightlife chapter.) The price tag on the majority of menu items will bring you within the cost figure shown above, but there are enticing exceptions that are more costly. Davis & Main is open for dinner seven days a week.

The Dining Room at the Berkeley
$$$ • 12th and E. Cary Sts. • 780-1300

The food is superb, the service is attentive, the atmosphere is sedate and tranquil, and it's an excellent place to watch everything

that's going on in the heart of Shockoe Slip. The menu includes items such as barbecued Atlantic salmon, Smithfield lean pork tenderloin, Summerfield Farm rack of lamb, roaster angler fish and seared sea scallops with Prince Edward Island mussels. The restaurant has an extensive wine list from a private collection. Breakfast, lunch and dinner are served daily, with a brunch on Sundays. Reservations are suggested.

duJour
$$ • 5806 Grove Ave. • 285-1301

A hospitable and accommodating place amid the Shops on The Avenues, duJour attracts a dedicated clientele. Voted "Best Outdoor Dining" by *Style Weekly*, duJour's sidewalk cafe adds extra seating capacity during warm-weather months. The innovative dinner menu features seasonal offerings of fresh fish, veal, beef, pasta, lamb, pork, chicken and vegetarian items. You can take a guest here with confidence, and it's a great place for Sunday brunch. duJour serves lunch and dinner Monday through Saturday. Reservations are suggested.

The Frog and the Redneck
$$$ • 1423 E. Cary St. • 648-FROG

Jimmy Sneed ("The Redneck" and former chef of the award-winning Windows on Urbanna Creek of early 1990s fame) and Jean-Louis Palladin ("The Frog" and formerly of Washington's Jean-Louis at the Watergate Hotel) have joined in this tour de force featuring regional dishes and classic French touches. Specialties include fresh seafood, homemade pastas, rotisserie, soups and stews. The wine list features American and French selections; the menu features American and French versions of selected dishes. Cartoons of the Frog and the Redneck festoon the walls.

This is a Richmonder favorite, having taken in countless awards for excellence. The restaurant is open for dinner Monday through Saturday. Reservations are suggested, especially on Friday and Saturday and at prime times during the week.

Graffiti Grille
$$$ • 403 N. Ridge Rd. • 288-0633

Decorated with, of course, graffiti, this restaurant in the West End has a notebook-style menu that tells the history of the restaurant, even though it's only a few years old. A nice beer and wine selection complement incredible entrée choices. Don't miss the Peppermint Patty pie for dessert. The Graffiti Grille is open for dinner Monday through Saturday.

Granite on Grove
$$$ • 5702 Grove Ave. • 288-3600

Granite on Grove is a newer restaurant in town, but already a favorite among many. And who can blame Richmonders because the restaurant is beautiful and the food is delicious. Dinner options include a spinach and avocado salad, shrimp and vegetable tempura, seared squab breast and pan-seared halibut. The wine selection is good, and a Tasting Menu is available. Dinner is served Monday through Saturday.

The Ironhorse
$$ • 100 S. Railroad Ave., Ashland • 752-6410

The Ironhorse in Ashland draws customers from as far afield as Fredericksburg and Williamsburg. The owners are very hands-on, and this shows in the food and service and in the warm way you'll be welcomed. The menu changes monthly and has included grilled duck, fresh seafood, lamb chops and certified Angus beef. The Caesar salads are whoppers. The Ironhorse serves lunch Monday through Friday and dinner Tuesday through Saturday. American Express cards are not accepted. Reservations are suggested for dinner and are necessary on weekends.

Konsta's Restaurant & Lounge
$$ • 2526 Floyd Ave. • 359-3122

Konsta's is one of Richmond's most beautiful restaurants. Its stained-glass windows, cherry paneling, marble-top tables, brass and glass accents, and original artwork create an upscale yet casual dining experience. The nouveau and continental cuisine includes Angus beef, veal, fresh seafood, and Greek and Italian favorites. Konsta's serves dinner Monday through Saturday, and lunch Monday through Friday. Reservations are suggested.

Lemaire Restaurant
$$$$ • Franklin and Adams Sts. • 649-4644

This restaurant in the Jefferson Hotel is perhaps the most elegant dining experience in Richmond. It includes seven different dining rooms, some large and some small enough that they are often booked for private parties. An eighth dining room is expected to open soon, decorated with glass and rod iron and overlooking Franklin Street. Entrees include offerings such as salmon, lamb chops, crab cakes, pork tenderloin and duck. A Tasting Menu with five different courses accompanied by select wines is available as well. Lemaire serves breakfast every day and dinner Monday through Saturday.

Millie's Diner
$$$ • 2603 E. Main St. • 643-5512

Bon Appetit magazine describes Millie's, a small, cozy diner-ish restaurant on E. Main Street just east of Shockoe Bottom and at the foot of historic Church Hill as "the best symbol of an updated Richmond." *Travel & Leisure* and *National Geographic Traveller* magazines also have taken note of Millie's great food and reputation. Nationally acclaimed for its inspired "global eclectic" menu and ambiance, Millie's draws a diverse crowd — business executives, artists, students, travelers — Richmonders from all over town who enjoy good food. The menu changes every few weeks, offering creative American food with a variety of ethnic influences. The wine and beer list is international and extensive. Millie's serves lunch and dinner Tuesday through Sunday, with expanded hours for Saturday and Sunday brunch, and accepts early evening dinner reservations for parties of eight or more.

The Track
$$$ • 2915 W. Cary St. • 359-4781

The Track is in the Carytown area across from the Byrd Theater and offers steak, seafood and special menu items amid a casual, relaxed atmosphere built around a horse-racing motif. A dependable and consistent source of good food, The Track is among Richmond's fine small restaurants — a quiet place for a great meal. The restaurant serves dinner Tuesday through Saturday and recommends reservations.

All-Star Turf & Surf

Byram's Lobster House
$$ • 3215 W. Broad St. • 355-9193

Byram's has been a Richmond mainstay since the days when you could count the good restaurants on one hand. It continues to have a loyal following and is a great place for live lobster, other kinds of seafood, prime steaks, Greek food and pasta. Byram's doesn't skimp on the size of its servings. The salads are masterpieces and come with a basket of warm Italian bread and corn bread squares. The restaurant serves lunch and dinner daily, and brunch on Sundays. Early bird specials are offered from 3 to 6 PM Monday through Friday and from 2:30 to 5 PM on Sundays. Reservations are suggested.

Buckhead's Restaurant & Chop Shop
$$$$ • 8510 Patterson Ave.• 750-2000

Given the "Award of Excellence" by *Wine Spectator Magazine*, this wood-paneled, New York-style chophouse offers generous portions and one of Richmond's most extensive wine lists with choices to complement any of the appetizers, entrees or desserts. The staff personifies Southern hospitality and possesses an uncommon knowledge of the food and wines. Buckhead's offerings include salmon, steaks, chops and weekly specials. Buckhead's is open for dinner seven days a week except Sundays in the summer. Reservations are recommended.

Chetti's Cow and Clam Tavern
$ • 21 N. 17th St. • 644-4310

It's casual and offers steaks, but the emphasis is more on things like the Shockoe Bottom Clam Bake (a sampler of steamed shellfish), crabs, oysters on the half shell, Spaghetti Chetti (with mussels, scallops, shrimp and clams) and spaghetti with clam sauce. It touts itself as the "Home of The Moister Oyster Shooter." Chetti's serves dinner Tuesday through Saturday.

Sam Miller's Warehouse
$$ • 1210 E. Cary St. • 644-5465

Sam Miller's is one of Shockoe Slip's originals, and it's one of our favorite places. It offers a comfortable, clublike setting, live Maine lobsters, fresh Chesapeake Bay seafood, prime rib and other popular entrees. The restaurant serves lunch and dinner daily. Reservations usually are not necessary, but it never hurts to make them, just in case.

See our Nightlife chapters for more information about the evening happenings at Sam Miller's.

The Tobacco Company Restaurant
$$$ • 1201 E. Cary St. • 782-9555

Without question, this is the showplace of Richmond. If you want to dazzle clients, impress your visiting relatives or just plain have dinner at a place you'll never forget, this is the place to come. The restaurant covers three floors of an old warehouse and is filled with more than 400 19th-century artifacts and antiques, including a brass elevator from New York's Con Edison building that carries guests through a plant-filled atrium.

The menu is extensive: steaks, prime rib, lobster, veal, shrimp, scallops, salmon, rainbow trout, chicken, crab, Virginia ham and pasta. A second serving of prime rib is on the house if you finish off the first one. The Tobacco Company serves lunch and dinner daily and a brunch on Sunday. The bar stays open until 2 AM. Reservations for dinner are accepted until 7 PM. (See our Nightlife chapter for additional information.)

Awash in Specialties of the Sea

Awful Arthur's Seafood Company
$$ • 101 N. 18th St. • 643-1700
$$ • 7408 W. Broad St. • 672-9385

Awful Arthur's has a real fish-house atmosphere complete with a roll of paper towels at each table. It's very casual and specializes in soft-shell crabs, steamed crabs, oysters, clams, shrimp and fish but also offers pasta dishes and the Awesome Burger (6 ounces of ground chuck). A full wine list specializes in Virginia varieties. Awful Arthur's serves lunch Monday through Saturday and dinner seven days a week at its 18th Street location, and lunch and dinner daily with a Sunday brunch at its Broad Street location.

The Blue Marlin
$$ • 7502 W. Broad St. • 672-3838

The New Orleans-style music, pictures of old-time fishermen and a giant blue marlin decorate this tasty restaurant in the West End. All entrees come with homemade bread and salad topped with Goldfish crackers and a tangy Italian dressing. The creamy grits are delicious, and the homemade cobbler, no matter what fruit, shouldn't be missed. The Blue Marlin is open for lunch Monday through Friday and for dinner every night.

Brookside Seafood
$$ • 5225 Brook Rd. • 262-5716

Brookside is one of the best seafood experiences the Richmond area has to offer. Its extensive menu includes a variety of fresh local seafood cooked to perfection. The Brookside Special is a generous portion of scallops and shrimp fried with mushrooms and onions. The restaurant is open for lunch and dinner seven days a week and offers a Sunday brunch. Reservations are suggested.

The Crab House
$$ • 4040-B Cox Rd. • 270-3555

Although it might be tough, try not to fill up on the homemade hush puppies and butter that are served by the bowl as a complimentary appetizer. The crab legs are the specialty here, but everything is good, including the oysters, cream of crab soup and variety of fish entrees. Live entertainment fills The Crab House at least twice a week. Located in Innsbrook, this seafood splendor is open for lunch and dinner daily.

Crab Louie's Seafood Tavern
$$ • 13500 Midlothian Tnpk. • 275-2722

A lot of people swear by this place and its fresh seafood served in an 18th-century Colonial tavern setting in the Sycamore Square Shopping Center. Specialties are fresh fish and crab entrees, plus homemade relishes and homemade breads. Crab Louie's is open seven days a week for lunch and dinner. Reservations are suggested.

Hard Shell
$$ • 1411 E. Cary St. • 643-2333

The Hard Shell, in Shockoe Slip, is one of the best seafood restaurants in town. It offers a wide selection of seafood, from calamari and chowders to crab cakes and seafood quesadillas. Also on the menu are vegetarian and non-seafood dishes such as filet mignon, ribs and chicken fajitas. The decor features dark wood, ceiling fans and brick walls painted with mariners' advertisements. The Hard Shell serves lunch Monday through Friday and dinner Monday through Saturday. The patio is a great place to enjoy live music on week nights.

Skilligalee Seafood Restaurant
$$ • 5416 Glenside Dr. • 672-6200

Skilligalee is probably Richmond's most popular seafood place. Near Reynolds Metals' headquarters and within easy reach of downtown via I-64, it has five dining rooms, three working fireplaces and a salty decor that includes marine artifacts, ship models and decoys. The fare offers a complete seafood menu including soft-shell crabs and shad roe in-season, five to six fresh fish specials daily and steaks. Reservations are suggested for parties of five or more. The restaurant is open for lunch Monday through Friday and for dinner seven days a week.

Matt's Tavern and Comedy Club
$$$ • 109 S. 12th St. • 643-5653

More than half the entrees here are seafood, but you'll also find prime rib, burgers, sandwiches and breast of chicken. The Louisiana-style shrimp will set your mouth on fire. This location is across the street from the Omni Richmond. You'll be pleased to know that Matt Moran's mother's recipe for bread pudding has survived and is still on the menu.

Lunch and dinner are served seven days a week. The comedy club downstairs is written up in our Nightlife chapter. Reservations are required for the comedy club.

Surf Side Grill
$$ • 1714 E. Franklin St. • 644-8704

If you like straightforward food served without fancy or trendy trimmings, then you'll like Surf Side. Hush puppies come with entrees, and crab cakes are made without fillers. Side dishes are excellent and a blackboard lists an array of daily specials. You'll also find a mixed grill and, for dessert, Key lime pie. The atmosphere is very casual with beachy prints, ceiling fans and surfboards mounted on the walls. Surf Rider serves lunch Monday through Friday and dinner Monday through Saturday.

Awesome Steak and Chops

Lone Star Steakhouse & Saloon
$$ • 2001 Southpark Rd., Colonial Heights • 520-1009
$$ • 8099 W. Broad St. • 747-8783
$$ • 10456 Midlothian Tnpk. • 272-0391

While this is part of a chain, Lone Star Steakhouse gets rave reviews from local restaurant critics. The walls are wooden, the floor is plank, cold longneck bottles fill the tables and there's country music in the air. Waitresses wear "Don't Mess with Texas" T-shirts, and the menu features eight cuts of steak, chicken, ribs and a Bubba Burger. You'll find great steaks,

and you'll have a great time. (And you can even throw peanut shells on the floor like everybody else does.) Lunch and dinner are served daily.

Outback Steakhouse
$$ • 7917 W. Broad St. • 527-0583
$$ • 2063 Huguenot Rd. • 272-4500

Outback Steakhouse is part of a chain, but it is an immense favorite of locals. It has a comfortable, down-home atmosphere and a menu that's filled with big juicy steaks, chicken, ribs, chops and shrimp. The 14-ounce steak is called the Crocodile Dundee, and other lingo and decor are suitably Down Under. Outback serves dinner daily and does not take reservations.

Ruth's Chris Steak House
$$$$ • 11500 Huguenot Rd. • 378-0600

In the restored manor house of Bellgrade Plantation, Ruth's Chris offers a comfortable ambiance that's suitable for family or business dining. The menu includes prime steaks and chops, plus live Maine lobster and seafood. Ruth's Chris uses U.S. Prime corn-fed beef. (Only 5 percent of available beef is this type.) Portions are large. Desserts include hot apple pie and Raspberry Ruth, an ice cream freeze of vanilla ice cream and Chambord dusted with nutmeg. The restaurant serves dinner seven days a week, and the lounge opens at 4 PM. Reservations are suggested.

Topeka's Steakhouse 'N Saloon
$ • 1776 N. Parham Rd. • 346-3000

You might feel like you *are* in Kansas when you walk into this steakhouse. Topeka's specialty is, of course, the steaks, but you'll find a nice variety of other entrees, including rotisserie chicken, honey-lime salmon and ribs. The peanuts come by the bucket here. Located in the West End, Topeka is open for lunch and dinner every day.

Bastions of the Fan

Avalon
$$ • 2619 W. Main St. • 353-9709

Avalon is stylish in atmosphere and comprehensive in its variety of great food and drink. Innovative cuisine is emphasized. On the menu you'll find escargot, crab cakes, filet mignon and chicken dishes, plus delicious pastas and seafood salads. It has a wide selection of microbrewery beers, and the restaurant's wine selections are excellent. (See our Nightlife chapter.) Avalon serves dinner daily.

Bogart's
$ • 203 N. Lombardy St. • 353-9280

Specialty sandwiches and burgers are mainstays of this cafe, known for its casual atmosphere and walls covered with Bogart movie posters. Bogart's serves lunch and dinner in the front (cafe) part of the restaurant Monday through Saturday. Bogart's opens its popular Back Room jazz/blues club for appetizers and music on Friday and Saturday nights. The club has a $5 minimum purchase per person and does not admit anyone younger than 21. (See our Nightlife chapter for more information.) Reservations and American Express cards are not accepted.

Caffe Di Pagliacci
$$ • 214 N. Lombardy St. • 353-3040

Caffe Di Pagliacci is a great place for great Italian food, from the traditional to the classic gourmet. For more information, see the restaurant's listing under the "Italian" heading.

Commercial Taphouse and Grill
$ downstairs; $ upstairs • 111 N. Robinson St.
• 359-6544

Downstairs you'll find a spirited crowd enjoying pub fare and the focus on the restaurant's unusual selection of microbrewery beers. Upstairs is a dining room with a short but eclectic menu served in an atmosphere that is reminiscent of a quiet, avant-garde New York restaurant. The restaurant serves dinner daily.

Helen's
$$$ • Robinson and Main Sts.
• 358-4370

Helen's is a comfortable and eclectic place with a lot of personality, even sort of a 1920s bistro feel. The food is great and includes grilled salmon, sirloin, roast loin of lamb and Peking chicken. Helen's is the genuine article when it comes to a cozy restaurant with good food, and it has been a Fan favorite for more than a decade. Helen's serves dinner daily.

Joe's Inn
$ • 205 N. Shields • 355-2282

Joe's is an enduring (about 20 years) Fan favorite that offers breakfast, sandwiches, Spaghetti à la Joe and à la Greek, subs and homemade dishes. The atmosphere is casual, but it gets very busy at night so be sure to put your name on the list for a table as soon as you walk in the door. Joe's serves breakfast, lunch and dinner seven days a week. (See our Nightlife chapter for more information.)

Konsta's Restaurant and Lounge
$$ • 2526 Floyd Ave. • 359-3122

Upscale yet casual in atmosphere, Konsta's prepares its own brand of nouvelle and continental cuisine. For more information, see Konsta's listing in the "Accent on Continental" section of this chapter.

The Lighthouse
$ • 1627 W. Main St. • 353-4060

Decorated with pictures of lighthouses, this restaurant has a full range of food styles, including Greek, Italian and American. If you're with a big group, the Greek nachos are a great appetizer (or a great meal for two to share). And the vegetarian sub and French fries are the best in town. But above all, save room for Richmond's best cheesecake, topped with either blueberries or strawberries. It's thick and fluffy, and the owner swears he'll never share the recipe. The Lighthouse is open for dinner daily.

Robin Inn
$ • 2601 Park Ave. • 353-0298

The service here is fast, the prices are reasonable, and the restaurant has been family-operated for more than 30 years. Patrons come from all over town. Specialties include spaghetti, lasagna and pizza. Robin Inn isn't fancy, but it is a place where you'll immediately feel comfortable and at home — and the food is great. They even deliver. Lunch and dinner are served Tuesday through Sunday.

Sidewalk Cafe
$ • 2101 W. Main St. • 358-0645

Sidewalk Cafe features a mix of steaks, barbecue, seafood, Italian and Greek fare, plus quick-service deli sandwiches. With a two-story black-and-white mural of "Miss Sidewalk Cafe" on the side of the building, it's hard to miss this inexpensive neighborhood spot that attracts a lively crowd. It's open seven days a week for lunch and dinner and later (see our Nightlife chapter for more information on the "later").

Soble's
$ • 2600 W. Main St. • 358-7843

Soble's serves seafood, beef and deli items in a deli/bar atmosphere. It's a well-patronized place and features a great outdoor patio and raw bar offering oysters on the half-shell, fresh crabmeat and king crab legs. Their bacon cheeseburger is a must. The restaurant serves lunch and dinner. (See our Nightlife chapter for more.)

Southern Culture
$$ • 2229 W. Main St. • 355-6939

This restaurant ignites the gastronomic experience by blending Cajun, Creole, Caribbean, Mexican and pure Southern flavors with confidence and flair. Dessert portions are large enough to serve two. There's a large bar downstairs (see our Nightlife chapter) with lots of booths and an upstairs (quieter) main dining room. The atmosphere is reminiscent of New Orleans with a few touches of 1950s kitsch. Dinner is served daily.

Strawberry Street Cafe
$ • 421 Strawberry St. • 353-6860

A Fan tradition, Strawberry Street Cafe is popular for its salad bar that is set up in an old-fashioned bathtub on legs and its homemade burgers, pastas, vegetarian lasagna, beef and chicken. It has a casual atmosphere, a large wine selection and a children's menu. Local artists do impressionistic chalkboard art.

Lunch and dinner are served seven days a week, and there's a weekend brunch. (See our Nightlife chapter.)

Best Virginia (North Carolina and Tennessee) Barbecue

Allman's Barbecue
$, no credit cards • 9130 Jefferson Davis Hwy.
• 271-9710

Allman's specialties include a pork plate and ribs plus homemade apple pie and peach cobbler. It's got hush puppies, black-eyed peas, greens and cole slaw, and it'll arrange a take-out Pig-Out Party (tell Allman's how many people and it'll prepare the works) on two-day's notice. Allman's is open for lunch and dinner Monday through Saturday.

Bill's Barbecue
$ • 331 Church Rd. • 747-3980
$ • 927 Myers St. • 355-9905
$ • 5805 W. Broad St. • 282-8539
$ • 6555 Mechanicsville Tnpk. • 746-2429
$ • 3100 N. Boulevard • 355-9745
$ • 700 E. Main St. • 788-1261
$ • 8820 W. Broad St. • 270-9722
$ • 10101 Brook Rd., Glen Allen • 553-0826
$ • 11230 Midlothian Tnpk. • 794-9849
$ • 45 Broad St., Manakin Sabot • 784-0256
Credit cards are not accepted at any location.

Established in 1930, Bill's has been synonymous in Richmond with the word "barbecue." It's a popular place, and it specializes in Virginia-style barbecue, freshly squeezed limeades and lemonades, family-made pies (including regional sweet potato pies, lemon chess pies and cream-topped icebox fruit pies) and special breakfast items. Service is quick, and the restaurants are well-run. Bill's opens

---

INSIDERS' TIP

Wine connoisseurs will enjoy Buckhead's top-rated wine list, recently given the "Award of Excellence" by *Wine Spectator* magazine.

early (about 7 AM) and stays open until well after the dinner hour, seven days a week. Children eat for free when accompanied by an adult on Wednesdays from 4 until 8 PM.

Carolina Bar-B-Que
$, no credit cards • 3015 Nine Mile Rd. • 649-3424

If you like your barbecue Carolina-style, this is your place. You'll also find deviled crab, shrimp, fish and bologna burgers. You can stop by for lunch or dinner seven days a week. On Friday and Saturday the place stays open until 3 AM.

Extra Billy's Steak & Bar-B-Que
$ • 5205 W. Broad St. • 282-3949

"Where there's smoke there's barbecue," the saying goes, and it is usually hard to miss the aroma as you approach Extra Billy's. It has a large seating capacity and is near The Shops at Willow Lawn. Specialties are a barbecue sandwich and plate, baby back ribs, a brisket plate and prime rib. Extra Billy's is open for lunch and dinner Monday through Friday. On Saturday it opens for dinner only.

The Farm House
$$ • 7519 Jefferson Davis Hwy. • 271-6472

This place is nationally known for its barbecue sauce and ribs. Red carpeting starts on the floor and runs right up the wall. The Farm House will feed you breakfast, lunch and dinner Tuesday through Sunday. Reservations are recommended for parties of eight or more.

Houndstooth Cafe
$$ • U.S. 301 and Rt. 54, Hanover Courthouse • 537-5404

The walls are decorated with hunt prints and brass horns, there are formal curtains at the windows and Coalport china graces the shelves. A stuffed fox dressed in a red jacket smiles from a corner. Not your usual kind of barbecue place, but that's what this restaurant in the small, historic village of Hanover Courthouse is famous for. It's also known for its fresh seafood and other dishes, all well-prepared. The dining rooms are relaxed, and the bourbon-laced Derby pie is decadent. The restaurant serves lunch and dinner Tuesday through Saturday and is closed Sunday and Monday.

Smokey Pig Restaurant
$ • 212 S. Washington Hwy. (U.S. 1), Ashland • 798-4590

The Smokey motto is "I Dig the Pig," and there are pig pictures and pig ornaments galore. Specialties, in addition to ones you might expect, such as baby back ribs, hush puppies and homemade desserts, include crab cakes. It's a popular, family-operated place for locals and for travelers. Smokey Pig observes lunch and dinner hours Tuesday through Sunday and closes on Monday.

Breweries

Legend Brewing Company
$ • 321 W. 7th St. • 232-3446

Legend brews a variety of beers, including a lager, pilsner, porter and different monthly specialty beers. The food is spicy, but always good. You'll find a variety of salads, sandwiches, pastas and more. Legend, located just across the James River, is open daily for lunch and dinner.

Richbrau Brewing Company & Restaurant
$$ • 1214 E. Cary St. • 644-3018

The big draw of this microbrewery is the beer and ale produced on premises. But the club-like atmosphere (see our Nightlife chapter) provides an interesting background for lunch or dinner. The menu includes a signature dish, Sonoma shrimp sauteed in olive oil and tossed with sun-dried tomatoes, carmelized garlic, spinach and cappellini. Also on the menu are a mixed sausage grill, beer-battered fish and chips, specialty sandwiches and salads. Lunch and dinner are served seven days a week, and an appetizer and bar menu is available until 1 AM.

British Pubs

Fox and Hounds British Pub
$$ • 10455 Midlothian Tnpk. • 272-8309

Steak-and-kidney pie, shepherd's pie, fish and chips and a lot of American options are here along with a billiard room and cozy dining in The Library. Lunch and dinner are served daily. The pub offers live music Mondays, and often on Thursdays, Fridays and Saturdays.

Penny Lane Pub
$ • 207 N. 7th St. • 780-1682

Penny Lane has seven imported beers on tap and offers British fare, steaks, chops, lamb and seafood. The atmosphere is informal, and the owner and his staff are attentive. Penny Lane Pub serves lunch Monday through Friday and dinner Monday through Saturday. Reservations are recommended for parties of four or more for Saturday dinners.

Potter's Pub
$$ • 7007 Three Chopt Rd. • 282-9999

British pub dishes here include steak-and-mushroom pies, and fish and chips. Steak and seafood also are on the menu. Potter's is a popular place at night, and the crowd sings along with the band Tuesday through Saturday (see the Nightlife chapter). Potter's serves lunch Monday through Friday and dinner Monday through Saturday. Reservations are recommended.

Siné
$ • 1327 E. Cary St. • 649-7767

This brand new Irish pub and restaurant in Shockoe Slip has a wide selection of food and a full-service bar. For more information, see the "Nightlife" chapter.

Cajun

Cobblestone Brewery
$ • 110 N. 18th St. • 644-2739

With pool and foosball, live music and 30 microbrews on tap, this is a popular spot for casual, relaxed dinning — and perhaps some taste testing. The food is best described as a Cajun/Jamaican blend: seafood and steaks, primarily, with blackboard specials. Cobblestone offers a side dinning room for large and private parties. Located in the lively Shockoe

Bottom, it's a good place to stay all night. (See our Nightlife chapter.) The cobblestone is closed on Sundays and Mondays.

Gumbo Ya-Ya
$$ • 2232 W. Main St. • 358-9292

Cajun food is one of the new entries on the local restaurant scene, and Gumbo Ya-Ya helped launch its introduction. The menu offers just about everything you'd expect: jambalayas, gumbo, red beans and rice, crawfish, and lots of dishes featuring shrimp and spicy sauces. Five sauces compliment the pastas, all of which are vegetarian. And, of course, always be sure to listen for chef Jason Purkey's nightly specials. The restaurant serves dinner seven days a week.

Medley's
$$ • 1701 E. Main St. • 648-2313

This New Orleans-style Cajun and Blues bar features authentic Cajun and French cuisine, including Creole Jambalaya, Medley's Etoufee, Andouille sausage, as well as turtle, alligator, crawfish, assorted fish, chicken and steak. It's open Monday through Saturday for lunch and dinner, and Sunday for brunch only.

Caribbean

Winnie's Caribbean Cuisine
$$ • 200 E. Main St. • 649-4974

Winnie's began serving Caribbean cuisine long before it became trendy. Spanish, Portuguese, Dutch, African and East Indian influences blend in the menu. Recorded reggae music and Caribbean colors and decor add to the atmosphere. Lunch is served Monday through Friday and dinner is served Monday through Saturday (including an all-you-can-eat buffet on Friday). Winnie's is closed on Sunday.

Carryout

Almost any restaurant will be happy to fix carryout meals if you call in advance. Some,

---

INSIDERS' TIP

Strawberry Street Cafe has their salad bar in, of all places, a claw-foot bathtub.

such as Bottoms Up Pizza, will even deliver within specified geographical bounds and within certain periods of the day. Though most of the customers for these places take their food to go, most have tables. For starters, here is a list of some local favorites in the carryout business.

Belle Kuisine

$ • 3044 Stony Point Shopping Center • 272-2811
$ • Broad St., Shops at Willow Lawn • 282-2266
$ • 3426 Pump Rd. • 360-1964

Belle Kuisine's peanut butter cookies and Heath bar cookies are out of this world. But the main events are the lunch and dinner entrees (including pastas), the salads and the locally produced specialty foods. Lunch and dinner are served Monday through Saturday, and a Sunday brunch is offered at the Willow Lawn location.

Dominic's of New York

$ • 1600 Willow Lawn Dr. • 673-2586
$ • 4502 W. Broad St.
$ • 10901 Hull Street Rd.
$ • 3700 W. Kroger Ctr. (behind Chesterfield Towne Ctr.)
$ • 12640 Jefferson Davis Hwy.

Even if you're not shopping for hardware or do-it-yourself items at Lowe's, Dominic's is an excellent reason for visiting Lowe's locations in the Richmond area. Dominic's operates out of mobile kitchens in front of Lowe's and the cuisine offers, among other things, a cheese steak sandwich that beats anything you'll find in south Philly — drippy, heaping with meat and those great fried peppers and oozing with cheese. There are five kinds of steak sandwiches, five kinds of chicken sandwiches, sausage sandwiches and hot dogs.

Fantaste

$ • 1201 W. Main St. • 355-1889

Fantaste's offerings are covered in the following "Lunch Places" section. Pick up and delivery times are available seven days a week.

Homemades by Suzanne

$ • 10 S. Sixth St. • 775-2116
$ • 102 N. Railroad St., Ashland • 798-8331

Homemades by Suzanne's specialties are covered later in this chapter in the "Lunch Places" section.

Incredible Edibles

$ • 1 N. Belmont Ave. • 353-3356

In keeping with its name, Incredible Edibles offers temptations that range from tarragon chicken and chicken-and-artichoke pasta salad to some of the most fantastic baked goods and desserts you'll find anywhere. Breakfast, lunch and dinner are offered Monday through Saturday at the Belmont location.

Konsta's Bakery and Pastry Shoppe

$ • 2526 Floyd Ave. • 359-3122

This little neighborhood gourmet bakery and pastry shop mixes the tastes of Europe with Southern hospitality. It offers a variety of homemade breads, pies, decorated cakes, pastries and muffins, plus a full line of deli goods and boxed lunches to go.

Mainly Pasta

$ • 2227 W. Main St. • 359-9304

If it's pasta, it has to be here! In addition to gourmet pastas, you'll find fresh salads, desserts and box lunches. The pasta is made fresh, by hand. They are closed Sunday and Monday.

Mediterranean Bakery & Deli

$ • 6516 Horsepen Rd. • 285-1488

This bakery and deli welcomes visitors in at least a half-dozen scripts and languages outside the door. When you leave you'll carry home goodies that easily could have been picked up from a street vendor in Beirut. It's a good idea to call ahead and place your order for faster service. Their menu features falafel, spinach and feta cheese pies and all sorts of exotic blends, like breast of chicken on pizza bread.

Sally Bell's Kitchen

$ • 708 W. Grace St. • 644-2838

"The most famous take-out going," Sally Bell's is a genuine Richmond institution. It has a secret recipe for making deviled eggs and potato salad. Its box lunches are popular, so be sure to call ahead. Open Monday through

Friday, 10 AM to 4 PM, Sally Bell's only serves lunch: sandwiches, ham biscuits, cupcakes and the like. It also caters.

Stonewall Market
$ • 4917 Grove Ave. • 358-3821

Stonewall Market, in a fashionable section of the West End, is much more than your average run-of-the mill grocery store and will prepare box lunches and deli trays to go. Call in advance.

Tokyo Teriyaki
$ • 918 W. Grace St. • 355-7517

A good place to sample Japanese food, Tokyo Teriyaki specializes in teriyaki and tempura along with dishes such as chicken katsu, fish katsu and miso soup. While it mainly deals with take-out orders, there are a few tables, and servers are helpful and knowledgeable.

Ukrop's Carryout Cafe
$ • 3522 W. Cary St. • 353-0676
$ • 10001 Hull Street Rd. • 745-4920
$ • 11361 Midlothian Tnpk. • 379-1444
$ • 12601 Jefferson Davis Hwy. • 748-7142
$ • 9645 W. Broad St. • 965-0530
$ • 5700 Brook Rd. • 264-1595
$ • 40 Colonial Sq. • 520-4800
$ • Heritage Bldg., 10th and Main Sts.
• 648-5633
$ • 7324 Bell Creek Rd. • 746-4441
$ • 9782 Gayton Rd. • 740-9167
$ • 13700 Hull Street Rd. • 739-9845
$ • 8028 W. Broad St. • 270-9621
$ • 253 N. Washington Hwy. • 798-1305
$ • 6401 Centralia Rd. • 796-1120
$ • 3000 Stony Point Rd. • 323-0306
$ • 1008 Sycamore Sq. • 794-7074
$ • 7035 Three Chopt Rd. • 288-5263
$ • 3460 Pump Rd. • 364-1480

Operated by the famous Richmond grocery chain, the Ukrop's carryout cafes are hard to beat when it comes to freshness and quality. They have a detailed menu, and you can watch food being prepared on the spot, or you can fix your own — for breakfast, lunch or dinner. All locations are open Monday through Saturday, except for the Ukrop's location in the Heritage Building (Fresh Express, a cafeteria-style cafe with all sorts of lunch items) which is not open on Saturday. The Cafe location in the Village Shopping Center is the talk of the town and is one of the best. The Pump Road location features an outdoor garden cafe.

Vie de France
$ • 1501 E. Cary St. • 780-0748

In the atrium of James Center II, Vie de France offers an extensive array of croissants, muffins, Danish pastries and a lunch menu with a decidedly country-French flair. Specials are posted daily. A sizeable seating area is available should you want to eat in. Party trays and catering are a specialty.

Caterers

The Richmond area has a lot of excellent caterers. The Bell Atlantic Yellow Pages' listing of caterers covers six pages, and the list includes the names of many local restaurants. Here are the names and phone numbers of a few:

Catering by Jill
8574 Sanford Ct. • 262-5787

Jill (actually owner Jack Halpern) specializes in corporate catering, weddings and catering for motion-picture crews when they are on location in Richmond. But he also fixes box lunches. The food is "eclectic American," meaning just about anything from ham biscuits to fajitas — and then some.

duJour
5806 Grove Ave. • 285-1301

The menu is always changing, offering up the season's best ingredients. duJour offers imaginative treatments of seafood, meat and poultry. For more information on the restaurant, see the listing in the "Accent on Continental" section.

INSIDERS' TIP

Some Richmonders maintain that the deviled eggs at Sally Bell's Kitchen are the best in the world.

Homemades by Suzanne
102 N. Railroad Ave., Ashland • 798-8331

Suzanne has a loyal following and an excellent reputation. She has several restaurants, mentioned elsewhere in this chapter, which have grown out of her catering business. Her specialties include homemade breads, salads, soups and desserts.

Houndstooth Cafe
U.S. 301 and Rt. 54, Hanover Courthouse • 537-5404

Known for its seafood and barbecue, Houndstooth Cafe does it all: food, drinks, mixed drinks, beer and wine, soft drinks and desserts. It provides for wedding receptions, rehearsal dinners, corporate functions, and much more. See the Houndstooth Cafe's entry in the Barbecue section.

I Cater
6937 Lakeside Ave. • 266-3992

We have put on a number of events catered by I Cater. Food and service are first class, and this business is careful to adhere to budget limits.

Incredible Edibles
1 Belmont Ave. • 359-2825

This gourmet food shop handles small and large events, including business meetings, cocktail parties, weddings, rehearsal dinners and box lunches for any occasion.

Konsta's
2526 Floyd Ave. • 359-3122

Konsta's promises "a celebration with a flair." It handles off-premises buffets, corporate events, receptions and outdoor events. See the restaurant's entry in the "Accent on Continental" section.

Mr. Patrick Henry's Inn
2300 E. Broad St. • 644-1322

Located on historic Church Hill, Mr. Patrick Henry's has a long history of catering throughout the Richmond area. The Inn is known for its grilling and smoking of seafood and poultry. See our write-up in the "Alive with History" section for more about the Inn's restaurant.

Chinese

China Kitchen
$ • 9157-B Atlee Rd. • 746-9103

The decor is simple and unpretentious; pop Chinese tunes play in the background; and the food is excellent. The menu is extensive and offers combination meals. Many customers come in for carryout orders. China Kitchen serves lunch Monday through Friday and dinner Sunday through Friday.

Golden Dragon
$ • 3028 W. Cary St. • 359-4062

This Chinese restaurant is a bit of an adventure with some unusual and exotic dishes on the menu that you might not expect to find. The food is well-prepared, and sauces are excellent. Reservations are not required. Lunch is served Tuesday through Saturday. Dinner is served seven days a week.

Hunan East Gourmet
$ • 4415 W. Broad St. • 353-1001

This restaurant serves an all-you-can-eat lunch buffet daily as well as dinner. It is very popular with Richmonders who know good value and good food, and it features Hunan and Szechuan cuisines. Lunch and dinner are available seven days a week.

Joy Garden
$ • 2918 W. Broad St. • 358-8012

One of our personal favorites and for many years Joy Garden was Richmond's only Chinese restaurant. Its specialties include Cantonese, Szechuan and Hunan dishes. Joy Garden serves dinner seven days a week. Reservations are suggested on weekends.

Mandarin Palace
$ • 2811 Stratford Hills Shopping Ctr. • 272-8020

Don't let the shopping center address scare you off. The former chef for a U.S. Ambassador established the longtime Richmond favorite that is not far from the Forest Hill Avenue exit on the Powhite Expressway. Dinner is served daily and lunch is served every day

but Sunday. You usually do not need reservations.

Peking Restaurant
$ • 8904 W. Broad St. • 270-9898
$ • 1302 E. Cary St. • 649-8888
$ • 5710 Grove Ave. • 288-8371
$ • 7100 Mechanicsville Tnpk., Mechanicsville
• 730-9898
$ • 13132 Midlothian Tnpk. • 794-1799
$ • Rt. 1 and Rt. 10, Chester • 751-9898

With its attentive service and good food, Peking Restaurant has developed a loyal clientele. The menu covers a wide range from Peking specialties to Szechuan, Mandarin and Hunan dishes. Dinner is served at all locations every day. Lunch is served Monday through Friday. Sunday features an all-you-can-eat buffet.

Tiki-Tiki Restaurant
$$ • 8917 Patterson Ave. • 740-7258

Tiki-Tiki offers Cantonese, Szechuan, Polynesian and American dishes served in an Oriental atmosphere. Lunch and dinner are served daily.

Yum Yum Good
$ • 5612 Patterson Ave. • 673-9226

The name, you might think, is a bit silly. But the atmosphere is warm, and the food and service are critically acclaimed. The luncheon menu features a long list of specials, and the evening menu offers Hunan, Cantonese and Szechuan dishes, plus some interesting variations. Yum Yum Good is a popular place for carryout food. Dinner is served seven days a week and lunch every day but Sunday. Reservations are not required.

Chinese Fast Food

Two popular places for fast-food counter service and carryout Chinese food are Hunan Express at 10833-B W. Broad Street, 388 Southpark Circle and 11500 Midlothian Turnpike, and Ming's Dynasty in the Hungry Brook Shopping Center at Parham Road and U.S. Route 1.

Coffeehouses and Bagel Shops

Belle Kuisine

$ • **3044 Stony Point Shopping Center** • **272-2811**

$ • **Broad St., Shops at Willow Lawn** • **282-2266**

$ • **3426 Pump Rd.** • **360-1964**

See the full write-up for this lunch and dinner spot in the "Carryout" section of this chapter.

Bev's

$ • **2911 W. Cary St.** • **204-2387**

Bev's has a great selection of coffee to go with the wraps, salads, soups, sandwiches and baked goods that are offered. And to top off a great meal is homemade ice cream. Located in Carytown across the street from The Byrd Theatre, Bev's is open every day.

Chesapeake Bagel Bakery

$ • **Chesterfield Towne Center** • **794-1600**

$ • **10839 W. Broad St.** • **346-3300**

$ • **Broad St., Shops at Willow Lawn** • **285-5000**

Fourteen varieties of fresh-baked bagels, nine flavors of cream cheese, sandwiches, salads, homemade soups, desserts, party platters and a large variety of beverages — everything is here for eat-in or carryout feasts built around bagels or croissants. Chesapeake Bagel is open seven days a week.

Coffee & Co.

$ • **2928 W. Cary St.** • **355-2040**

A gourmet coffeehouse and bakery, Coffee & Co. is open seven days a week. It's a pleasant place to relax with great coffees, espresso drinks or house-blend cappuccinos. Sample croissants, bagels, muffins, cookies, brownies, cakes, fresh-baked bread and other works of the baker's art. On weeknights there are Word Parties — monologues, poetry and book readings, plays and folk singers.

Java Outpost

$ • **3433 W. Cary St.** • **359-0868**

If you're looking for a delicious sandwich (or muffin or pastry) and a soothing cup of coffee (or tea or chai) for lunch, then Java Outpost is where you should go. Sandwiches include turkey and brie, San Francisco style seafood salad and smoked gouda. Located in Carytown, this coffeehouse has plenty of seating upstairs, downstairs and on a small patio out front. Java Outpost is open every day.

FYI

Unless otherwise noted, the area code for all phone numbers listed in this chapter is 804.

Manhattan Bagel

$ • **5401 Glenside Dr.** • **266-1558**

$ • **4028 Cox Rd.** • **346-4889**

$ • **9411 Burge Ave.** • **275-6165**

$ • **10461 Midlothian Tnpk.** • **560-9448**

You'll find 18 varieties of bagels baked fresh daily. The full-service grill is open for breakfast and lunch and serves sandwiches and six kinds of cream cheese.

Puddin' Head

$ • **1211 W. Main St.** • **355-2739**

This cafe in the trendy area of W. Main seems to be a favorite among Fan District residents and VCU students. Not only is there a large variety of coffee and tea, but it also offers pastries, boxed and light-fare lunches, a variety of teapots and other fine bakery items. Local artwork hangs on the walls, and a jazz pianist plays an upright piano at lunch Tuesday and Thursday (except in the summer months). Here you'll find all of the coffees and pastries you'll need for a delightful break in the day. Puddin' Head is open from sunup to sundown Monday through Saturday.

World Cup

$, no credit cards • **204 N. Robinson St.** • **359-5282**

Classical music plays, shelves are lined with travel books and current magazines, and there are plenty of things to nibble on. Come here for civilized beginnings to the day, for lunch or to unwind after a hectic day. World Cup opens up bright and early in the morning seven days a week.

Delis

Boulevard Restaurant & Deli
$ • 5218 W. Broad St. • 282-9333

The Boulevard Restaurant & Deli is a popular spot not far from the Shoppes at Willow Lawn, and it serves a breakfast menu all day. It specializes in quality Kosher meats, homemade soups, salads and desserts. It also carries Virginia wines. The deli is open for lunch Monday through Friday and dinner Friday and Saturday.

Boychik's Deli
$ • 4024-B Cox Rd. • 747-1030

Boychik's gets its bagels from New York, and a variety of choices are available fresh each day. In addition to bagels and fish platters, potato knishes and matzo ball soup, Boychik's has cheeseburgers, western omelettes, steak dinners and Italian entrees. Boychik's is open for breakfast, lunch and dinner Monday through Saturday and for breakfast and lunch on Sunday.

Coppola's
$ • 1116 E. Main St. • 225-0454
$ • 2900 W. Cary St. • 359-6969

This is the headquarters for Italian meats and for Heros, meatball sandwiches and vegetarian subs. It is open for lunch and dinner Monday through Saturday. The downtown location is closed on weekends.

Hickory Hams Cafe & Deli
$ • 4040 G. Cox Rd., Glen Allen • 747-4534

Hickory Hams, in the Innsbrook Shoppes, serves a variety of sandwiches, soups and salads. This Atlanta-based company also offers spiral-sliced hams and turkeys and serves lunch and dinner Monday through Saturday.

Manhattan Deli
$ • 9550 Midlothian Tnpk. • 330-3845

It's in a Midlothian Turnpike shopping center and it may be far too clean and courteous to be a true New York delicatessen, but local restaurant critics say it does an excellent job of capturing the spirit. An array of beer fills the shelves, display cases show off cheesecakes, and there are first-rate Reubens, sailors, subs, four varieties of franks, soups and bagels. A chalkboard lists daily specials. Manhattan Deli is open for lunch and dinner Monday through Saturday.

New York Delicatessen
$ • 2920 W. Cary St. • 355-6056

Specialties here include New York-style deli sandwiches, clubs and subs, salad bowls and platters, omelettes, smoked fish, Nova and whitefish. Deli meats and fish come from New York, and the bagels are fresh. The New York Delicatessen has been in business for more than 50 years. Breakfast, lunch and dinner hours are observed seven days a week.

Padow's Ham & Deli
$ • The Shops at Willow Lawn • 358-4267
$ • 1110 E. Main St. • 648-4267
$ • 9720 Midlothian Tnpk. • 330-4267
$ • 900 E. Broad St. • 225-9333

Padow's to Richmonders means "ham." For more than 50 years Padow's has been the local king of Smithfield ham, country ham, honey-glazed ham and slab bacon. You can buy the whole ham at Padow's or you can get them to put together sandwiches and platters. They also carry Virginia peanuts and other delicacies.

Sue's Country Kitchen
$, no credit cards • 1213 Summit Ave. • 353-5408

To be sure, Sue's carries the hot-lunch specials with meat, vegetables and rolls you'd expect from a country kitchen. But the deli fare here is the real standout — hot pastrami and Swiss on rye, sailors, creamy potato salad, soups and rich desserts. Sue's serves lunch Monday through Friday.

Family Restaurants

Dabney's Restaurant
$ • 1501 Robin Hood Rd. • 359-8126

The buffet and menu here include a lot of good solid food: things like meat loaf, baked and fried chicken, crab cakes, beef Stroganoff, buttery spoon bread and warm rolls. Dabney's serves lunch and dinner seven days a week.

Elli's Restaurant
$ • 10392 S. Leadbetter Rd., Ashland • 550-3400

All entrees here are priced less than $10, and there's a wide selection — from steaks to spaghetti. Lunch and dinner are served seven days a week. Elli's emphasis is on family fare and prices. The Airpark Shopping Center is just off Interstate 95 near the Atlee-Elmont exit, but call for directions if you're not familiar with the area. The restaurant is closed on Sundays.

Fuddruckers
$ • 8317 W. Broad St. • 747-4779

This place is popular for its easygoing atmosphere and for its delicious burgers. Fuddruckers grinds its own beef daily and makes its own buns, so you can imagine how tasty the end result is. Children, and those not having to watch a waistline, also love Fuddruckers' shakes and malts, handmade with whole milk, and hand-dipped ice cream.

The little ones also enjoy Monday nights when they are entertained by costumed characters, leaving Mom and Dad more time to savor their meals. There's also live music on Tuesday nights. Fuddruckers serves lunch and dinner seven days a week. In summer, the restaurant stays open until 11 PM.

Shoney's
$ • 10093 Brook Rd. • 261-9307
$ • 8901 Brook Rd. • 553-8395
$ • 5310 Oaklawn Blvd., Hopewell • 748-6834
$ • 12531 Jefferson Davis Hwy., Chester • 748-9087
$ • 11500 Midlothian Tnpk. • 222-6226
$ • 9963 Hull St. • 266-2459
$ • 7009 W. Broad St. • 672-2802
$ • 8415 W. Broad St. • 747-1655
$ • 7101 Staples Mill Rd. • 745-4950
$ • 7137 Mechanicsville Tnpk. • 730-2572

This is family eating that is affordable, enjoyable and tasty. The 10 metro-area locations of this chain are popular with tourists and visitors alike. The gigantic all-you-can-eat breakfast bar attracts a lot of loyal followers and not only offers traditional breakfast foods but also low-fat and low-cholesterol selections (plenty of fresh fruit, low-fat English muffins, low-fat milk and cholesterol-free Bundt cake) for the health conscious as well as cereals such as Captain Crunch and Trix for the younger crowd. The menus for breakfast, lunch and dinner are extensive. Shoney's offers 50¢ off Senior Meals, regular specials such as Family Night when children 12 and younger eat free, and a $2.99 Breakfast Bar from 6 to 8 AM on Friday. The Shoney's restaurants are open seven days a week.

Fast Food

For fast food the way it used to be served, and for fast-food architecture that looks like something out of the '50s, try one of the following restaurants. The burgers and fries are great at all of these places.

Bullets, with locations at 7712 W. Broad St., 1501 Eastridge Rd., 2224 Chamber-layne Ave., 10100 Midlothian Tnpk., 400 E. Belt Blvd., 6600 Mechanicsville Tnpk. and 4802 W. Broad St.

Dairy Queen
$ • 2311 W. Broad St. • 359-4780
$ • 10101 Brook Rd. • 553-1252
$ • Cloverleaf Mall • 276-3825
$ • 5711 Hull Street Rd. • 276-0115
$ • I-95, Atlee/Elmont Exit • 550-2775
$ • 11964 Iron Bridge Plaza, Chester • 748-4817
$ • 8830 Jefferson Davis Hwy. • 271-7990
$ • 4844 S. Laburnum Ave. • 222-0700
$ • 11500 Midlothian Tnpk. • 379-5256

Dairy Queen serves frozen yogurt and soft ice cream and specializes in custom ice cream cakes. This is the home of the Blizzard, a frozen thicker-than-a-shake concoction of soft ice cream blended with fruits, candies and cookies.

Fondue

The Melting Pot
$$ • 9704 Gayton Rd. • 741-3120

Creamy cheese fondues are in the spotlight here. But you also can enjoy other specialties: filet mignon, teriyaki sirloin, chicken and fresh seafood. The Melting Pot has tables with built-in burners filled with peanut oil or spice bullion. Everything from appetizers to dessert is a do-it-yourself cooking experience. Dinner is served daily.

French

La Petite France
$$$ • 2912 Maywill St. • 353-8729

Marie Antoinette and Paul Elbling brought gourmet French cuisine to Richmond when they opened La Petite France a quarter of a century ago. They, and their restaurant, have become Richmond institutions. You can't go wrong here if you like great food! Lunch is served Tuesday through Friday. Dinner is served Tuesday through Saturday. Reservations are strongly suggested.

Greek

Athens Tavern
$ • 401 N. Robinson St. • 353-9119

The Athens Tavern was the original Greek restaurant in Richmond. Our friends who really know Greek fare say it's the best in town. If you're looking for good guvetsi, baklava, moussaka and other great food in a tavern atmosphere, why not check out the original article? Dinner is served seven days a week, and reservations are recommended for large parties.

The Crazy Greek
$ • 1903 Staples Mill Rd. • 355-3786

This is a busy place, maybe because it serves Italian and Greek dishes. Portions are generous, prices are extremely reasonable, and the restaurant is very family-friendly. Lunch is served Monday through Friday and dinner is served Monday through Saturday. Reserva-

tions are recommended for parties of five or more.

Dena's Grecian Restaurant
$$ • 11314 Midlothian Tnpk. (Sassafras Shopping Ctr.) • 794-9551

Voted "The Best Greek Restaurant" in *Richmond Magazine,* Dena's offers Greek as well as American and Italian cuisine in a casual atmosphere. The food is top-class, and the service is excellent. The restaurant is next to Chesterfield Mall. Dena's is open for lunch and dinner Monday through Friday, but for dinner only on Saturday. The restaurant is closed Sunday. Reservations are recommended for parties of five or more.

The Greek Islands Restaurant
$ • 10902 Hull St. • 674-9199

Restaurant critics rave about this place as one of the best restaurants in town. The Greek Islands is family-operated. Specialties include chicken lemonato, stuffed grape leaves, lamb chops, Shrimp Mikonos and homemade bread. The restaurant serves dinner daily. Reservations are suggested.

Trak's Greek and Italian Restaurant
$$ • 9115 Quioccasin Rd. • 740-1700

A small, family-run place with a relaxed atmosphere that allows you to linger over a meal, Trak's gets great reviews. The truest taste of what Trak's is all about is in its Mediterranean Sampler. It includes all of the specialties of the house: dolmades, tiropita, spanakopita, real feta cheese, Greek olives, tomatoes, pepperoncini and Greek caviar. Trak's serves lunch and dinner daily, except for Saturdays in the summer.

Zorba's
$ • 9068 W. Broad St. • 270-6026

The fare here is not intended for the gourmet but for those who want to savor big platters of Greek and Italian specialties. Doggie

---

INSIDERS' TIP

Havana '59 doesn't just tolerate smoking, it encourages it. Try the fine selection of cigars. Sorry, no Cubans.

bags are so common the staff offers to box leftovers before one even digs in. Zorba's is open daily for lunch and dinner.

Indian

Farouk's House of India
$ • 3033 W. Cary St. • 355-0378

Farouk's was Richmond's first Indian restaurant and serves North Indian food, like vindaloos and biryanis, in a warm, friendly atmosphere. Lunch is served Tuesday through Sunday, dinner is daily, and a brunch is offered on Sundays.

India House
$ • 2313 Westwood Ave. • 355-8378

Entrees include Indian specialties made with chicken, lamb, vegetables, rice and seafood. The restaurant gets consistently excellent reviews and is one of the few restaurants in town to make all of the *Critics' Choice* lists. Lunch is served Monday through Friday, and dinner is served Monday through Saturday.

Passage to India
$ • 6856 Midlothian Tnpk. • 745-5291

At Passage to India you can specify how you want your curry: mild, medium or hot. The cuisine is excellent, and the menu is wide-ranging. Restaurant critics love this place. The restaurant serves lunch Monday through Saturday and dinner seven days a week.

Italian

Amici Ristorante
$$ • 3343 W. Cary St. • 353-4700

Amici is truly one of the greatest restaurants in town. The service, ambiance and food are all excellent — a real dining experience. The extensive menu includes fresh homemade pasta, seafood, veal and game. Amici's classic approach to Northern Italian cooking and its attractive presentations make every meal one to remember. Amici's has had a four-star rating for six years running and has been praised by *Bon Appetite* and *Southern Living* magazine.

Reservations are a must. Dinner is served daily and lunch is served Monday through Saturday. Patio dining is available.

Caffe Di Pagliacci
$$ • 214 N. Lombardy St. • 353-3040

This cozy, award-winning neighborhood restaurant in the Fan District serves homemade Italian fare from the traditional to the gourmet. Family-owned and operated, its specialties include fresh pasta, seafood, veal, incredible desserts plus espresso and cappuccino. Dinner is served Monday through Saturday. Reservations are accepted.

DeFazio's
$$ • 4032-B Cox Rd. (Innsbrook) • 747-5500

Specialties include Northern Italian food, veal, local seafood, spit-roasted chicken, beef and what DeFazio's calls "the best Grand Marnier soufflé in the state." The atmosphere is casual. DeFazio's serves lunch Monday through Friday and dinner daily. Reservations are suggested.

Candela's
$ • 14235 Midlothian Tnpk. • 379-0910

This light, bright trattoria bridges two worlds in that it appeals to serious diners with excellent gourmet fare and to casual diners and take-out clientele with delicious pasta and pizza. Lunch and dinner are served daily. Reservations are suggested.

Franco's Ristorante & Cafe
$$ • 9031-1 W. Broad St. • 270-9124

The Northern- and Southern-style Italian menu here is vast and varied. Owner Paolo Randazzo expertly executes classic Parmigianas, fra diavolos and fettuccines.

INSIDERS' TIP

For a change of pace, try lunch with a Japanese architectural flair at the Lora and Claiborne Robins Tea House at the Lewis Ginter Botanical Garden.

Photo: Spike Knuth

Members of the Greek Orthodox Cathedral serve up Greek food and entertainment at their annual festival in June.

Servings are large, and the restaurant is a favorite of local critics (and of visiting celebrities such as Frank Sinatra). Lunch and dinner can be savored here Monday through Saturday.

The Greenhouse
$$ • 6624 W. Broad St. (Hyatt Richmond) • 285-1234

Here you will find a unique collection of eclectic and colorful contemporary art paired with a creative menu of Northern Italian cuisine plus steaks, lamb chops and seafood. Dinner is served daily, and reservations are suggested.

Julian's
$ • 11129 Three Chopt Rd. • 346-1004
$ • 2617 W. Broad St. • 359-0605

Julian's opened its doors on W. Broad Street in 1947 and made possibly the first pizza in Richmond. It is family-owned, offers homemade bread and pasta and has built a stable reputation that Richmonders have come to count on. Lunch is served every day but Sunday, and dinner is served daily. Reservations are recommended for groups of eight or more.

La Grotta
$$$ • 1218 E. Cary St. • 644-2466

Great food and on-the-ball service give La Grotta a solid four-star rating. The decor is breezy with stucco, brickwork and plants, and casual dress is the norm. If your destination is Shockoe Slip and your mood is Italian, then La Grotta is the place. Lunch is served Monday through Friday and dinner is served seven days a week.

Lakeside Restaurant
**$$ • 13550 Harbour Point Pkwy.
• 739-8871**

In the Brandermill Inn and Conference Center, this restaurant offers all diners a view overlooking the lake between Brandermill and Woodlake, and you also can watch your entrees being prepared in an open kitchen. The menu provides a classic variety of American, Italian and seafood dishes. Lakeside serves breakfast, lunch and dinner seven days a week. Reservations are suggested.

L'Italia
$$ • 10610 Patterson Ave. • 740-1165

This has been consistently considered one of the best Italian restaurants in Richmond for more than 20 years. Chef Vincenzo "Gino" DiLiberto, who attended the Culinary Institute of Milan, and his wife, Maria, prepare entrees from scratch every day. Dinner is served Tuesday through Sunday.

Mamma Zu
$$ • Pine and Spring Sts. • 788-4205

In a former corner market in Oregon Hill, Mamma Zu opened in 1994 to rave reviews. It draws an eclectic crowd and is one of the newest see-and-be-seen spots. It offers a variety of inventively prepared Italian food and has the best value in a great house wine you'll find anywhere in Richmond.

The menu is posted on a blackboard, and it helps to know a little Italian when you read it. (Although the staff will do an excellent job of explaining it.) The family of the former owner of the famous A. V. Ristorante Italiano on New York Avenue in Washington, D.C., runs the restaurant. Mamma Zu serves lunch Monday through Friday, and dinner Monday through Saturday. Reservations are not accepted.

Monte Calvo's
$$ • 5703 Staples Mill Rd.• 266-3314

Monte Calvo's has good pasta, veal and seafood, and it is a place where you'll feel comfortable dressed casually or for business. The restaurant serves dinner Tuesday through Sunday. Reservations are suggested.

The Olive Garden Italian Restaurant
**$ • 7113 W. Broad St. • 672-6220
$ • 9750 Midlothian Tnpk. • 330-7391**

These restaurants, again, are part of a chain, but their fresh pasta is made daily, and their wide range of Italian cuisine and huge bowls of salad have made them popular. Droves of customers show up for lunch and dinner, served seven days a week.

Sal Frederico's
$$ • 1808 Staples Mill Rd. • 358-9111

Sal Frederico once operated Capri, which in days gone by was the Italian restaurant in Richmond. Sal has developed a very strong following at his present location. Specialties are Veal alla Sal, veal chops, salmon marinara and chicken cacciatore. You'll never go wrong at Sal's — the atmosphere is friendly, and the service and food are excellent. Sal's serves lunch Monday through Friday and dinner every day except Sunday.

The Spaghetti Warehouse
**$ • 10099 Brook Rd. (Virginia Ctr. Commons)
• 553-4966**

Antique signs and memorabilia (including a trolley car) decorate this fun restaurant. Among house specialties are a 15-layer lasagna and veal and chicken varieties of Parmigiana and piccata. There are lots of spaghetti seasonings and sauces, all part of an extensive Italian menu. It's a great place for families, and the wait staff really caters to children. The restaurant serves lunch and dinner seven days a week. Even though it's a warehouse, reservations are suggested for parties of 10 or more.

INSIDERS' TIP

If you like a show with your sirloin, an evening at Kabuto Japanese Steak House is sure to please. A chef expertly prepares your meal on a sizzling tepanyaki table while you watch.

Theresa's Italian Villa
$$ • 1212 N. Concord Ave. • 261-4043

Family-owned, warm and friendly, Theresa's specializes in veal, pasta, lasagna and seafood. The restaurant, located at the corner of U.S. Highway 1 and Parham Road, is open for lunch and dinner seven days a week. Reservations are suggested.

Japanese

Hana Zushi Restaurant
$ • 1309 E. Cary St. • 225-8801

This sushi bar offers Japanese food including traditional tempura, teriyaki, sukiyaki, cutlets, noodles, donburi and sushi. Hana Zushi is open for lunch Monday through Friday and for dinner Monday through Saturday.

Kabuto Japanese House of Steak
$$ • 8052 W. Broad St. • 747-9573
$$ • 13158 Midlothian Tnpk. • 379-7979

You're also in for a touch of showmanship here at Kabuto, where the chef prepares your meal "Hibachi Style" at Teppan Yaki tables. Kabuto serves sushi nightly except Monday, lunch Monday through Friday and dinner seven days a week. Reservations are suggested.

Kanpai Japanese Steakhouse
$$ • 10438 Midlothian Tnpk. • 323-4000

Tables surround gas-fired grills, and the cook's showmanship is as great as the food. Dishes include steak, chicken, shrimp, scallops and lobster. Dinner is served seven days a week.

Saito's
$$ • 611 E. Laburnum Ave. • 329-9765

Saito's features traditional Japanese "homestyle" cooking and has two tatami tables available for traditional seating on the floor. Saito's special is a combination of several items offering variety, especially helpful for the first-time customer. Lunch is served Tuesday through Friday. Dinner is available Tuesday through Saturday. Reservations are suggested.

Korean

V.I.P. Restaurant
$$ • 7437-B Midlothian Tnpk. • 675-0511

While a variety of milder Chinese dishes are one the menu here, it's the gutsy Korean fare that is the main attraction. V.I.P. prepares many dishes over individual gas burners at your table, and a single serving of an entree is often large enough for two people. Spices and peppers are used heavily, and side dishes are an adventure. Lunch and dinner are served seven days a week.

Lunch Places

Applebee's Neighborhood Grill & Bar
South of the James:
$ • 900 Moorefield Park Dr. • 330-3954
$ • 10823 Hull Street Rd. • 276-3855
$ • 2611 Old Hundred Rd. • 768-4259
North of the James:
$ • 5400 W. Broad St. • 673-1721
$ • 9601 W. Broad St. • 747-0583
$ • 10151 Brook Rd. • 266-6095
$ • Parham Rd., Regency Square Mall • 740-5782
$ • 4306 S. Laburnum Ave. • 226-9390

Applebee's offers sandwiches and burgers in a casual atmosphere and an all-you-can-eat rib special Sunday, Monday and Tuesday. But its also offers a Lightning Lunch from Monday to Saturday, a lunch it promises within 14 minutes or you get it free. It's part of a chain, but it's so popular that it deserves mention here. Applebee's restaurants are open seven days a week.

Becky's
$ • 100 E. Cary St. • 643-9736

Becky's has a following of regulars that makes it almost club-like. At lunchtime on Monday through Friday you'll find things such as breaded veal cutlet, slabs of roast beef with gravy and slow-cooked green beans. The restaurant also serves breakfast beginning at 7 AM.

Chesapeake Bagel Bakery

$ • 10839 W. Broad St.• 346-3300

$ • Broad St., Shops at Willow Lawn
• 285-5000

The full write-up for this full-service lunch spot is in the "Coffeehouses and Bagel Shops" section.

Chez Foushee

$ • 203 N. Foushee • 648-3225

Chez Foushee has an interesting roundup of sandwiches including grilled London broil, turkey and smoked Gouda, house pimento cheese, Foushee garden pocket and albacore tuna salad. Everything is upscale including the decor and the magazines in the reading rack. And everything is homemade, including soups, fresh pasta salads, sandwiches, hot entrees and desserts (with offerings such as Key lime pie, white chocolate cheesecake and lemon butter cake). Chez Foushee offers full catering service and will deliver box lunches or prepare them for pickup.

Chiocca's Park Avenue Inn

$ • 2001 Park Ave. • 355-9219

There are not very many tables here, but it's a longtime favorite gathering place for regulars who know the sandwiches are great. It is not open on Monday.

The Dairy Bar

$ • 1602 Roseneath Rd. • 355-1937

For nearly 50 years, this has been a popular place for breakfast and lunch. Longtime Richmonders still call it "Curles Neck Dairy Bar," its former name. Breakfast specialties include herring roe, eggs and salt herring. Lunch specialties include club sandwiches, probably the best milk shakes in town and ice cream. The Dairy Bar serves lunch (and breakfast) Monday through Saturday.

Fabulous Foods

$ • 2029 Huguenot Rd. • 320-0615

The atmosphere is relaxing and tearoom-like. Fruit salads, nut-studded chicken salads, rich casseroles, pot pies, hot and cold soups and assorted sandwiches are the typical fare. For dessert you'll find lemon chess pie and bread pudding. Fabulous Foods is in the Huguenot Village Shopping Center and is open Monday through Saturday.

Fantaste

$, no credit cards • 1201 W. Main St.
• 355-1889

Fantaste has only 16 seats, so you need to arrive early if you want to get one at lunchtime. Specialties include homemade daily specials, muffins, teriyaki chicken, classic Greek and Caesar salads and fresh desserts. Fantaste is open Monday through Friday.

Gooseberry Cafe

$ • 5205 S. Laburnum Ave.
• 222-3295

If you are in the neighborhood of the Richmond International Airport at lunchtime, this is where you should head. The name "Gooseberry" says it all — neat decor, courteous service and good food. It's a popular weekday lunch spot with people who work in offices nearby. Lunch and dinner are served Monday through Saturday.

High's Express

$ • 10 S. Thompson St. • 355-8804

The subs at this edge-of-Carytown restaurant can't be beat. The bread is warm and crunchy and the ingredients are always fresh. Be sure to try the limeade, some of the best in Richmond. After lunch, High's has a great selection of ice cream and sundaes. Lunch is served Monday through Saturday.

INSIDERS' TIP

Just about everyone has heard the restaurant-speak "86 the special" (rhymes with "nix" and means "we're out of it"), but did you know "41" is lemonade, "80" is a glass of water, and "55" is root beer. Now, if someone yells "95!" at you, it's not a drink. They think you're trying to walk out on a check.

Homemades by Suzanne
$ • 102 N. Railroad Ave., Ashland
• 798-8331
$ • 10 S. Sixth St. (in the Atrium)
• 775-2116

This is a bright, clean place with excellent food, and it's convenient to just about everything downtown. There are homemade soups, a famous shrimp salad, chicken salad, potato salad, made-from-scratch brownies, pastries and pies, and cream puffs filled with custard and whipped cream. You can eat here or get boxed lunches to carry out. Suzanne's is open Monday through Frida at both locations as well as on Saturdays in Ashland. Smoking is not permitted.

Johnson's Grill & Restaurant
$ • 1802 E. Franklin St. • 648-9788

Johnson's serves breakfast and lunch Monday through Saturday beginning at 6 AM. The lunch menu includes home-cooked items, fresh vegetables, homemade bread and desserts. Johnson's is a longtime favorite for down-home food. Take-out orders are a specialty. This is soul food at its best. No smoking or alcohol is permitted.

Manhattan Bagel
$ • 5401 Glenside Rd. • 282-3334
$ • 9411 Burge Ave. • 275-6165
$ • 4028 Cox Rd. • 346-4889
$ • 10461 Midlothian Tnpk. • 560-9448

See our "Coffeehouses and Bagel Shops" section for the full write-up for this luncheon stop.

Perly's
$ • 111 E. Grace St. • 649-2779

Perly's Delicatessen is club-like and has a loyal following. The menu ranges from deli sandwiches and soups to gazpacho and vegetarian fare. The place is casual and friendly. It also serves great breakfasts.

Steve's Restaurant
$ • 110 N. Fifth St. • 649-3460

The friendly atmosphere and fast service here is coupled with basic food homemade specials, Italian dishes, corned beef and cabbage. Lunch is served Monday through Friday.

Photo: Metro Richmond Convention and Visitors Bureau

Once the commercial center of the city, Shockoe Slip's former tobacco warehouses now house clubs, bars and restaurants.

Mexican and Southwestern

Bandito's Burrito Lounge
$ • 733 W. Cary St. • 343-1177

As you might guess, burritos are the specialty here, and there's quite a variety of them— from chicken and beef filled to pork, seafood and vegetable stuffed. But all of Bandito's other dishes are good, too, including the quesadillas, salads, and chips 'n' salsa or cheese. The margarita menu is complete with other drinks as well, and a great selection of Mexican beer. The atmosphere at Bandito's is fun, and it's filled with all age groups. Attached next door is Bandito's new Diablo Room, where live bands play throughout the week. Open for lunch and dinner every day, the full menu is available until 12 AM and appetizers until 2 AM.

Cactus Cafe
$ • 5713 Hopkins Rd. • 275-9030

"California-style" Mexican cuisine is the specialty at Cactus Cafe. New management has updated the menu and daily specials have been added. New items include grilled rib eye steak, a shrimp and black-bean chimichanga and chiles rellenos. Lunch and dinner are served Monday through Saturday.

Casa Grande
$ • 3528 Pump Rd. • 360-7774
$ • 7818 W. Broad St. • 755-2388

Casa Grande serves good Mexican food at reasonable prices. The sizzling cast-iron skillet for the fajitas creates drama as it is brought to the table. Lunch and dinner are served seven days a week.

Chili's Southwest Grill and Bar
$ • 3528 Pump Rd. • 360-7774
$ • 9111 Midlothian Tnpk. • 320-6132

While Southwest Texas and Mexican food are the specialties here, you'll also find delicious hamburgers. Living up to its name, Chili's is a popular place for the grill and bar crowd. Lunch and dinner are served seven days a week.

El Matador
$ • 1903 Betty Ln. • 285-3813

You can bring your whole group here and eat a whole lot of very good Mexican food, then get a bill low enough to make you want to do the Mexican hat dance (but don't try it because you'll be too full). Lunch and dinner are served seven days a week.

Mexico Restaurant
$ • 6406 Horsepen Rd. • 282-7357
$ • 2845 Hathaway Rd. • 320-1069
$ • 5213 Williamsburg Rd., Sandston
• 226-2388
$ • 7334 Bell Creek Rd., Mechanicsville
• 559-8126

This bright, colorful restaurant offers distinctive Mexican food that goes beyond standard fare. For example, if you thought Mexi-

can dishes were all ground beef, beans, lettuce and taco sauce, try this restaurant's Mole Poblano made with chicken. Lunch and dinner are served seven days a week.

Tex-Mex Cafe
$ • 3511 Courthouse Rd. • 745-6440

If you're looking for Mexican food in south Richmond, this is the place — housed in an authentic dining car. The fajitas are a real treat, with sizzling chunks of meat that have a smokey flavor that comes from mesquite grilling. Here you'll also find a good selection of burritos, chalupas, tacos, enchiladas and other beef, chicken and sausage dishes with a Southwestern flavor. Lunch is served Tuesday through Friday and dinner is available Tuesday through Saturday. The restaurant is closed on Sunday and Monday. Reservations are suggested for six or more. (See our Nightlife chapter for more information on the Tex-Mex Cafe.)

Museum and Garden Cafes

Carriage Court Cafe at Maymont
$ • 1700 Hampton St. • 358-7166

The Cafe is in the cobblestone courtyard of the Carriage House at the 100-acre Maymont park and museum. (See our Attractions chapter.) Lunchtime fare of gourmet-style sandwiches and salads is offered. Catering is by A Movable Feast. (See the "Carryout" section.) There's ample free parking. Lunch is available Wednesday through Friday from April through early October.

Lewis Ginter Botanical Garden
$ • 1800 Lakeside Ave. • 262-9887

Lunch at the Lewis Ginter Botanical Garden at Bloemendaal is served in the Lora and Claiborne Robins Tea House Monday through Saturday year round, and on Sunday during April and May. Fresh menu selections are provided by the Bull & Bear Club.

Wickham's Garden Cafe at the Valentine Museum
$ • 1015 E. Clay St. • 649-9550

The magnificent walled garden at the Valentine Museum is a great place to enjoy a tranquil lunch. The cafe looks out onto the garden through walls of French doors. Popular menu items are tarragon chicken salad and turkey Havarti sandwiches. Lunch is available daily. Only cash and checks are accepted.

Zeus Gallery
$$$ • 201 N. Belmont Ave. • 359-3219

Local art exhibits are featured here. The menu changes frequently but usually includes beef, chicken, seafood, pasta and vegetarian dishes. Brunch is served on Saturday and Sunday. Dinner is served daily.

Other Casual Places

Allison's
$$ • 404 Westover Hills Blvd. • 230-1800

Allison's specializes in seafood and ribs. Lunch and dinner are served Tuesday through Sunday and breakfast also is available on weekends. Allison's is not open on Monday.

Anthony & George's Restaurant
$$ • 7505 Staples Mill Rd. • 266-4182

The pasta, steaks and prime rib are great, and the service is excellent. Here you'll find a broad menu and a comfortable atmosphere. Lunch is served Sunday through Friday, and dinner is served seven days a week.

Bamboo Cafe
$ • 1 S. Mulberry St. • No phone

The Bamboo offers homemade soups and desserts, sandwiches, steaks, seafood and chicken in a casual atmosphere. Lunch and dinner are served seven days a week.

Bistro R
$$ • 10190 W. Broad St. • 747-9484

This American bistro has a California feel about it and is a favorite West End place to see and be seen. Chef Robert Ramsey is a gold medal winner, and the menu features Mediterranean-style fish, pasta and grilled items. Vegetable dishes are exquisite. Lunch is served Monday through Friday, and dinner is served Tuesday through Saturday. Bistro R

is closed Sunday. Candlelight at dinner provides an elegant atmosphere, yet it's casual enough for an impromptu dinner with friends. Reservations are suggested.

Bubba's
$ • 4000 Williamsburg Rd. • 236-3262

Bubba's is everything the name implies, including pool table, pinball machines, country music on the jukebox, gun-rack-equipped pickups in the parking lot and guns mounted on the wall. The menu also is what you might expect and includes bologna burgers, fried chicken sandwiches, pizza and Bubba's popular 21-piece shrimp dinner with cole slaw and fries. Lunch and dinner are served seven days a week.

Buddy's
$ • 325 N. Robinson St. • 355-3701

Home cooking, along with sandwiches and burgers, is served here. The atmosphere is very casual. Lunch and dinner are served seven days a week and a "late breakfast" is served on Sunday morning.

Cary Street Cafe
$$ • 2631 W. Cary St. • 353-7445

Fresh seafood, steaks, chicken, sandwiches, salads, pizza and homemade soups are the fare, with a hearty dose of vegetarian dishes. Every night, the cafe offers live music with open-mike events. Lunch and dinner are served Monday through Sunday, with a brunch on Sundays offering omelets, waffles and a big breakfast burrito.

Casablanca
$ • 6 E. Grace St. • 648-2040

The food here is superior, and the decor does a pretty good job of making you feel like you are in Rick's American Cafe on the set of the famous 1940s movie. The menu of main courses and sandwiches is creative, and dishes are named for Peter Lorre, Sydney Greenstreet and others associated with the film. Specials of the day are always outstanding, and the place shows promise of becoming a Richmond classic. Lunch is served on weekdays, and dinner and late-night fare (see our Nightlife chapter too) are served every day with brunch on Sunday.

Charley's Stony Point Cafe
$$ • 3088 Stony Point Rd. • 323-3984

Signature dishes — chicken, onion soup and pasta — steaks, seafood and sandwiches are served in this popular place. Charley's serves lunch and dinner seven days a week and brunch on Sunday.

Chiocca's
$, no credit cards • 425 N. Belmont Ave. • 355-3228

A snug, homey neighborhood place, Chiocca's has been a longtime favorite where many customers are regulars — well-known to the staff and to others. Food is basic and good. Dinner is served every day and lunch Wednesday through Monday.

Chugger's Old City Pub
$ • 900 W. Franklin St. • 353-8191

The cozy pub-like atmosphere here provides a setting for some of the best and most reasonably priced food in town, including a roast beef sandwich on a Kaiser roll drenched in natural juices that is unquestionably the most delicious you will find anyplace. The sweet Bermuda onion deep-fried in cayenne-enriched butter is a must as an appetizer. Draft beer comes in small, medium and large glasses, the latter being pitcher-sized. It's all a far cry from the old Chesterfield Tea Room that occupied this site for many, many years. Lunch and dinner are available here seven days a week.

Dot's Back Inn
$ • 4030 MacArthur Ave. • 266-3167

Here you'll find standard lunch fare such as Rosie the Riveter's Lunch Pail (a grilled cheese sandwich and a bowl of homemade soup). It's an old-fashioned neighborhood hangout with old-fashioned prices and World War II headlines on the wall. Lunch and dinner are served Monday through Saturday.

Goodfella's
$ • 1722 E. Main St. • 643-5022

If you're headed for "The Bottom" and want bar fare and progressive rock, then Goodfella's may just be made to order. It serves dinner only and is not open Sunday or Monday.

Hill Cafe
$ • 2800 E. Broad St. • 648-0360

A popular spot on historic Church Hill, Hill Cafe offers innovative nouvelle cuisine. It has a casual, neighborhood atmosphere and is furnished with 1910 vintage church pews. Daily lunch and dinner specials are offered and take-out is available. This is a popular spot for Sunday brunch. Hill Cafe is open for lunch and dinner every day but Monday.

Jan's
$ • 9501 Woodman Rd. • 266-5303

This is a pleasant, comfortable spot on the North Side that's easy on the wallet and that offers an appealing family-style menu: soup/salad bar, pizza, subs and steaks. Lunch and dinner are available Monday through Saturday. Jan's is closed on Sunday.

The Jewish Mother
$ • 8982 Quioccasin Station Shopping Ctr. • 740-1400
$ • 10921 Midlothian Tnpk. • 379-1400

The Jewish Mother is a place for people of all ages who like to color on the walls, enjoy good music (perhaps a classical guitarist for Sunday brunch or a blues band in the evening) and eat delicious food. The menu features great omelettes, deli sandwiches, soups, crepes, salad platters and kids' meals. The

---

FYI

Unless otherwise noted, the area code for all phone numbers listed in this chapter is 804.

INSIDERS' TIP

Many say that Edgar Allan Poe's inspiration for the "enchanted garden" in his famous "To Helen" came from a private garden where he played as a child, what is today the site of the Linden Row Inn.

ZEUS GALLERY & cafe

HOURS

MONDAY – THURSDAY
5:00 p.m. - 10:00 p.m.

FRIDAY – SATURDAY
5:00 p.m. - 11:00 p.m.

SUNDAY
9:00 a.m. - 2:00 p.m.
5:00 p.m. - 10:00 p.m.

201 N. Belmont Avenue • 359-3219

restaurant serves breakfast, lunch and dinner seven days a week.

Palani Drive
$ • 401 Libbie Ave. • 285-3200

The large selection of coffees and teas is a nice complement to the healthy selection of wraps, salads, sandwiches and smoothies at Palani Drive, a newer restaurant at The Shops at Libbie and Grove. After ordering at the counter, diners can choose between a booth, table, couch or bar stool to sit and eat. Palani Drive is open every day.

Melito's
$ • 8815 Three Chopt Rd. • 285-1899

In addition to world-famous hotdogs, Melito's serves American-style food that includes daily specials. Its varied menu and location makes Melito's a super-popular West End gathering spot. Lunch and dinner are served Monday through Saturday. Reservations are suggested on weekends.

North Pole
$$ • Route 6 (Patterson Ave.), Crozier • 784-4222

This place is in the horse country of Goochland County, and its food and ambiance are comfortable and unassuming. Featuring Italian, seafood and steak, it is a great destination for good food and fine wine. Dinner is served Thursday through Sunday.

O'Toole's Gay Nineties
$ • 4800 Forest Hill Ave. • 233-1781

Barbecue, pizza, stir-fry, seafood, beef and ribs are served here, and if you time it right you can participate in an Irish sing-along. O'Toole's is open for lunch and dinner daily. (See our Nightlife chapter for more on O'Toole's.)

Out of Bounds
$ • 2701 W. Broad St. • 355-7390

Televised sports and a long bar flanked by pool tables hold center stage at this casual spot on W. Broad near Boulevard. Don't look for anything fancy on the menu, but there's plenty of variety ranging from reasonably priced pasta dishes and pizza to chicken and 16-ounce T-bone steaks. Lunch and dinner are served daily.

Philip's Continental Lounge
$ • 5704 Grove Ave. • 288-8687

Known simply as "Phil's," this has been the "in" place for locals in the West End since before World War II. The menu includes club and sailor sandwiches, meat loaf, burgers and baked chicken. Phil's is open daily.

Red Oak Cafe
$ • 1601 Hockett Rd., Manakin-Sabot • 784-2330

If you're looking for great food at an unexpected location in the country, this Goochland

County restaurant offers a delightful and casual atmosphere and diverse dishes from applewood-smoked rainbow trout to grilled salmon, plus great desserts. Lunch is served every weekday, dinner is daily, and brunch is served on Sunday.

Shackleford's
$$ • 10496 Ridgefield Pkwy. • 741-9900

Hidden in the corner of the Gleneagles Shopping Center on Ridgefield just west of Pump Road, Shackleford's offers a mixed American grill cuisine. Innovative dishes and a comfortable, informal atmosphere make it a popular place. Lunch and dinner are available daily.

The Slip at Shockoe
$ • 11 S. 12th St. • 643-3313

The fare here includes chicken, meatballs, shrimp and sandwiches. There's dancing after 10 PM Friday through Sunday on a lighted dance floor. Breakfast and lunch are served Monday through Friday. Dinner is served Thursday through Saturday.

Stuffy's Subs
$ • Parham Rd. & Rt. 1. • 264-4770
$ • 7304 Staples Mill Rd. • 266-8917
$ • Gayton Crossing Shopping Center • 741-8100
$ • 324 Libbie Ave. • 285-7995
$ • 411 N. Harrison St. • 359-6800
$ • 2930 W. Broad St. • 355-5100
$ • 261 Wadsworth Dr. • 330-3205
$ • Genito & Coalfield Rds. • 744-9122
$ • Huguenot & Robius Rds. • 320-3403
$ • Chesterfield Meadows East • 748-7789
$ • Laburnum & Williamsburg Rds. • 226-1471

Each independently owned, Stuffy's has a wide variety of subs—you can even get any of the options stuffed in a pita). The Great Garden is a delicious vegetarian sandwich, and the meatball sub is one of the best around. Most Stuffy's locations are open daily.

The Tavern at Triangle Park
$ • 7110-F Patterson Ave. • 282-8620

Crab cakes, grilled chicken salad, vegetarian burgers, pasta and fresh fish are among the specialties. The enclosed deck is heated in the winter and open in the summer. The Tavern at Triangle Park has a mix of casual ambiance and good food that makes it one of the West End's most popular watering holes. Come here early for dinner because the place fills up fast. Lunch and dinner are served daily.

T.J.'s Restaurant and Lounge
$$ • Franklin and Adams Sts., Jefferson Hotel • 649-4672

T.J.'s serves sandwiches — and maybe the best burger in town — seafood, steaks, prime rib and pasta in a casual setting. Service begins in late morning and runs until midnight daily. T.J.'s offers a great Sunday brunch.

Village Cafe
$ • 1001 W. Grace St. • 353-8204

The Village Cafe is on the edge of the VCU campus. It's an interesting place to go if you have plenty of time and want to catch up on some of the latest trends in counterculture fashions or if you just want to gaze out of the big windows at the passing scene on Grace Street. If the Village Cafe takes its name from Greenwich Village, then it's apt. The menu is varied, but the food here takes second place to other attractions in this lively and unique neighborhood. Breakfast, lunch and dinner are available seven days a week. T.J.'s offers a great Sunday brunch.

Pizza

Bottoms Up Pizza
$ • 1700 Dock St. • 644-4400

Bottoms Up, at 17th and Dock streets, is one of the really "in" places in Richmond. One draw is its interesting location, not only is it in an old building in Shockoe Bottom, but it's along part of the old canal and practically under the three railroad trestles that pass overhead. But the big draw is its variety of exceptional toppings that include seafood, fruit and unusual vegetables — all used to produce a truly gourmet pizza. Bottoms Up is open for lunch and dinner seven days a week.

Peter's Pizza Plus
$ • Gayton Crossing Shopping Center • 740-5050

You can eat in or carry-out, but don't expect delivery from this family-style restaurant. Decorated with different holiday items, Peter's has some of the best pizza in the West End, if not all of Richmond. You'll also find a great selection of pasta dishes and subs. Plus, a few classic video games, including Ms. Pac Man, round out the experience. Peter's is open for lunch and dinner every day but Sunday.

Piccola Italy Pizza & Subs
$ • 1100 W. Main St. • 355-3111

Piccola Italy, in the VCU area, has some of the best pizza in town. The place is open seven days a week and stays open until midnight weekdays and until 2 AM on weekends.

Steve's Pizza
$ • 1299 W. Broad Street Rd., Oilville
• 784-0166

Steve's has some of the best pizza in the area. The establishment is in a red barn on the portion of Broad Street Road that runs through Oilville, reasonably close at hand if you live in the far West End or if you work in Innsbrook. Quantity and quality are both excellent. (A medium deluxe here would qualify as a large at most pizza places in town.) You also can get a half-pound hamburger and a one-pound lettuce salad with all of the fixings. Count on about 15 to 20 minutes for your pizza with homemade crust to be prepared. Or, call in your order in advance as most people do. Steve's is closed on Monday and Tuesday, but on other days it is open for dinner.

Something Different

In the mood for something eclectic, unusual or just plain different? Maybe a dinner cruise or a gourmet meal in a turn-of-the-century farmhouse? Or maybe you just need to sit beneath a ceiling fan with a pina colada in a balmy Cuban atmosphere. The following places offer a variety of atmospheres and food — hopefully something that will suit your mood.

Annabel Lee
$$$ • 4400 E. Main St. • 644-5700

Passengers can enjoy a buffet lunch, brunch or dinner while this riverboat cruises the James. Served from the ship's complete on-board galley, the menu includes traditional Virginia favorites and Chesapeake Bay specialties.

Two-hour "Lunch On The River" cruises take place Wednesday through Saturday, and there is a two-hour "Sunday Brunch" cruise. A special three-and-a-half-hour plantation lunch trip downriver to Westover, Evelynton and Berkeley plantations is provided Tuesday; it includes not only a buffet lunch at midday but also a continental breakfast at 10 AM departure. Three-hour dinner cruises depart Wednesday through Sunday. Boarding starts a half-hour before departure, so be sure to call the above phone number for schedule information. Reservations are recommended. Smoking is permitted on the outer decks only.

David's White House Restaurant
$$ • 3560 Courthouse Rd., Providence Forge • 966-9700

The menu is broad-ranging, with dishes like the Plantation Platter, Oysters Weyanoke and other specialties. In a restored turn-of-the-century farmhouse in Providence Forge (midway between Richmond and Williamsburg via U.S. Highway 60), the restaurant is operated by David Napier, one of the original owners of Indian Fields Tavern. Napier's culinary capabilities are well-known by Richmonders who are devoted to fine food.

The restaurant serves dinner Wednesday through Sunday and brunch on Saturdays and Sundays. Reservations are recommended.

Havana '59
$$ • 16 N. 17th St. • 649-CUBA

The owners of Havana '59 have gone to great lengths to create an authentic atmosphere of Havana in the days when it was a city of pleasure with a balmy sensuality that affected visitors and natives alike.

Fresh fruit drinks and Cuban and American diner fare are part of the scene, harkening back to the glory days of Sloppy Joe's and Floridita. This place is designed for good friends, good food, good fun and a good cigar. Havana '59 is open for dinner seven days a week, and it stays open until 2 AM.

Homer's Sports Grill
$ • 14 N. 18th St. • 643-2222

Homer's features what it calls the

"eatertainment" concept — high-tech audio and laser disc video presentations combined with delicious down-home fare. Everything is made from scratch and prepared to order, from the home-baked breads to the signature fried chicken.

The prime rib is slow-roasted daily and the barbecue ribs come with a choice of three sauces. Known as the watering hole for sports celebrities, Homer's is the place for sports fans to see and be seen. The atmosphere is highlighted by a beautifully crafted granite and copper bar. Homer's offers the latest last call on food and drink in town, seven nights a week.

Liberty Valance
$ • 7017 Forest Hill Ave. • 320-4276

The jukebox plays country tunes, and the spirits of the Old West and of John Wayne are alive and well here in the decor and theme, as well as in drinks called Miss Kitty and Calamity Jane.

Entree portions are for big appetites and feature beef, ribs and great desserts. You can even get a root beer float served in a glass cowboy boot. Liberty Valance serves lunch Tuesday through Saturday and dinner Tuesday through Sunday.

Mystery Dinner Playhouse
$$$ • 9826 Midlothian Tnpk., Best Western Governors Inn • 649-CLUE

Solve a comedy murder mystery while enjoying a four-course dinner! Characters in the mystery serve your meal. In the process, they pass along clues to help you solve the evening's crime. Group discounts are available.

Since this is a dinner theater, call the number listed above to check the theater schedule and to make reservations, which are required.

The Palm Court at The Jefferson
$ • W. Jefferson at Franklin St. • 788-8000

The Palm Court at The Jefferson Hotel is a great place for afternoon tea, which is served Thursday through Sunday from 3 to 4:30 PM. Sunday brunch is served in the lower lobby with the grand stairway as a backdrop. It's a great place to give visitors a taste of the quintessential South.

Poe's Pantry and Pub
$$ • 2706 E. Main St. • 648-2120

At the end of E. Main Street across from Tobacco Row, Poe's offers friendly service and a casual atmosphere. Its large glassed-in eating area is a nice place to relax and imagine what this neighborhood might have looked like in the days when Poe edited the *Southern Literary Messenger* about a dozen blocks up the street, or when the Confederate Navy Yard was just down the hill.

Menu items, while basic, are tagged with names such as Tell Tale Hearts of Artichoke and Raven Chili. Lunch and dinner are served daily. Light fare is available as late as 2 AM.

The Border Chophouse & Bar
$$ • 1501 W. Main St. • 355-2907

From bratwurst and potato pancakes to chili and enchiladas, the menu here is what the restaurant's name implies. You might think this eclectic place is slightly off the wall, but there's never a dull moment. The signature chili comes in mild, half-and-half and "widowmaker" versions. Lighter choices on the menu include salads, vegetarian chili and reduced-fat versions of standard menu items.

It's the only restaurant in Richmond with a stuffed cow. If you're a visitor or newcomer to Richmond, this is one of those must-see places. Visiting travel and restaurant writers love it! The Border packs 'em in seven days a week.

Soul Food

Johnson's Grill & Restaurant
$ • 1802 E. Franklin St. • 648-9788

This is an ideal spot in the Bottom for down-home food. It's described more fully in the Lunch Places section of this chapter.

Woody's Inn
$ • 2128 W. Cary St. • 353-1346

The chicken wings are special. Be aware that Woody's has real soul atmosphere in that it is a hot spot for jazz lovers, so if you want a quiet meal, go early. On the other hand, if jazz is your kind of music, plan to stick around and enjoy it. Woody's is open for dinner seven days a week and stays open until the wee hours on weekends.

Southern

Freckle's Restaurant
$ • 5724 Patterson Ave. • 288-3354

If you're a good ol' boy, you'll love Freckle's. The amazing thing is that a lot of its clientele includes Main Street bankers and West End country-club members. The owner holds court at a center table, and the cooking is real down-home, with great breakfasts. Regular dinner specials include fried catfish (Wednesdays), fresh-cut New York strip (Thursdays) and homemade backfin crab cakes (Fridays). Just about everybody thinks the crab cakes are the best in town. Breakfast, lunch and dinner are served seven days a week. Sunday breakfast is served until 2 PM. The restaurant has an outdoor patio and grill.

Magnolia
$ • 3207 N. Boulevard • 359-9441

This restaurant, in the Holiday Inn near The Diamond, is one of the best in Richmond. The focus is on Southern food, including Virginia-cured ham, Virginia seafood, fried chicken and country biscuits topped with gravy. But Magnolia also offers delicious steaks cooked to order and escargot di Napoli and fettuccine Caprice. A soup and salad bar are included in the price of all entrees. Presentation and service are first class. Lunch and dinner are available daily.

McLeans Restaurant
$ • 10372 Leadbetter Rd. • 550-2421
$ • 4001 W. Broad St. • 358-0369

Salt herring, country ham, buckwheat cakes, roe and eggs, and free grits with gigantic breakfasts are the staple at McLeans. Specializing in county-style cooking, McLeans is home of "The Biggest Breakfast in Town." For lunch and dinner you'll find hamburgers and sandwiches and things like bean soup and meat loaf smothered in gravy. Breakfast is served Monday through Friday and lunch is served seven days a week. Carryout is available.

Street Vendors and Food Courts

Street vendors with their food carts are seemingly everywhere downtown and in other parts of the city at midday, and they offer fare that ranges from the basic to the gourmet. Lots of people like to pick up their lunches from these sources, then find a sunny spot in the plazas of the James Center, in the MCV area around 12th and Marshall streets or elsewhere to enjoy a picnic break with a few friends. Food carts usually are set up about 11 AM on weekdays and stay on site until about 3 PM.

Food courts in shopping centers also are favorites for eat-in or to-go fare. Shopping centers with major food courts (including on-site tables and seating) are 6th Street Marketplace, Cloverleaf Mall, Virginia Center Commons, Regency Square, The Shops at Willow Lawn and Chesterfield Towne Center. Most have about a dozen food vendors. All are open during regular mall hours, are wheelchair accessible and offer designated nonsmoking sections.

24-hour Eats

Aunt Sarah's Pancake House
$ • I-95 & Willis Rd. • 271-1070
$ • Glen Allen • 266-3177
$ • 4205 W. Broad St. • 358-8812
$ • Ashland • 798-7627
$ • 7927 W. Broad St. • 747-8284
$ • 8201 Midlothian Tnpk. • 323-0639

We can't resist continuing to mention Aunt Sarah's under this heading. For years its W. Broad Street location was a favorite all-night gathering spot. Alas, no more. The good news

---

INSIDERS' TIP

Some parents used to tell their children that Gen. Lee and his horse, Traveller, came down from the monument at night so Traveller could have a drink of water and something to eat.

is that all locations still remain open until at least 3 AM on Friday and Saturday. If you're looking for pancakes, breakfast dishes and homestyle cooking for breakfast, lunch or dinner, this is the place to head.

Denny's
$ • 803 E. Parham Rd. • 261-3687
$ • 6598 W. Broad St. • 288-7553
$ • I-95 and Rt. 10, Chester • 748-5010

This 24-hour chain restaurant has your typical American fare: steaks, burgers and fries and an assortment of breakfast items. They also have a good children's menu.

River City Diner
$ • 1712 E. Main St. • 644-9418

This 50s-style restaurant in Shockoe Bottom offers typical diner food but on a grand scale. A popular breakfast spot (don't miss the cinnamon-raisin French toast), the River City Diner isn't exactly a 24-hour eat, but it's sure close. The hours are as follows: Tuesday through Thursday, 8 AM to 12 AM; Friday and Saturday, 8 AM to 3 AM; and Sunday and Monday, 8 AM to 3 PM.

Third Street Diner
$ • 218 E. Main St. • 788-4750

The minute you step inside the door here you'll be transported back into the 1950s diner atmosphere, jukebox and all. Richmonders love it, and the restaurant serves breakfast all day and all night, plus blue-plate specials, homemade desserts and a few Greek dishes such as spanikopita and grape leaves. The atmosphere is casual, and the diner is open 24 hours a day, seven days a week.

Vegetarian

Vegetarian dishes have become so popular that most Richmond restaurants today have at least one or two vegetarian entrees on the menu. Here are two that concentrate on vegetarian dishes.

Back to Roots
$ • 321 N. Second St.

This is an all-natural vegetarian cafe with an African-American bent. It offers a daily soup and salad special for take-out or eat-in.

Indochine
$$ • 2923 W. Cary St.
• 353-5799

See the "Vietnamese" section for an in-depth write-up of this family friendly restaurant.

Panda Garden
$ • 935 W. Grace St. • 359-6688

This Chinese restaurant located near VCU has a predominantly vegetarian menu. In fact, half of its luncheon buffet is filled with vegetarian dishes, made mostly with meat substitutes. It starts daily at 1 PM.

Main Street Grill
$ • 17th and Main Sts. • 644-3969

This neighborhood spot, even though it serves meat during the day, has a vegetarian menu at night — and it serves Stone Age sourdough hotcakes for breakfast and has vegetarian specials at lunch. Customer favorites are refried beans, hummus, tabouli and wheatberry chili. Across the street from the Farmers' Market, it features whatever is in season. It closes on Monday, but otherwise serves breakfast, lunch and dinner daily and is open until midnight. (See our Nightlife chapter for more on the Main Street Grill.)

Vietnamese

Chopstix
$ • 3129 W. Cary St. • 358-7027

This small restaurant seats only 36 people. Here you can try things such as shrimp on sugar cane, marinated and grilled beef, exotic stews, a vegetarian plate, fried spring rolls filled with meat and vegetables, delicious soups and

---

INSIDERS' TIP

Good places to pig out are the Rib Festival and the Greek Festival — both annual events.

Many fine restaurants are within easy walking distance of Richmond's older neighborhoods.

stir-fry dishes. There also are roll-your-own dishes with paper-thin crepes and vegetable accompaniments. Lunch and dinner are served Monday through Saturday.

Indochine
$$ • 2923 W. Cary St. • 353-5799

French-Vietnamese food, the specialty here, is visually more dazzling but milder and less challenging to the constitution than traditional Vietnamese food. Indochine is comfortable, hospitable and very accommodating, not only to families with children but also to vegetarians. The menu notes that most of the stir-fry dishes can be prepared without meat. The list of entrees is tantalizing, so come prepared to make some difficult choices.   Dinner is served Monday through Saturday.

Saigon Gourmet
$ • 11033 Hull Street Rd. • 745-0199

Favorites here are crispy spring rolls, steamy noodle soup and grilled items that come with salad, rice noodles and rice paper for wrapping. The atmosphere is stark but spar-

kling clean, bright and airy. Saigon Gourmet is open for lunch every day but Monday and dinner seven days a week.

Saigon Restaurant
$ • 903 W. Grace St. • 355-6633

The setting is simple, and there's a no-fuss ambiance about this place, but the food is good and moderately priced. You'll find that the fare stacks up against similar dishes that are more expensive at other places. The literati from around town are faithful supporters. Lunch and dinner are available Monday through Saturday. It's closed on Sunday.

Vietnam Garden
$ • 3991 Glenside Dr. • 262-6114

From spring rolls to Vietnamese ravioli, this restaurant offers a full array of Vietnamese cuisine (including what it says is "low-fat" Vietnamese barbecue). The restaurant, when it opened in 1992, quickly captured the tastebuds of local restaurant critics. Vietnam Garden serves lunch Monday through Friday and dinner every day.

Shockoe Bottom is the liveliest place in Richmond to go for nightlife, and it's the place to be on weekends.

Nightlife

Shockoe Bottom is still THE place to go for nightlife. Richmond's newest clubs, restaurants and bars continue to pop up in old warehouses and office buildings throughout this abandoned industrial area surrounding the Farmers Market on 17th Street near downtown.

In historic Shockoe Slip, an established nightlife area a few blocks up the Cary Street hill from the Bottom, you can dance, listen to live music, laugh with professional comedians and go bar-hopping at numerous restaurants and clubs in restored tobacco warehouses and historic buildings.

Head west on Main Street to the Fan District and you'll find live music and a friendly, neighborhood atmosphere at the many restaurants and bars along Main Street and throughout this eclectic historic community near downtown.

Other popular nightspots are at Innsbrook and at area hotels. Richmond also has many neighborhood bars and pubs where you can meet and chat with friends over a cold one while you watch an interesting parade of local characters.

With so many colleges and universities here, there's a good supply of talented local musicians. Clubs also book groups from Virginia Beach, North Carolina and other nearby areas. To find out who's playing where and when, check the listings in the Weekend section of the *Richmond Times-Dispatch*, *Style Weekly*, the *Richmond Music Journal* or *Punchline*. Local radio stations can also fill you in: Call the Q94 and XL02 Info Line, 756-4636; or B103.7, Info Line, 272-9692. For concert tickets, call TicketMaster at 262-8100.

When all the clubs close, you can have a late-night (or early morning) breakfast at the River City Diner, a '50s-style restaurant in the Bottom with booths and jukeboxes that's open all night on the weekend. If you can't get a table there, try the 3rd Street Diner, the 4th Street Cafe or McLean's at 4001 W. Broad Street. See our Restaurants chapter for more information.

For those who have a taste for the arts, there's the Richmond Symphony plus a wide range of musicals, plays, dinner theaters and dance performances. Fans of the silver screen will find a good selection of new as well as classic films, and there are special events and concerts at the Richmond Coliseum, the Classic Amphitheatre at Strawberry Hill, Richmond's Landmark Theater, the Carpenter Center, 6th Street Marketplace, Innsbrook, Dogwood Dell, The Boulders, Kanawha Park and Paramount's Kings Dominion. If you like spectator sports, you'll find plenty of year-round college action as well as professional baseball, hockey and auto racing.

In this section, we've listed some of the most popular nightspots arranged in the following categories:

Shockoe Bottom
Shockoe Slip
The Fan
Dancing
Sports Bars & Billiards
Karaoke
Irish Pubs
Movie Theaters

The list of movie theaters is organized by section of town. For information about Spectator Sports, Annual Events, Attractions or The Arts, please see those chapters of our book.

As we go to press, some of the nightclubs and restaurants will undoubtedly be coming under new management or changing their hours and entertainment schedule, so be sure to call ahead before you go. Don't try to lock a club into any one type of music or crowd. They can be rock'n'roll one night and jazzy the next.

Cover charges vary depending on the entertainment, and a lot of clubs don't charge cover fees. To be on the safe side, be prepared to pay anywhere from $1 to $5, or call ahead. Crowds vary from college students to 40-something couples. Also, please be aware that Virginia ABC laws prohibit the sale or consumption of alcohol after 2 AM, so most clubs have "last call" around 1:30 AM and close at 2 AM. All listings in this chapter accept major credit cards unless otherwise noted.

Shockoe Bottom

FYI

Unless otherwise noted, the area code for all phone numbers listed in this chapter is 804.

To get to the Bottom from downtown, drive east on Cary Street down the hill across 14th Street. You'll go under an overpass and drive beside railroad trestles through what looks like the wrong part of town. But it isn't. This is the liveliest place in Richmond to go for nightlife, and it's the place to be on weekends. Most of the clubs are on 17th and 18th streets between Cary and Grace streets.

A lot of clubs don't have cover charges. Those that do charge from $1 to $5, depending on the club and the band. You must be 21 to enter most of the clubs with live music on weekend nights, but many clubs in the Bottom offer entertainment on Thursday night for the college crowd. Street parking is available, and there is a parking lot near the Farmer's Market on 17th Street.

Area 51
1713 E. Main St. • 643-5100

Themed around the secret government alien-research area in Arizona that was featured in the film "Independence Day," this club offers a variety of music including alternative, dance, rap, etc., every day and live music two to three times a month. The 21 to 30ish crowd hangs out at the bars. There is a full-service bar, and the health-conscious cuisine is easy on the wallet. Try the bean cakes, tortillas and sauteed dinner specials.

Alley Katz
10 Walnut Alley • 643-2816

This is where the college crowd hangs out to listen to live local, regional and national bands every Wednesday through Saturday. Depending on the band, the crowd here may also include a mix of people of all ages. A varied beer menu is available that includes about 30 different microbrewed beers.

Bottom's Up Pizza
1700 Dock St. • 644-4400

Bottom's Up Pizza serves the best pizza in town at its popular see-and-be-seen hangout in the Bottom under the Triple-Pass of railroad tracks. On weekends, the Butter Bean Quartet plays jazz from 7 to 11 PM. There's a good mix of groups and singles age 25 and older. The dress is mostly casual, but you see everything from jeans to tuxedos. The decor is typical of the area: exposed bricks, ceiling beams, neon accent lights and two outdoor decks. As you might expect, it's always crowded here.

Catch 22
1718 Main St. • 343-1560

This dance club and restaurant in the Bottom features a martini bar with more than 50 concoctions to choose from. Listen to music from the '70s, '80s and current Top-40 tunes while you sip the night away. Dining is available in the Vitello Room. Reservations are accepted.

Cobblestone Brewery
110 N. 18th St. • 644-2739

Bands play a variety of music here on Friday and Saturday night including acoustic, reggae and folk. Pool tables and Foosball are available. The menu is eclectic, with seafood specials, steaks and blackboard specials. Some of the most requested beers are Cobblestone Beers, Harpoon India Pale Ale and Francis Kaner wheat beer. An outdoor patio is open weather permitting. For more information, see the Restaurants chapter's "Brewery" section.

Havana '59
16 N. 17th St. • 649-2822

One of the hottest clubs in the Bottom, Havana '59 features a stylish Cuban atmosphere with potted plants, ceiling fans, imported cigars and a menu with items such as

More than 100,000 people enjoy the sights and sounds of the Big Gig every year.

spicy black bean soup, wood-oven-baked pizza and fried calamari.

Across from the historic Farmer's Market, Havana '59 looks like an old garage from the '50s with large roll-up garage doors at the entrance. These are raised during warm weather to create an open front and even more of a balmy Cuban atmosphere. Havana '59 attracts a varied clientele. The dress is stylishly casual. This club is so popular, there is almost always a crowd waiting to get through the door on the weekends. There is an outdoor deck on both the second and third levels.

Homer's Real Sports Grill
14 N. 18th St. • 643-2222

This Bottom bar features four project screen TVs, and satellite reception so you won't miss any televised sport events. The crowd here tends to range from mid-20s to mid-30s. Homestyle comfort foods are served — fried chicken, ribs, burgers and a few pasta dishes. Patrons here prefer the six beers on tap that always include at least two locally brewed Legend beers. A full-service bar is available.

Liquid Assets
1727 E. Main St. • 343-0236

This popular neighborhood bar-and-grill-style restaurant with booths and bar offers music and dancing. A dozen beers including microbrews and imports are available on tap. The crowd is usually around age 25, and the dress is casual. Photos of the customers and the staff decorate the walls above the booths. Munchies include slammers (small burgers), chicken fingers and 25¢ wings.

Main Street Grill
1700 E. Main St. • 644-3969

This is a small, folksy, low-key place in an old, grill-style restaurant. You'll find a variety of entertainment here for people who don't like to watch television. On Thursday nights you can enjoy Old-time Jam, featuring Appalachian-style mountain music, and on Fridays and Saturdays the grill offers a variety of live music, cabaret-style acts and even poetry readings. The third Friday of every month is Irish Music Jam.

Musicians have an open invitation to participate in the Old-time Jam and the Irish Music Jam. There is a regular core of musicians that usually appears, and as many as 15 musicians have been known to bring their fiddles, banjos, mandolins, harmonicas and dulcimers. They all play for free, so be prepared for the passing of the hat. Tuesday is slide night. Bring your favorite slides and put on a show.

Established in 1953, the grill is the oldest restaurant in Shockoe Bottom. Known as the "Home of the Paco," the restaurant serves a popular pita sandwich and features vegetarian food, homemade desserts, beer, wine and herbal teas. Like most of the places in the Bottom, it's not unusual to see people waiting outside to get a seat on weekends.

The Main Street Grill does not accept credit cards.

Poe's Pantry and Pub
2706 E. Main St. • 648-2120

This cozy neighborhood bar, decorated with a raven, photographs of Poe and old Richmond, offers live music Wednesday through Saturday night. There's an Open Blues Jam every Wednesday night and bluegrass bands play every other Saturday. In a renovated gas station at the top of the Bottom, the pub attracts a mixed crowd of friendly regulars. Be sure to try the ribs. A full-service bar is available.

Other Bottom Bars and Restaurants

The Bottom has a growing number of great restaurants that are described in more detail in our Restaurants chapter including Awful Arthur's Oyster Bar, a casual seafood restaurant; River City Diner, a '50s-style diner that's open all night on weekends; and Rock Bottom Cafe, great for a slice of pizza to go. For more elegant dining and a change of pace, you'll also find several top-rated restaurants, such as The Frog and the Redneck and The Hard Shell.

Shockoe Slip

Just up Cary Street from the Bottom is the Slip with its established clubs, restaurants and boutiques housed in renovated warehouses and buildings. Metered parking is available along the street or in one of several pay-to-park lots.

Richbrau Brewing Company
1214 E. Cary St. • 644-3018

Rock 'n' roll bands play here at the pub on weekends, and there's an adjoining dance club with party music, rock 'n' roll, lights and bubbles. (It used to be the Bus Stop.) In the pub, the atmosphere is friendly, and the decor is similar to an old English pub with a restaurant. Upstairs there are three billiard rooms with 9-by-4 and professional tables. There's also Foosball and darts. The billiards lounge can be rented for private parties.

Behind the scenes are a lot of stainless steel barrel fermenters and cool storage tanks connected with a complex array of pipes and valves — all brewing flavorful concoctions of beer. The pub regularly brews and serves Golden Griffin, a light ale; Old Nick, a pale ale; and Big Nasty, a porter. Fruit beer, seasonal beer and guest beers from other brew pubs are also offered. A full-service bar is available. An executive chef offers a spirited cuisine with dishes made with beer or wine, or foods that complement them such as barbecue duck burritos, Sonoma shrimp, chili, steaks, seafood, beer bread and Big Nasty pecan pie. For the less adventurous, there are also sandwiches. See our Restaurants chapter for more information.

Sam Miller's Warehouse
1210 E. Cary St. • 644-5465

The well-established Sam Miller's was one of the original restaurants in Shockoe Slip. Acoustic acts play here on Thursdays. The restaurant specializes in Chesapeake seafood and prime rib and offers soup, sandwiches and late-night munchies. A full-service sit-down bar and lounge-style seating are available. You'll find a good mix of people in their mid-20s, 30s and 40s mingling in the casual, antique-filled atmosphere.

Matt's Pub and Comedy Club
109 S. 12th St. • 643-JOKE, 644-0848

An established nightspot in the Slip, the Comedy Club features two live performances by professional comedians every Friday at 8 and 10:30 PM, and Saturday at 8 and 11 PM. Shows are about an hour and 40 minutes and include two entertainers. Drinks, sandwiches and appetizers are served during the shows in a nightclub atmosphere downstairs from Matt's Pub. A full-service bar is available.

The crowd dresses comfortably, and the intimate atmosphere makes the Comedy Club a favorite of comedians all over the country. It seats about 100 people and has been compared to comedy rooms in New York.

Upstairs, Matt's Pub serves pasta, pub specials, beef entrees, crab cakes, and a variety of tortillas and pitas. If you plan to dine before the show, make dinner reservations for about an hour and a half before showtime. The shows usually sell out by noon on Friday, so make your reservations early. Admission is $9 per person, but be sure to ask about the cash discounts. Special dinner and show package tickets are also available.

The Tobacco Company
1201 E. Cary St. • 782-9431

The Tobacco Company offers live music on the first floor and dancing in the basement (the Tobacco Company Club) of its renovated tobacco warehouse. Known for its three-story atrium and antique furnishings, The Tobacco Company features a working exposed-cab elevator formerly of the Consolidated Edison building in New York. On the first-floor cocktail level, you can enjoy Top 40, jazz, pop rock, blues and acoustic groups every day but Sunday. The atmosphere is upscale and comfortable. You can sit at the bar, at a table or in an intimate grouping of chairs and couches.

Downstairs, the Tobacco Company Club has one of the most popular sunken dance floors in Richmond. The first Wednesday of the month, there's live music. All other times, DJs play a variety of Top-40 dance music. There are two full bars, and sandwiches and appetizers are available. Business travelers and people of all ages come here. The con-

servative crowd is mostly 25 and older. Collared shirts are required, and khakis and button-downs prevail. Most people wear nice casual or business attire. The club opens at 8 PM and starts getting full around 10 PM. The cover charge is usually about $5.

The Fan

This renovated historic neighborhood near Virginia Commonwealth University is home to a number of timeless corner bars and restaurants that exist primarily to serve local college students, businesspeople and residents, but they come alive with visitors from other parts of town on the weekends. Most of the popular, relatively new restaurants are on Main Street from the VCU area to the Boulevard. Mingling with the crowd is the entertainment here. Only a few places have live music and dancing. For more information about their menus and hours, see our Restaurants chapter.

Avalon
2619 W. Main St. • 353-9709

This Fan restaurant offers one of the largest import and microbrewed beer lists in area with more than 50 selections plus weekly beer specials. One side features a large sit-down bar and standing area, and the other side offers table seating. Old movie star photos add a touch of glamour. The global nouveau cuisine changes seasonally and features pastas, salads, steaks, crab cakes, seafood and even duck. Grill items and sandwiches are available late at night. As you might expect it's very crowded here on weekends, especially after 11 PM. This is the restaurant where restaurant people go.

Bogart's Backroom
203 N. Lombardy St. • 353-9280

Listen to live music — predominantly jazz and rhythm and blues — every Friday and Saturday from 9:30 PM to 1:30 AM at this small intimate club in the back room of Bogart's cafe-

---

INSIDERS' TIP

The Richmond Jazz Society sponsors jazz musicians and events in the Richmond area. To find out who's playing where, call them at 643-1972.

style restaurant. The atmosphere is laid-back, and you see everything from suits to jeans and a lot of people in their late 20s to 40s. The decor is dark and woody with exposed bricks. High-backed booths provide a sense of privacy, and advertisements from the 1940s and 1950s add to the nostalgic charm. A full-service bar and appetizers are available. Open since the 1970s, Bogart's is one of the oldest clubs in the city area. The cover charge is usually about $3.

Cary Street Cafe
2631 W. Cary St. • 353-7445

This casual restaurant features live blues, bluegrass or rock 'n' roll bands on some Thursday, Friday and Saturday nights. There's no room to dance, but there is a full service bar and a menu that has everything from affordable entrees to sandwiches, pasta dishes, vegetarian dishes and really good burritos.

Davis & Main
2501 W. Main St. • 353-6641

After everyone else has closed their kitchens, try Davis & Main. The complete menu featuring classic American grilled food is served until 1 AM. A full-service bar is available.

Fan Bar & Grill
1731 W. Main St. • 358-6611

You'll find mostly college students and younger 20-somethings at this new fan hangout, especially since local college students receive a discount. Fridays and Saturdays feature live jazz with The Jason Jenkins Trio. Homemade pizzas are the specialty on this extensive menu. Closed on Mondays.

Gumbo Ya Ya
2232 W. Main St. • 358-9292

Listen to zydeco and New Orleans-style jazz, blues and rock 'n' roll at this funky New Orleans-style restaurant and bar. As you might expect they have Mardi Gras beads dangling from the bar along the booths, and they serve Hurricanes and New Orleans beer such as Dixie lager, Dixie Blackened Voodoo, and Dixie Crimson Voodoo, plus microbrewed beer from Abita Springs, Louisianna.

The laid-back, fun-loving crowd is usually between 25 and 40, and the owners encourage them to take some beads with them. Popular late-night snacks include "Ya-Ya Balls," a mixture of crabmeat and crawfish; chicken wings, better known as "gator wings," and jalapeno pepper poppers. For a really crazy time, go to the Mardi Gras Ball the Thursday before Fat Tuesday. It's a formal masquerade with live music, featuring the crowning of the "King of Baccus," who will reign supreme over the restaurant — at least for the evening.

Joe's Inn
205 N. Shields Ave. • 355-2282

This is a classic Fan favorite, with Greek specialsseafood, pizza, sandwiches and Spaghetti à la Joe. It's a casual, noisy place with two rooms full of booths and tables — great for meeting friends and tablehopping.

The Sidewalk Cafe
2101 W. Main St. • 358-0645

This is a favorite place for a lively crowd of regulars and THE place to go if you want to meet young people in Richmond. The menu features inexpensive Greek food, spaghetti, subs and deli sandwiches. A full service bar is available, and the kitchen is open until 1:30 AM every day.

Sobles
2600 W. Main St. • 358-7843

This enduring Fan restaurant is more open and well-lit than some of the other corner bars in the Fan. Cozy booths and tables offer a chance to chat and see old friends. It has a great outdoor patio, and it's known for its fresh-cut french fries, great cheeseburgers, spiced shrimp and raw bar, offered seasonally.

Southern Culture
2229 W. Main St. • 355-6939

Order a spicy Cajun, Creole or Gulf Coast style meal here for a late-night meal or try one of their luscious desserts, large enough for two. Downstairs there's a large bar and lots of booths with a casual jazzy New Orleans ambiance. Regulars here tend to be somewhat sophisticated and interested in the arts.

Strawberry Street Cafe
421 Strawberry St. • 353-6860

This casual restaurant in the middle of the Fan district is probably best known for its bathtub salad bar. It's upscale yet casual atmosphere makes it a great place to talk with friends over a glass of wine or dessert. The menu is eclectic, and the pace is busy.

The Border Chophouse & Bar
1501 W. Main St. • 355-2907

Bottled beer and spicy food is the norm in this narrow, rowdy restaurant where everyone seems to know everyone else. Rock'n'roll and folk music is live on Saturday nights.

Dancing

Cafine's
401 E. Grace St. • 775-CAFE

Every Friday night at 8 PM, Cafine's hosts "Swing Out," a chance for members of the 21-and-over crowd to try their hand at swing dancing. Located just off the Virginia Commonwealth University campus, Cafine's charges $8 for "Swing Out" with lessons and $4 without.

Catch 22
1718 Main St. • 343-1560

See the "Shockoe Bottom" section of this chapter for a full write-up for this new dance club and restaurant.

Club Boss/Club Colors
534 N. Harrison St. • 353-9670

Club Boss is famous for its Retro Night, hosted by Q94, during which all of your favorite songs from the 1980s are alive and kicking. Thursdays are College Night, and Fridays are Latino Night. Club Colors takes over on Saturdays with Cabaret Night. Every night,

however, welcomes a younger, primarily college-aged crowd.

Club Fahrenheit
119 N. 18th St. • 783-2608

One of the only clubs in Richmond that has a long line waiting to get in, Club Fahrenheit is *the* place to be on Thursday, Friday, and Saturday if you're young and like to dance. Red windows filled with bubbling water, two large dance floors and people packed from wall to wall are the elements that give this dance club the feel of New York City.

Glenn's Restaurant
1509 Chamberlayne Ave. • 321-3444

Glenn's is a popular family-owned restaurant and nightclub that opened in 1937. Rhythm and blues and Top-40 music plays in the disco Wednesday through Saturday and attracts the 30-something crowd. Jazz and oldies play on Friday from 4 to 9 PM, followed by live music until 1:30 AM. Lunch, dinner and appetizers are available. The dress is casual.

Lightfoot's — Hyatt Richmond
6624 W. Broad St. • 285-1234

Tuesday is ladies' night, the most popular event at this dance club with music by local radio DJs and special giveaways. Wednesday nights are jazz nights for the 50-plus crowd. Local and regional bands play Top-40 dance music Friday and Saturday. The crowd includes a mix of professionals and the 30-to-45 crowd.

Most people wear business attire or nice casual clothes (collared shirts and jeans). The decor features a dance floor surrounded on two sides by raised seating areas, high-back cushioned chairs and a marble bar. A full-service bar and appetizers such as sandwiches, quesadillas, buffalo wings and chicken strips are available. It's best known for its after-work drink specials and complimentary shrimp buffets.

INSIDERS' TIP

Entertainment legends like Billie Holliday, James Brown, Bill "Bojangles" Jackson, Lena Horne, Nat King Cole and Cab Calloway played at The Hippodrome Theater, 528 N. Second St., in Jackson Ward during its heyday.

Little Texas Saloon & Grill
6922 Staples Mill Rd. • 262-9652

As the name implies, this bar began with a predominantly country music atmosphere. However, rock 'n' roll has made its invasion on Little Texas. Tuesdays feature complimentary line-dancing lessons. Wednesdays are hosted by WKLR 96.5 The Planet, a classic rock radio station. Pop music takes over on Thursday nights, the most popular Little Texas night, which is hosted by Q94 FM. Friday is country night, hosted by K-95 FM. Fridays and Saturdays feature All-You-Can-Eat crab legs.

Midway Lounge
Lee-Davis Rd. • 746-8630

The Midway Lounge in Mechanicsville is one of the oldest and most popular country music dance spots in the area. DJs play a mix of music Wednesday through Saturday. The format includes Top-40 and rock 'n' roll music along with country. Dancing lessons are available on Wednesdays (couple line-dancing for $3) and on Thursdays (line-dancing for $2). Dress is neat but casual — jeans, nice slacks, collared shirts and country wear. Food, liquor, beer and wine are available. There is a $2 minimum cover charge on weekends.

Peppermint Lounge — Howard Johnson
2401 W. Hundred Rd., Chester • 748-6321

Dance the night away to Top 40, beach music and Rhythm and Blues behind the red-and-white candy-striped door. Live music is offered on Fridays; DJs take over on other nights. There's a small dance floor. A full-service bar and food are available. Ask about the steak dinner and dance special. Dress is casual.

Razzle's—Best Western
9848 Midlothian Tnpk. • 330-0007

DJs play a variety of Top-40 dance music here on Mondays, Fridays and Saturdays, but mix it up on other nights. On Tuesday, it's beach and shag music, and Wednesday is

rock 'n' roll night with XL102 FM. On Thursday night, Razzle's turns into a comedy club, with live, stand-up comedians. Look for live beach bands on Sunday nights. Located in the Best Western Hotel, Razzle's is usually packed on the weekends, with about 100 couples on the dance floor and about 600 people between the ages of 21 and 40. A full-service bar, buffet dinner and snacks are available.

The Tobacco Company Club
1201 E. Cary St. • 782-9431

See the listing under the Shockoe Slip section for more information.

Vision's Dance Club — Holiday Inn Executive Conference Center
1021 Kroger Ctr. Blvd. • 379-3800

You can shag, bop, hop, boogie or line dance at this South Side club where DJs offer a variety of music Friday through Sunday. It's country night on Wednesdays when Vision's offers complimentary line-dancing lessons. They offer everything from beach music, to Top 40, rhythm and blues, and country. Collared shirts and jeans are the norm. The club offers a huge dance floor and lots of brass and bricks. Liquor, beer, wine and appetizers are offered. The atmosphere is friendly, and the service is good.

Sports Bars & Billiards

Bottom Billiards
117 N. 18th St. • 643-4323

If you're looking to play pool, grab a drink, and have a deli snack, then Bottom Billiards is the place for you. This new club offers seven tournament-quality professional pool tables from 5 PM to 2 AM, Wednesday through Saturday.

Damon's
4024 Cox Rd. • 965-9550

With a full bar and walls covered in sports memorabilia, Damon's is the place to be after

INSIDERS' TIP

If you need to ride home in a cab, don't expect to hail one in the street. Have a bartender call a cab company in advance so your ride will be ready when you are.

work. Great music, live NTN trivia, and several big screen TVs round out this sports bar and full-service restaurant known best for its ribs.

Homer's Real Sports Grill
14 N. 18th St. • 643-2222

See the listing under Shockoe Bottom for more information.

Mulligan's Sports Grille
8006 W. Broad St. • 346-8686
1323 W. Main St. • 353-8686
7073 Mechanicsville Tnpk. • 730-8686
11146-A Hull St. • 744-8686

This popular sports bar offers four locations: West End, The Fan, Mechanicsville and Midlothian. Live danceable music is offered every Thursday, Friday and Saturday, with DJ music on Wednesdays. Mulligan's also sponsors chartered trips to sporting events and big holiday parties on St. Patrick's Day and Cinco de Mayo with giveaways, bands and contests. Decorated with sports memorabilia, Mulligan's has sit-down bars, a dining area, a large dance floor and band room. You can play pool, video games and darts, and you can watch thousands of satellite channels on big screen and regular TVs.

After work, you'll find a lot of business people enjoying the club's happy-hour specials, and at night there's a good mix of people. Families with children are welcome. Mulligan's specializes in steaks and ribs. Dining room reservations are a good idea. Dress is casual.

The Playing Field
7801 W. Broad St. • 755-7700

The Playing Field is a great place to "play" with a group of friends or with a private party. Located in Richmond's West End, it has almost 30 pool tables as well as dart boards and tables for foosball, snooker and shuffleboard. The Playing Field also has a full-service bar and a complete menu.

Sharky's Bar & Billiards
4032 Cox Rd. • 273-1888

Giant fish tanks and underwater scenes painted on the walls explain Sharky's name as do the 14 pool tables. You'll also find a good selection on the juke box, live music

three nights a week, an outdoor patio and great appetizers at this fun Innsbrook hang out.

Side Pocket
2012 Staples Mill Rd. • 353-7921

You can play pool, darts, video games, chess, checkers, backgammon or watch TV while you enjoy your favorite brew at this West End hangout in the Crossroads Shopping Center. Sandwiches, shrimp, chicken wings and other snacks are available as well as daily meal specials. This is a very casual place with reasonable prices and a good mix of people. Nine-ball tournaments are held here part of the year.

Karaoke

Caddy's
13312 Midlothian Tnpk. • 794-3007

Grab the mike and be a star at this South Richmond restaurant where karaoke singing is a popular attraction Tuesday through Thursday nights from 9 PM to 1:30 AM. Thursday night is also ladies' night with special prizes and contests.

Dog Town Lounge
7051 Forest Hill Ave. • 323-9435

Located on Richmond's South Side, this new blues lounge offers "Nick's Karaoke" for a younger crowd with DJ Kevin. The fun starts at 9 PM. The Dog Town Lounge also offers blues bands and open mic nights throughout the week.

Gus' Italian Cafe
7358 Bell Creek Rd. • 730-9620

In Mechanicsville, at the Hanover Square Shopping Center, this friendly, low-key, casual restaurant offers karaoke singing on Wednesday from 8 to 12 PM, and on Saturday from 9 PM to 1 AM. A full-service bar is available, and the menu includes everything from pizza to steak.

The Jewish Mother
Quiocassin Station Shopping Center
• 740-1400
South Park Mall, Colonial Heights
• 520-2222

On Wednesday nights, both the West End

and South Side locations of this fun deli and bar are the place to be for karaoke. The singing gets started around 9 PM, and there is a cover charge.

Mulligan's Sports Grille
1323 W. Main St. • 353-8686

Wednesday nights at 9 PM, the karaoke gets going at this sports bar in The Fan. For more information on Mulligan's, see the Sports Bars & Billiards listing.

Peppermint Lounge—Howard Johnson
2401 W. Hundred Rd., Chester • 748-6321

Every Thursday night starting at 7 PM, David Allen lets Richmonders be singing sensations with karaoke. For more information on the Peppermint Lounge, see the listing under Dancing.

Vision's Dance Club—Holiday Inn Executive Conference Center
1021 Kroger Ctr. Blvd. • 379-3800

You won't want to miss Thursday nights at Vision's, when the karaoke gets crazy. For more information on this South Side club, see the listing under Dancing.

English & Irish Pubs

Fox & Hounds British Pub
10455 Midlothian Tnpk. • 272-8309

Located on Richmond's South Side in the Pocono Green Shopping Center, this British Pub has been a community favorite for more than 14 years. Originally a British grocery story, the Fox & Hounds now offers 15 different beers on tap, 85 different bottled beers and a complete menu. Outdoor dining is available year round as is the non-smoking dining room that's decorated like an Old English library, complete with a fireplace. Mondays through Saturdays, you'll find live entertainment, including acoustic, DJ, and folk music. The Fox & Hounds has eight pool tables, three dart boards, and is open until 2 AM, seven days a week.

O'Tooles Restaurant & Pub
4800 Forest Hill Ave. • 233-1781

This Irish pub in Westover Hills is another favorite sing-along place where the customers are part of the entertainment. A variety of live music is offered occasionally on Friday and Saturday, and Thursdays always feature piano music. Best known for its St. Patrick's Day party, this is a great place for a fun time. The menu features chef specials, steaks, seafood, ribs, Italian dishes and sandwiches. A full-service bar is available.

Potter's Pub
7007 Three Chopt Rd., Village Shopping Center
• 282-9999

Join acoustic musician John Small, a legendary favorite at this West End pub, Tuesday through Saturday beginning at 9:30 PM. Almost everything he plays is a request. You can dance a little if the spirit moves you, sing a little and even try your luck at an occasional limbo contest. Audience participation is a big part of the show, so if you want to chill out and sit in a corner, this is not the place for you.

The dinner menu features hardy English items, such as fish and chips, chicken pot pie, crab cakes, and chef specials. A full-service bar is available, but most people drink the European beer on tap, such as Guinness or Bass. They also serve layered black and tans. Dress is casual. Dinner reservations are recommended if you want to get up front near John.

Rare Olde Times
10602 Patterson Ave. • 750-1346

An full Irish staff will wait at you when you visit this authentic Irish pub in Richmond's West End. Live Irish and American folk music makes for great entertainment Tuesdays through Sat-

---

INSIDERS' TIP

If you like jazz, be sure to try "Fridays at Sunset," an outdoor summer party with live jazz at Kanawha Plaza that begins around 6 PM every Friday and goes "all night." Kanawha Plaza is located downtown at Clay and Eighth streets.

urdays, which tends to draw an older crowd. Open since 1994, Rare Olde Times offers a full range of Irish beer, including Guinness, Stout, Bass and Harp, as well as Irish cuisine.

Siné
1327 E. Cary St. • 649-7767

This brand new Irish pub and restaurant in Shockoe Slip was built, painted, and decorated with Irish materials and by Irish craftsman. A wide selection of food, a full-service bar and intriguing iron and wood working make Siné a popular spot for both families, couples and people of all ages. Gaelic for "that's it," Siné will soon have live acoustic music on its planned outdoor patio.

Movie Theaters

Here's a list of movie theaters by area. To find out what's playing, just check the "green section" or the entertainment section of the *Richmond Times-Dispatch*. Many offer gift certificate books and have special children's matinee series. See the Arts chapter for information about alternative, foreign language and art films.

Different Cinemas

Byrd Theatre
2908 W. Cary St. • 353-9911

Richmond's oldest movie palace, replete with an original Wurlitzer theater organ, the Byrd Theatre was built for $900,000 and opened on Christmas Eve 1928. It became a Virginia historic landmark in 1977 and is the only old-style movie palace left in Richmond. Eddie Weaver and other local organists still play the theater's Wurlitzer organ — the largest in the area. The Byrd offers 99¢ movies and other entertainment. In 1985 it restored its stage and, off and on, has produced shows starring jazz artists and its Byrdette chorus line.

Features Dinner Cinema
8809 W. Broad St. • 747-6300

This is the place to go if you want to munch and sip while you take in a movie. Features shows second-run movies on four screens and is non-smoking.

Chesterfield County

Chester Cinemas
  13025 Jefferson Davis Hwy., Chester
  • 796-5911
Cloverleaf Mall Cinema 8
  7201 Midlothian Tnpk. • 276-6600
Genito Forest Cinema 9
  11000 Hull St. • 276-8100
Midlothian 6 Cinemas
  7901 Midlothian Tnpk. • 272-9300
Southgate Cinemas
  5955 Midlothian Tnpk. • 233-2777
Southpark Mall Cinemas
  374 Southpark Mall, Colonial Heights
  • 526-8100
United Artists Theatres
  Huguenot Rd. and Midlothian Tnpk., Chesterfield Towne Ctr. • 379-7800

West End

Byrd Theatre
  2908 W. Cary St. • 353-9911
Features Dinner Cinema
  8099 W. Broad St. • 747-6300
Ridge Cinema 7
  1510 E. Ridge Rd. • 285-1567
Willow Lawn Cinemas 4
  Willow Lawn Mall
  • 282-7383
Westhampton Cinema 1 & 2
  5706 Grove Ave. • 288-9007
West Tower Cinemas
  8998 W. Broad St., • 270-7111

Ashland

Ashland Theatre
  203 England St. • 798-3990

Hanover

Virginia Center 14
  10091 Jeb Stuart Pkwy. • 261-5411

Since guest rooms in the area's nearly 170 hotels and motels now exceed 12,000, you'll probably be able to find just about anything you want in terms of accommodations with up-to-date amenities.

Accommodations

There was a period of time in the late 1980s when new hotels opened in Richmond at the rate of one every other month. Such a boom is upon us again. Every year since 1997, new hotels are either under construction or are being planned or proposed.

Many developers worry that this recent surge might lead to a flooding of the market. Guest rooms in the area's nearly 170 hotels and motels exceeds 12,000. What this means to you is you'll probably be able to find just about anything you want in terms of accommodations with up-to-date amenities.

What follows is not a complete listing of all the hotels, motels, and bed and breakfast inns in the area, but a brief overview of the range of options, including some of our favorite recommendations.

Price Code

The dollar sign ($) code with each entry indicates what it will cost for one night's lodging during the week for a room with two people. It works as follows:

Less than $50	$
$51 to $85	$$
$86 to $120	$$$
$121 and up	$$$$

Keep in mind that rates are subject to change and that weekend rates often are substantially less. All hotels and motels described in this chapter accept the major credit cards unless otherwise noted.

Most places have nonsmoking rooms available. We've noted exceptions. The hotels and motels listed in this chapter are handicapped accessible and do not allow pets unless otherwise noted. If you have special needs, be sure to inquire about hotel services when you make reservations. It's always wise to call ahead and make reservations because when

a major convention hits town, rooms can be difficult to find at the last minute.

For your convenience, hotel accommodations are listed geographically: downtown, east, north, south and west.

Hotels and Motels

Downtown

Berkeley Hotel
$$$$ • 1200 E. Cary St. • 780-1300

This European-style hotel is centrally located in historic Shockoe Slip, two blocks from the State Capitol and amidst numerous shops. It has 55 traditionally decorated guest rooms, an excellent restaurant, valet parking for room and dinner guests and a complimentary health club. The largest of its three meeting rooms will accommodate 150 people, the smallest, 12. Its Governor's Suite has a 25-foot vaulted ceiling, two baths (one with a Jacuzzi) and three terraces with a skyline view of the city.

Commonwealth Park Suites Hotel
$$$$ • 901 Bank St. • 343-7300

At the edge of Capitol Square, this prestigious hostelry is convenient to state government offices as well as the financial district. For informal dining, there is the comfortable Maxine's restaurant on the premises. All 59 rooms are suites and there are three meeting rooms. The hotel offers room service and 24-hour valet parking. Pets are allowed.

Crowne Plaza
$$$ • 555 E. Canal St.
• 788-0900; (800) 227-6963

The Crowne Plaza is a 299-room (15 suites), full-service hotel with a spectacular view of the James River. It has an indoor swimming pool and health facilities complete with a Jacuzzi, a sauna and exercise equipment. The Crowne Plaza offers more than 10,000 square feet of meeting space in 10 rooms which, along with its restaurants, are on its second floor and easily reached from the hotel's covered parking deck.

Historic District Hotel
$$$$ • 301 W. Franklin St. • 644-9871

This former Holiday Inn is the home of legislators when the state's General Assembly is in session, and it's a popular overnight place for bus tours. It has 204 rooms, three suites and four meeting rooms. An outdoor pool on the top of the hotel is also available. There is a restaurant with a second-floor view of historic Franklin Street and a first-floor lounge off the lobby.

Jefferson Hotel
$$$$ • Franklin and Adams Sts.
• 788-8000; (800) 424-8014

The Jefferson has no peer in Richmond. Built in 1895 and totally renovated in the 1980s, it has everything you would expect of a legendary grand hotel. Upper and lower lobby areas are connected by a magnificent stairway that easily could have been a model for the one in *Gone with the Wind* — in fact, local legend will try to tell you it was the staircase.

There are 275 guest rooms and 26 suites. Its 23,000 square feet of meeting space includes 12 versatile rooms plus a Grand Ballroom resplendent in gold detail. A state-of-the-art fitness center is available to guests. The hotel is the home of a gourmet restaurant, Lemaire, and of T.J.'s Restaurant and Lounge. (See our Restaurants chapter for more on T.J.'s.)

Linden Row Inn
$$$$ • 100 E. Franklin St.
• 783-7000; (800) 348-7424

Linden Row is a modern restoration of

seven antebellum townhouses, three Garden Quarter buildings and a carriage house (now the dining room for inn guests, which is written-up in our Restaurants chapter). Its 70 guest rooms, including seven parlor suites, are appointed with Empire furnishing and modern amenities. Each room is climate-controlled and offers remote control cable TV. If you feel like working out, there's a YMCA one block away. There's one meeting room that will accommodate as many as 32 persons theater-style, and suites also can be used for meetings. If you like history, you'll love Linden Row and its central location.

Omni Richmond
$$$$ • 100 S. 12th St.
• 344-7000; (800) THE OMNI

The four-star, ultramodern Omni enjoys a strategic location in the James Center adjacent to Shockoe Slip and Richmond's financial district, and it is just a few blocks from the State Capitol. Each of the Omni's 353 first-class guest rooms feature in-room movies, a mini-bar and an executive desk. The eight parlor suites and two hospitality suites have separate areas for entertaining. There are 42 Omni Club rooms on two floors with a private lounge and concierge. About 14,000 square feet of meeting space is available in 13 rooms, and the hotel has an indoor pool and underground parking. The Omni is the home of Caffe Gallego (see our Restaurants chapter).

Richmond Marriott
$$$$ • 500 E. Broad St.
• 643-3400; (800) 228-9290

The Marriott, with 30,000 square feet of meeting space and a direct connection to the Richmond Centre, is action central. It has 401 guest rooms including two presidential suites, four hospitality suites and four executive suites. Allie's American Grille offers a great selection, and the lounge, Triplett's, provides fun entertainment. The hotel has an indoor pool, hydrotherapy whirlpool, saunas, a weight room, a

FYI

Unless otherwise noted, the area code for all phone numbers listed in this chapter is 804.

INSIDERS' TIP

For a beautiful view of the James River, the Crowne Plaza always manages to please.

tanning salon and aerobics instruction. Complimentary guest parking is available in an adjacent 1,015-space lot. The hotel has a game room and an in-house audiovisual company where you can rent movies and VCRs.

East

Airport Hilton
$$$ • 5501 Eubank Rd.
• 226-6400; (800) HILTONS

This Hilton has 160 guest rooms (including 122 suites), a restaurant and lounge called Wings, an outdoor pool, an exercise room and a volleyball court. Its six meeting rooms cover 4,500 square feet, and the 2,000-square-foot Flight Deck provides outdoor meeting space perfect for a catered affair. Guest suites are ideal for small meetings of as many as 12 people.

Best Western Airport
$$ • 5700 Williamsburg Rd., Sandston
• 222-2780; (800) 528-1234

As its name implies, this hotel is conveniently located near Richmond International Airport and is ideal for those making a pit-stop in Richmond. It offers 122 guest rooms. More than 1,100 square feet of meeting space are available in four rooms. There's an outdoor pool plus a restaurant and a lounge on premises.

Courtyard by Marriott
$$$ 5400 Williamsburg Rd., Sandston
• 652-0500, (800) 321-2211

Called the "hotel designed by business travelers," this Courtyard by Marriott offers 142 guest rooms, three suites, two meeting rooms, an indoor pool, a whirlpool and a minigym. Both a restaurant and lounge are on the premises.

Days Inn Airport
$ • 5500 Williamsburg Rd., Sandston
• 222-2041; (800) DAYSINN

Days Inn Airport has 100 guest rooms and one meeting room that will accommodate as many as 35 people, theater-style. Mom & Pa's restaurant is right next door. The hotel has outdoor entrances and offers its guests access to an outdoor pool. Pets are allowed.

Holiday Inn Airport
$$ • 5203 Williamsburg Rd., Sandston
• 222-6450; (800) 964-6886

This is the largest airport hotel, with 230 guest rooms and four suites—all recently renovated. It has seven meeting rooms covering almost 7,000 square feet. Together these rooms are capable of handling theater-style seating for as many as 600 people. There is a restaurant on premises, and pets are allowed with a deposit. New additions include an outdoor pool and state-of-the-art exercise facility.

Photo: Michael Ryan Croxton

The list "Slept here" reads like a roll call to history. That's no surprise because the Executive Mansion is the oldest continuously inhabited governor's mansion in the country.

Hampton Inn Airport
$$$ • 5300 Airport Square Ln., Sandston • 222-8200; (800) HAMPTON

With an outdoor swimming pool, 125 guest rooms, a hospitality suite and a free deluxe continental breakfast, this Hampton Inn provides comfortable accommodations near the airport. It has two small meeting rooms. And there's a 100 percent satisfaction guarantee.

Legacy Inn/Airport
$ • 5252 Airport Square Ln., Sandston • 226-4519

All 123 rooms in this hotel are located on the ground-floor. Twelve rooms come with kitchenettes, so be sure to call ahead and reserve one if you desire such. An outdoor pool provides for some relaxation. Though pets are welcome at the hotel, they do require that you leave a deposit, usually about $20.

Wyndam Garden Hotel
$$$ • 4700 S. Laburnum Ave. • 226-4300; (800) 628-7601

The Wyndam's ground-floor atrium complex consists of an indoor heated pool, a whirl-pool, an exercise gym, saunas and meeting and banquet rooms. A buffet breakfast is served daily in the atrium, the hotel's Garden Cafe offers casual dining and No Entertainment is an exciting lounge. There are 155 guest rooms and suites and 11 meeting rooms.

North

Best Western Hanover House
$ • 10296 Sliding Hill Rd., Ashland • 550-2805; (800) 528-1234

People who work nearby gather regularly for after-hours fun at this hotel's restaurant. Hanover House has 93 guest rooms and six meeting rooms. An outdoor swimming pool is also available for a little fun after the meetings. HBO and the Disney channel come free in each room.

Best Western Kings Quarters
$ • 16102 Theme Park Way, Doswell • 876-3321; (800) 528-1234

Just north of Ashland, this is the most convenient place to spend the night if you plan to visit Paramount's Kings Dominion. This Best

Western has 248 rooms and one suite. There is a restaurant on premises and an outdoor pool and tennis courts. Small pets are allowed. When Kings Dominion is open, the rates increase quite a bit.

Comfort Inn Ashland
$$ • 101 Cottage Green Dr., Ashland • 752-7777

This Comfort Inn is just off I-95 in the town of Ashland. Just down the street from Randolph-Macon College, this is a good place to stay if you're visiting a student or attending a college event. The hotel offers a free continental breakfast and *USA Today*, an outdoor pool and a health center. Accommodations include 126 rooms and two suites, all of which offer free Cinemax and HBO.

Holiday Inn Ashland
$$ • 810 England St., Ashland • 798-4231; (800) HOLIDAY

Holiday Inn Ashland has 167 guest rooms and one suite. There are three meeting rooms. It has an outdoor swimming pool, fitness center, restaurant and lounge on premises. The motel is situated amid a cluster of fast food restaurants and shops.

Holiday Inn North
$$ • 801 E. Parham Rd. • 266-8753; (800) HOLIDAY

This North Side Holiday Inn offers 82 guest rooms, a restaurant and an outdoor swimming pool. The Parham Road location just off I-95 is convenient for thru-state travelers, and the hotel is only about five minutes from the businesses and action of downtown Richmond.

Knight's Inn
$ • 9002 Brook Rd. • 266-2444;

This Knight's Inn has 63 rooms, a restaurant, and an outdoor swimming pool on the premises. It is near the intersection of Parham Road and Brook Road where there are several shopping centers and fast food restaurants.

Quality Inn
$$ • 5701 Chamberlayne Rd. • 266-7616

Formerly the Virginia Inn, the Quality Inn is at the intersection of Interstate 64 and I-95. Located only a short distance from Azalea Mall

and countless other shops and restaurants, this hotel offers 104 guest rooms and an outdoor swimming pool. It also has one small meeting room that seats about 25 people.

South

AmeriSuites Arboretum
$$$ 201 Arboretum Place • 560-1566

Located on Richmond's Southside, AmeriSuites offers 128 guest suites, 33 TCB (Taking Care of Business) suites for business travelers, two meeting rooms, an outdoor swimming pool and a 24-hour on-site fitness center. Also, all guests have access to the American Family Fitness center that's within walking distance for a minimal charge. Each suite includes a kitchenette, iron and ironing board and a coffee maker. Although a restaurant is not on the premises, Chili's restaurant offers free delivery to AmeriSuites' guests. A complimentary continental breakfast is included with a stay.

Best Western Governor's Inn
$$$ • 9826 Midlothian Tnpk. • 323-0007; (800) 528-1234

The Governor's Inn offers 80 guest rooms, four of which have jacuzzis. The hotel also has three suites and two very large meeting rooms. On the premises you'll also find an outdoor swimming pool and hot tub and the Razzles lounge. Guests receive a complimentary continental breakfast.

Brandermill Inn
$$$ • 13550 Harbour Pointe Pkwy., Midlothian • 739-8871; (800) 554-0130

The 60 guest rooms here are all two-level suites and overlook the wooded banks of a 1,700-acre lake. The inn offers a boardroom and a conference room for meetings, and it has an outdoor swimming pool, an indoor Jacuzzi and a health spa. Its Lakeside Restaurant (see our Restaurants chapter) specializes in American-Italian cuisine and seafood, and it has a nightclub lounge. Boat rentals are also available.

Comfort Inn
$$$ • 2100 W. Hundred Rd., Chester • 751-0000; (800) 228-5150

This Comfort Inn has 112 guest rooms plus

an additional 10 suites complete with a hot tub. There are two meeting rooms. There is a restaurant, outdoor swimming pool and indoor exercise room on the premises. A deluxe continental breakfast buffet comes free with your stay.

Comfort Inn Corporate Gateway
$$ • 8710 Midlothian Tnpk.
• 320-8900; (800) 228-5150

At the Gateway, you'll find a Bob Evans restaurant, a courtyard pool and four meeting rooms, all backed by 150 guest rooms and five suites. Guest accommodations include large rooms with king-size beds and a seating area for entertaining. Also included are refrigerators, coffee makers, cable TV, microwaves, complimentary continental breakfast and a newspaper.

Econo Lodge
$ • 6523 Midlothian Tnpk.
• 276-8241; (800) 55ECONO

This motel on Chesterfield County's Midlothian corridor has 72 economy-priced guest rooms. The hotel is near the extensive shopping areas of Cloverleaf Mall and Chesterfield Towne Center. This Econo Lodge doesn't offer breakfast but just next door you'll find a Waffle House.

Hampton Inn
$$$ • 12610 Chestnut Hill Rd., Chester
• 768-8888; (800) HAMPTON

At Exit 61A on I-95 S., this new 66-room Hampton Inn provides free deluxe continental breakfast and a complimentary morning newspaper. It shares an outdoor swimming pool, banquet room and exercise facilities with the Comfort Inn next door. Only two suites are available here so call well ahead if you're interested.

Holiday Inn Select
$$$ • 1021 Koger Blvd., Koger South Conference Center
• 379-3800; (800) HOLIDAY

Part of the Koger Center off Midlothian Turnpike, this Holiday Inn has extensive meeting facilities. Its 11 meeting rooms will handle from 10 to 1,000 people in theater-style seating. There are 235 guest rooms, six suites and

one executive suite. A fitness center next door offers indoor/outdoor tennis, racquetball, a soccer field, a baseball diamond, basketball courts and a running trail. The inn has a restaurant and an outdoor swimming pool. Rooms come equipped with coffee pots, microwaves, refrigerators, voice mail and data ports.

Holiday Inn — Southeast (Bells Road)
$$ • 4303 Commerce Rd.
• 275-7891; (800) HOLIDAY

At the Bells Road exit on I-95 S., this comfortable 170-room hotel is convenient for interstate travelers. Over the years it has volleyed back and forth between a Holiday Inn and Howard Johnson but is now back to the former. It has three meeting rooms, a restaurant, a lounge and an outdoor pool. Pets are allowed.

Howard Johnson Chester
$$ • 2401 W. Hundred Rd., Chester
• 748-6321; (800) I GO HOJO

This Howard Johnson, home of the Peppermint Lounge, also used to be a Holiday Inn. It has 166 guest rooms and two meeting rooms. A restaurant and an outdoor swimming pool can be found on the premises and you're only 10 minutes north of South Park Mall.

La Quinta Inn
$ • 6910 Midlothian Tnpk. • 745-7100; (800) 531-5900

If you like to shop, there are a number of large malls and small shopping centers nearby the La Quinta Motor Inn. Here you'll find 130 guest rooms, two small meeting rooms and an outdoor swimming pool. With your stay you get free local calls and a free continental breakfast. The hotel also provides night security. Pets are allowed.

Sheraton Park South
$$$ • 9901 Midlothian Tnpk. • 323-1144; (800) 628-7601

One of the best hotels in this part of Richmond, the Sheraton Park South has 195 guest rooms, one suite, nine meeting rooms, a popular restaurant called the Cafe Palm and a bar called the Ivy. For conventions and banquets, the facility can accommodate groups ranging from 10 to 400. The hotel offers a club floor for corporate travellers, with slightly larger rooms equipped with a desk and computer hook-ups.

Amenities include an indoor-outdoor swimming pool, a sauna, a Jacuzzi and an exercise facility. Jogging trails wind around adjacent lakes. Richmond portrait artist Toby Sheorn's work can be seen throughout the hotel.

Super 8 Motel
$$ • 2421 Southland Dr., Chester
• 748-0050; (800) 843-1960

Just off I-95 at State Route 10 and U.S. Highway 301, this motel offers four specially-designed handicapped rooms, 44 guest rooms and two suites. A free continental breakfast comes with the cost of a room. There's a restaurant adjacent to the motel.

West

Amerisuites Innsbrook
$$$ • 4100 Cox Rd., Glen Allen
• 747-9644; (800) 833-1516

Part of the sprawling Innsbrook Corporate Center, Amerisuites has 126 guest suites, 12 TCB (Taking Care of Business) suites for business travelers, two meeting rooms, an outdoor swimming pool and a fitness room. Kitchenettes and room service are available, and the motel is convenient to Interstate 295. A free continental breakfast is provided.

Comfort Inn Conference Center
$$ • 3200 W. Broad St. • 359-4061;
(800) 866-0553

Meeting facilities here include five rooms with a capacity of 550 in theater-style seating. There are 190 guest rooms and six suites. Access for handicapped individuals is available at the front door and from the parking deck. If you want to relax, there's an outdoor pool. Short-term leases are available — call for rates.

Comfort Inn Executive Center
$$ • 7201 W. Broad St.
• 672-1108; (800) 221-2222

This Comfort Inn, just off the Broad Street exit on I-64, has 123 guest rooms, a conference room a small meeting room and an outdoor swimming pool. Some rooms come with whirlpool tubs (at a slightly higher cost). This part of town has plenty in the way of restaurants, shopping centers and nightlife

Courtyard by Marriott
$$$ 3950 Westerre Parkway
• 346-5427, (800) 321-2211

Located one block east of the Innsbrook Corporate Center, this hotel offers 154 guest rooms, 10 suites, two meeting rooms, an indoor pool, a whirlpool, Jacuzzis and a fitness center. The Courtyard's restaurant is open for breakfast every day, and dinner is served Monday through Thursday. The lounge is open Monday through Thursday, evenings only.

Courtyard by Marriott
$$$ • 6400 W. Broad St.
• 282-1881; (800) 321-2211

Across Broad Street from Reynolds Metals Company's corporate headquarters, the Courtyard by Marriott has 144 guest rooms, 13 suites, two small meeting rooms, an outdoor swimming pool, whirlpool and exercise pool. There is a restaurant on the premises , which is open for breakfast daily and dinner Monday through Thursdays. There are a number of restaurants nearby, including a Denny's.

Days Inn — West Broad
$$ • 2100 Dickens Rd.
• 282-3300; (800) DAYSINN

Just off the I-64/Broad Street exit, this Days Inn motel has 180 newly renovated guest rooms, one small meeting room, an outdoor swimming pool and exercise facili-

---

INSIDERS' TIP

Visitor information, if it can't be found at your hotel's front desk, is available from the Metro Richmond Visitors Centers at Richmond International Airport, at 1701 Robin Hood Road, in the 6th Street Marketplace at 550 E. Marshall Street, and from the Virginia Tourist Information Center in the Bell Tower just inside Capitol Square at E. Franklin and 9th streets.

ties. Pets are allowed with a $5 deposit, and guests are provided with a complimentary continental breakfast. Weekly, monthly and group rates are available.

Embassy Suites Hotel
$$$$ • 2925 Emerywood Pkwy.
• 672-8585; (800) EMBASSY

With an indoor swimming pool, a sauna and steam room, full-service fitness facilities, 226 suites and eight meeting rooms that can handle up to 450 persons theater-style, this hotel is just off W. Broad Street near the I-64 interchange. It has a restaurant and treats guests to a free cooked-to-order breakfast. Suites come equipped with coffee makers, microwaves and refrigerators.

The Inn of Virginia
$ • 5215 W. Broad St. • 288-4011

The 141-room Inn of Virginia was formerly the Red Carpet Inn Executive Center. Here you'll find such amenities as laundry facilities, banquet rooms, an outdoor swimming pool and monthly rates. The Inn is near The Shops at Willow Lawn.

Fairfield Inn
$$ • 7300 W. Broad St.
• 672-8621; (800) 228-2800

A total of 124 guest rooms are available in this inn, along with an outdoor swimming pool. Fairfield Inn offers nonsmoking rooms and serves a free continental breakfast with your stay. Fairfield Inn is the economy chain of Marriott International.

Hampton Inn
$$$ • 10800 W. Broad St.
• 747-7777; (800) HAMPTON

If you have business in the Innsbrook area or are visiting friends in the West End, this is a convenient place to stay. This Hampton Inn offers 136 guest rooms, one meeting room with audiovisual equipment, an outdoor swim-

ming pool, free deluxe continental breakfast, a complimentary *USA Today*, free local phone calls and voice mail and data ports. Your stay comes with a 100% satisfaction guarantee.

Holiday Inn Central
$$ • 3207 N. Boulevard
• 359-9441; (800) HOLIDAY

At the Boulevard exit from I-95, the Holiday Inn Central is a place where you will find flowers everywhere, even in its Magnolia Restaurant and Lounge (see our Restaurants chapter), which was recently rated by the *Richmond Times Dispatch* as "the best restaurant in north Richmond." It has an outdoor swimming pool, 183 guest rooms and one suite. Its eight meeting rooms have 8,000 square feet of space and are capable of handling as many as 450 people, theater-style. Connecting rooms are available.

Holiday Inn Crossroads
$$ • 2000 Staples Mill Rd.
• 359-6061; (800) 368-8889

The Holiday Inn Crossroads is the only scheduled in-town pickup point for the Washington-Richmond airport ground shuttle. It has 143 guest rooms, six suites, an outdoor pool, a restaurant and four meeting rooms with a capacity of 225 people in theater-style seating.

Richmond Hotel and Conference Center
$$ • 6531 W. Broad St. • 285-9951

This hotel has 280 guest rooms, four suites and nine meeting rooms capable of handling as many as 575 persons. To accompany your meetings or functions, the catering department will prepare anything from a coffee break to a full dinner. The hotel's lounge, Kicks Sports Bar, is one of Richmond's popular nightspots. There's also a quieter place to unwind called The Club. This hotel has a fitness club and an indoor swimming pool.

Hyatt Richmond
**$$$$ • 6624 W. Broad St.
• 285-1234; (800) 233-1234**

The West End's prestige hotel, the Hyatt has 372 guest rooms and suites surrounding a 9,000-square-foot indoor-outdoor pool and garden courtyard, all recently renovated. It is the home of a popular restaurant: the plant-filled Greenhouse Restaurant. You will also find Lightfoot's lounge, a longtime West End favorite.

Recreational facilities, in addition to the swimming pool, include a health club, lighted tennis courts and a jogging course through the business complex with exercise stations. Topping it all off are 24 meeting rooms encompassing 28,000 square feet, with the largest room capable of accommodating almost 7,000 people theater-style. There are over 600 complimentary parking spaces.

Prestige Inn and Suites
$$ • 1501 Robin Hood Rd. • 353-0116

If you hear the crack of a baseball bat and the whiz of a passing fly ball, it's because this motel is next to the Diamond, home of the Richmond Braves (farm team to the Atlanta Braves). The Prestige Inn and Suites, formerly the Diamond Lodge and Suites, offers 115 rooms, 20 two-room suites, a restaurant and an outdoor pool. Just off I-95 and I-64, the motel is only minutes from downtown.

Ramada Inn West
**$$ • Parham and Quioccasin Rds.
• 285-9061; (800) 272-6232**

Near Regency Square shopping center, Ramada Inn West has 105 newly renovated guest rooms, 14 suites, three meeting rooms capable of handling as many as 225 people theater-style, a fitness room and an outdoor swimming pool. It serves a complimentary continental breakfast. This area is teeming with restaurants, shops and entertainment. Ridge Cinema is just up the road should you want to catch a movie.

Residence Inn by Marriott
**$$$$ • 2121 Dickens Rd.
• 285-8200; (800) 331-3131**

If you like lots of elbow room, one of the 80 suites here should do the job. In most suites you'll find a cozy fireplace, and all come with full kitchens. This is an ideal place for those

INSIDERS' TIP

When the Virginia General Assembly is in session, you can bet on seeing your senator or delegate hanging about the Commonwealth Park Suites Hotel.

planning an extended stay. Ask for details on these special rates.

The hotel offers an outdoor pool and free access to the Richmond Athletic Club's exercise facilities that are just down the road. The Residence Inn is located just off W. Broad Street near I-64, close to a number of shops and restaurants. Your stay comes with a continental breakfast, and pets are allowed with a fee of $125.

Quality Inn West
$$ • 8008 W. Broad St. • 346-0000

This newly renovated 194-room Quality Inn, formerly the Best Western James River Inn, has one meeting room that encompasses 1,200 square feet. The hotel offers free van shuttle service to the airport and Amtrak station. Among its many amenities are an outdoor swimming pool, an American Family Fitness Center, free local phone calls, cable TV (pay-per-view and HBO) and a complimentary continental breakfast.

Bed and Breakfast Inns

It is necessary to make advance reservations at all Richmond bed and breakfast inns. Some rooms in the inns, but not all, have private baths, and most are nonsmoking. So be sure to inquire about these things if they are important to you.

A central reservation service for bed and breakfasts in the Richmond area and in Williamsburg, Petersburg and Fredericksburg is operated in Richmond by Bensonhouse at 353-6900. They can help you find an inn that matches your needs and preferences. There is no fee for this service. Also, try visiting www.bensonhouse.com.

Hanover County

The Henry Clay Inn
$$$ • 114 N. Railroad Ave., Ashland • 798-3100

Named after local Henry Clay just as Ashland was named for Clay's home, this mag-

nificent inn qualifies as a bed and breakfast but on a grander scale than most. It has 15 rooms, three suites, private baths, Jacuzzis, fireplaces, grand porches with rocking chairs, a highly acclaimed restaurant serving homestyle food and an art and gift gallery.

Adjacent to Randolph-Macon College, it is the perfect place for parents to stay when visiting their kids at school. The inn has a cozy, small-town, bygone-era feel about it, even though it was rebuilt from the ground up in 1992. The inn's Drawing room provides the perfect setting for receptions, seminars, meetings, and other special occasions. Awaken to the kitchen's fresh-baked bread and enjoy ample helpings of homemade specialties. See our Restaurants chapter for more information on the Henry Clay kitchen.

FYI

Unless otherwise noted, the area code for all phone numbers listed in this chapter is 804.

Charles City County

Along historic State Route 5 and within about a 25-minute drive from downtown Richmond are:

Edgewood Plantation
$$$$ • 4800 John Tyler Memorial Hwy., Charles City • 829-2962

This Victorian mansion drips with history, charm and romance. It has six bedrooms in the house and two rooms, Prissy's Quarters and Dolly's Quarters, in a cabin behind the main house. Ten fireplaces, period canopy beds, period clothing decorating the rooms, museum antiques, candlelight breakfasts and a pool. The location is convenient for those who want to tour the James River Plantations. Be sure to make an appointment to enjoy the Edgewood's relaxing Victorian tea in the afternoon. Williamsburg is a pleasant 25-minute drive to the east, and Richmond and Petersburg are about the same distance to the west.

North Bend Plantation
$$$$ • 12200 Weyanoke Rd., Charles City • 829-5176

Built in 1819 for Sarah Harrison, sister of U.S. President William Henry Harrison, this manor home is surrounded by 250 acres of land and served as Gen. Sheridan's headquarters during the Civil War. Furnishings include colonial antiques and a fine collection of rare books. The plantation desk used by Gen. Sheridan still has labels affixed from 1864. The five guest rooms all have private baths. Comfort and hospitality are hallmarks. A billiard room is available, and a swimming pool and horseshoe, croquet and volleyball facilities are on-site. The hosts serve a full country breakfast.

Piney Grove at Southall's Plantation
$$$$ • 16920 Southall Plantation Ln., Charles City • 829-2480

On the National Register of Historic Places, this secluded country retreat in Virginia's James River Plantation Country offers four spacious rooms with private baths, fireplaces, refrigerators and coffee makers. Guests enjoy the parlor library with its books on Virginia history, the nature trail, the gardens and the pool. The hosts at Piney Grove serve mint juleps or hot toddies (depending on the season), Virginia wines and plantation breakfasts.

Fan District

Emmanuel Hutzler House
$$$$ • 2036 Monument Ave. • 355-4885

This enormous 8,000-square-foot Italian Renaissance house was constructed in 1914 in the heart of one of Richmond's most prestigious historic districts. It features mahogany paneling, leaded-glass windows, coffered ceilings with dropped beams and a marble fireplace in the guests' living room. It has four spacious rooms, each with a private bath, one with a Jacuzzi. The house is within walking distance of museums, restaurants and historic sites. Full breakfasts are prepared on the weekends and continental-plus breakfasts, during the week. Other amenities include cable TV, in-room phones, central air, off-street parking and TC the resident cat.

Summerhouse
$$$ • Monument Ave. • 353-6900

This splendid 1909 Greek Revival home was recently renovated by its new owners. The millwork has been faithfully reproduced and is complimented by brightly colored walls,

fireplaces and detailed windows throughout. Decorated with a continental flair, the house features crystal chandeliers, antiques, oriental rugs, gilded antique mirrors and framed artwork. The kitchen was featured in a spring 1990 issue of *Southern Living* magazine. Twin-or queen-bedded guest rooms with a private bath and wet bar are available. This home is ideal for couples — ask about their special honeymoon and anniversary packages.

Church Hill

Mr. Patrick Henry's Inn
$$$ • 2300 E. Broad St. • 644-1322

The Inn has a gourmet restaurant (see our Restaurants chapter), an English-basement pub and a garden patio. Four suites have fireplaces, private baths and kitchenettes, and some have private balconies. Guests are just a hop from Richmond's thriving entertainment district, the Bottom, not to mention the shops and restaurants of Shockoe Slip. And don't miss out on the nearby St. John's church where this inn's namesake got his name in American history with such fiery speeches as "Give me liberty, or give me death." The Inn is closed on Sundays.

The William Catlin House
$$ • 2304 E. Broad St. • 780-3746

Tastefully restored, the William Catlin House (c. 1845) is a Richmond classic. Its five rooms and two suites are comfortably furnished with period antiques and modern amenities. If you are into history and like restored homes, you'll love this hideaway on Church Hill. It is close to the Bottom and Shockoe Slip, as well as the state Capitol.

Chesterfield

Amber Grove Inn
$$$ 16216 Genito Rd. • 639-7717

Centered on 25 acres, this late-1800s farmhouse offers the feel of the country just 25 minutes from downtown Richmond. Private baths accompany three bedrooms and one suite, the latter of which has a large jacuzzi on a private deck. Although a full country breakfast is served to all guests, the Amber Grove offers a four-course gourmet dinner to overnight guests for an extra charge. Period and contemporary antiques fill the inside, and farm animals and gardens decorate the outside of this quaint inn, nestled in Richmond's southside.

Henrico Country

Virginia Cliffe Inn
$$$ 2900 Mountain Rd. • 266-7344

Four rooms, all with private baths, are available in this plantation-style house. Out back is a fully equipped cottage, perfect for newlyweds and families. All guests enjoy a homemade country breakfast of casseroles, omelets, biscuits and more. Meal requests are both encouraged and fulfilled. Flower beds and a swan-filled pond add to the outdoor beauty.

Corporate Apartments

Corporate executives in the process of moving to Richmond can arrange temporary housing in a variety of ways.

Prices will vary according to the degree of luxury you desire. Typically, however, extended-stay apartments will run you less than a regular hotel stay.

ExecuStay by Marriott
565-B Southlake Blvd.
• 379-6661, (888) 840-7829

ExecuStay is the business traveler's home away from home. Fully furnished and professionally decorated one-, two- and three-bedroom apartments are available and customized to the renter's request—choose from contemporary, traditional and country style. Each apartment can include an answering machine, TV, VCR, washer and dryer, and all apartments include a fully equipped kitchen with a dishwasher and microwave. Pet accommodations are available. The minimum stay at ExecuStay is 30 days.

Extended StayAmerica
6811 Paragon Place • 285-2065,
(800) EXT-STAY

Near Glenside Dr. in Richmond's West end, Extended StayAmerica offers fully furnished studios on a daily and weekly basis. Each studio includes a full kitchen, recliner, cable TV, data port and voice mail. Laundry facilities are available on the premises.

Homestead Village
10961 W. Broad St. • 747-8898
241 Arboretum Place • 272-1800

Homestead Village offers weekly accommodations that include weekly housekeeping, laundry facilities, personalized voice mail, data port and fully equipped kitchens. The facilities are located in both the West End and on the Southside of Richmond.

King Corporate Apartments and Guest Suites
3900 Forest Hill Ave. • 233-2970

King Corporate Apartments offers fully furnished accommodations complete with kitchenware and cable television. There is a minimum stay requirement of seven days.

The Lions Inn
905 W. Grace St. • 355-7265

This extended-stay facility has been part of the Richmond community for more than 13 years. Built in 1870, this Italianate-style home offers six bedrooms with three shared bathrooms, rented on a weekly basis. Each room has cable TV, including HBO and Cinemax. Although The Lions Inn does not serve any meals, a number of restaurants are within walking distance.

Marriott Residence Inn
2121 Dickens Rd. • 285-8200;
(800) 331-3131

In the West End near the Broad Street exit from I-64, the Residence Inn has studio penthouses with fireplaces, kitchens and a daily maid service.

StudioPLUS
10060 W. Broad St. • 747-0840,
(888) 788-3467
6807 Paragon Place • 285-7050

StudioPLUS offers furnished suites with all the luxuries of home: fully equipped kitchens with microwave and full-size refrigerator, computer data ports, free local phone calls, expanded cable television, on-site laundry facilities, a fitness center and an outdoor pool. StudioPLUS offers daily and weekly rates.

TownePlace Suites by Marriott
4231 Park Place Court
• 747-5253, (800) 257-3000

TownePlace Suites fits in perfectly as part of Richmond's booming Innsbrook business community. The Marriott-owned facility offers studio, one- and two-bedroom suites that are available on a semi-weekly, weekly or monthly basis. The suites include full kitchens, housekeeping twice weekly and separate living and working areas. An outdoor pool, exercise room and laundry facilities are on the premises, and pets are welcome.

Wingate Inn Richmond Airport
491 International Centre Dr., Sandston
• 222-1499, (800) 228-1000

Located just one mile from the airport, the Wingate Inn is designed for the business traveler, as daily, weekly and monthly rates are available. All suites and guest rooms include a cordless, two-line, speaker phone; computer data port; coffee maker; iron and ironing board; and a safe. The hotel has a free, 24-hour Business Center that offers faxing, copying, Internet access, computers and printers. An indoor pool, whirlpool, fitness center and board room also are available. A complimentary continental expanded breakfast is included with a stay.

The nearest state park that offers camping facilities is the Pocahontas State Park in Chesterfield County, just 20 minutes from downtown.

Campgrounds

If you like hunting, fishing, bird-watching, hiking, or just being outdoors, you'll find some of the most beautiful scenery, native wildlife, and well-managed state and national park campgrounds within an hour or two of Richmond. To the west, you can camp high atop the majestic Blue Ridge Mountains, in secluded valleys and meadows, or beside lakes and rivers. To the east, you can camp under pine trees or beside the ocean dunes, so close to the seashore that you can hear the waves.

From backpacking and wilderness camping to deluxe resort facilities, there are more than 400 private and government-owned campgrounds in Virginia. Some have drive-in sites, others can be reached only by boat or by foot.

Information Sources

You'll get a good idea of how many parks and campgrounds are near the Richmond area if you look at the state map published by the Virginia Tourism Development Group. Some information about the campground facilities and phone numbers are included. If you would like more information, we suggest that you contact the following organizations:

Virginia Tourism Corporation
901 E. Byrd St. • 786-2051

This state office will send you a state map and information about attractions and state and national parks and campgrounds in Virginia.

Virginia Division of State Parks
203 Governor St., Ste. 306 • 786-1712

This state office will send you information about state parks and cabin facilities.

Virginia Campground Association
2101 Libbie Ave. • 288-3065

This association provides a directory of private campgrounds in Virginia.

Campgrounds

If you want to camp close to Richmond, the nearest state park that offers camping facilities is the Pocahontas State Park in Chesterfield County, just 20 minutes from downtown. This is the only campground in the metropolitan area that offers a complete outdoors experience.

There are also a few private campgrounds in the area that cater to people who are just looking for a place to stay. If you're from out of town and you plan to visit Paramount's Kings Dominion amusement park, or if you need a campground near the Richmond area, Paramount's Kings Dominion Campground and the Americamp Richmond-North are both popular.

Camping seasons and fees are subject to change, so we suggest you call ahead to verify the information in the following campground listings.

Pocahontas State Park
10301 State Park Rd. • park office, 796-4255; reservations, (800) 933-PARK • campsites: $18 per night includes water and electricity

Area residents come here to enjoy the outdoors in a full-service park environment that's close to home. The park is also within easy travel distance of historic attractions in Richmond and Petersburg. Camping is available from March through November.

INSIDERS' TIP

If you have a Ukrop's valued customer card or your *Richmond Times Dispatch* Press Club Pass, present it for a discount on admission to participating attractions and events.

New, large wooded sites for tents or recreational vehicles are expected to be available sometime in 1998. Camping and a few primitive cabins are also available for groups.

One of the original six state parks built by the Civilian Conservation Corps, the Pocahontas State Park opened in 1936. The park includes more than 7,600 acres of forest land surrounding Swift Creek Lake and Beaver Lake in Chesterfield County, just 20 minutes from downtown Richmond.

An Olympic-size pool, trails, biking, freshwater fishing and canoeing as well as wildlife and history programs are available. Be sure to visit the wildlife exhibits at the visitors center and find out more about what the park has to offer. The park staff will be happy to help you plan your visit.

The sites include a tent pad, picnic table and grill. Additional facilities include modern bathhouses, hot showers, concessions, rowboats, canoes, paddleboats and a dump station. A maximum of six people or one family is allowed at each site.

Holidays and weekends are very busy, and reservations are recommended. (During the week, you probably won't need one.) Individual and group reservations may be made through the park's reservation number. Walk-in reservations are also handled at the State Parks Office in downtown Richmond, 203 Governor Street, Suite 306. Major credit cards are accepted. The park grounds are open year-round. Special activities are seasonal.

To get there, take Exit 61B off I-95, then go west on Route 10 to Route 655, Beach Road.

Americamps Richmond-North
11322 Air Park Rd., • 798-5298
• **campsites: pull through with full hookups $23.70 per night plus tax; tents $18.70; water and electric $21.70.**

Sites are available for tents and recreational vehicles at this partially wooded campground just off I-95, about 15 minutes north of Richmond. Take the Lewistown Road exit and follow the signs. Facilities include camp store, laundry, game room, playground and pool. It's open all year. Major credit cards are accepted.

Kings Dominion Campground
I-95 and Route 30, Doswell • 876-5355
• **cabins: $58.50 per night; campsites: $22.50 per night; with water and electricity $27.00; with sewer hookup $31.**

This shady campground offers log cabins, and tent and recreational-vehicle sites in a woodsy area adjacent to Paramount's Kings Dominion. Sites with modern hookups are available. Cozy log cabins include a queen-sized bed and a set of bunk beds. Bring your own linens. Outdoor grills are provided for cooking. A maximum of six people may stay in each cabin. For more than four people in a cabin, an additional charge of $5 per person is assessed.

Be sure to ask about special packages and amusement park tickets for campers. The park is about a five minute walk from the camp. A free shuttle service is available to and from the park.

Campground facilities include a large swimming pool, a playground, a game room and a complete camp store and laundry. A convenience store and several fast-food restaurants are nearby on Route 30. Hot showers and bathhouses are provided.

Reservations are recommended. Call at least one month in advance to reserve a site for holidays. Call two weeks in advance for other times. There may be a minimum stay requirement for weekend and holiday reservations. The campground is open all year. Off-season rates are available when Kings Dominion is closed, usually from September to April. Major credit cards are accepted.

To get there from I-95, take the Doswell Exit and go east about a mile on Route 30. The campground is on the right after you pass Paramount's Kings Dominion.

FYI

Unless otherwise noted, the area code for all phone numbers listed in this chapter is 804.

Photo: Tom Thorp

Aquariums, nature centers and parks welcome visitors from all over.

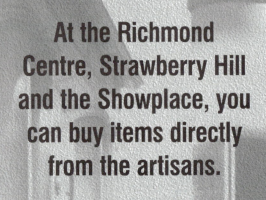

At the Richmond Centre, Strawberry Hill and the Showplace, you can buy items directly from the artisans.

Shopping

If you like strolling on sidewalks and browsing through interesting boutiques and galleries, you'll have fun exploring Shockoe Slip, Carytown and the Shops at Libbie and Grove. For serious shoppers, Richmond also has numerous shopping malls anchored by one or more of the area's major department stores: Belk, Hecht's, Peebles, Dillard's, JCPenney and Sears.

In addition to the malls and shopping areas, there are specialty stores to please every shopper looking for everything from designer clothes to exotic foods.

Bargain shoppers will discover that Richmond has its share of discount stores selling goods from electronics to shoes. There are also a number of vintage clothing and consignment stores where you can find everything from retro fashions to baby clothes in like-new condition for a fraction of the original cost. You'll also find great deals on everything from name-brand clothing to housewares and pottery at the outlet shops in Williamsburg, just 45 minutes east of Richmond.

For groceries, we think you'll find the some of the best service and produce in town at Ukrop's, a local, family-owned grocery chain, where they treat customers like guests. Employees go out of their way to make sure you have an enjoyable shopping experience, and it's not unusual to see the owners greeting customers. Just about everyone in town has a story about Ukrop's to tell. They've completely redefined the grocery shopping experience.

For those who like poking around in dusty antiques stores, you'll be delighted to know that Richmond has a wealth of shops in the metropolitan area and surrounding counties. You can go on a number of antiquing expeditions without seeing the same store twice.

We also have several excellent craft shows at the Richmond Centre, Strawberry Hill and at the Showplace where you can buy items directly from the artisans.

If you're looking for unusual or distinctive gifts, you'll find out-of-the-ordinary items at the gift shops at the Science Museum of Virginia, the Richmond Children's Museum, the Museum and White House of the Confederacy, the Valentine Museum, the Virginia Museum of Fine Arts, Maymont and the Lewis Ginter Botanical Garden.

In this chapter, we explain what you can expect to find at our major shopping areas and malls. We also cover some of the nearby shopping meccas, and at the end of the chapter, we highlight those special shops you just won't want to miss. All stores are open during regular business hours unless otherwise noted.

Unique Shopping Areas

Carytown
Cary St. from the Boulevard to the RMA

You'll be surprised at the variety of shops, boutiques, restaurants and food stores in this nine-block shopping area that extends from the Boulevard to the RMA beltline just west of the Fan District. There are more than 250 stores and professional offices lining both sides of the one-way street, in shopping courts, alleys and along side streets. It's also the site of the Byrd Theatre, a national historic landmark that still operates as a movie and entertainment theater.

Carytown began in the 1930s with the construction of the Cary Court Shopping Center, and it's been growing ever since. The old First Baptist Church has been renovated for retail use and includes Annette Dean (women's and childfren's fashions), Acacia Regional Cuisine, Martin Furnishings (interior design) and Karina's Hair.

You'll also find Oriental rug dealers, art galleries, coffee and tobacco shops, florists, card and party shops, bakeries, seafood stores, wine and cheese shops, antiques stores, fine furniture stores, clothing and lingerie stores, a pet shop, bicycle shops, a kitchen shop and piano shops. The businesses seem to have developed spontaneously in no particular order, so you might be in an Oriental rug store one minute and a pet store the next. Stroll up and down the sidewalks and browse through the stores that appeal to you. Shopping here is a unique experience and a lot of fun on a pleasant day.

Carytown stores include Schwarzschild Jewelers, Tiffany's (bridal wear and consulting), The Groom's Corner, Jean-Jacques Bakery, Bangles & Beads (costume jewelry and supplies), The Silk Jungle (home furnishings), Vogue Flowers & Gifts, Amazing Pets, Agee's Bicycle as well as Two Wheel Travel (bicycle shops), Carytown Coffee & Tea, Tobacco House, Mongrel's (unusual and creative cards and gifts), Ellman's Dancewear, NYFO Black & White (women's clothing), Premiere Costumes, For the Love of Chocolate (everything chocolate), City Shoes, Children's Market Exchange, Skirt and Shirt (clothing), La Lune (jewelry and clothing), Brazier Fine Art, Gravity Skateboard Shop, Glass & Powder Board Shop, Art Antics/Phenomenon Gallery, Plan 9 Records, The Phoenix (women's clothing), Narcissus (women's clothing and accessories), Pink (fashionable clothing, cards, gifts and jewelry with a New York flair), The Top Drawer (lingerie and night wear), ...But is it Art? (gallery and gift store), Second Time Around (antiques and collectibles), Martha's Mixture (antiques), Lane Sanson (international gifts, jewelry and furnishings), Narnia (children's books), The Compleat Gourmet (kitchen equipment and accessories), Garden Designs (planters and garden accessories), Road Runner (running supplies), House of Lighting, Richmond Piano, The Hall Tree (consignment), Sally Huss Gallery, Soak (natural bath and body essentials), Devin's (women's clothing), Anthill Antiques, Whatever (interior consignment), The Dalston Line (home furnishings), Guitar Works, All Fired Up (paint your own ceramics), Pennyrich (women's clothing), Tortoise Shell (art and home furnish-

FYI

Unless otherwise noted, the area code for all phone numbers listed in this chapter is 804.

ings), Thomas-Hines Antiques, Beck & Little (toys and comic books), Luxor Vintage Clothing, St. Tropez (women's clothing), River City Cellars (wine and gourmet foods), World of Mirth (40s, 50s, and 60s collectibles), Tropical Treehouse, Ten Thousand Villages (world handicrafts), Old World Accents (Christmas store), Bygones Vintage Clothing, The Byrd Theatre, Actualize (personal training and massage), Dominion (skateboards), Need Supply Co. (women's and men's clothing), Merrymaker Fine Papers, One Eyed Jacques (games), Leo Burke Furniture, Old Dominion Camera Shop, Wrap it Up (balloons and supplies), The Antique Gallery, The Honey Shop (natural foods), Wine & Beer of Carytown, Lex's of Carytown (clothing and gifts), Glass Boat (women's clothing and furniture), Storehouse (furniture), Carytown Photo, Etc. for the Home, The Aquarian Bookshop, Ellwood Thompson's Natural Market, Baker's Crust Bread Market and Starbucks.

On side streets, you'll find Owen Suter's Fine Furniture, Annette Dean Consignments, The Art & Frame Shop, Incredible Edibles and Niblick and Cleek (golf clothing).

If you want to see it all, allow yourself plenty of time, park and walk up one side and down the other. There are more than 25 places to eat, so you can stop for lunch or refreshments if you get tired. Popular restaurants are the New York Deli, The Track, Chopstix and Amici's. (See our Restaurants chapter for more information.) There are also a number of sidewalk cafes that are perfect for people-watching.

You may also want to visit the annual Carytown Watermelon Festival in August, when the merchants association sponsors a weekend street party with special activities.

Parking is available along Cary Street, side streets or at free parking decks — one at Crenshaw and Dooley and one at Sheppard and Colonial. Shop hours vary. Most of the stores are open from 10 AM to 5:30 PM, Monday through Saturday. Some stay open later depending on the season, and a few stores are also open on Sunday.

Gaskins Place
Gaskins Road and Patterson Avenue

This smaller shopping plaza ranges from the large stores to the small shops. For grocery and convenience shopping, you'll find Ukrop's, CVS Pharmacy and 7-Eleven. And for the fun, eclectic shopping, check out Roomers (bed, bath, and home furnishings), Vogue Flowers (balloons, cards and gifts) and Celtic Colours (British and Irish imports). When you're ready for a snack, stop in for a sweet treat at The Little Yogurt Shop.

Shockoe Slip
Cary St. from 10th to 13th Sts.

Near downtown, historic Shockoe Slip offers cobblestone streets, restaurants, hotels, boutiques, art galleries, antiques shops and clothing stores in a quaint three-block area of Cary Street known for its renovated tobacco buildings and warehouses.

Special shops here include La Lune (silver jewelry and clothing from Bali), NK Designs (women's fashions and accessories), Shockoe Espresso (coffeehouse), Beecroft & Bull Ltd. (fine men's clothing and furnishings), Rare Gems Gallery, Frances Kahn (women's clothing), The Toymaker of Williamsburg, Fornash (diamonds and fine jewelry), and Antique Boutique (heirlooms, accessories, unusual gifts, jewelry). You'll also find My Romance (unusual gifts), The Fountain Bookstore, Glass Reunions (specializing in blown and stained glass), Cudahy's (art and fine crafts) and a number of other clothing, jewelry and antiques shops.

Be sure to allow time for lunch, dinner or drinks while you're here. Shockoe Slip has earned a reputation for having excellent restaurants and clubs with live music, comedy and dancing. See our Restaurants and Nightlife chapters for more details.

Shockoe Slip also hosts many special events in the downtown area such as the Halloween Pumpkin Party sponsored by the merchant's association. Christmas brings a bustle of activity, special shows and events, twinkling lights and a sense of magic to the Slip.

Street parking is limited, but there are several parking lots around the area within easy walking distance. Most of the stores open at 10 AM Monday through Saturday and stay open until 5 or 6 PM. Some stay open later on Friday and Saturday nights, and a few stores are open on Sunday.

Patterson Avenue
Westview to Maple avenues

This small but growing shopping area is parallel to The Shops at Libbie and Grove, but north a few streets. Along Patterson Avenue you'll find Yellow Umbrella Fresh Seafood, Freda (women's clothing), Shades of Light, Plaids & Stripes (home furnishings), Pretty Paper, Mosmiller Florist, A. Roman Antiques, Jingles (bridal boutique), Westhampton Pastry Shop, The Butterfly (consignment boutique) and The Toy Center. There's also a variety of restaurants to choose from, including James Café.com (American), Yum Yum Good (Chinese) and SuperStar's Pizza.

The Shops of Libbie and Grove "On the Avenues"
Libbie and Grove Aves.

This charming shopping area in the West End might remind you of an exclusive boutique area in a small resort town. About 45 specialty shops and restaurants line both sides of the street in one- and two-story buildings and Victorian-style homes with awnings, friendly porches and sidewalk cafes. Attorneys, doctors, Realtors, interior designers and travel agents have also set up shop here, renovating old buildings and adding to the neighborly ambiance. Shops begin on Libbie Avenue within about two blocks of Grove Avenue and continue on Grove Avenue for a block or two on either side of the intersection.

The Arcade on Grove is one of the newest additions to the shops here. Modeled after a European-style shopping arcade with a gazebo and handpainted wall murals, The Arcade on Grove offers a collection of specialty shops unlike any other place in Richmond. Shops include Morning Glory (garden pots, tools and accessories), Market Place (gifts), Open House (gifts for the kitchen and home) and the Arcade Cafe (lunch and carryout).

Walk a block in any direction and you'll find a variety of specialty shops offering women's fashions, jewelry, baskets and plants, fabrics, antiques, home fashion accessories, gifts, country crafts and decorative items, art galleries, children's clothing, books and more. Local merchants own the shops, so you'll enjoy personalized service and attention.

Shops here include Thistles (fine leather goods), Monkey's (women's clothing), The Happy Cook (gourmet kitchen shop), Goodnight Grove (interior design), Jermie's Needlework and Linens, The Complete Fly Fisher, Created by You (paint your own ceramics), Madelyn's (women's clothing), J. Emerson Inc. (fine wines and cheese), Cachet Ltd. (gifts and interior accents), Signature Flowers, Added Dimensions (women's clothing), Kim Faison Antiques, WhipperSnappers (children's clothing), One Thing at a Time (stationary and personalized gifts), Cottage Stitchery (needlepoint accessories), Early & Co. (French antiques), Rothchild Jewelers, Suitable for Framing, Irresistibles (women's clothing), Paper on the Avenue, Kneeknockers (children's clothing), Chadwick Antiques, Levys (women's clothing), The Flag Center, John Barber Art Ltd. (original maritime paintings and lithographs), The Shoe Box, Grove Avenue Coffee & Tea, Cabell Shop (women's clothing), Frillseekers (unique art and gifts), Peter Blair (men's clothing), The Knitting Basket, Moto-Photo, Ardley (women's clothing), Robert Blair Antiques, and Paper Plus.

Combine your shopping with lunch, or visit the avenues in the evening for a movie at the Westhampton Theatre and dinner at duJour or the Peking. duJour is one of Richmond's best neighborhood cafes and specializes in fresh, innovative cuisine. You can relax and dine at the sidewalk cafe when the weather permits. The Peking is a well-established restaurant, specializing in authentic Szechuan and Mandarin cuisine. If you prefer faster food, try a sandwich at Luna Grove or a wrap at Palani Drive.

Free parking is available along the streets or in parking lots behind the shops — use the entrance from Libbie Avenue or behind Grove Avenue Grill on Maple Avenue. Store hours range between 9 AM and 5 PM, Monday through Saturday.

6th Street Marketplace
550 E. Marshall St. • 648-6600

You'll find a number of specialty boutiques and restaurants at this downtown marketplace between the Carpenter Center on Grace Street and the Marriott on Broad Street. The narrow, two-level center is probably best known among locals for its ornate walkway that spans Broad Street.

Built in 1987, 6th Street Marketplace caters mainly to downtown office workers at lunch time and to visitors attending conferences and events at the Richmond Centre and the Coliseum. Festival Park, an open area between the marketplace and the Coliseum, is also the site of many special events, including the Friday Cheers concert series sponsored by Downtown Presents. (See our Annual Events chapter for more information.)

Some of the shops here include Gerri's Gifts (country crafts and gifts), Bridges (authentic African goods), Footlocker, Radio Shack, Golf Unlimited (golf accessories), Georgetown Jewelry, 6th Street News (newsstand) and Shoes Etc.

You'll also find the Blue's Cafe & Bistro and numerous fast food places in the food court including Subway, Pasta Lovers, Steak Escape and Dragon Wok.

Free two-hour validated parking is available from participating merchants with a $10 purchase. Shops are open 10 AM to 6 PM, Monday through Friday; 10 AM to 4PM on Saturday; they are closed on Sunday.

Sycamore Square Shopping Village
Sycamore Square and Crowder Drs.
• 320-7600

This quaint shopping village in Chesterfield County off of Midlothian Turnpike will remind you of Williamsburg with its Colonial-style buildings and high-pitched cedar-shake roofs. There are numerous shops, specialty boutiques, art galleries, professional offices and a Ukrop's, all arranged in clusters to resemble a small town. Crab Louie's, a popular seafood restaurant, is also here, as well as the Italian Café and a family restaurant called Milepost 5. See our Restaurants chapter for more information.

Specialty shops include Sycamore Pewtersmith, Penelope (women's fashions), The Parrot (dress shop), Down the Garden Path (garden shop), R.S.V.P. (party services and gifts), Herbs, Etc. (herbs and related gifts), Toys, Trains and Teddy Bears, Pottery Wines & Cheese, Kathleen's Fudge & Sweet Sensations, and Talbot's (women's apparel) is also nearby.

Shops are open from 10 AM to 5 PM, Monday through Saturday. Some are open earlier or later, and they are all closed on Sunday.

Major Shopping Malls and Centers

Chesterfield Towne Center
Huguenot Rd. and Midlothian Tnpk.
• 794-4660

Decorated with palm trees and skylights throughout, this South Side mall has the ambiance of a tropical paradise, especially on a sunny day. It's the largest in the area, with more than 125 shops, services and restaurants including Belk, Hecht's, Dillard's and Sears. At Chesterfield Towne Center, you'll find stores that no other mall in the area has, including Journey's (shoe store), Gantos (stylish women's fashions), Northern Reflections (casual wear for men and women) and San Rio Surprises (a children's accessory store). Other popular stores here include Structure, Ann Taylor, Eddie Bauer, Fink's Fine Jewelry, Wicks 'n' Sticks (a candle shop)and Cocoanut Jewelry. There's also a nine-screen movie theater, plenty of fast food restaurants in the Palm Court, the Chesapeake Bagel Company, Spinnaker's Restaurant and Boston Market.

At the customer service desk in the Palm Court, you'll find strollers, wheelchairs, shopping bags, stamps and gift certificates.

The mall also offers Club Mom, which features special seminars, workshops, fashion events and provides discounts for members, both moms and dads. To register, just visit the Palm Court on the first Tuesday of each month. The mall sponsors holiday and community events and a mall-walker program. Frequent walkers receive awards such as T-shirts and warm-up jackets based on the number of miles

they walk. If you're a frequent shopper, be sure to join the Play and Save shoppers club. You'll receive coupons, discounts and free shopping bags every time you shop, plus you can play special mall games to win big prizes. To join, just stop by the customer service desk and ask for information.

Stores are open 10 AM until 9 PM, Monday through Saturday and 12 to 6 PM on Sunday.

Cloverleaf Mall
7201 Midlothian Tnpk. at Chippenham Pkwy.
• 276-8650

The south side's Cloverleaf Mall opened in 1972 and has been a favorite mall of Richmond shoppers ever since. Anchored by Hecht's, JCPenney and Sears, the mall offers more than 60 stores and services arranged in a complex that makes shopping easy and quick. In addition to its user-friendly layout, Cloverleaf also has stores with moderately priced merchandise which make it more value-oriented than other shopping centers. In 1987, the mall added the food court and a movie theater building and completed significant renovations.

Some favorite stores here include Kay Bee Toys, Rainbow Shops (women's and children's clothing), Victoria's Secret, Limited Express, Sea Dream Leather (leather boots, bags, belts and accessories), Ingle's Nook (country and classic home decorations and accessories), Babbage's (computer software and Nintendo), Cavalier (popular young men's fashions), Foot Action USA (sports shoes), The Avenue Plus (women's fashions), Dynamics (men's clothing), Blockbuster Music, Friedman's Jewelers and Spencer Gifts.

While you're here, you can enjoy a snack or a meal at numerous fast food restaurants in the food court or you can visit the Piccadilly Cafeteria. You can also see a movie at the Cloverleaf Cinema 8. Family-oriented events and community activities (art shows, health screenings, etc.) are held here frequently.

If you want to shop the whole mall, we suggest that you park in the back of the mall near Hecht's and JCPenney and enter through the food court. For shopping bags, gift certificates, strollers, wheelchairs, stamps and gift wrapping, visit the information booth near the center of the mall.

Store hours are 10 AM to 9 PM, Monday through Saturday; 12 to 6 PM on Sunday.

Fairfield Commons
Nine Mile Rd. at Laburnum Ave. • 222-4167

This mall opened in 1967 as Eastgate Mall and became Fairfield Commons in 1990 when the mall was sold to Interstate Properties, a New Jersey-based shopping center owner. Anchored by Peebles and CVS Pharmacy, the mall has a pleasant, airy look.

Other stores here include A&N (men's and women's casual apparel), Dynamics (men's clothing), Kay-Bee Toys, Footlocker and FootAction, Afterthoughts (accessories), Payless Shoe Source, Radio Shack, Sam Goody, General Nutrition Center (a.k.a. GNC), Alpha Jewelers and Simply Fashions.

Restaurants include Shoney's, Far East Café and Dot's Soup and Salad inside Peebles.

Near the Richmond International Airport, the mall serves shoppers in eastern Henrico and Hanover, Charles City and New Kent counties. Wheelchairs, strollers, shopping bags and information are available at the Security/Information desk. A 24-hour information line, 222-4167, provides recorded information about mall stores and events such as community, school and cultural programs sponsored by the mall.

Store hours are 10 AM to 9 PM Monday through Saturday; 12:30 to 5:30 PM on Sunday.

Gayton Crossing
Gayton, Gaskins and Quioccasin Rds.

This West End strip center is one of the largest in the entire metropolitan area. Anchored by both Hannaford and Ukrop's grocery stores, the center's shopping mix includes home furnishings and entertainment, men's, women's and children's apparel and shoes, pet care, health and beauty products, gifts, restaurants and miscellaneous services.

Some of the more interesting shops include Arts Limited (custom frame shop and art gallery), Carol Pipes Interior Design (commercial and residential interior design), Shoe Trends (women's fashion shoes), Jos. A Bank Clothiers (traditional clothing for men and women), Melting Pot Restaurant, Pat's (women's specialty clothing and accessories),

Plaid Racket (tennis rackets, accessories and clothing for the entire family), Canine Design (dog and cat grooming and tattooing), Gayton Animal Hospital (specialized medical care for pets), Mail Boxes, Etc. (postal, business and communication services), Travel Agents International (business and vacation travel agency), Frenchy's Bakery (homemade breads, rolls and assorted specialties), Karen's Homemades (homemade breads, sandwiches, salads and vegetarian products), Peter Pizza Plus (pizza and other Italian specialties), Barnett's Hallmark (cards and gifts), Paper & Party (cards, balloons and other party supplies), Shir-Rudolf's Collectibles and Gifts, Sycamore Pewtersmith (quality gifts and housewares), Wild Bird Center (bird feeders and accessories), Toys That Teach (children's creative learning toys), Around the Home, Good Food Grocery, Blockbuster Video, Starbucks and Einstein Brothers Bagels.

Regency Square
Parham and Quioccasin Rds. • 740-7467

Anchored by Hecht's, JCPenney and Sears, Regency Square lives up to its reputation for being one of *the* places to shop in Richmond. All of the department stores are the largest in the area, with unmatched merchandise selection and quantities. About a third of the stores can only be found in Richmond at Regency Square. Some of the special shops in this west end mall include Warner Bros. Studio Store, The Disney Store, Banana Republic, Natural Wonders (gift items related to nature and science), Brooks Brothers (traditional men's and women's apparel), Circuit City Express (state-of-the-art personal electronic equipment and gifts), Nordic Track, Eddie Bauer, Cach (unique women's clothing and accessories), Guess, Deck the Walls (print and frame shop), Bath & Body Works, Nine West, The Body Shop, Godiva Chocolatier, The Great Train Store and Yankee Candle.

Other popular stores include Ann Taylor, Laura Ashley, Laura Ashley Child, The GAP/GAP Kids, Gymboree, The Limited, Sea Dream Leather, Britches of Georgetowne (exclusive men's clothing) and Crabtree and Evelyn (fine English toiletries)

While you're here, you can order a fresh cup of gourmet coffee from The Coffee

Don't forget to bring your shopper's eye to Richmond's festivals.

Beanery Ltd. — the aroma is irresistible, and you can grab a quick bite to eat or a frozen yogurt at numerous fast food restaurants in the Food Court. If you prefer a leisurely lunch or dinner, try Applebee's.

If you want to combine a movie with your shopping trip, the Ridge Theatre is just a few blocks away across Parham Road.

For shoppers' convenience, the mall offers "Regency Services" at the Concierge Desk. If you can't find something or you're not sure if the mall has it, the staff will use a computerized listing of merchandise and services available in all of the mall's stores to help you locate it. Just call or fax them a note, 740-SHOP or (800) 431-SHOP. Strollers, wheelchairs, gift registry, gift certificates, shopping bags, even disposable diapers for emergen-

cies are also available at the Concierge Desk on the upper level.

Mall hours are 10 AM until 9 PM, Monday through Saturday; and 12 to 6 PM on Sunday.

River Road Shopping Center
6200 River Rd. at Huguenot Rd.

If you're looking for designer fashions for women, this is the place to shop. In the west end, the River Road Shopping Center features Frances Kahn and Talbot's. The center also includes the Kellog Collection (home furnishings and accessories), Jack Kreuter Jewelers, Azzurro (Italian restaurant)and Shenanigans (toy store).

Shop hours vary, but most are open 10 AM to 5:30 PM Monday through Saturday. Some shops stay open until 8 PM on Thursdays.

Shops at Willow Lawn
5000 W. Broad St. at Willow Lawn Dr.
• 282-5198

At the intersection of Broad Street and Willow Lawn Drive near Staples Mill Road, Willow Lawn was a popular strip shopping center for many years and was remodeled several years ago to include an enclosed mall area and a food court.

Anchored by Dillard's, Tower Records and Video, Barnes and Noble Bookstore and Hannafords Grocery Store, Willow Lawn features more than 80 stores including Kitchen Kuisine (Virginia products and wines, fine kitchen wares, gift baskets), Structure, The Limited, Cocoanut Jewelry (unique jewelry), Kay-Bee Toys, Victoria's Secret, Rack Room Shoes, The Nature Company (ecological and earth gifts), The Bombay Company (classic home accessories and furnishings), Picture Parts (framing and art) and Lillian Vernon (retail version of the catalog operation).

The Food Court and other restaurants include a dozen international eateries one of which is the Seattle favorite Starbucks Coffee. While you're there, take a few minutes to watch the Cinnabon employees make fresh cinnamon buns. For a lively bar or a great salad, visit Ruby Tuesday restaurant. You'll find Belle Kuisine, Padow's Hams and Deli and Chesapeake Bagel Bakery. The newest restaurant, Graywolf Grill, spices things up with its Mongolian barbecue. There's also a four-screen cinema here as well as the Barksdale Theatre.

Store hours are 10 AM until 9 PM, Monday through Saturday; 12:30 to 5:30 PM on Sunday.

Stony Point Shopping Center
Forest Hills Ave. and Hugenot Rd.

Anchored by Ukrop's, this popular strip shopping center offers about 40 interesting shops including Alchemist (crystals and palm reading), Bears 'N More (unusual and designer stuffed animals), Belle Kuisine (gourmet food, wine and beer boutique and restaurant), Charley's (restaurant), Good Foods Grocery (health food), Just For Comfort Shoes (women's shoes), Kitchen Kuisine (gourmet kitchen accessories and cooking classes), La Grande Dame (better large-size ladies' clothing), Papeterie (gifts and stationery), Pet Pros (pets, supplies and grooming), J. Altis, Ltd. (men's clothing), Stogie's (cigar and tobacco shop), Barbara's Hallmark, Toys that Teach, and Willis Optical. Most stores are open Monday through Saturday from 10 AM to 9 PM. A few of the stores are open on Sunday.

Virginia Center Commons
10101 Brook Rd., Glen Allen • 266-9000

On U.S. Highway 1 about a half-mile north of Interstate 295, Virginia Center Commons offers a growing selection of stores and boutiques. Anchored by JCPenney, Dillard's, Hecht's and Sears, the mall offers a growing number of popular shops, seasonal displays and activities. An antique carousel, one of only 150 still operating in the world, has become a permanent attraction for shoppers to ride and enjoy. The 75-year-old carousel is near Sears, and rides are offered for a small fee during mall hours.

Situated in a spacious open area of Glen Allen, the mall features terrazzo tile floors, brick columns, palm trees and sky lights. There are more than 100 stores here including the largest Disney Store in the state, Ingle's Nook (home accessories and gifts), Tailors Row (men's fashions), The GAP/GAP Kids, The Finish Line (value-priced sportswear and shoes), The Coffee Beanery, The Limited, Express, Structure, Bath & Body Works, The Athlete's Foot, Sea Dream Leather (leather clothes and accessories), Rees Jewelers (independently owned jewelry store), Things Remembered (keepsakes and gifts) and T-Shirts Plus (custom designed T-shirts).

Ruby Tuesday, the mall's full-service restaurant, is so popular that the average waiting time for a table is about a half-hour. There is also a wide variety of fast food restaurants in the Food Court, including Wendy's, Manchu Wok, Luca's Pizza and Deli Delite. Kids of all ages like to visit the Candy Express and Fun-N-Games arcade.

Virginia Center Commons also offers special events and family entertainment nearly every weekend, including the magical Santa's Castle at Christmas. Frequent shoppers may participate in valuable prize drawings and receive a free gift when they spend $50 or more at the mall. Ask at the customer service desk for more information. The mall is also home to the Bear Footers, a walking club sponsored by Henrico Doctor's Hospital. All registered walkers may walk the mall before it opens, from 7:30 until 10 AM Monday through Friday. Gift certificates, shopping bags and wheelchairs are also available. Ask for more information at the customer service booth.

Stores are open 10 AM to 9 PM, Monday through Thursday; 10 AM to 9:30 PM, Friday and Saturday; and 12 to 6 PM on Sunday.

Nearby Shopping

Colonial Heights

Southpark Mall
230 Southpark Cir. • 526-3900

This beautiful shopping mall south of Richmond in Colonial Heights opened in 1989 and has grown so rapidly that it's known by some as a shopper's paradise. Anchored by Hecht's, Dillard's, JCPenney and Sears, the mall offers about 90 stores and services. Restaurants include Morrison's Cafeteria and The Jewish Mother. There are also several fast food restaurants.

In addition to the 800,000-square-foot center, the Southpark complex includes two large strip-shopping centers, Southpark Crossing and Southpark Square, plus ParkSouth, an office/service specialty center, and other outparcels that include JC Penney, Pier 1 Imports, music stores, restaurants, a travel agency and banks.

Southpark has a reputation for spectacular Easter and Christmas displays and attracts shoppers from out-of-state during these seasons. At Christmas, a special train transports visitors through a winter wonderland including an elves' workshop, a gold mine and caves. There's also a 32-foot-tall Christmas tree that

Photo: City of Richmond Parks, Recreation and Community Facilities

The Carillon stands in remembrance of the Virginians who died in World War I.

stretches high into the sky dome and Santa's house built into the side of a snow mountain. At Easter, the mall offers a similar train ride through seasonal exhibits.

Southpark is conveniently located directly off Interstate 95 S. at Exit 54 (Temple Avenue). Stores are open 10 AM to 9 PM, Monday through Saturday; 12:30 to 5:30 PM on Sunday.

Fredericksburg

Massaponax Outlet Center
904 Princess Anne St. • (540) 898-3242

About 45 minutes north of Richmond at the intersection of I-95 and U.S. 1, the Massaponax Outlet Center opened in 1990 and offers about 30 brand-name stores including Springmaid Wamsutta (linens), Bass (shoes and apparel), Corning (dishes and cookware), Oneida (silver), Van Heusen (men's and women's apparel), Kitchen Collection, Fredericksburg Pottery and Full-O-Beans (coffee, tea and gift baskets). The area also includes a Wyte Stone Suites Hotel, Comfort Inn and the Spotsylvania County Visitors Center. Hungry shoppers will find a Cracker Barrel Restaurant, Aunt Sarah's Restaurant and a food court in the outlet center. Stores are open 10 AM until 9 PM, Monday through Saturday; 12 to 6 PM, Sunday.

Williamsburg

There are many special places to shop and browse in Williamsburg for clothing, crafts, home accessories, furniture, gifts and the like. The discount outlets are especially popular.

Prime Outlets
5715-62A Richmond Rd., Lightfoot
• (757) 565-0702

You'll find top designer and fine name-brand clothing and other products at 20 to 70 percent off the usual market price. This list of tenants is too long to list here but includes scores of well-known names.

From Richmond take Interstate 64 east to Exit 234 in Lightfoot then take Route 60 east for about 2 miles. Prime Outlets is on the right.

Williamsburg Outlet Mall
6401 Richmond Rd., Lightfoot
• (757) 565-3378

There are more than 60 factory outlet stores in Williamsburg's only enclosed mall. Shops here also offer 20 to 70 percent off retail prices. A variety of food is also available. From Richmond take I-64 east of Lightfoot exit 234. Go left onto Route 60 and look for the mall on the right.

Williamsburg Pottery Factory
Route 60 W., Lightfoot • (757) 564-3326

The Pottery is a sprawling complex of 32 Quonset-style huts, outbuildings and warehouses with 8,000 parking places. It's not so much a factory as it is an international array of goods displayed along miles of shelves. You'll find pottery, but you'll also find fine crystal, plants, dried and silk flowers, baskets, microwave ovenware, folk art, woodwork, lamps, home accessories, glassware and more. People come here by the busload to shop 'til they drop. On the same grounds are the Pottery Factory Outlets with more than 20 outlet stores.

From Richmond, take I-64 east to Lightfoot. Take exit 234 to Route 60 (International Parkway). It's on the left.

Specialty Shopping

Antiques & Collectibles

There are literally hundreds of antiques stores within an hour's radius of the Richmond metropolitan area, and there are numerous weekend auctions where you might find a good deal. If you enjoy spending your weekends

INSIDERS' TIP

Gift shops in Richmond-area museums, gardens and historical sites are a good place to go to find unusual gifts, plants and accessories.

poking around in shops, there are a few areas in Richmond that are especially well known for their antiques shops including the 300 block of Broad Street in downtown Richmond, Carytown; U.S. 301 north of Richmond; and U.S. 1 north of the city. Ask the dealers if they can recommend other stores nearby. Here are a few popular places to get you started.

Alexander's Antiques & Auctions
7114 Midlothian Tnpk. • 674-4206

Every Thursday at 6:30 PM, Alexander's holds the area's largest antique auction. The thousands of antiques that are up for grabs are listed by noon the day before on Alexander's website (www.alexanders antiques.com) as well as in the *Richmond Times-Dispatch.*

Antique Village
10203 Chamberlayne Ave.
• 746-8914

Allow plenty of time to explore the treasures offered here by 7 permanent dealers and collections from 30 others. Items include jewelry, toys, art pottery, postcards, furniture, glassware, advertising items, tobacco items and more.

Berry's Antiques
318 W. Broad St. • 643-1044

Shoppers will find a variety of antiques such as furniture, lighting and collectibles at this reputable downtown store.

Billy's Dodge City
12083 Washington Highway, Ashland
• 798-9414

Just 2 miles south of Ashland, this antique center has been around so long, over 17 years, that it's a landmark. About a dozen individual shops offer a blend of old and new antiques and collectibles including lamps, shades, quilts, candles, sterling, coins, jewelry, glassware, crocks, crafts, dolls, reproduction furniture and more.

Bradley's Antiques
101 E. Main St. • 644-7305

Bradley's carries something for everybody,

but they specialize in 18th century paintings and furniture. They also offer estate jewelry.

Caravati's Salvage Yard, Inc.
104 E. 2nd St. • 232-4175

Caravati's buys and sells architectural antiques and restoration materials from old buildings.

Chippenham Antique Center
8004 Midlothian Tnpk. • 320-4440

There are about 150 dealers here, and you should allow about 3½ hours to seriously browse this general collection of antiques and collectibles.

Collectors' Old Book Shop
15 S. Fifth St. • 644-2097

This antique book shop is described in the "Bookstores" section of the chapter.

Etc. for the Home
3506 W. Cary St. • 358-2040

Mostly by consignment, Etc. sells antique furniture, lamps, paintings and more. Shoppers will also find some new gift items in this Carytown shop.

Gates Antiques
12700 Old Buckingham Rd. • 794-8472

Established in 1961, Gates Antiques specializes in 18th and 19th century furnishings. Their collection includes primarily American pieces and some English antiques for the home or office. One of the largest dealers on the East Coast, Gates offers antiques that vary from pieces in the rough to fully restored items. They also carry decorative accessories such as lamps and china. One of the foremost antique authorities in the state, they offer appraisals, repairs and classes on antiquing.

The Glass Lady
7501 Iron Bridge Rd. • 743-9846

As the name implies, The Glass Lady is dedicated to discontinued patterns of china, crystal and unique collectibles. This South Side antique shop features selections from more than 250 companies, including 800 older, limited-edition collector plates. The shop buys, sells, trades and offers consignments, lay-a-way and gift certificates.

Governor's Antiques & Architectural Materials
8000 Antique Ln. • 746-1030

Best known for their collection of antique architectural materials, Governor's Antiques is located in Mechanicsville off Meadowbridge Road near I-295. Governor's also offers antique furniture, glass and jewelry.

Martha's Mixture
3445 W. Cary St. • 358-5827

One of the most popular antique stores in the Richmond area, Martha's Mixture is located in the heart of Carytown. As their slogan says, they sell antiques "that are fun to live with."

The Millstone
U.S. Hwy. 301 • 746-3988

This store specializes in American furniture before 1840 and Canton porcelain. You'll also find Oriental rugs, lamps and classic accessories.

Serendipity
5615 Patterson Ave. • 281-7888

The motto at this West End antique shop is, "We offer everything from farm tables to gilded glass." And they do, focusing on primitive pieces to the very sophisticated. Serendipity keeps a stock of very interesting items, purchased from estate sales and private owners.

World of Mirth
3005 W. Cary St. • 353-8991

At this unusual store in Carytown, you'll find collectibles from the '40s to the '60s including vintage housewares, furniture, lamps, toys, cards and books. You'll also find funky eclectic gifts like velvet Elvis mouse pads.

Civil War Items

The Haversack Store
1201 E. Clay St. • 644-4936

Located in the Museum of the Confederacy, this store offers all kinds of Civil War items, including flags, ornaments, books and more. See the "Bookstores" section for more information.

Owens & Ramsey Booksellers
2728 Tinsley Dr. • 272-8888

Owens Books offers thousands of Civil War books including new, used and rare editions. See the "Bookstores" section for more information.

Richmond Arsenal
7605 Midlothian Tnpk. • 272-4570

This Civil War Shop will buy, sell or trade artifacts. It carries original muskets, carbines, accoutrements, buttons, canteens, uniforms, leather goods, bullets, artillery shells, prints, relics and metal detectors.

African-American Specialty Shops

African House
834 W. Grace St. • 359-8469

Shoppers will find everything from books and greeting cards to jewelry, incense, clothing and beads, all relating to Africa and its heritage. The African House is located close to the campus of Virginia Commonwealth University.

Ghana House by Rawqartz
517 N. Harrison St. • 355-2963

This African boutique features clothing, jewelry, crafts and arts from Ghana, Nigeria, Senegal and Ivory Coast including wooden masks and sculptures. You'll find it between Grace and Broad streets near Virginia Commonwealth University.

One Force Books
217 E. Clay St. • 644-0332

See the write-up in our "Bookstores" section for more information.

Consignment and Vintage Clothing

Bygones Vintage Clothing
2916 W. Cary St. • 353-1919

Next to the Byrd Theatre in Carytown, Bygones sells vintage clothing, accessories and jewelry for men and women.

Children's Market & Exchange
2926 W. Cary St. • 359-6950

The Children's Market and Exchange in Carytown buys seasonal secondhand clothing and equipment. You'll find a range of sizes from infant to 14, plus cotillion dresses and

jackets for young girls and boys. All items are in excellent condition.

Clothes Rack
2618 W. Cary St. • 358-4693

The Clothes Rack accepts donated and consignment clothing and household items by appointment only.

Exile
822 W. Grace St. • 358-3348

This downtown store offers clothing, jewelry and collectibles from the '40s to the '70s.

Halcyon — Vintage Clothing
117 N. Robinson St. • 358-1311

A Fan District favorite, this shop features clothing, jewelry and accessories for men and women from 1890 to 1970.

The Hall Tree
12 S. Thompson St. • 358-9985

At the west end of Carytown, the Hall Tree accepts consignment clothing suitable for the shopping season. Shoppers can feel confident that items sold here have passed strict quality checks and are in excellent condition.

Urban Artifacts
1208 W. Main St. • 355-9692

This fun shop in The Fan has a mid-century focus with a mix of both vintage and modern items. Shoppers will find clothing, furniture, jewelry, kitchen items and more.

Bookstores

The Aquarian Bookshop
3519 Ellwood Ave. • 353-5575
Willow Lawn Shopping Center • 285-6264

Along with tarot card readings and workshops, The Aquarian has new age, personal growth and recovery books. Called the "soul supplier," The Aquarian also has magazines, jewelry, crystals, tapes and videos and gift items.

Barnes & Noble
1532 Parham Rd. • 527-0051
1601 Willow Lawn Dr. • 282-0781
1200 Huguenot Rd. • 378-3651

One of the largest bookstores in the area,

Serendipity in Richmond

5615 Patterson Avenue

Richmond, Virginia 23226

(804) 281-7888

Farmers Lane of Serendipity

Farmers Lane Road

Jetersville, Virginia

(804) 561-6880

Barnes & Noble stocks nearly everything you could want in about 30 different categories for adults alone. Their wide variety of titles goes way beyond the bestsellers. They also have an extensive juvenile section and can special order titles from a database of more than 160,000 publishers.

Special events such as author signings, children's story hours and guest speakers on topics such as gardening and learning how to use the Internet are offered weekly. You'll also find a variety of gifts for readers, calendars, journals, coffee mugs, maps, music tapes and CDs.

Book People
536 Granite Ave. • 288-4346

In its 18th year, this neighborhood bookstore calls itself "an old-fashioned bookstore," in the sense that there's nothing slick or fancy about it—just books and people who know books. Shoppers will find both new and used books as well as collector's books. Book People offers an out-of-print book search as well.

Borders Books & Music
9750 W. Broad St. • 965-0733

Borders offers the complete book-buying experience. Shoppers can sit and relax in the cafe and enjoy the espresso bar, pastries and sandwiches while they listen to music and read

or browse through the rows of books and publications. Over 120,000 titles in every imaginable category are offered along with Borders famed selection of out-of-town newspapers and international magazines and foreign language publications. There's also a separate children's area.

Special events are offered several times a week including open-mike poetry readings, children's story hours, author signings and workshops. Borders also has a music department and carries book-related gift items, calendars and greeting cards.

Books-A-Million
9131 Midlothian Tnpk. • 272-1792
8093 W. Broad St. • 270-1487
Southpark Shopping Center • 526-7068

With over 700,000 titles and more than 100 categories, this store offers a lot of everything and some bargain books, too. All top-ten hardback books are 33 and 1/3 percent off all the time, and it have a gigantic sale section where you can buy a lot of books for a little bit of money. It also has an extensive children's section and a Hallmark store.

Carriage House Bookshop Ltd.
404 N. Harrison St. • 359-2365

Located near Virginia Commonwealth University, this shop specializes in college textbooks and school supplies. It also carries literature and art-related paperbacks, greeting cards and posters. Used textbooks and trade books are available.

Carytown Books
2930 W. Cary St. • 359-4831

You'll find about 5,000 titles in paper and hardback on Virginiana and a variety of general topics at this Carytown book shop. And, if you can't find it, the staff takes pride in providing quick turnaround for specially ordered books. The store also carries a large selection of magazines, including British publications, university publications and literary magazines. It does not carry children's books since Narnia, a bookstore that specializes in books for kids, is directly across the street. Periodically, it sponsors author signings, and poetry and prose readings both on and off-site. Carytown Books is a member of Book Sense, a national association of independent bookstores that sponsored the 1999 Tony awards.

Cokesbury
3700 West End Dr. • 270-1070

This bookstore in the West End specializes in religious and Christian books, gifts and supplies including candles, robes, bibles, etc. It also has an African-American section and a women's interest section.

Collector's Old Book Shop
15 S. Fifth St. • 644-2097

Housed in the English basement of the Barrett House built in 1834 by the wealthiest man in Richmond, this shop sells out-of-print and rare books including books about Virginia, the Civil War, children's books, biographies and more.

Edward T. Rabbit & Co. — Books for Children
7029 Three Chopt Rd. • 288-2665

Established in 1984 at the Village Shopping Center, Edward T. Rabbit's mission is to bring books and children together. You'll find a wide selection of books for all ages of children, from babies to teenagers, along with a variety of related items, such as stuffed animals, posters, puzzles and audio and video tapes that help bring the books to life. In addition, the shop offers story hours, read-aloud workshops for parents and teachers, author signings and readings, costumed character appearances and more. Special ordering is available.

B Dalton Bookseller
11500 Midlothian Tnpk. • 794-7241

Located in Chesterfield Towne Center, B Dalton offers a wide selection of books on a variety of general topics. It carries a special section of books related to Richmond, Virginia, and the surrounding area including travel guides, cookbooks and coffee table books. Owned by Barnes and Noble, you'll find the same special ordering services, calendars, book-related gift items and discounts for frequent buyers.

VCU E^2 Bookstore (energy squared)
1111 W. Broad St. • 828-1678

On the campus at VCU, this store offers new and used textbooks, plus the top-ten bestsellers, general trade books, computer books, and business-related publications. It has a popular buyback program for used books. It also sells VCU hats, clothing and other licensed paraphernalia, and they offer an extensive selection of art supplies. E^2 now offers a coffee shop, large screen TVs, a music center, Internet centers and community programs and workshops.

The Fountain Bookstore
1312 E. Cary St. • 788-1594

The focus of this eclectic bookstore is a high level of customer service. The staff at this small, friendly shop in Shockoe Slip goes out of its way to help you find the books you want, and it delivers to nearby locations in the downtown area and to businesses that order large quantities of books. The Fountain offers a wide selection of books about Richmond and the Civil War and sponsors author signings. It also offers a hard-to-find/out-of-print search service.

The Haversack Store at the Museum of the Confederacy
1201 E. Clay St. • 644-4936

This small shop inside the Museum of the Confederacy offers a good selection of books

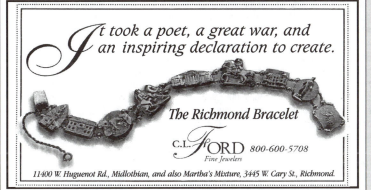

related to the Civil War, including biographies, general histories and books about women and the Civil War. You'll also find a variety of gift items and souvenirs related to the Civil War and the Victorian era, such as children's toys, jewelry, flags, calendars and ornaments.

J. Sargeant Reynolds Community College Bookstore
1651 E. Parham Rd. • 371-3266

This college bookstore offers new and used textbooks, a buyback program, trade books, and a great selection of computer software at affordable prices. It also sells college paraphernalia and school supplies.

Library of Virginia Shop
800 E. Broad St. • 692-3524

As the name suggests, this shop inside the Library of Virginia offers a strong collection of over 110 publications on Virginia's history and culture that's published by the Library of Virginia. The shop also carries other books related to Virginia, reference books and educational publications related to reading, writing, genealogy, and computers. And surprisingly, although the library doesn't have a children's section, the shop maintains a large children's section with books and related dolls, toys, puzzles, gifts and games to encourage reading. You'll also find a delightful selection of journals, cassette tapes, decorative accessories and reproduction jewelry from other museums and libraries.

Narnia Children's Books
2927 W. Cary St. • 353-5675

This popular bookstore in Carytown offers a great selection of books for kids from babies through teens and even some books about growing up for adults. But the primary focus is on books for kids up to about age 12. In addition to books, they also offer books on tape, music for kids and plush toys related to popular books. Book signings and costumed characters are scheduled periodically.

One Force Books
217 E. Clay St. • 644-0332

One Force Books specializes in literature about African Americans and Africans. You'll also find cards, artwork and prints.

Owens Books
2728 Tinsley Dr. • 272-8888

Owens Books offers thousands of Civil War books including new, used and rare editions. You'll find books on military history, Americana, Virginiana and the South as well as fine art prints and maps. Free monthly catalogues are available.

Phoenix Rising
19 N. Belmont Ave. • 355-7939

Located near The Fan, Phoenix Rising is Richmond's only gay and lesbian bookstore. Along with books, shoppers will find jewelry, music, bumper stickers, clothing, greeting cards and more.

Richmond National Battlefield Park Bookstore
3215 E. Broad St. • 226-1981

This is the one-stop Civil War shop for educational material about the war. The focus is on books about the Civil War, military history of the war and the Eastern Theater of the war. Several-hundred titles including general histories and specialized studies like regimental studies and biographies. It also has a selection of related videos, cassette tapes of music and some CD-ROMs.

Science Museum of Virginia Store
2500 W. Broad St. • 367-9187

This amazing shop inside the Science Museum of Virginia is worth a visit, even if you don't want to tour the museum. You'll find a variety of science-related books and publications on science education, experiments, astronomy and nature. They also carry an extensive selection of science toys, games and experiments, rocks and minerals, telescopes, and some jewelry and apparel.

INSIDERS' TIP

Virginia Center Commons has a 75-year-old antique carousel that shoppers can ride for a small fee.

Tower Records, Video, Books
1601 Willow Lawn Dr. • 673-6424

Although this national chain is known mostly for its music and videos, it does have a nice selection of books that focus on music, movies and pop culture.

Valentine Museum Shop
1015 E. Clay St. • 788-4178

Inside the Valentine Museum, this gift shop offers books primarily about Richmond and Virginia history, along with cookbooks related to the city and state. It also carries books that complement the museum's exhibits such as books about textiles and the history of toys. You'll also find jewelry, kids' toys and other gifts and souvenirs.

Very Richmond Gallery and Gifts
1051 E. Carey St. • 644-3613

In the James Center Atrium, this shop offers a collection of Richmond- and Virginia-related items including an extensive selection of books on the city, the state and the Civil War. You'll also find prints, original art, jewelry, mugs, T-shirts, cards, furniture, Civil War relics and other memorabilia. It specializes in custom gift baskets and sponsors events, such as book signings and art shows, monthly.

The Virginia Book Company
900 W. Franklin St. • 359-1222

This college bookstore primarily serves students at Virginia Commonwealth University. They offer new and used books and have a book buyback program. You'll also find standard college supplies here.

Virginia Commonwealth University East Campus Bookstore
601 N. Tenth St. • 828-0336

Serving primarily students on the VCU medical college campus, this is one of the few medical bookstores in the state. It carries textbooks for medical, dental, and allied-health students and provide books for hospitals and medical institutions in the area. The store also carries medical equipment needed by students such as stethoscopes and complete diagnostic kits. In addition, the store maintains over 6,000 reference titles that are open to students and the public.

Virginia Museum of Fine Arts, The Museum Shop
2800 Grove Ave. • 367-0891

Inside the Virginia Museum of Fine Arts, this popular shop offers a wide variety of beautifully illustrated books on artists, painting, photography, pottery, glassmaking, sculpture, textiles, etc. It also has books on travel, architecture, interior design and gardening, plus a children's section with art books and classic literature titles. As a complement to the museum's exhibits, the museum develops its own series of reproductions that include everything from postcards to jewelry.

You'll find a wide selection of unique and unusual gift items including Virginia-made by crafts and art. It also has designer jewelry, slides, postcards, notecards, gift wrap and posters. Prices are surprisingly moderate.

Virginia Union University Bookstore
1500 N. Lombardy St. • 355-4610

This college bookstore primarily serves students at Virginia Union University. It sells new and used books and has a buyback program. It also sells school supplies, school spirit items and greeting cards.

Waldenbooks
Cloverleaf Mall • 276-8811
Virginia Center Commons • 262-9479
Regency Square Mall • 740-1253

Waldenbooks is the mall bookstore chain that focuses on stocking bestsellers and popular books, and providing easy ordering for any titles that they don't carry. It sells calendars, greeting cards, magazines and children's gift items. For directions to the malls, see the "Major Shopping Malls" section of this chapter.

Other Special Stores

Many of our popular stores are included in the descriptions of the shopping areas and malls. These are some other special places that deserve mention.

Alpine Outfitters
11010 Midlothian Tnpk. • 794-4172
7107 W. Broad St. • 672-7879

This was one of the first stores in Richmond that specialized in outdoor equipment and apparel. You'll find skiing and camping equipment, canoes and backpacks for sale or for rent. The staff offers free advice and is very knowledgeable about outdoor adventures in the area. They can also provide information about climbing, kayaking and ropes classes in the area as well as maps of trails in the Blue Ridge Mountains.

Circuit City
1321 Huguenot Rd. • 897-0856
2040 Thalboro St. • 257-4321
9900 W. Broad St. • 273-6850

Headquartered in Richmond, Circuit City carries appliances, computers, radios, televisions, audio equipment and just about everything that's electronic. The store will install car stereos. It's known for having a great selection and competitive prices.

Festival Flags Unlimited Inc.
322 W. Broad St. • 643-5247

In 1971, a flag of colorful design was flown for a party, and in 1975, another flag was flown to announce the birth of a son. Since then, the two flags have flown into a thriving business and created a tradition in Richmond. This is the company that started the decorative flag industry. It's as original as Betsy Ross. The flags are known for their unique designs and quality fabrication. Owner Millie Jones and the staff at Festival Flags specialize in custom work as well as national and state flags. Free catalogues with over 150 stock items are available.

Franco's
5321 Lakeside Ave. • 264-2994
11400 W. Huguenot Rd. • 378-5220
8900 W. Broad St. • 270-4891

Franco's has offered traditional clothing for men and women for more than 20 years in the Richmond area. It also offers professional tailoring services and custom-made suits.

Ignatius Hats
959 Myers St. • 354-0726

A graduate of Virginia Commonwealth University, Joe Ignatius Creegan moved to New York City in the late 1980s to build his career as a milliner and then moved back to Richmond in the early 1990s. He creates and constructs one-of-a-kind hats and patterned hats which are now sold through City Shoes. His styles include natural straw braid hats, caps, costume work, and women's hats in suiting and wools. He'll create a custom hat just for you, or you may choose a fabric or leather to add a personal touch to one of his patterned hats.

Jefferson Clothing
9130 W. Broad St. • 527-1515

This family-owned store is known for its service-oriented sales staff and its meticulous alterations department. The men's departments dominate the store and offer high quality suits, tuxedos, slacks, shirts, ties and accessories at discount prices plus casual clothing from jeans to swimwear. There's also a small but well-stocked ladies' department that specializes in suits and accessories but also carries separates and dresses.

Pleasants Hardware
2024 W. Broad St. • 359-9381
3540 Pump Rd.

Established in 1915, Pleasants has a reputation for providing personal service and advice. They have "most anything," including one of the best selections of brass, porcelain and iron fixtures, knobs, keys, keyholes, hinges and other furniture hardware and fixtures in the area.

Saxon Shoes
1527 Parham Rd. • 285-3473

In the Ridge Shopping Center, Saxon Shoes has the largest selection of shoes in Richmond. This store is also known for having hard-to-find sizes and designer shoes. It carries men's, women's and children's shoes.

Stein Mart
7801 W. Broad St. • 672-8556
9746 Midlothian Tnpk. • 330-3363

This small department store sells name-brand items at low prices, including ladies', men's and children's clothing, shoes and accessories, linens and household items.

T.J. Maxx
201 Wadsworth Dr., Midlothian Market
• 330-3008
9125 W. Broad St. • 346-3113
This department store sells name-brand items at low prices and carries primarily men's, women's and children's clothing and some household items.

Museums, cultural organizations and the city and county parks and recreation departments offer special enrichment programs and classes for young people during the summer and occasionally throughout the year.

Kidstuff

From toddlers to teens, young people can exercise their bodies and stretch their imaginations at some very special places and events in the area. You'll also find amusement parks, sporting events, festivals and parades that the whole family will enjoy.

Many of the places listed here are also listed in other sections of this book, especially in the Attractions and the Annual Events chapters. At the risk of being redundant, we've included some of the same information here for your convenience. This chapter is organized into the following categories: "Major Kidstuff" the most popular kids attractions in the area; "Travel through Time," engaging historical sites; "Museums"; "Out of Doors," places where the kids can breathe fresh air while they romp; "Indoor Entertainment"; "Enrichment Programs," music, art, acting, drama and science classes and programs for young people; and "Annual Kids' Events," which includes special events in the Richmond area that are especially popular with kids.

Major Kidstuff

Paramount's Kings Dominion
Rt. 30 and I-95, Doswell • 876-5000

If you love rides and getting wet, this is your kind of place. Paramount's Kings Dominion is a 400-acre family entertainment park with seven different theme areas and more than 40 different rides including seven world-class roller coasters. Kids love the wild, messy, hands-on entertainment of the 3-acre Nickelodeon park and the "excellent" Wayne's World theme area with a replica of Wayne's basement. See our Attractions chapter for details about the rides.

If you visit the park between May and September, wear your bathing suit under your clothes or pack it along with some towels in a backpack so you can enjoy the water-park

rides and splash pools. There are lockers, showers and changing rooms inside the water-park area which is in the middle of the park.. There's also a grill-style restaurant here with relatively inexpensive food and a picnic area filled with tables and umbrellas. It's one of the best places in the park for lunch.

Before going on rides, kids will need to be measured to determine what they can ride safely. There are measuring points throughout the park, so if the first few you see are busy, just keep walking toward the rides you plan to go on.

Small children will enjoy the splash pool, the gentler rides in the water park and the Kidzville area with its construction-company play area filled with ballrooms, slides, tunnels and towers. Yogi's cave is always a favorite and there's even a special first-time roller coaster that parents can ride with their kids. Once you've braved that, you can move up to the transitional Scooby Doo roller coaster, which is more thrilling than it looks. You'll also find the Busytown Cafe, a children's restaurant designed after Richard Scarry's children's books. Splat City is a favorite for kids of all ages and gives parents a chance to run through sprinklers or just sit and watch. The Mega Mess-a-Mania show is a lot of fun — if you sit down front, you might get a chance to be in the show and you're sure to be splattered with Gak and Slime. Sit up high if you want to avoid the mess.

The whole family can experience the thrill of high-speed professional auto racing at the Days of Thunder racing simulator. It has special stationary seats for anyone who does not want to be in simulator seat. If you need a break from the rides, there are a variety of live performances and animal shows. The park also has evening fireworks shows, musical street parties and concerts.

Arrive early and spend the day. Food inside the park is expensive, and many people pack a picnic lunch and eat in the park areas just outside the entrance. There's a lot of walking, and it gets hot, so dress comfortably. Season passes for individuals and families are a bargain for locals who like to come here often.

Many companies and employers in the area offer discount tickets. Just ask at work and watch the ads. Admission is $33.99 for ages 7 and older; $24.99 for ages 3 to 6; and $28.99 for seniors age 55 and older. Children age 2 and younger get in free. Call (800) 553-7277 to purchase season passes.

The park is open daily from Memorial Day weekend through Labor Day. It's open only on weekends from the end of March until Memorial Day, and from Labor Day until October. The park is closed a few days each season for special events, so it's best to call first to make sure it's open the day you plan to visit.

FYI

Unless otherwise noted, the area code for all phone numbers listed in this chapter is 804.

To get here, take Intersate 95 North from Richmond and look for the well-marked Kings Dominion exit at Doswell.

Maymont
1700 Hampton St. • 358-7166

Pick a pleasant day, pack a picnic and head for a great day outdoors at Maymont, a 100-acre Victorian estate in the middle of the city. Use the Spottswood entrance and start with a visit to the children's farm and the animal habitats. Be sure to bring some quarters so the kids can get a handful of food for the animals, and bring your camera to capture their delight at petting rabbits, goats, cows, horses and sheep.

Then head down the walking path to the animal habitats where you'll find bears, foxes, bison, owls and hawks. If you want to keep going, you'll end up in the Japanese gardens where the kids can jump across the pond on stepping stones and search for giant goldfish and turtles while you enjoy the serenity and beauty of the Japanese landscaping, arched bridges, pathways and sculptures.

On your way back, be prepared for a steep climb back up the hill to the animal farm. At the top, you can get your picnic from the car, spread a blanket on the grass near one of the gardens or under a giant shade tree and re-

lax. Drinks, snowcones, ice cream and some fast foods are available at a nearby concession stand.

If you want to continue your tour of the park, you can walk or take the tram to the Nature Center on the other side of the park and see the indoor exhibits. The carriage collection near the nature center is also interesting, and you'll probably see a few peacocks wandering around. There's a concession stand and a gift shop here. Older children might enjoy a tour of the Maymont House. Guided 30-minute tours of the mansion are offered in the afternoon until 4:30 PM. When you're ready to leave, catch the tram and ride back to the Children's Farm.

Weather permitting, concession stands are open in spring, summer and fall. Bicycles, pets, alcohol, kites and automobiles are not allowed in the park. Dress comfortably for walking, as the terrain is hilly and some of the slopes are quite steep. The grounds are open daily and close at night. The house, Nature Center, barn and gift shop are closed on Monday. Admission is free, but a $3 donation is suggested for the house tour. Fees are charged for carriage and tram rides. Self-guided tour information is available at the Nature Center.

Maymont is on the north bank of the James River, just east of the Boulevard Bridge and south of Byrd Park.

Children's Museum of Richmond
740 Navy Hill Dr. • 643-KIDO, 788-4949

This museum provides hands-on learning experiences for children to expand their awareness of and respect for the diverse world in which we live — its art, nature and people. Kids ages 2 to 12 come here to explore and be creative. They can play in a grocery store, doctor's office, ambulance or television news studio and see themselves on camera. While mom and dad watch, they can try their skills at Computers for Kids, dress in costumes and act out their fantasies on stage. They can even put on a miner's hat and go spelunking in a 40-foot replica of a Virginia limestone cave. In the art studio, children paint, sculpt, make collages and create masterpieces. Seasonal themes focus on cultures throughout the world and offer a full slate of related activities. The whole family will enjoy professional music, drama, puppetry and dance performances.

The museum also sponsors nature programs, cooking demonstrations, art exhibits, storytelling, a theater group for children and Peanut Butter 'n Jam, a summer concert series for families. Call 788-4949 for a list of events.

Be sure to bring a camera and flash or a video camera. If you want to go somewhere for lunch, you can walk a few blocks to the 6th Street Marketplace where there are lots of casual places to eat.

The museum is on Navy Hill Drive, formerly known as 6th Street, off Jackson Street near Interstates 95 and 64 in downtown Richmond. Parking is free. Admission is $3 for children and $4 for adults. Children younger than 2 are admitted free.

Science Museum of Virginia
2500 W. Broad St. • 367-6552;
(800) 659-1727 event line;
36STARS 24-hour skywatch info.

The Science Museum of Virginia, in the historic Broad Street Train Station, offers more than 250 hands-on exhibits and participatory programs to encourage visitors to explore the exciting world of science. You'll find very few, if any, "Do Not Touch" signs here. The museum also offers large-screen-format films projected on a five-story-high domed screen in the Ethyl Universe Theatre. The sensation of being part of the movie action is so strong, you'll feel like you've been on a ride at an amusement park. Planetarium shows are also available.

Interactive exhibits feature astronomy, aerospace, chemistry and physics, computers, crystals, electricity and telecommunications. Allow plenty of time for the aviation exhibits where you can fly a plane on a computerized simulator or test-fly a variety of paper airplanes. You'll also see one of the world's largest pendulums — suspended from the center of the dome in the rotunda — demonstrating the rotation of the earth.

The museum offers special events and activities every weekend and schedules special exhibits periodically. The second Saturday of

each month is Super Second Saturday with special events and science-related projects for 3- to 10-year-olds.

In the spring, the museum usually offers a major visiting exhibit. Popular displays in recent years include sea creatures, bears and giant robotic dinosaurs. In March, a special weekend exhibit entitled Bay Days celebrates the sights and sounds of the Chesapeake Bay. In November, the museum presents the Model Railroad Show, and December features Joy From the World with decorated trees and holiday customs from around the world as presented by representatives of Richmond's international community. The first day of summer is celebrated with the Scooper Bowl ice cream party and Spring N2 Summer celebration on the front lawn of the museum.

This is a great place to go as a family. It's also neat to just walk around the historic old train station with its domed ceiling and interesting spaces. Weekday afternoons and anytime in September and January are good times to visit if you want to avoid the crowds. Spring is typically a very busy time with a lot of school groups. Allow yourself plenty of time to see everything. You can easily spend half a day here. Lunch is available at the Cosmic Cafe inside the museum. There are several fast-food restaurants nearby, or you can pack a picnic lunch and eat on the grounds. Picnic tables and a few vending machines are available. Admission to the exhibit area is $4.50 for seniors, $4 for youths and $5 for adults. With one theater show, admission is $7.50 for seniors, $7 for youths and $8 for adults.

A 24-hour skywatch information line, 36STARS, offers information about constellations and astronomical features visible in the evening sky.

Travel through Time

Agecroft Hall
4305 Sulgrave Rd. • 353-4241

Take the whole family on the "Tudor Tykes" tour of Agecroft Hall, a 15th-century Tudor-style manor house moved here from England to save it from destruction. Learn about the lives of Tudor and Stuart children and enjoy a stroll through the magnificent gardens over-

Photo: Trilby Studio

Children can feed the animals at the Maymont farm.

looking the James River. Reservations are required. The cost is $5 for adults, $4.50 for seniors, and $3 for children age 12 and younger. Agecroft is closed on Mondays.

Henricus Park/Citie of Henricus
601 Coxendale Rd., Chesterfield County
• 706-1340

Soak up some history at the Citie of Henricus, a partially reproduced 1600s town on the James River in Chesterfield County. Henricus, now known as Farrar's Island, was established by Sir Thomas Dale in 1611 when the London Company sought a better loca-

tion than Jamestown for its colony. This second English settlement was wiped out in 1622 by an Indian massacre. The site now includes a palisade with watchtowers, a storehouse, a necessary building and commemorative monuments. Future development plans include the construction of a visitors center and a replica of what is believed to be the nation's first hospital.

A 2.5-mile round-trip hiking trail through Henricus Historical Park offers spectacular views of the river, and commemorative markers relate interesting tidbits of history. The trail is well-shaded, and there are plenty of

INSIDERS' TIP

Each June, the Richmond Children's Museum hosts a Soap Box Derby race at 10th and Cary Streets. Parents can help their kids build a racer. Call the museum, 788-4949, in February for registration and kit information.

benches for resting or picnicking. If the kids have a lot of energy to burn, continue your hike through the adjacent Dutch Gap Conservation Area where you'll see beaver, deer and wild turkeys. Interpretive tours with an experienced guide can be arranged in advance. Call 706-1341.

On Citie of Henricus Publick Day, celebrated on the third Sunday in September each year, the park sponsors a historic re-enactment of the lives of the settlers, a 17th-century Church of England morning-prayer service, games, food and tours. Old-fashioned games such as hoop-rolling, bowling, stilt-walking and tree-stump checkers take you back to a simpler time. Families will also enjoy Indian storytelling and puppet shows, and you can try your skill at candle-making or building a wattle-and-daub hut with a thatched roof.

To get here from Route 10, take the Old Stage Road and follow the signs to Dutch Gap Landing at the end of Coxendale Road.

Meadow Farm at Crump Park
3400 Mountain Rd., Glen Allen • 672-5100

Combine some history with a romp in the country. Open March through early December, Meadow Farm is a 19th-century living-history museum where costumed interpreters re-create life on Dr. John Mosby Sheppard's middle-class farm in the 1860s, just before the outbreak of the Civil War. Unlike many historical attractions, this one focuses on the middle class instead of the rich and famous.

This is a great place to visit with children. You can tour the farmhouse, barn, a 19th-century doctor's office, blacksmith's forge, smokehouse, kitchen, orchard and crop demonstration fields. In the barnyard, you'll find a pig, chicken, sheep, cows, ducks and horses.

Living history events and re-enactments throughout the year create a lot of excitement and activity here on weekends. Events include Sheep to Shawl in April, the Civil War Encampment and Battle in late May, an Old Fashioned Fourth of July, Civil War Days in September, the Harvest Festival in October and the Yuletide Fest in December.

Meadow Farm's 50 acres of pasture and woodlands also provide a natural environment for a variety of plants and animals. There are about 2 miles of nature trails where you'll discover delightful opportunities to see hawks, quail and deer.

Changing exhibits focusing on Virginia and Henrico County life are displayed in the orientation center, and a video about the farm is shown here. There's also a gift shop.

From downtown, take I-95 N. to Interstate 295 W. (Exit 36). Take the Woodman Road S. exit to Mountain Road. Go right on Mountain Road and follow the signs. There are plenty of parking spaces. Picnic tables and playground equipment are available at nearby Crump Park. The grounds are open daily most of the year. The buildings are closed on Monday. Call for information about hours and winter closings. Admission is free.

The Old Jail — Chesterfield County Museum Complex
corner of Krauss and Ironbridge Rds.
• 748-1026

Visit this old jail and see a replica of an old pillory where offenders were exposed to public scorn. Next to the Chesterfield County Museum, the jail was built in 1892 and used for prisoners until 1962. Today it depicts the life of prisoners during the late 1800s and early 1900s. The Old Jail also includes historical exhibits of the police and fire departments.

Richmond National Battlefield Park
3215 E. Broad St. • 226-1981

Children enjoy walking in the battlefield areas and seeing the Civil War dirt works and old homes. Living history programs and re-enactments are performed on special occasions to help bring history to life. There are also weekend walks and talks, and a Junior Ranger program for children ages 6 to 12. For more information, see our Attractions chapter.

Scotchtown
corner of Rts. 54 and 685, Hanover County
• 227-3500

Go for a weekend picnic and history tour at Scotchtown, Patrick Henry's home during the Revolutionary War from 1771 to 1778. One of Virginia's oldest plantations, Scotchtown is about 9 miles west of Ashland. The restored wood-frame Colonial home was built between 1717 and 1719 and is furnished with authentic 18th-century antiques. You can see the kitchen, which is in a separate building; the basement that includes a small museum and wine cellar; and the dry well, which was used to keep meat and other perishable food fresh. The house is surrounded by about 40 acres of farm and woodland. Docents conduct tours.

Costumed guides and living history presentations are offered at special events such as the Scottish Festival and Games in May. Also, during the first full weekend in December, Scotchtown presents candlelight tours of the house, plays and special decorations illustrating Christmas customs in the 18th, 19th and 20th centuries.

Some picnic tables and benches are provided. Scotchtown is open April through October. Scotchtown is operated by the Patrick Henry Scotchtown Committee in cooperation with the Association for the Preservation of Virginia Antiquities. Call for admission prices.

St. John's Church
2401 E. Broad St. • 648-5015

Bring history to life: Take the family to a free re-enactment of Patrick Henry's famous "Give me liberty, or give me death" speech at historic St. John's Church in a restored section of Church Hill. Every Sunday at 2 PM from Memorial Day to Labor Day, actors portray George Washington, Thomas Jefferson, Patrick Henry and other patriots in re-enactments of the Second Virginia Convention of 1775. Seating is limited, so try to arrive by about 1:30 PM. Costumed interpreters conduct tours and assist visitors. Admission is $3 for adults, $2 for seniors, $1 for students ages 7 to 18 and free to anyone younger than 7.

State Capitol and Capitol Square
Ninth and Grace Sts. • 698-1788

A free 30-minute tour of the historic Capitol building is a favorite among school children. The Capitol is home to Virginia's most treasured work of art, the statue of George Washington by Jean Antoine Houdon and several famous paintings. Older kids may enjoy visiting as session of the General Assembly — held for 60 days in even years and 30 days in odd years — and seeing their representatives at work. Sessions begin in mid-January. To get in, ask for a pass from the Capitol hostesses on the second floor of the Rotunda. In sunny weather, enjoy a picnic on the lawn. For more information see our Attractions chapter.

Museums

Virginia Aviation Museum
5701 Huntsman Rd. • 236-3622

In the Richmond International Airport, this museum, now a division of the Science Museum of Virginia, displays an extensive collection of vintage and historically significant aircraft as well as navigation devices and memorabilia dating from 1914 to World War II. In June, the museum presents "Flight Day" with special activities, planes and children's activities.

Admission to the museum is $5 for adults; $4 for seniors and $3 for children ages 4-12; and free to children younger than 4. It's open daily from 9:30 AM to 5 PM.

Virginia Fire and Police Museum, Steamer Company No. 5
200 W. Marshall St. • 644-1849

Built in 1849, this is Richmond's only surviving firehouse from the Civil War period, and it's one of the oldest firehouses in the country. The museum features hand-drawn, horse-drawn and early motorized fire-fighting apparatus. The museum also offers changing exhibits about interesting and historical aspects of firefighting and police work such as the role of African-Americans on the police force and the use of horses. A 19th-century working police station with jail cells will be developed soon. More than 100,000 school children are trained in fire safety here each year. The museum is open Monday through Friday from 10 AM to 4 PM as well as weekends by appointment. Suggested donations for admission are $2 for adults, $1.50 for seniors, and $1.50 for children ages 8 to 18. Children ages 7 and younger get in free. Police and fire personnel and their families are admitted free. The facility may be rented for parties, meetings and other occasions.

Virginia Museum of Fine Arts
2800 Grove Ave. • 367-0844; 367-0859 tours and group visits

Create art together any Sunday afternoon

in the Children's Art Resource Center and tour the fascinating galleries. This museum presents a panorama of world art from ancient times to the present and has gained an international reputation for its collections. While you're here, you can have lunch in the Arts Cafe or on the patio. The museum also offers many wonderful programs and classes. For more information, see our chapter on The Arts. Admission is free, but a $4 donation is suggested.

Outdoor Fun

Berry Picking
variety of locations

"You-pick-'em" farms are scattered throughout the area. Many advertise in area newspapers, others just put signs along the roads. Drive through rural Hanover County and you're sure to pass several. Look for strawberries in April, blueberries in June, blackberries in July and pumpkins in October. Most farms provide buckets or boxes, but you may want to bring your own containers just in case.

Thousands of people visit the Ashland Berry Farm at 12623 Old Ridge Road, 227-3601, to pick fresh strawberries and blackberries each year. Everyone hops on a flat-bed truck for a bumpy ride to the fields, where you'll find acres and acres of berries. A guide points out where the picking is good and leaves you to pick as much as you want. You can eat as much as you like for free. When you're ready to go, you wait in the field road for the next ride back to the weighing station. While you're here, you can also visit a petting farm and greenhouse. Concessions are available.

City and County Parks

The metropolitan area has so many great parks, you could probably visit a different one every weekend for a year. Many of the large parks offer playing fields, picnic areas, fishing and walking trails. A few family favorites include: Rockwood Park in Chesterfield County where children enjoy hands-on exhibits in the log-cabin Nature Center; Dorey Park in Henrico where young children can play on well-kept playground equipment, feed ducks, fish and

fly kites; Poor Farm Park in Hanover with over 5 miles of mountain-bike trails; James River Park in Richmond with walking trails, great river views, and kayaking and canoe runs; and Byrd Park in Richmond with three large lakes, fishing, remote-controlled boat races, paddleboat rentals and tennis courts. For more information, see our Parks and Recreation chapter.

Laurel Skate Park
10301 Hungary Spring Rd. • 67-BOARD

When your kids get bored skate boarding around your neighborhood, bring them to this special skate park in the Laurel Recreation Area and let them try their skills on a variety of ramps and obstacles, a freestyle skate area and a 6-foot-deep combination bowl. The park is open daily, weather permitting, for skateboarding and in-line skating. The recreation area also includes athletic fields, sports equipment and concessions. For information and a schedule, call 67-BOARD or 672-5100.

Lewis Ginter Botanical Garden
1800 Lakeside Ave. • 262-9887

Follow your children around the garden paths at this botanical garden where thousands of plant species are artfully arranged across 80 acres to provide spectacular displays throughout the year. Lewis Ginter Botanical Garden is known for its extensive collection of daffodils, day lilies, rhododendrons and azaleas. You'll also enjoy seasonal floral displays and a cottage garden planted with herbs and species roses surrounding Bloemendaal, a charming Victorian manor house that now serves as a visitor center, gift shop and staff office building. There's also a special children's garden area planted with vegetables and flowers from Asia, Africa and North and South America, a perennial garden, oriental garden and an island garden that includes Venus's flytraps, a bug-eating plant that fascinates children. Please don't feed the plants!

Lewis Ginter Botanical Garden offers a variety of hands-on activities, workshops, basic gardening classes, lectures, tours and everything from concerts to camps for kids. Allow yourself about an hour for a self-guided tour through the gardens, and wear good walking

Lewis Ginter Botanical Garden offers nature camps for kids.

Photo: Lewis Ginter Botanical Garden

shoes for grassy and pebbled paths. Maps and information are available at the admissions booth. Admission is $5 for adults, $4 for seniors and $3 for children ages 2 to 12.

Richmond Raft Company
4400 E. Main St. • 222-7238

If your family likes getting wet and loves adventure, try an exciting whitewater raft ride on the James River. This full-service outfitter offers several scenic trips on the Falls of the James through the center of the city. You don't have to be experienced. Each trip begins with an orientation session and safety instructions. All equipment is provided, and your guide will teach you along the way. Up to six people plus a guide may travel in each raft.

The "Falls of the James" and the "Lower Section" trips include moderate Class IV rapids and are not recommended for children younger than 12. Younger children are encouraged to try the "Upper Section" trip which involves milder Class I and II rapids, more swimming and scenic rafting. Children must weigh at least 50 pounds to participate. This trip lasts three to four hours and is popular with youth groups and birthday parties.

Trip costs range from $35 to $50. Discounts are available for groups of 18 or more. Reservations are required. Call two or three weeks in advance for your choice of trip times. For more information, see our Attractions and Tours chapter.

Spectator Sports

You'll find plenty of spectator sports in the area that the whole family will enjoy. Take your kids to see Richmond Braves baseball, Renegades ice hockey, Richmond Rage basketball, college basketball and football, or a Kicker's soccer match. For more information, see our Spectator Sports chapter

Three Lakes Nature Center and Aquarium
400 Sausiluta Dr. • 261-8230; 24-hour information line, 652-FISH

Kids'll enjoy spending an hour or two looking at the fish in the 50,000-gallon outdoor aquarium, the largest in Central Virginia, and playing with the interactive exhibits in the Nature Center. They'll also like feeding the ducks and running down the paths woven throughout the 127-acre park where plant, fish, bird and animal-life abound.

The Nature Center is on the edge of one of the park's three spring-fed lakes. You can stroll around the deck and view the aquarium from above, or you can go below for an underwater view of the same kinds of fish that live in the park's lakes. You'll come face-to face with largemouth bass, bluegill, redear sunfish and black crappie.

Special exhibits focusing on the aquarium, lakes, wetlands, animal life and the forest fill the upper level of the Nature Center. You'll learn about the environment and the plants and animals that live here as well as how to maintain and preserve them. The center also presents classes, workshops and special programs. Call for information.

In addition to the Nature Center, the park offers fishing, hiking, two picnic shelters, play equipment, an exercise trail and an observation deck.

Three Lakes Park is off Wilkinson Road at Sausiluta Drive. Call for more information or to schedule group tours.

Travelland
Corner of Robin Hood Rd. and the Boulevard • 358-5511

Take a few minutes to let your children scramble aboard a train or the aviation exhibits at the small outdoor park area at Travelland, just outside the Richmond Visitor's Center. There is no charge to see the exhibits.

Indoor Entertainment

Discovery Zone
1530 N. Parham Rd. • 270-3376

This high-energy playground is for kids age 12 and younger. They can play as long as they want in a giant, padded, screened-in rumpus rooms with tunnels, ball rooms, climbing ropes, towers, every type of sliding board imaginable and more. Parents can join their kids for free or just flop at a bench or table and watch the action. Be sure to bring extra money

for the arcade games and allow plenty of time for the kids to cash in their game tickets for candy and toys. Socks are required. Try to avoid rainy days and weekends when the crowds are overwhelming.

Libraries
Call the libraries near you to find out about their free weekly story hours and special children's activities. After the librarians read stories, they often invite the children to work on a related art project. Occasionally, the libraries also sponsor professional children's storytellers and entertainers.

Theatre IV Productions
114 W. Broad St. • 783-1688

Based at the Empire Theatre, Theatre IV offers a Family Playhouse series for children, and its children's touring theater is the second largest in the nation. It also offers a Broadway Series as well as a Theatre Gym series of innovative works by guest artists. See our Arts chapter for more information.

Ultrazone — Laser Adventure
889 Research Rd. • 378-0448

Play an exciting game of laser tag in a high-tech adventure maze, complete with special "smoke" and lighting effects. On Monday and Tuesday, Ultrazone is open for reserved private functions only. Call for information about hours, rates and special times for children younger than 12.

Enrichment Programs

One advantage of living in or near a metropolitan area is the tremendous cultural resources available for families. Many museums and cultural organizations offer special enrichment programs and classes for young people during the summer and occasionally through-

---

INSIDERS' TIP

If you need help shuttling your kids and teens to and from school, recreation activities or anywhere else in the Richmond area, Kidz Transport will pick them up and run the roads for you in Richmond and Chesterfield, Eastern Goochland, Western Henrico and Hanover counties. Last-minute or prescheduled service is available. Call 330-0177.

out the year. The city and county parks and recreation departments also offer numerous arts, crafts and cultural activities as well as nature programs for children. The following is a list of the most popular.

Cat's CAP, St. Catherine's School
6001 Grove Ave. • 288-2804

During the summer months, children can enroll in music, art, writing, drama and a variety of other enrichment classes taught at this private school in the West End. The Creative Arts Program (CAP) Courses are filled on a first-come, first-served basis on registration day. Arrive early to make sure that your child gets in the program. Call in early spring for a course schedule.

Hand Workshop Inc.
1812 W. Main St. • 353-0094

This center-city art studio offers a broad spectrum of summer classes for children and teens including pottery, painting, cartooning, textile art, fabric painting, tile-making and more. Classes are usually scheduled for one or two weeks and are taught by area professionals. Call in the spring for a course schedule and sign up early. The classes fill up fast.

Children's Museum of Richmond
740 Navy Hill Dr. • 788-4949

The Children's Museum offers special programs throughout the year for kids as old as 12. You'll find everything from one-hour craft workshops for toddlers to mask-making, cartooning, painting and an extensive dramatic acting workshop. Call for a course schedule.

Science Museum of Virginia
2500 W. Broad St. • 367-6552

The Science Museum offers a variety of classes during the year. Children conduct experiments with area scientists. Call for a course schedule.

SPARC
1205 Main St. • 355-2662

Kids from ages 5 to 18 can study acting, singing and dancing with top area professionals at SPARC, the School of the Perform-

FYI

Unless otherwise noted, the area code for all phone numbers listed in this chapter is 804.

ing Arts in the Richmond Community. Programs begin in the fall with skills-building activities for beginners, intermediate and advanced students. In the winter, children have a chance to use their skills in actual performances presented by SPARC and in association with area theaters. During the summer, children prepare for a major musical presented on a local stage after an intensive six-week summer camp. Core classes are taught at First English Lutheran Church at 1603 Monument Avenue. Special one-hour weekly programs are also offered for schools and day-care centers.

Virginia Museum of Fine Art
2800 Grove Ave. • 367-0844

Art classes for children and teens are taught by area professionals during the museum's summer workshop program. Children may choose from a variety of classes including painting, sculpture, and pottery. The workshops are hands-on and include some instruction in art history.

Annual Events

Richmond Children's Festival
Arts Council • 355-7200

This delightful outdoor festival celebrates children and the arts. The weekend event held at Discovery Park in October features music, drama and other professional performances for young people, crafts, roving entertainers and food. The activities usually feature a different cultural theme each year. Thousands of families attend. Discovery Park is at the science museum located at 2500 W. Broad St. Best of all, it's all free. Watch the daily paper for details.

State Fair of Virginia
600 E. Laburnum Ave., Strawberry Hill • 228-3200

Every September, the State Fair returns with something for everyone. There are craft displays, blue-ribbon winners, livestock displays and demonstrations, midway rides and games, Italian sausages and corn dogs, big-name entertainment shows, magic shows, side shows, a circus and lots and lots of exhibits by companies and organizations from all over the state. To enter a competition, call 228-3200 or (800) LUV-FAIR. Many employers and companies offer discount tickets. Ask at work or watch the ads. The admission ticket, which costs around $12 in advance, includes all the rides and attractions. Ask about special ticket prices for children.

Parades

The biggest parade in the area is the Jaycee's Christmas Parade in December on Broad Street. Arrive early for a good view and bring blankets, chairs and snacks. If you stay for the whole parade, you'll need to allow at least two hours. You may also want to bring some cash for balloons or souvenirs. Other popular parades include the St. Patrick's Day Parade, the Grand Illumination and the Ashland Holiday Parade. See our Annual Events chapter for more information.

Tackiest Christmas Decorations Tour

See our Annual Events chapter for a full write-up of the route 'o extreme decoration.

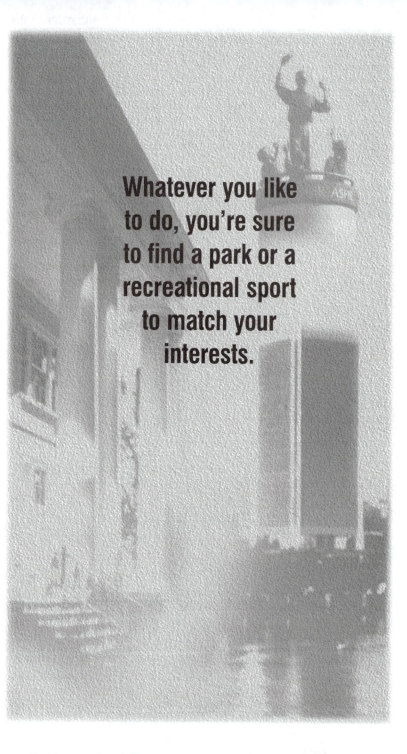

Whatever you like to do, you're sure to find a park or a recreational sport to match your interests.

Parks and Recreation

The Richmond area offers a unique urban wilderness along the James River, some of the best smallmouth bass fishing in the nation, more than 60 parks and more than 5,000 acres of park land. Some have historical significance; others offer play equipment, hiking, nature trails, fishing, boating or picnicking. Many parks provide opportunities for community fun with festivals, charity runs, pet walks and educational programs.

Participant sports action abounds for youth, adults and seniors. Sports enthusiasts will find organized soccer, baseball, softball, basketball, volleyball, tennis and swimming teams established by recreation departments throughout the area as well as bicycling, canoeing, kayaking, sailing, rock climbing, ice skating, roller skating, spelunking and more.

Whatever you like to do, you're sure to find a park or a recreational sport to match your interests. In this chapter, we've organized information about parks and recreational activities by jurisdictional areas. The City of Richmond and each surrounding county has a Department of Recreation and Parks that is responsible for park facilities and sponsors or co-sponsors organized sports, community events and senior programs for residents. Some programs are also open to nonresidents. If you would like more information, maps or brochures, contact the Department of Parks, Recreation and Community Facilities in Richmond, 780-6091; Chesterfield County, 748-1623; Henrico County, 672-5100; or Hanover County, 798-8062.

General information about soccer, swimming, bicycling, canoeing and other sports that are not necessarily organized by jurisdictional area is included after the city and county information. Golfing is so popular, we cover it in a chapter of its own.

Parks

City of Richmond

Richmond Department of Parks, Recreation and Community Facilities
900 E. Broad St. • 780-5733

The city's Department of Parks, Recreation and Community Facilities maintains and operates the city parks including the James River Park System, historic city cemeteries and community centers. The city also coordinates and sponsors organized sports programs and maintains dozens of ball fields and sports facilities that are available for residents and league play. A variety of classes, programs and events for youth and adults including arts and crafts, sports, music, games, dance and nature programs are also offered daily at community centers and other park facilities.

Picnic shelters and community centers may be reserved for group or special events; call 780-7391 for facility reservations. If you have questions about activities, contact your neighborhood recreation center. To find out which center is nearest you, call the recreation department's citizens' assistance coordinator at 780-7000. Call the general phone number, 780-5733, for more information on any of the following Richmond parks.

Battery Park
Hawthorne Ave. and Overbrook Rd.

This park features tennis courts, a playground, a community center and a swimming pool. It was the site of gun batteries during the Civil War.

Broad Rock Sports Complex
2401 Broad Rock Blvd.

This park offers tennis courts, soccer and baseball fields.

Brown's Island Park
S. Seventh St.

Brown's Island Park is at the end of Canal Walk. Benches overlooking the James River provide scenic resting spots. This is the usual site of the World Rib Championship and the annual rubber duckies race to benefit the Big Brothers. A variety of weekend events is also held here. The park has been closed temporarily until work is completed on the canal. It is expected to reopen in late 1998.

Bryan Park
Bellevue Ave. and Hermitage Rd.

Bryan Park is famous for its Azalea Gardens. There are tennis courts, three picnic shelters, a fishing lake, tot lot, playground, soccer complex (under construction), and wooded and open spaces.

Byrd Park
Boulevard and Idlewood Ave.

Byrd Park offers three lakes, fishing, paddleboat rentals (summer only), two picnic shelters, an exercise and fitness course, ball fields, tennis courts, a tot lot, a soccer complex, the Carillon (a World War I memorial) and Dogwood Dell, an outdoor amphitheater where the Festival of Arts is held each summer. (See our Annual Events chapter for more information. Tennis is especially popular here. It's also the site of the Richmond Children's Festival, Arts in the Park, the 4th of July Celebration, the Christmas Eve Nativity Play, and the annual Run for the Arts.

Chimborazo Park
E. Broad St. near 32nd St.

This park has an exercise cluster with equipment that's accessible for people with disabilities. The park was the site of the Chimborazo Field Hospital — the largest in the world during the Civil War (see The Civil War chapter). The park now serves as the headquarters of the National Battlefield Park System.

City Golf Range
400 School St. • 780-4074

This public golf range features all-weather tees and natural turf tees, target greens, a practice bunker and a pro shop. Lessons are available. Open from mid-February to mid-November, the range is lighted and handicapped-accessible. Buckets of balls are available for a fee.

Forest Hill Park
Corner of Forest Hill Ave. and 41st St.

This park used to be the site of the Forest Hill Amusement Park and was the end point of the Forest Hill streetcar. The park offers a picnic area, lake, walkways, two shelters, tennis courts, a meeting house and a small azalea garden.

Gillies Creek Park
Stony Run Dr. and Williamsburg Rd.

This park features the only Frisbee golf course in the area. There are also lighted ball fields and horseshoe pits. A BMX bike trail

Maymont's 100 acres can provide many strenuous hikes or leisurely strolls.

and a regulation croquet course are under construction.

James River Park
22nd St. and Riverside Dr.
• 780-5311, (800) 697-3373

This is Richmond's urban wilderness park, known as one of the only places in the nation that offers urban whitewater canoeing and kayaking. There are also excellent opportunities for rock climbing and rappelling, and it's one of the best places in the country for smallmouth bass fishing. Walking along the trails affords great views of the river. Educational programs are offered on weekends or by appointment for groups.

The park has five sections — Main, Pony Pasture, Huguenot Woods, North Bank and Belle Isle.

The Main section of the park is on the south side of the river between the Boulevard and Lee bridges. Flatwater and whitewater canoe trips begin here. Information, maps, trail guides, interpretive tours and restrooms are at the visitors center, which is accessible from the parking lots at 42nd and 22nd streets.

Pony Pasture is on the south bank of the river, 2 miles downstream from the Huguenot Bridge on Riverside Drive. Fishing and birdwatching are excellent here. An easy whitewater canoe run begins here and ends at the visitors center. Huguenot Woods is also on the south bank, directly under the Huguenot Bridge, and is a good place to begin a flatwater canoe trip.

The North Bank section is on the north side of the river at the end of Texas Avenue. A pedestrian bridge crosses railroad tracks and the canal down to the edge of the river. Fishing is good here too.

Belle Isle is directly under the Lee Bridge and may be reached by pedestrian bridge from the Tredegar Street side or from the 22nd Street parking lot on the south bank of the river bed when water levels are below 5 feet. The toll-free number listed provides access to river level information at the Westham Gauge. A wheelchair route is also available.

The island is the site of the notorious Civil War prison, and the remains of the historic iron foundry can still be seen. Bike and walking trails feature interpretive signs, and the whitewater rapids offer excellent kayak and canoe runs for highly skilled boaters. The fishing is good here, and it's free, but you must comply with state licensing regulations. Contact the Virginia Department of Game and Inland Fisheries, 367-1000, for more information. There's also a floating fishing pier at the old granite quarry pit. Swimming is not recommended because of fast-moving water, rocks, rapids and dangerous undertows.

Jefferson Hill Park
21st and E. Marshall Sts.

This park features a bandstand, tot lot, exercise trail and a beautiful view of the south side of the city. A steam train is buried under the hill from an October 2, 1925, cave-in. A commemorative plaque is at the sealed entrance to the tunnel off 18th Street.

Kanawha Plaza
Clay and Eighth Sts.

This landscaped plaza features a fountain with a pool. It's a popular lunch spot for downtown workers and the site of numerous events including "Fridays at Sunset," an outdoor summer party with live jazz that begins around 6 PM every Friday and goes "all night." (See our Annual Events chapter.)

Libby Hill Park
28th and E. Franklin Sts.

Libby Hill Park is one of the original three parks in the city's parks system. It features the Confederate Soldiers and Sailors Monument (see our Monuments chapter), a small park house and a great view of the south side of the city. The walkways, seating and antique lighting add to the atmosphere.

Maymont Park
1700 Hampton St. • 358-7166

This beautiful, 100-acre Victorian estate is operated by the Maymont Foundation with assistance from the Richmond Department of Recreation and Parks. For more information about the park, see the Attractions chapter or call the Maymont Foundation at the number listed.

Monroe Park
Belvidere and W. Franklin Sts.

Near Virginia Commonwealth University and Richmond's Landmark Theater, Monroe Park was the site of the first Virginia State Fair in 1854. The park offers walking paths, benches, a park house and a decorative fountain.

Nina F. Abady Festival Park
6th Street Mktpl.

This park is downtown at 6th Street Marketplace between the Coliseum and the Crystal Palace. Concerts and other special events, such as Friday Cheers are held here. For information about upcoming events read the daily and weekend pages of the *Richmond Times-Dispatch*, the weekly list of events published by *Style Weekly* every Tuesday, or call Downtown Presents at 643-2826.

Oregon Hill Linear Park
Along Belvidere St.

This small park parallels Belvidere Street and covers about a five block area from Idlewood Avenue to Riverside Park. A beautiful backyard-size park, it's best known as a neighborhood green space for casual outdoor activities.

Powhatan Hill Park
Williamsburg Rd. and Northampton St.

This park offers tennis courts, a playground, a comfort station and a community center. The name of the park comes from the legend that Chief Powhatan used the area for a tribal campground in Colonial times.

Smith-Peters Park
900 block of Catherine St.

Located in the Carver neighborhood, this park offers a tot lot, half-court basketball, a walking trail and picnic facilities.

INSIDERS' TIP

The parks and recreation departments in each county and the city offer a smorgasbord of activities for kids throughout the year. Call for information about sports, parks, classes and events in your area: 780-5944 in Richmond; 672-5100 in Henrico County; 798-8062 in Hanover County; and 748-1623 in Chesterfield County.

Travelland
Robin Hood and Hermitage Rds.
• 358-5511

Full-size exhibits of a train, a jet plane and other modes of transportation are here at the Tourist Information Center. This is a great place to let the kids climb and explore.

Chesterfield County

Chesterfield County Recreation and Parks
600 Wagner's Way • 748-1623

Chesterfield offers about 20 parks including Henricus Historical Park at the site of the second major English settlement in Virginia; Point of Rocks Park overlooking the Appomattox River; Rockwood Park with its popular nature center; and Pocahontas State Park, the nearest state park to the metropolitan area.

Residents may also participate in varied sports and recreation programs including traditional sports leagues, fencing, karate, gymnastics, horseback riding and lacrosse. Some of these are outlined in the Sports and Recreation section in this chapter. The county also offers classes and programs in rock climbing, spelunking, gem hunting, nature programs, dance, self defense for women, herb gardening and arts and crafts. Boating, canoeing/ kayaking, ocean fishing, scuba diving, sailing, bateau rides and group skiing trips are also offered. Special events include Rainbow of Arts (an arts and crafts festival in the fall), Kite Day and a series of free summertime outdoor concerts with the Richmond Symphony. The department even sponsors summer camps, a lecture series, Civil War study groups and activities and programs for seniors and people with disabilities.

Unless another phone number is given, all Chesterfield County parks can be reached at the general number, 748-1623.

Bensley Park
2900 Drewrey's Bluff Rd.

This park opened in 1988 and features a picnic area, play equipment, softball and baseball fields, a football field, tennis courts, a concession area and a community center.

Ettrick Park
20400 Laurel Rd.

Near the Amtrak train station on Laurel Road, this park offers football, baseball and softball fields, plus a community building where a variety of programs and activities are offered for all ages. The modern one-story building includes a kitchen, several large meeting rooms and an arts-and-crafts area. It is available for rent for gatherings and parties.

Fort Stevens Historical Park
Pams Ave. and Norcliff Rd.

This 2-acre park opened in 1988 and features trails around Civil War embankments and a picnic area.

Goyne Park
5300 Ecoff Ave.

This park offers playing fields, tennis courts, a picnic shelter and play equipment. An undeveloped area has woods, fields and a small stream.

Harrowgate Park
4200 Dean Dr.

This neighborhood park has tennis courts, playing fields, picnic and playground areas and a fitness trail.

Henricus Historical Park
601 Coxendale Rd. • 706-1340

On the banks of the James River at the site of the second major English settlement in Virginia, this park features a walking trail with views of the river, a visitors center and a partial reconstruction of the Citie of Henricus. Visitors may also explore the adjoining Dutch Gap Conservation Area, an 805-acre wildlife area with beavers, deer, wild turkeys and bass fishing. It's accessible from Dutch Gap Boat Ramp and the Henricus Park Boat Landing. (Additional information is included in the Attractions chapter under Citie of Henricus.)

Huguenot Park
Robious Rd.

This 57-acre park is heavily wooded and features azalea gardens, playgrounds, athletic fields, a skateboard area, tennis and basketball courts and a fitness trail. Wheelchair tennis is available here.

Iron Bridge Park
Va. Hwy. 10, across from Chesterfield Airport

This 367-acre park features four softball fields, a baseball field, four tennis courts (two with artificial clay surfaces), two outdoor handball/racquetball courts, a volleyball area and a handicapped-accessible basketball court. There are also 3 miles of nature trails, a 5-mile mountain bike trail and a boardwalk crossing Reedy Creek Marsh. Concession stands are available.

Matoaca Park
1900 Halloway Ave.

This park features tennis courts, playing fields, a lighted basketball court, picnic shelter and play equipment.

Pocahontas State Park
10301 State Park Rd. • 796-4255

This full-service state park offers camping, hiking, swimming, biking, fishing and educational programs. You can also rent row boats, canoes and paddle boats. The park includes more than 7,600 acres of forest land surrounding Swift Creek Lake and Beaver Lake. It is described in detail in the Campgrounds chapter.

Point of Rocks Park
Enon Church and Ruffin Mill Rds.

This 190-acre site is in a remote area at Enon Church and Ruffin Mill roads. From Richmond, take Interstate 90 south to Hopewell, Exit 61. Go east on State Route 10 for 4.8 miles. Turn right on to Enon Church Road. The park is about 2 miles on the left. Visitors walk on trails and boardwalks through a marsh teeming with plants and wildlife to an observation deck overlooking the Appomattox River.

Robious Landing Park
5800 James River Rd.

This 60-acre park recently opened. It has a picnic area, volleyball nets, a car-top boat launch, and several other areas under development.

Rockwood Park
3401 Courthouse Rd.

This is the oldest and most popular park in Chesterfield. It includes the Rockwood Nature Center, which is housed in a log cabin. The center features hands-on exhibits and wildlife and environmental displays related to the area. It also offers an archery range, garden plots, 3.5 miles of nature trails, picnic shelters, play equipment, ball fields, tennis courts and restrooms.

Warboro Athletic Complex
3204 Warboro Rd.

Built on top of a landfill, this recreation area includes soccer fields, a playground and 72 acres of open space.

Henrico County

Henrico County Recreation and Parks
8600 Dixon Powers Dr. • 672-5100

Henrico County operates about 30 park facilities. We've included a sampling of them here. For more information or for group reservations at certain parks, call the parks department at the number above.

Henrico County offers a diversified schedule of sports and special programs for youth and adults including sailing, kayaking, canoeing, rock climbing, skiing, spelunking and hunting. Other activities and programs include martial arts, arts and crafts, trips, dancing, summer playground programs, preschool activities, gardening and more. Some of these options are explored in the Sports and Recreation section of this chapter.

The county also offers special programs for people with mental or physical disabilities, and they have a very active seniors program. For information about county-sponsored activities or to find out how to contact other sports associations in the area, call the listed number.

Confederate Hills
302 Lee Ave.

This Highland Springs park offers tennis, a croquet course and a picnic area. There is

---

FYI

Unless otherwise noted, the area code for all phone numbers listed in this chapter is 804.

Photo: Tom Thorp

Three Lakes Park offers fishing, hiking, play equipment and an exercise trail.

also a recreation center with meeting rooms, a large multipurpose room and a kitchen.

Crump Memorial Park
3400 Mountain Rd. • 672-5100, 672-1367

In Glen Allen, this park features the 150-acre Meadow Farm, a restored pre-Civil War middle-class farm. It's used as a living history museum interpreting rural life in the 1850s. The park offers picnic shelters, nature trails, play equipment and horseshoes. Civil War reenactments, encampments and holiday events are scheduled throughout the year. (For more information, see our Attractions chapter.)

Deep Bottom Park
9525 Deep Bottom Rd.

Picnicking and pier fishing are available at this public boat landing in Varina. Boaters have access to the James River. The county is planning a 58-acre park next to the landing, and there is a canoe launch here with direct access to the scenic Four Mile Creek.

Deep Run Park
9900 Ridgefield Pkwy.

This 167-acre park offers five picnic shelters, two ponds, soccer and football fields, basketball courts, play areas, an exercise trail and a multiuse outdoor area. A pedestrian/bike trail connects the recreational areas.

Dorey Park
7200 Dorey Park Rd. • 795-2334

Off Darbytown Road, Dorey is one of Henrico's largest parks. Amid its 400 acres are seven picnic areas, tennis courts, ball fields, an equestrian ring, exercise and hiking trails and a small fishing pond. A new recreation center in a renovated dairy barn recently opened and includes three classrooms, two conference rooms, a multipurpose room, an arts and crafts room, an activity room and a kitchen. In fall, this is the site of Christmas in September, an annual arts and crafts show with more than 140 exhibitors.

Glen Allen Softball Complex
2175 Mountain Rd.

Formerly known as North Run, this 12-acre facility includes four lighted baseball fields. With a concession stand, picnic area and shelter, this park is very popular for tournament and league play.

Hidden Creek
2415 Brockway Ln.

This 7-plus-acre playground features tennis courts and a memorial for the *Challenger* Space Shuttle crew erected by students in the county's afterschool program.

Laurel Skate Park
10301 Hungary Spring Rd.
• 67-BOARD, 672-5100

In the Laurel Recreation Area, this ¾-acre facility includes a street skate area with a variety of ramps and obstacles, a freestyle skate area and a 6-foot-deep combination bowl. The park is open daily, weather permitting, for skateboarding and in-line skating. The recreation area also includes athletic fields, play equipment and concessions.

Osborne Boat Landing
Osborne Tnpk. and Kingsland Rd.

This has been the site of several Bass Masters Tournaments. The boat landing is on the James River.

Pouncy Tract
4751 Pouncy Tract Rd.

Next to the Short Pump Middle School, this park offers beach volleyball, a playground, baseball, softball and soccer fields, a picnic shelter and a walking trail.

Short Pump Park
3401 Pump Rd.

This is a neighborhood park with playing fields, a picnic shelter and softball, soccer and football fields.

Three Lakes Park
Wilkinson Rd. at Sausiluta Dr.
• 262-4822

Three Lakes Park features a 50,000-gallon outdoor aquarium — the largest in Central Virginia — plus a Nature Center and a 90-acre park where plant, fish, bird and animal life abound.

Surrounded by a lush forest, the Nature Center is on the edge of one of the park's three spring-fed lakes. You can stroll around the deck and view the aquarium from above, or you can go below for an underwater view of the same kinds of fish that live in the park's lakes. You'll come face-to-face with largemouth bass, bluegill, red ear sunfish and black crappie.

The upper level of the Nature Center is filled with special exhibits focusing on the aquarium, lakes, wetlands, animal life and the forest. Visitors learn about the environment, the plants and animals that live here and how to maintain and preserve them. Classes, workshops and special programs are also available.

In addition to the Nature Center, this 90-acre park offers fishing, hiking, two picnic shelters, play equipment, an exercise trail and an observation deck.

Vawter Street Park/Glen Lea Recreation Area
4501 Vawter Ave.

This 352-acre park offers a scenic nature trail, picnic facilities, play equipment and soccer, softball and football fields.

Hanover County

Hanover County Parks and Recreation
200 Berkley St. • 798-8062

Hanover County has five parks and offers elementary school playgrounds for public use in the summer. The county also rents canoes and maintains a boat launch area on the Pamunkey and South Anna rivers. To rent a canoe or reserve a park facility, call the Hanover County Parks and Recreation Department.

Hanover County co-sponsors youth and adult sports leagues. A variety of recreational programs are offered including summer camps, nature and wilderness camps, sports clinics and classes on archaeology, boating skills, roller-skating, dance, horseback riding, fine arts, computer skills, languages, photography, cooking, music and more. Some of these are outlined in the Sports and Recreation section of this chapter.

The county also offers adult classes in a variety of subjects including kayaking and Jazzercise. For registration and schedule information, watch the local newspapers. A complete list of activities, sports leagues and programs is published periodically in the *Herald Progress*.

For more information about any of the Hanover County Parks, call the general information number, 798-8062.

Cold Harbor Battlefield Park/ Garthright House
Va. Hwy. 156, Cold Harbor

About 50 acres surrounding the historic Garthright House, once used as a field hospital during the Civil War, have been developed as one of Hanover's parks. In Cold Harbor, the park, known by locals as Garthright Park, includes a 2-mile trail system with interpretive signage that leads visitors through Civil War trench works and rifle pits. (See our Civil War chapter.)

Courthouse Park
U.S. Hwy. 301

South of Hanover Courthouse, this 363-acre park offers soccer/athletic fields, a pond, a jogging trail, concession stand and shelter. Only about 50 acres of the park site have been developed.

Hanover Wayside
U.S. Hwy. 301

Five miles south of Hanover Courthouse, Hanover Wayside is a 36-acre park with a picnic shelter and tables, ball fields, tot-lot, playground and a 6-acre pond. The Atlee Ruritan Club maintains the park as a community project.

North Anna Battlefield Park
Verdon Rd.

Developed by General Crushed Stone Quarry, this 75-acre park was donated to Hanover County in 1996. Located adjacent to General Crushed Stone Quarry in Doswell, the park contains trench works with rifle pits from the Battle of North Anna that are considered to be some of the most pristine examples of Civil War earthworks in existence. Explore the park and learn its history through an interpretive trail system. The park is open daily during daylight hours.

Poor Farm Park
Hwy. 54, Ashland

Near Patrick Henry High and Liberty Middle schools, Poor Farm Park is about 3 miles west of Ashland on Va. 54. Its 270 acres include an outdoor amphitheater, nine soccer fields, archery range, nature trails, orienting course, picnic shelter, grills and a toddler play area. Sand volleyball courts, horseshoes and 5 miles of mountain bike trails are also available. An outdoor concert series, the Hanover Humane Society's Pet Walk and the county's annual Heritage Faire are held here. (See our Annual Event chapter for more information.)

Sports and Recreation
City of Richmond

For information about recreational activities and sports programs in Richmond, call the city's Department of Park, Recreation and Community Facilities, 780-6208, or the community center nearest you. A comprehensive list of all the community centers in Richmond is provided in the phone book. For information on senior activities, call 780-6087 or 780-8590.

Youth Sports

Baseball

For Little League baseball, there are four

INSIDERS' TIP

The late Col. Charles H. Reed of Richmond played a key role in the rescue of the Royal Lipizzan stallions in Czechoslovakia during World War II.

leagues for children from about ages 6 to 15 including Metro, South, East and West Richmond. The youngest children play T-Ball to learn the fundamentals of the game. Fields are provided by the city. Teams are open to girls and boys.

Basketball

Most of the community centers sponsor teams, with play beginning in early January. Participation is free. City Championships are held in late March. Teams are also organized by the Boys Club, 353-3246, and the Jewish Community Center, 288-6091.

Cheerleading

Cheerleading squads for girls age 16 and younger are formed at all recreation centers that offer football and basketball. The squads are trained by volunteers and cheer at Saturday games. Participation is free. A cheerleading jamboree is held each fall at the Arthur Ashe Center.

Football

Most of the community centers sponsor football teams in the fall, beginning in September. Participation is free. City Championships are in November.

Soccer

The Richmond Department of Parks, Recreation and Community Facilities coordinates soccer teams through community centers to provide opportunities for boys and girls ages 5 to 16 to learn the fundamentals of the game. Teams compete on a regular schedule from mid-September through mid-November and April through June.

Teams are offered for different age levels, and coaches are trained volunteers. Practices are after school hours, and games are usually held on Saturdays. Playoffs are at the end of the fall season for the City Soccer Championships. The city also sponsors a traveling team.

More information about soccer is included at the end of this chapter.

Tennis

In cooperation with area tennis associations, the recreation department offers more than 140 tennis courts throughout the city for individual or group play. Competitive and instructional tennis programs are available for youth ages 6 to 16.

Volleyball

Children's coed volleyball programs are available at some community centers. Call for more information.

Adult Sports and Activities

Basketball

There are several adult leagues including the Industrial League, composed of teams formed by businesses, the Open League and the Church League.

Softball

The recreation department provides facilities for adult softball in cooperation with the Amateur Softball Association. Men's, women's and coed teams are formed according to ability levels.

Volleyball

The Richmond Volleyball Club sponsors leagues and outdoor tournaments played on grass, sand and asphalt courts. Men's, women's and coed teams are formed according to ability levels. Call 358-3000 for more information.

Other Sports

The city's community centers offer a vari-

Wildlife Returns to the James

During the past ten years, as the water has become cleaner and full of oxygen, the James River has experienced an explosive return of wildlife, most spectacularly indicated by a pair of nesting bald eagles inside the James River Park System at Williams Island. The pair gives Richmond bragging rights as the only capital city in the contiguous 48 states with an eagle's nest inside city limits.

The return of the eagles and other wildlife such as river otters and ospreys is largely attributed to the growing populations of fish such as shad, striped bass and small mouth bass. There have also been consistent sightings of flathead and blue catfish, and even the Atlantic sturgeon, which can grow as large as 800 pounds, has been found again in the James River as far inland as Richmond.

Several factors and events have played a role in renewing the health of the once polluted river. In 1969 and 1971, hurricanes Camille and Agnes damaged some of the dams along the James which enabled the river to flow more freely. Almost immediately after these dam breaks, biologists and naturalists noticed an improvement in the wildlife supported by the river as shad were able to migrate farther upstream. Since then, additional holes in the dams have been created by the state, and the river now runs freely all the way from Lynchburg to the Atlantic Ocean.

As a direct result of the holes in the dams and the introduction of fish ladders, shad will be able to migrate another 130 miles upstream from the Boscher Dam to Lynchburg. The growing shad population is seen as the key to the continued return of wildlife since its eggs and the young fish are a source of food for other fish, mammals and birds. Within a few years, the population of osprey, otters and eagles along the river is expected to increase dramatically.

— continued on next page

Improvement in water quality at the James River has led to happier fish and anglers.

The growth of the shad population is also expected to further encourage the striped bass population since they prey on smaller fish such as shad and bream. With the opening up of the dams, and the seasonal moratorium on catching them, the striped bass population has made such a strong return to the river that some say it's difficult to catch anything but a striper.

In addition to the breaks in the dams, implementation of the Clean Water Act was a major factor in cleansing the river. The Clean Water Act enacted in the 1950s regulates sewage treatment plants and pipelines and prohibits the dumping of raw sewage in the river. It has had a significant long-term effect on the renewed health and oxygenation of the James.

The natural beauty of the clean, free-flowing river and the return of the wildlife has in turn attracted more people. James River fishermen enjoy some of the best small mouth bass fishing in the country; canoeists, rafters and kayakers seek the thrill of the whitewater rapids; and naturalists relish the quiet joy of wildlife sightings. Still others accept the challenge of rock climbing along the river banks and bridge ruins.

It's inspiring to think that this urban wilderness, in the shadow of the city's skyline, is thriving once again. It's even more fantastic when you realize that you can get off at a city bus stop and walk down to it.

ety of classes and activities for adults including fencing, boxing, aerobics, yoga, walking clubs, weight training, tennis, volleyball, basketball, martial arts, self defense and swimming. They also offer arts and crafts, photography, sculpture, dance, chess, bingo, safety classes, trips and more.

In addition, self-guided fitness trails with written instructions and equipment for exercising are at Byrd Park, Pine Camp Arts Center, Reid Community Center, Chimborazo Park and Canoe Run Park. Also several gymnasiums at city schools are available for residents to use. For more information call your local community center.

Senior Citizen Activities

In cooperation with local seniors organizations, the city offers a wide variety of activities, programs, trips, clubs and events. Programs and services are based on geographical areas. The Linwood Robinson Senior Citizen Center at 700 N. 26th Street in Church Hill also offers daily activities including crafts, recreational activities, trips and tours. For more information, call 780-6087.

Chesterfield County

Contact the Chesterfield Department of Parks and Recreation, 748-1623, or watch for articles and ads in the *Richmond Times-Dispatch* and county newspapers for information about how to register for any of the sports listed below.

Youth Sports

Baseball

There are three Little League baseball leagues in Chesterfield. Children register directly with the Huguenot and Central Chesterfield leagues, or they may join the Chesterfield Baseball Club through their neighborhood athletic association. This is the largest club and includes about 30 athletic associations.

Several thousand children play baseball each year, from T-Ball (age 5 and older) to teams for youths to age 18. Most of the fields are provided and maintained by the county. Girls and boys may join. The season begins in March and ends in July. There are several postseason tournaments. For information, call the Department of Parks and Recreation, 748-1623.

Basketball

There are five basketball leagues for children — Chesterfield, Ettrick-Matoaca, Bon Air/Southampton, Chester Jaycees and Chesterfield Girls. Girls teams play in all the leagues.

The season is from November to mid-March, but registration begins as early as August. Teams are open to children age 6 and older. Skill development and sportsmanship are stressed with the youngest players, and competition is low-key. The focus becomes more competitive with children age 8 and older.

Cheerleading

Hundreds of cheerleading teams are formed through the neighborhood athletic associations for football and basketball teams according to age levels. Championships are held at the end of the seasons.

Football

The Chesterfield Quarterback League plays from August to November and includes teams from about 30 athletic associations in the county. Flag football teams are available for children around age 6, and older groups play tackle football. Teams are formed according to age. Championships are held at the end of the season. The county provides and maintains the fields.

Lacrosse

The Chesterfield Lacrosse Club plays in the Midlothian area each spring. Boys and girls in high school and middle school are eligible to participate. Call the Department of Parks and Recreation for more information.

Softball

The Chesterfield Girls Softball League offers slow-pitch softball to girls ages 6 to 18. The season is from March to July. The Chesterfield United Girls' Softball League includes mostly fast-pitch teams at the high school level. Participation is open to girls age 10 and older, and the season begins in May.

Tennis

Tennis lessons are available for youths age 10 and older. Classes are usually taught at Iron Bridge Park and the Byrd Athletic Complex. Fees vary.

Adult Sports

Basketball, softball, football, soccer and volleyball leagues are available for adults age 18 and older. Contact the recreation department for details.

Senior Citizen Activities

Special programs and activities for seniors include walking programs, trips, tennis, volleyball, exercise classes, softball and the Golden Olympics. The Ettrick and Bensley community centers offer regular programs and activities for seniors.

Other Activities

Fencing

Boys, girls and adults may participate in fencing throughout the year with the Chester Knights Fencing Club. Call the Department of Parks and Recreation at 748-1623 for more information.

Challenge Course

This is a ropes course designed to promote initiative and confidence and strengthen group dynamics, communication and teamwork. Life-altering experiences are common among participants. Request a copy of the course brochure from the Chesterfield Recreation Department for more information. This is ideal for groups, classes and scout troops. High- and low-course options are available. Instructors are extensively trained and certified.

Therapeutic Sports

Specially designed programs for people who have mental or physical handicaps include adaptive swimming, wheelchair tennis, horseback riding, basketball, bowling, miniature golf, hiking, softball and Little League baseball. The recreation department also sponsors social activities and the annual Rainbow Games for youths and young adults age 7 to 21 who have disabilities. The events include track and field, swimming and instructional clinics.

Gymnasiums

Various school gymnasiums are open for the public periodically. Contact the recreation department for scheduling information. There is no fee for residents to use the facilities.

Henrico County

Contact the Henrico County Recreation and Parks Department, 672-5100, for information about any of the sports listed below.

Youth Sports

Baseball

Area Little League baseball teams include Bethlehem, Chamberlayne, Glen Allen, Glen Lea, Highland Springs, Lakeside, Sandston, Tuckahoe, Varina and Virginia Randolph. Girls and boys ages 6 to 17 are invited to participate.

Basketball

Registration is usually held in October, with tryouts in November. Youths age 8 to 17 may participate. Teams are formed according to age levels. Standings are not kept for younger players; the emphasis is on instruction. About 650 kids are involved in the program each year.

Football

Information about football programs is available from the county. There are numerous leagues that play in the Metro Youth Football Association including Bethlehem, Chamberlayne, Glen Lea, Highland Springs, Kanawha, Laurel, Sandston, Tuckahoe, Varina and Virginia Randolph. Leagues play teams from throughout the metropolitan area.

Girls Softball

Girls age 6 to 17 may participate in area softball leagues including the Bethlehem Girls, Western Girls, Old Dominion Girls, Tuckahoe, Western Henrico, Varina, Chamberlayne and Virginia Randolph.

Adult Sports

Basketball

Basketball teams play at the Moody, Byrd and Tuckahoe middle schools in the winter from November through March and in the summer from June through August.

FYI

Unless otherwise noted, the area code for all phone numbers listed in this chapter is 804.

Baseball

An over-30 Baseball League plays in the spring and summer. Call 672-5156 for further information.

Golf

The county sponsors two adult golf tournaments each year. The Best Ball Tournament is held in June, and participants play at three area courses. The Two-Man Scramble is held in October at the Belmont Golf Course.

Volleyball

Coed volleyball is offered in the fall, winter and spring. Games are usually played at the Brookland Middle School.

Senior Citizen Activities

People age 55 and older can participate in a variety of activities including the Senior Games, trips, special programs, billiards, bowling, golf, softball, tennis, volleyball, water aerobics and walking clubs.

Other Activities

Henrico County offers coaching clinics for adults who coach youth sports. For information contact the county. About 15 school gymnasiums are open for basketball and other activities during December, January and February. Call the county for a list of schools and a schedule.

Special Programs

A variety of activities for people who have mental or physical disabilities are offered through the county including dances, picnics, crafts, workshops, martial arts, bumper bowling, basketball, softball, swimming and training for the Special Olympics.

Hanover County

Contact the Hanover County Department of Recreation and Parks at 798-8062 for more information about the sports listed below.

Youth Sports

Baseball

Youths age 6 to 18 may participate in baseball leagues from T-ball to Little League to the teen leagues. Fundamentals are stressed in T-ball, but older children play competitively and try out for teams. In Hanover, leagues operate in Atlee, Ashland, Mechanicsville, Beaverdam, Montpelier and Rockville. The season is usually March through July. There are championship playoffs at the end of the season, and all-star teams are selected to represent the area in postseason competition.

Basketball

Basketball leagues in Hanover County include the Ashland Youth Recreation Association and the Hanover Youth Recreational Association. Teams compete within their league from November through March. Teams are formed by age levels for kids 6 to 18.

Football

Teams are formed in the fall based on age and weight. There are three football leagues in Hanover County — Ashland, Blue Star and Mechanicsville. All the leagues play in the Metropolitan Youth Football Association and compete with teams throughout the Richmond area. The season is generally from August through November.

Softball

Leagues in Ashland, Mechanicsville, Atlee and Rockville form teams for youth ages 6 to 18. Girls' fast-pitch teams are also available. Teams play within their leagues from March through July.

Adult Sports

There are numerous men's, women's and coed softball leagues. For information about these leagues and to find out about adult basketball, volleyball, softball or bowling leagues, call the Hanover Parks and Recreation Department.

Senior Citizen Activities

The county offers dances with live bands, trips, bowling leagues, softball, aerobics, a bridge club, newsletters and other activities for seniors including an annual picnic at Wayside Park and a luncheon each year in Mechanicsville.

Other Metro Area Recreational Activities

Ballooning

Balloons Over Virginia
9988 Unit 10 Licking Hole Rd., Hanover County Airport • 798-0080

If you'd like a top-of-the-line view of Hanover County and the surrounding areas, the best way to get it is through Balloons Over Virginia. Richmond's only hot air balloon company offers two flights per day (at sunrise and two hours before sunset) by reservation only. The flight lasts about an hour, depending on weather and winds. Afterwards, enjoy a First Flight Celebration. Each ride costs about $200, with a two-person minimum.

Bicycling

Tour the Richmond area by bicycle, and get a closer look at parks, monuments and intriguing architecture. There are several bi-

---

INSIDERS' TIP

Tubing on the James is offered every Saturday afternoon in August by the Richmond Parks and Recreation Department. Float with a tour guide from the Pony Pasture to the Visitors Center for just $3. The fee includes a tube, life jacket, tour and shuttle service. Call 780-5311 for a reservation.

cycle tours on state-maintained roads in the area, and mountain bikes are permitted at Pocahontas State Park, Belle Island and Poor Farm Park. Maps and information on bike tours in the metropolitan area, Washington, D.C., and the Blue Ridge Mountains are available from Two Wheel Travel, 2934 W. Cary Street, 359-2453; or Rowlett's at Broad Street and Staples Mill Road, 353-4489.

Group rides around the area are regularly sponsored by the Richmond Area Bicycling Association (RABA), 266-BIKE. Bike rentals are available from Two Wheel Travel. Rates start at $15. Following is a sampling of a few popular and relatively easy rides. Be sure to get a map for specific directions.

Windsor Farms Tour

This 30-minute ride will take you through this residential neighborhood beginning at Locke Lane and ending at Cary Street Road. You'll ride by Agecroft Hall and the Virginia House — you may want to allow time to visit these historic attractions.

Battlefield Park Tour

This ride will take you on suburban and rural routes that pass by a Civil War fort, a marina and farmland. This route begins and ends at Fort Harrison off Va. Highway 5 (New Market Road) in eastern Henrico County.

Bellona Arsenal Tour

This route starts at Huguenot and Buford roads and travels through suburban and scenic rural areas of Chesterfield County. Steep hills on this tour provide a good workout.

Ashland Breakfast Club Ride

This tour leaves on Saturday mornings from the Laurel Park Shopping Center at Woodman and Hungary roads and travels about 10 miles to Hardee's in Ashland by way of backroads and the Old Washington Highway. Many riders take a variety of extension trips on the way back.

Bowling

Tenpin bowling is available at nine alleys in the area. Instruction and leagues for se-

niors are offered by some of the county and city departments of parks and recreation and at area bowling alleys. You'll also find numerous employer and church leagues throughout the area. Bumper bowling for kids is available at some of the alleys.

AMF Hanover Lanes
7313 Bell Creek Rd.
• 559-2600
6540 W. Broad St., Sunset Bowl
• 282-0537
8037 Shrader Rd., Major League
• 747-9620.

AMF Hanover Lanes on Bell Creek Road is the largest bowling center in Virginia. The 59,000-square-foot facility features 56 lanes and showcases the latest bowling equipment manufactured by AMF. The center also includes bumper lanes, a large game room, a billiards room, a pro shop and a spacious concourse area.

Bowl America
5018 Williamsburg Rd. • 222-5183
11532 Hull Street Rd. • 744-1500
7929 Midlothian Tnpk. • 320-7115

Choose from three Bowl America locations for league play, lessons or parties. All locations feature snack bars, automatic scoring, pro shops and anywhere from 36 to 52 lanes, depending on the location. Special DJ music nights are offered on Friday and Saturday nights at the Hull Street (southwest) and Williamsburg Road (eastern Richmond) centers.

Plaza Bowl
523 South Side Plaza • 233-8799

This is the only venue in town for duckpin bowling. Plaza Bowl offers 24 duckpin lanes, concessions and video games. You can bowl for $2 a game.

Ten Pin Coliseum
325 Belt Blvd. • 233-9801

DJ music on Saturday nights keeps things rolling at this South Side alley. Reservations are accepted. Party packages, bumper bowling, video arcade games and billiard tables are available.

Canoeing and Kayaking

The James River and other nearby rivers offer a variety of flatwater and whitewater trips. See the description of the James River Park in the City of Richmond Parks section of this chapter for more information.

Virginia Whitewater, a book by Richard Corbett, provides detailed descriptions of canoe and kayak trips in the state. Copies are available from Alpine Outfitters, 672-7879, or Blue Ridge Mountain Sports, 794-2004. Canoes and camping equipment can also be rented from Alpine Outfitters. The Hanover Parks and Recreation Department, 798-8062, also rents canoes.

Instruction and trips are offered through local departments of parks and recreation and by these private organizations.

Adventure Challenge
8225 Oxer Rd. • 276-7600

Combine the scenery and wildlife of the James River and other local waterways with the exhilaration of kayaking for an unforgettable experience that could become lifelong passion. Certified American Canoe Association instructors offer white water and sea kayaking lessons and guided trips on the James River, the Chickahominy River other local rivers and on eastern shore waterways. Kayak touring trips on flatwater also are offered, as well as sit-on-top trips. Youths age 10 or older, and adults are invited to participate. Parent/child combinations are encouraged.

A two-day beginner course costs about $125 for each participant. After-work and one-day tours for those who have had a beginners course or the equivalent, cost about $60. All of the necessary equipment will be provided. During the winter, Adventure Challenge also offers chartered, one-day ski trips to Wintergreen and Massanutten ski resorts in Virginia, and to White Tail resort in southern Pennsylvania. Rates vary depending on the package you choose.

Peak Experiences/Passages Adventure Camp
11421 Polo Circle, Midlothian • 897-6800

Kids ages 8 to 16 team up with Passages counselors for an exciting fun filled week or two of kayaking, canoeing, rock climbing and rappelling on Richmond's Belle Isle in the James River Park. About a day and a half is spent on each activity. Day camps are scheduled from mid-June through August. Activities begin at 8:45 AM and end at 4:45 PM each day. All equipment and meals are provided by the camp.

Passages counselors are experts in the field of outdoor adventure and enjoy working with kids. A better than 1-to-4 counselor to camper ratio ensures safety and individualized attention. Campers are grouped according to age and skill levels and progress at their own pace. Registration usually begins in March. Sessions are filled on a first come/first served basis. The cost for a one-week session is $399; two weeks is $770.

Passages also offers overnight trips on the James River and out-of-town trips to the New River Gorge in West Virginia and to the Ocoee River in Tennessee and North Carolina. Corporate team-building sessions are also available.

Peak Experiences offer kayaking classes for adults. The two-day basic course is $125 and the one-day advanced course is $65, both including equipment.

Richmond Raft Company
4400 E. Main St. • 222-7238;
(800) 540-7238

Explore the flatwater and rapids of the James River on an adventurous raft ride with experienced guides. Choose from several trips that vary in length and difficulty. A mild, scenic trip is available for children under age 12. See our Attractions chapter for detailed information on the company's services.

Fishing

The James River is one of the best smallmouth bass streams in the nation, and it's also a good place to catch catfish, bream, muskie and largemouth bass.

From its headwaters near Covington to the fall line at Richmond, the upper James River is ideal for smallmouth fishing. The lower James River from below Richmond to the Chesapeake

Bay is warmer and has more salinity, which makes it a great place for largemouth and striped bass. Catfish, bream and other panfish are found in both sections of the river.

You can find good fishing spots at several places in the James River Park (see previous listing in this chapter), and the Virginia Department of Game and Inland Fisheries maintains 14 boating access points. There are also several private marinas, launch sites and canoe and boat liveries that offer rentals near the access points.

For information on boating regulations and a list of public fishing waters in Virginia, plus license requirements and angling tips, contact the Virginia Department of Game and Inland Fisheries, 4010 W. Broad Street, Richmond, Virginia 23230, 367-9369.

If you are interested in fishing in the Chesapeake Bay, the ocean or other tidal rivers that flow into the Bay, you can get a copy of a *Guide to Virginia Saltwater Fishing*, published by the Virginia Saltwater Fishing Tournament, 968 S. Oriole Drive, Suite 102, Hauser Building, Virginia Beach, Virginia 23451, 491-5160. We also suggest a book by Bob Gooch, *Virginia Fishing Guide*, published by University Press of Virginia.

Horseback Riding

Richmond's proximity to many parks and rural areas offers numerous opportunities for horseback riding, a very popular sport in the area. There are many local horse shows and several horse shows at the state fairgrounds. There is also an equestrian ring at Dorey Park in Henrico County. Information about area trails is available from the Virginia Commission of Game and Inland Fisheries, P.O. Box 11104, Richmond, Virginia 23230, 367-1000; Virginia Division of Forestry, P.O. Box 3758, Charlottesville, Virginia 22903, 977-6555; Virginia Division of State Parks, 203 Governor Street, Suite 306, Richmond, 786-1712.

Hunting

Hunting seasons in Virginia begin with dove hunting in September. The major seasons for deer, turkey, small game and black bear open in November and remain open for 60 to 90 days. For information about licensing, where to go, public hunting lands, methods of hunting and harvest figures by county, contact the Virginia Department of Game and Inland Fisheries, 4010 W. Broad Street, Richmond, Virginia 23230, 367-1000. *Virginia Hunting Guide* by Bob Gooch, published by University Press of Virginia, is a good hunting resource.

Rock Climbing

The old Manchester Bridge ruins on the south side of the James River under the new bridge are very popular with rock-climbing enthusiasts as is the Old Netherwood quarry on Belle Isle near 42nd Street. Take the pedestrian bridge to Belle Isle in the James River Park (see previous listing), and you'll see where people have climbed on the rocks and ruins. Courses in rock climbing are offered by some of the local departments of parks and recreation and also by Challenge Discovery and Passages Adventure Camp.

Challenge Discovery Outdoor Adventures
P.O. Box 36342, Richmond, VA 23235 • 639-1544

Rock climbing, high ropes, canoeing and mountain climbing classes and excursions are offered by this established adventure organization to promote teamwork and personal growth for youth ages 10 to 16 or adults ages 17 and older. Everything you need is provided.

Rock climbing is usually offered in Richmond at the Netherwood Quarry in James River Park near 42nd Street, and in northern Virginia. Mountain climbing trips to Mexico are also offered. Register about three to four weeks in advance to get a session that's convenient for you. Individual rates start at about $50 a day. Corporate and group team-building sessions are available.

Peak Experiences
11421 Polo Circle, Midlothian • 897-6800

Peak Experiences has the largest indoor rock climbing facility on the East Coast, and the routes change every two months. Rates for adults are $12, students are $10 and children aged 12 and under are $9. Shoes and harnesses are $3 apiece to rent. Peak Experiences welcomes new climbers as well as birthday parties, boy and girl scout troops, and more.

Soccer

Soccer is a well-established year-round sport in the Richmond area for children and adults. Recreational and competitive teams are formed for many different age groups and skill levels.

For children as young kindergarten-age, there are house leagues that are formed mainly along geographical lines. These emphasize the fun and fundamentals of the game. Try-outs are not required, and league standings are not usually kept.

Travel or select teams are for more skilled players from ages 9 through 18. These teams compete against other teams in the same age group, and standings are kept. They may play in tournaments and compete for the annual Virginia State Cup. Tryouts are usually required.

In addition to clubs and travel teams, the city and county departments of recreation and parks also offer recreational soccer programs (see information in previous sections of this chapter).

Youth Soccer

Teams for boys and girls age 5 and older are sponsored by about 20 community, recreation and sports organizations in the area. Games are played at schools, churches, parks and athletic fields. Players do not have to play on the team closest to them geographically, but they may not play for more than one team. Registration dates are usually publicized in local newspapers about two months before the season begins. For information, call volunteer Skitch Hogan, 285-8067.

The main organizations are Atlee Youth Sports (Mechanicsville and northeastern Hanover County), Chesterfield Soccer Club (Chesterfield County), Chickahominy Youth Soccer League (northern Henrico County, south-central Hanover County), Eastern Football Club United (Varina, Sandston, Highland Springs and eastern Henrico), F.C. Richmond (northern Chesterfield, Bon Air, South Rich-

mond), Midlothian Youth Soccer League (western, southwestern and northwestern Chesterfield), Pocoshock Valley Youth Soccer League (northeastern Chesterfield), Powhatan Soccer Association (Powhatan County), James River Soccer Association (Midlothian area), Richmond Neighborhood Soccer Association (Richmond north of the river), Richmond Strikers Soccer Club (western Richmond, western and northwestern Henrico).

The Richmond Metropolitan Youth Soccer League is the local organization that supervises competitive play for Richmond and Tri-Cities area travel teams and for those from Charlottesville, Spotsylvania, Culpeper and Orange.

Girls Soccer

Girls-only soccer is increasing in popularity, and local organizers expect even more participation during the next few years. The Central Virginia Girls Soccer League (CVGSL) promotes both recreational house leagues and competitive travel teams. Teams play in the spring and fall.

Girls age 9 through the 8th grade play a recreational interclub schedule within their age groups and travel to fields throughout the Richmond area.

Under the supervision of CVGSL, travel teams compete with teams in the same age group within the Richmond area and against other travel teams from Charlottesville and the Tri-cities area — Petersburg, Hopewell, Colonial Heights. Travel team tryouts are usually held in May or June.

For information on travel teams, contact Steve Row at 320-4619; for more on house leagues, talk with Laura Heidig at 378-8949.

Adult Soccer

The Capital Area Soccer Association, 794-5259, has divisions for men up to age 40, men age 40 and older, and women older than 30.

The Central Virginia Soccer Association, 744-2872, has a competitive program for men in the fall and spring. They also have a seven-a-side competitive program for men during the summer.

The Chesterfield Coed Soccer League, 748-1128 has a summer recreational program for men and women age 21 and older, and the Chesterfield Women's Soccer Association has two divisions for women. For ages 19 and older contact 359-6329; for ages 30 and older, contact 560-3579.

Swimming

There are about 100 public and private outdoor swimming pools in the Richmond area serving almost every neighborhood. The city of Richmond has about 10 pools where residents may swim and take lessons for free. There are also several indoor pools for winter swimmers.

Indoor swimming and lessons offered through the Richmond Department of Recreation and Parks are available at the Calhoun Community Swimming Pool, 436 Calhoun Street, 780-4751, and at the Swansboro Swimming Pool, 3160 Midlothian Turnpike, 780-5088.

FYI

Unless otherwise noted, the area code for all phone numbers listed in this chapter is 804.

You'll find indoor pools at the YMCA facilities at Chickahominy, 5401 Whiteside Drive, Sandston, 737-9622; Downtown, 2 W. Franklin Street, 644-9622; Tuckahoe, 9211 Patterson Avenue, 740-9622; Chester, 3011 W. Hundred Road, 748-9622; North Richmond, 4207 Old Brook Road, 329-9622; and Manchester, 7540 Hull Road, 276-9622

The following private clubs also have indoor swimming pools: Riverside Wellness and Fitness Center-Briarwood, 794-6880; Burkwood Recreation Association, Studley Road, 730-2472; Raintree Swim and Racquet Club, 1703 Raintree Drive, 740-1035; and the Jewish Community Center, 5403 Monument Avenue, 288-6091.

Competitive Swimming

Competitive swimming is open to children as soon as they learn to swim until they are 18. In recent years, some of the swimmers in Richmond have qualified for the Olympic trials.

There are five summer swimming leagues in the area — Greater Richmond Aquatic League, James River Aquatic League, Richmond Metropolitan Aquatic League, South Side Aquatic League and Chesterfield Aquatic Club. The leagues are composed mostly of private clubs and compete among themselves. All leagues have championships at the end of the summer season, and about 5,000 kids participate. Inquire at your pool for information.

There are also several year-round state teams in Richmond including the Team Richmond Aquatic Club (Burkwood Recreation Center), Poseidon (Riverside Wellness and Fitness Center), the Dolphin Club (Jewish Community Center), The Richmond Racers (Calhoun and Swansboro Pools) and NOVA (NOVA Aquatic Center). About 1,000 kids swim on the state teams and compete against swimmers from around the Commonwealth. They progress to regional and national competitions depending on their ability. Noncompetitive coaching is also available for year-round swimmers. The state teams usually offer 12-month or eight-month programs.

Tennis and Racquet Sports

Tennis instruction and leagues for youth and adults are offered by a number of private clubs and through county and city departments of parks and recreation. There are also several tournaments open to amateurs and professionals. Information on the tournaments is available several months in advance from tennis shops, clubs, tournament locations and the local news media. Entry fees vary.

The City Tennis Championships are played annually in May at Byrd Park. The competition is open to amateurs and professionals who live in the Richmond area. Matches are held during a four-week period. Tournaments include the Rated Championships (based on ability level), the Family Tournament, Seniors (age levels from 35 and older), Juniors (age levels from 12 and younger to 18) and the Adult Open (no age restriction).

The State Championships are held in August at Raintree Swim and Racquet Club. This tournament is open to men and women, professionals and amateurs. Participants must be Virginia residents. Prize money is awarded.

The City Clay Court Championships are held in July at the Jefferson-Lakeside Country

Art at the River combines nature, education, art and a get-wet experience in the James River.

Photo: City of Richmond Parks, Recreation and Community Facilities

Club. This tournament is for men only and precedes the State Clay Court Championships for men and women at Riverside Wellness and Fitness Center in July. There is also an Indoor State Tournament in December at the Country Club of Virginia for amateur and professional players who are residents of Virginia.

For 10-and-younger and 18-and-younger players, Futures Tournaments are held at a variety of clubs throughout the area during the summer. For 18-year-olds, there is also the MidAtlantic Championships in June. The location varies.

Racquetball courts are available in 13 clubs, and 11 facilities offer indoor tennis; eight clubs offer both. Most of the courts are in private clubs available to members and guests only. Here is a sampling of major private clubs.

American Family Health and Racquet Club
9101 Midlothian Tnpk. • 330-3400
5750 Brook Rd. • 261-1000
4300 Pouncey Tract Rd. • 364-1200
Facilities at each location include four racquetball courts.

Burkwood Recreation Association
9111 Burkwood Club Dr. • 730-1066
Facilities include eight outdoor hard tennis courts with lights and four hard indoor tennis courts.

Capital Club
1051 E. Cary St. • 788-1524.
Facilities include two racquetball courts and two squash courts.

INSIDERS' TIP

Adventure Challenge offers whitewater kayaking, sea kayaking and snow-skiing trips and lessons. Seasonal activities are usually scheduled every weekend. Call 276-7600 for more information.

Courtside Racquet and Fitness Center
13620 Genito Road • 744-4263

Facilities include two racquetball and three indoor tennis courts. This used to be called Courtside at Brandermill.

Courtside West
1145 Gaskins Road • 740-4263

Facilities include three racquetball and three indoor tennis courts.

Ironbridge Indoor Tennis and Fitness Club
7211 Iron Bridge Rd. • 271-4500

Facilities include four indoor tennis courts.

Raintree Swim and Racquet Club
1703 Raintree Dr. • 740-0026

Facilities include two racquetball, four indoor tennis courts and 10 outdoor tennis courts. (Two are covered; eight are lighted.)

Richmond Athletic Club
4700 Thalbro St. • 355-4311

Facilities include three racquetball courts.

Riverside Wellness and Fitness Center, Briarwood
11621 Robious Road, Midlothian • 378-1616

Facilities include four racquetball courts and four indoor and 13 outdoor tennis courts (10 clay and three hard with lights).

Robious Sports and Fitness Center
10800 Centerview Rd., Midlothian • 330-2222

Facilities include two indoor and eight outdoor tennis courts, plus six racquetball courts.

Westwood Racquet Club
6200 W. Club Ln. • 282-3829

Facilities include four indoor clay courts, 13 outdoor courts (11 clay, two hard), two racquetball courts and two squash courts.

Walking, Jogging and Running

There are a number of fitness and nature trails in area parks, but you'll see most people out walking, jogging and running in their neighborhoods or down Monument Avenue. Shopping malls are also popular for indoor walkers and walking clubs. If you are interested in a walking club, contact the YMCA, the YWCA or your local department of parks and recreation for more information.

The Richmond Newspapers Marathon is a sanctioned event and attracts hundreds of local runners each year. (See the chapter on Spectator Sports for more information about the marathon.) There are also numerous running events and walkathons to benefit local charities or nonprofit organizations. Two of the larger charity events are Run for the Arts and the March of Dimes Walkathon. Details and schedules are published through the local news media and posters around town.

Some popular trails for walking or jogging are in Maymont Park, James River Park, Powhite Park, Byrd Park, Petronius Jones Park, Pine Camp Park, Battlefield Park, Rockwood Park, Point of Rocks Park, Henricus Historical Park, Iron Bridge Park, Huguenot Park, Pocahontas State Park, Cheswick Park and Dorey Park.

Wrestling

There are several wrestling associations in the area for children from age 5 to 13 including the Metropolitan Youth Wrestling League, the Hanover Youth Wrestling League and the Chesterfield Youth Wrestling League. Children compete within their leagues according to weight and age. The emphasis is primarily on fundamentals and developing self-esteem. The season is usually December through February.

INSIDERS' TIP

Registration for youth sports is usually held about two months before the season begins. Look for information in the local newspapers or call your county or city recreation department.

Fitness Centers

There are numerous fitness centers throughout the area. Here's a sampling of some of the popular ones. You may also want to refer to this chapter's listings under Tennis and Racquetball.

American Family Health & Racquet Club
9101 Midlothian Tnpk. at the Arboretum • 330-3400
4300 Pouncey Tract Rd. • 346-9600
5750 Brook Rd. • 261-1000

This club offers free weights, cardiovascular programs, pools with retractable roofs, aerobics, basketball, racquetball, whirlpool and sauna, martial arts, aerobics, exercise classes and a nursery.

Clubfit
7421 Lee Davis Rd., Mechanicsville • 730-3390

This club offers Nautilus, racquetball, free weights, exercise equipment, aerobics, personal training, 55-and-older classes and saunas. Child care is available.

Courtside at Brandermill
13620 Genito Rd. • 744-4263

This club offers aerobics, cardiovascular machines, Nautilus, tennis, racquetball, karate, nutrition and diet programs and special children's programs.

Jewish Community Center of Richmond
5403 Monument Ave. • 288-6091

The JCC offers indoor swimming, racquetball, basketball, soccer, volleyball, aerobics, exercise machines, free weights, saunas, steam rooms, whirlpools and exercise programs for all ages.

Main Street Nautilus
8 S. Harvey St. • 353-0057

This club offers Nautilus and cardiovascular equipment including Lifecycles, StairMasters, treadmills, and rowing and ski machines. Aerobics, free weights and supervised workouts are available.

Mike's Olympic Gym
7495 Old Hickory Dr. • 746-5022

This gymnasium offers free weights, cardiovascular and Selecterized equipment, aerobics, sport specific training and nutritional guidance.

New Fitness for Ladies
1236 Concord Ave. • 262-2666
10440 Ridgefield Pkwy. • 740-6060
13554 Genito Rd. • 744-4466

A fitness club just for women, New Fitness offers aerobics, personal training, supervised childcare, free weights and maxicam equipment, which is designed specifically for women.

Richmond Athletic Club
4700 Thalbro St. • 355-4311

This club offers racquetball, aerobics, Nautilus, free weights, basketball, steam room and sauna, whirlpool and child care.

Robious Sports and Fitness Center
10800 Centerview Dr. • 330- 2222

This club offers indoor swimming, plus a gymnasium, outdoor track, racquetball, tennis, whirlpool, outdoor running, circuit training, free weights, saunas and fitness testing.

Work Out Wonder Gym & Fitness Center Inc.
433 England St., Henry Clay Shopping Center, Ashland • 798-4910

This club, also known as WOW Gym, offers free weights, Nautilus, Lifecycles, boxing, aerobics, massage therapy, treadmills, tanning beds and saunas. On-site physical therapy is also available.

YMCA
737 Coalfield Rd. • 379-5668
2 W. Franklin St. • 644-9622
4207 Old Brook Rd. • 329-9622
7540 Hull Street Rd. • 276-9622
9211 Patterson Ave. • 740-9622
4024-C Cox Rd. • 270-3866
300 England St., Ashland • 798-0057

The Y offers gymnasiums, swimming pools, individual and group exercise programs, running tracks and specialized exercise machines. YMCA programs are open to men, women and children.

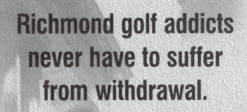

Richmond golf addicts
never have to suffer
from withdrawal.

Golf

From scenic riverside fairways to historic 1920s-style courses, there are more than 20 golf courses in the Richmond area. About half are open to the public, and the others are private clubs open to members and guests.

If you can escape for a weekend, you'll also find excellent golfing at well-known Virginia resorts in nearby places such as Wintergreen, The Homestead, Kingsmill and Tides Inn.

Unlike some northern states where the climate is too cold for winter golf, Richmond golf addicts never have to suffer from withdrawal. Although fewer people play from December to mid-March, golfing is a year-round sport in Virginia.

The best public courses are usually very crowded during midsummer and on the weekends. You'll have better luck getting a tee-time and avoiding the crowds if you try to play them in the fall when it's a little bit cold or it looks like it may rain.

If you're thinking of joining a private club, many of them have waiting lists and a few, such as The Country Club of Virginia and The Foundry, are by invitation only. You might be able to join one of the newer clubs such as The Dominion Club at Wyndham more quickly.

Courses

Belmont Golf Course
1600 Hilliard Rd. • 501-4653

Belmont is a public course that used to be the old Hermitage Country Club before it was purchased by Henrico County. It's a sloping, old-style, World War I-era course that has benefited from numerous improvements. Most of the holes are par fours. Several involve a creek and tricky out-of-bounds. Play Belmont in the late fall to avoid the crowds, as it has the lowest rates and is very popular. Special rates are available for seniors, juniors and Henrico County residents.

This 6350-yard, par 71 course costs: $17 on weekdays, $20 on weekends. Carts cost $11 per person. Reservations are required. Call a week in advance or as early as 7 AM on Monday for weekends.

Birkdale
8511 Royal Birkdale Dr., Chesterfield • 739-8800

This short, tight course is in an upscale neighborhood in Chesterfield, near Clover Hill High School. It's a long-hitter's course, similar to the Crossings (see the write-up in this chapter). Fees are seasonal and there are special rates for seniors.

Prices for this 6544-yard, par 71 range from $38-$41 on weekdays, $41-$46 on Fridays, and $46-$51 on weekends. Carts are included in the cost. Reservations are required. Call a week in advance.

Brookwoods Golf Course
7325 Club Dr., Quinton • 932-3737

Brookwoods is a public course with an available driving range. This mostly wooded course is a challenge with two lakes and plenty of hills. In fact, only one hole is flat. Because Brookwoods frequently hosts weekend tournaments, Monday is the least-crowded day to play. Special rates apply to seniors on weekdays.

This 6228-yard, par 72 course costs $26 on weekdays and $32 on weekends. Carts are included in the cost. Reservations are required.

The Crossings
800 Virginia Center Pkwy., Glen Allen • 266-2254

This is one of the most popular sites in the city for corporate outings and is often closed to the public. It used to be the old Ethelwood Golf Course, a private course owned by Hermitage Country Club. Almost every golfer in the area has played here several times. It's well-conditioned and has some unusual holes. Getting a tee-time on weekends is difficult. If you're lucky, you might get a chance to play during the week. Pull carts and coolers are not allowed. Walking is permitted before 9 AM or after 2 PM on weekdays, and on weekends after 2 PM. Special rates are available for nine-holes, ladies, juniors and seniors. Special winter rates are offered from October through March.

This 6619-yard, par 72 course costs $45 on weekdays, $52 on Fridays, $57 on weekends. Carts are included in the cost. Reservations are required. Call one week in advance.

Glenwood Golf Club
3100 Creighton Rd. • 226-1793

Like Belmont, playing this course is a good bargain. The fees are low, and it's just five minutes from downtown, making it very popular. It's tough to get a tee-time for the weekend. You'll have a better chance of getting a tee-time if you play during the week. Built in the 1920s, Glenwood is the oldest continuously operated course in Richmond. If you're a long-hitter, you'll love the low scores you can get on this tricky, rolling, short course. Special weekday rates apply for women, juniors and seniors. Also, late rates are offered after 3 PM.

This 6464-yard, par 71 course costs $17 on weekdays, $29 with cart; and $22 weekends, $34 with cart. Reservations are required for weekends and holidays. Call a week in advance.

Highland Springs Golf Course
300 Lee Ave. • 737-4716

Bordered by the Chickahominy River, this is a flat course, suitable for all levels of golfers. An easy course to walk, it features a lot of evergreens and water holes, very similar to courses in Florida. Bounded by the swamp on the left, a pond on the right, and a green surrounded by water; the number six hole is one

FYI

Unless otherwise noted, the area code for all phone numbers listed in this chapter is 804.

of the most challenging. Less than 10 minutes from downtown, this is one of the most conveniently located courses in the area. A full-service pro shop and snack bar are available.

This 6360-yard, par 70 course costs $30 on weekdays and $35 on weekends. Carts are included in the cost. Reservations are recommended. Call a week in advance.

The Highlands
8136 Highland Glen Dr., Chesterfield
• 796-4800

Because of the dramatic elevation changes on this course near the Pocahontas State Park, the Highlands offers a different terrain compared to other courses in the Richmond area. The course features a wooded setting, wetlands, lakes and abundant wildlife. It's not unusual to spot wild turkey or a deer as you tee up. Most of the holes are considered signatures holes. Walking is not permitted.

This 6711-yard, par 72 course costs $45 on weekdays and $55 on weekends. Carts are included in the cost. Reservations may be made a week in advance.

The Hollows Golf Course
14501 Greenwood Church Rd., Montpelier
• 883-5381

This 27-hole, semiprivate club west of Richmond in Montpelier features an easygoing, rustic atmosphere. The original front nine are open and the back nine are wooded. For those who want more challenge, the nine new holes offer bigger, more undulating greens.

A putting green is available, and walking and pull carts are permitted. Special rates available for nine holes, seniors and women.

This 6127-yard, par 70 course costs $19 on weekdays and $25 on weekends. Carts cost $7 for nine holes and $11 for 18 holes. Call after 1 PM on Wednesdays for weekend reservations.

INSIDERS' TIP

Champion golfers Bobby and Lanny Wadkins, Robert Wren, Vinny Giles, Nelson Broach and David Partridge are all native Richmonders.

Mill Quarter Plantation
Rt. 620, Powhatan • 598-4221

You'll find that this Chesterfield County course is similar to a private club and is one of the better public courses in the area. It's a long course with large greens that are usually in pretty good shape. Sneak out on a weekday to avoid the weekend crowds. Off U.S. Highway 60, it's popular with Midlothian and Chesterfield area residents. Special rates are available for nine-holes, weekday foursomes and seniors.

This 6943-yard, par 72 course costs $22 on weekdays, $36 with cart, and $28 on weekends after noon only, $42 with cart. Reservations are suggested for weekends or holidays. Call a week in advance.

River's Bend Country Club
11700 Hogan's Alley • 530-1000

Open since 1992, this well-conditioned, semiprivate club was originally designed as a private club. It features ravines, bluffs and the James River. The course is among the trickiest of the public clubs, and the finishing holes are challenging because of dramatic elevation changes. For example, on the 18th hole, you have to hit off a cliff down to a fairway that's about 200 feet below, and then across a 180-yard-wide ravine. This one is definitely for target golfers. Seasonal specials are available.

This 6671-yard, par 71 course costs $42 on weekdays and $52 on weekends, cart included. Reservations may be made up to a week in advance.

Royal New Kent Golf Course
3500 Bailey Rd. • 966-7023

When you play here, you'll think you're in Europe. This Scottish links style course is very open and windy, with lots of berms and bunkers. The fairways are trimmed with fields of tall waving grasses. Nominated as one of the best new courses in the country by *Golf Digest* in 1997, every hole is different and could be considered a signature hole. Midway between Richmond and Williamsburg, Royal New Kent is about 30 minutes from downtown Richmond. Take exit 214 off I-64.

This 7291-yard, par 72 course costs $85 (in season) and $65 (off season); $105 with a cart.

Royal Virginia
3181 Dukes Rd., Louisa • 457-2041

Some golfers claim that Royal Virginia is the most challenging course in Central Virginia, due to its length and level of difficulty. A few ponds and rolling hills, along with intricate ditch areas, make up this public course. Special rates apply to seniors.

This 7125-yard, par 72 course costs $33 on weekdays and $45 on weekends. Carts are included in the cost. Reservations are recommended.

Sycamore Creek
1991 Manakin Rd., Manakin-Sabot
• 784-3544

This Scottish-inspired course opened in 1992 and is a nearby and convenient alternative for West End golfers. The layout features a tremendous number of grass pot bunkers, rolling hills and mounds, and Tuckahoe Creek winds through the course. Even the best shotmaker will be challenged by the 15 water holes. Although this is a public course, you'll feel like you're playing at a private country club. Special fees apply to seniors and juniors.

This 6300-yard, par 70 costs $33 on weekdays, $35 on Fridays and $42 on weekends and holidays. Carts are included in the cost. Reservations are required. Call on Wednesday for weekends.

Golf Shops

Mulligan's
9127 W. Broad St., T.J. Maxx Shopping Center • 747-7277

If you're looking for something special or need a quick repair on your equipment, this West End shop has a good reputation for providing fast service and custom equipment.

Richmond Golf Center
5918 W. Broad St. • 288-4653
1105 Alverser Dr. (off Midlothian Tnpk.)
• 379-8333

This is Richmond's discount golf supermarket. It offers quality pro-line equipment, repairs, club fitting and tryout ranges. The stores are in the West End and Southside.

Pick a local team to root for, follow news about sports at the University of Virginia and Virginia Tech, and you'll have plenty to talk about.

Spectator Sports

From hard-driving auto races and professional baseball, to slam-dunkin' basketball and rock-em, sock-em action on the ice, Richmond has plenty of year-round excitement for sports enthusiasts.

Leading the list is the Richmond International Raceway, the Richmond Braves — top farm team for the Atlanta Braves—the Renegades hockey team, the Richmond Kickers professional soccer team and the Richmond Rage, a professional women's basketball team.

Plus, with four colleges and universities in the area, there's enough basketball and football to keep even the most avid fans happy, especially when you consider that two of the universities play at the Division I level.

Richmond is also only about a half hour away from a new pari-mutuel betting race track, Colonial Downs, in neighboring New Kent County, which opened in the fall of 1997.

If that's not enough, there's also tennis, a marathon, soccer, lacrosse, field hockey, professional wrestling and tractor pulls.

Since many people who work in the Richmond area have graduated from Virginia schools, sports provide lots of ammunition for friendly office rivalries. Pick a local team to root for, follow news about sports at the University of Virginia and Virginia Tech, and you'll have plenty to talk about.

Tickets are usually available at the gate for most sporting events in the area, with the exception of Winston Cup races and some of the games between local rivals such as the University of Richmond and Virginia Commonwealth University, Virginia Union and Virginia State, and Randolph-Macon and Longwood.

This chapter will acquaint you with the major spectator sports in the area. If you're interested in participant sports, you'll find that information in the chapter on Parks and Recreation.

Baseball

Richmond Braves
3001 N. Blvd., The Diamond • 359-4444

On a warm summer night, you can almost always catch a breeze and, if you're lucky, a foul ball at the Diamond, home of the Richmond Braves, the top minor-league team in the Atlanta Braves farm system.

Just one step away from the big leagues, the Richmond Braves compete at the elite Triple-A level, and local fans have seen more than one rising star. During the last few years, more than 50 former Richmond Braves have moved up to play in the majors.

The Braves have been a Richmond tradition since 1966, when the National League Milwaukee Braves moved to Atlanta following the 1965 baseball season, and Milwaukee's previous Triple-A franchise, the Atlanta Crackers found a new home in Richmond.

With features such as sky boxes and a restaurant behind first base where you can watch the games while you dine, the Diamond is considered one of the finest ballparks in the minor leagues. Several million fans have passed through its gates since it was built in 1985.

The sculpture of a giant Indian brave named Connecticut, seen peering over the top of a wall, adds to the atmosphere at the Diamond. On loan to the Diamond for several years by artist Paul DiPasquale, the sculpture was almost purchased by an outside interest and removed from the stadium. A fund-raising campaign headed by Signet Bank saved the sculpture, and Connecticut is now a permanent part of the ballpark.

If you arrive at the games early, you might get one of the free hats, gloves or other promotional items given to the first fans who arrive, or you might get a hug from Diamond Duck.

The home schedule usually runs from April through August. Located on the Boulevard, the Diamond is easy to get to from I-95 or I-64. General admission is $5 for adults and $3 for children 12 and younger as well as seniors.

Auto Racing

Richmond International Raceway
602 E. Laburnum Ave. • 345-RACE tickets

Richmond International Raceway (RIR) at the Virginia State Fairgrounds in Henrico County, put Richmond on the map as a major NASCAR city. RIR is one of only 16 Winston Cup race tracks in the country where you can see hard-driving truck and auto racing and some of the best racing teams in the U.S. The thoroughly modern track has more than 95,000 reserved seats and draws the largest crowd of any sports event in Virginia.

Each year, the raceway hosts two NASCAR Busch Grand National Series races, two Winston Cup Series races and a NASCAR Craftsman Truck Series race.

In September, RIR hosts a three-day race weekend beginning with "The Virginia is for Lovers 200" NASCAR Craftsman Truck Series race, followed by the "Autolite Platinum 250" NASCAR Busch Series Grand National, and ending with the Winston Cup Series on Saturday.

In November, RIR hosts "The Fall 300," a 150-lap race for NASCAR featherlite modified tour cars and a 150-lap race for NASCAR late-model stock cars.

In March, the excitement begins again with "The Hardee's Fried Chicken Challenge 250,"

NASCAR Grand National Series and "The Pontiac Excitement 400" Winston Cup Series.

Practices and timed trials are open to anyone with a race ticket. Children younger than 12 are admitted free to general admission races and preliminary practice sessions. Reserved seating only is available for Winston Cup races. Drivers may begin practicing as early as 9 AM on race day. Timed trials for the next day's race begin around 3 PM.

RIR has existed since the mid-1950s but was completely remodeled in 1988. The .75-mile track, the only one of its kind on the NASCAR circuit, is banked at 14 degrees in the turns. The 60-foot-wide track was expanded from its previous half-mile length to give the drivers more room to maneuver.

To accommodate the more than 100,000 fans coming and going to RIR, several streets in the area are converted to one-way streets on race days. If you want to avoid heavy traffic, read the local papers for transportation options and plan to arrive two or three hours before the race starts. Shuttle bus service is provided from several locations around town. Parking at RIR is free.

Seats sell out fast, so buy your tickets early. Raceway ticket and information offices are open all year. Camper parking spots with hook-ups are available through the State Fairgrounds. For information, call the fairground at 228-3200.

Winston Cup Race tickets cost $70 and $75. Other races cost about $30; children 12 and younger are admitted for free with paid adult.

Southside Speedway
12800 Genito Rd. • 763-3567

Every Friday night, beginning in late March and lasting through September, auto racing fans can watch NASCAR/Winston Series races at the Southside Speedway. Each week more than 70 competitors circle the .33-mile asphalt oval known as the "Toughest Short Track in the South." Free parking, full concessions and novelty items are available. Admission is $11; children ages 6-12 are $3; children younger than 6 are admitted for free.

Photo: The Richmond Braves

You can catch a Richmond Braves game from April through August.

Richmond Dragway
1955 Portugee Rd. • 737-1193

Richmond dragway opens the first Sunday in March each year and offers sanctioned drag racing programs each weekend through November.

Ice Hockey

Richmond Renegades
601 E. Leigh St., Richmond Coliseum
• 643-7825 tickets

The Richmond Renegades provide ice hockey fans with slam-bang action up and down the rink. More than 7,000 loud, boisterous, fight-loving fans add to the excitement. Formed in 1990, the Renegades play in the East Coast Hockey League at the Coliseum ("the freezer") in downtown Richmond. Games with rival teams from Roanoke and Hampton Rhoads are the most popular with fans. Ticket prices range from $8-$15.

Soccer

Richmond Kickers
3201 Maplewood Ave., Univ. of Richmond Stadium • 644-KICK

Just three years after the Richmond Kickers soccer team joined the United States Interregional Soccer League (USISL), they won the 1995 U.S. Open Cup and the USISL Premiere League championship.

The USISL is comprised of teams from eight regions throughout the country. The Kickers compete in the A League, which includes 24 teams in the Atlantic Division.

Coached by Frank Kohlenstein, the Kickers team includes recent collegiate standouts and selected international players. Since the Kickers were formed in 1993, more than eleven of their players have been drafted for major league soccer.

Fan support is excellent. Kickers' games have one of the highest attendance records in

INSIDERS' TIP

If you can't wait to find out who won the game, call the *Richmond Times Dispatch* Scoreboard at 649-6828 for a taped message with updated scores.

the entire league. More than 2,000 fans attend games at the University of Richmond Stadium. To get to the stadium from I-95, take the Powhite Exit and go 2 miles to Douglas Avenue. The stadium is at Douglas Avenue and McCloy Street. Tickets are available in advance at over 15 Arby's fast food restaurants around town, the ticket office or at the gate.

General admission is $8 for adults, $6 for youths age 17 and younger.

Marathon Running

Crestar Richmond Marathon
• 285-9495

The Crestar Richmond Marathon is one of the area's largest spectator sports and the most popular participant sports event in the area. More than 3,000 runners, joggers and wheelchair racers line up for the start each year. Sponsored in early November by the Crestar Bank, the marathon is sanctioned by the USA Track and Field and is a qualifier for all other marathons. The event includes a full 26.2-mile marathon and a 5-mile race.

Although some world-class runners participate, most of the racers are the same people you see jogging around town. Thousands of spectators turn out to cheer for friends, relatives and neighbors. It's a great excuse for a party or a curbside picnic. A variety of special activities downtown near the start and finish at Sixth and Broad streets add to the festivities.

If you're interested in participating, entry forms are available at www.rrrc.org before the race. For more information, call.

Tennis

Raintree Swim and Racquet Club
1703 Raintree Dr. • 740-0026

The annual men's and women's state tennis championships are usually held the first week in August at the Raintree Swim and Racquet Club. As many as 64 men and 64 women may compete on eight hard courts. Players must be Virginia residents. Prize money is awarded. Many of the winners have achieved high rankings in the men's and women's professional circuit. The champion-

ships are open to the public. Food and beverages are available. Admission is free.

Horse Racing

Colonial Downs Race Track
10515 Colonial Downs Parkway, New Kent
• 966-RACE

Colonial Downs, Virginia's first pari-mutuel betting race track, opened in the fall of 1997. The facility, in New Kent County between Richmond and Williamsburg, features a mile-and-one-quarter dirt track and a one-mile turf track. The grandstand facility offers a variety of dining options and an adjoining open-air racetrack area. Live standardbred harness racing runs every Monday through Wednesday at 4 PM from late May to early August. Thoroughbred races are held Fridays through Tuesdays at 3 PM in the fall.

College and University Sports

Virginia Commonwealth University
Sports Information Office
819 Franklin St. • 828-1RAM

Virginia's largest urban university, Virginia Commonwealth University sprawls in and around the downtown area and includes the Medical College of Virginia. Best known in sports for its men's basketball program, VCU also offers women's basketball and men's baseball. It does not have a football team. The Rams are members of the Colonial Athletic Association (CAA), NCAA Division I, that includes the University of Richmond, American University, East Carolina University, George Mason, James Madison, the College of William and Mary, UNC at Wilmington and Old Dominion University.

Basketball

Coached by Mack McCarthy, VCU has one of the strongest, most exciting, basketball programs in the state. In 1996, they won the regular season championship and tournament championship in the CAA and were invited to the NCAA tournament. In the 1980s, the Rams appeared in five NCAA tournaments and advanced to the quarterfinal of the NIT. The 1984-85 team was probably the best VCU team in history. At the end of that season, the Rams were ranked 11th by Associated Press and UPI polls. When they were in the Sun Belt Conference, the Rams won four regular season championships and three Sun Belt Tournaments, more than any other team in the league.

Since 1974, 16 VCU players have been drafted into the NBA, including Kendrick Warren, Gerald Henderson, Calvin Duncan, Rolando Lamb, Mike Schlegel and Bernard Hopkins.

Known by many fans as the "cardiac" Rams, the team has earned a reputation for playing fast-paced, exciting games frequently decided at the final buzzer.

An average of 5,500 fans attend each game at the Richmond Coliseum, the largest basketball facility in the state with a seating capacity of 10,716. General admission is $8 for adults and $4 for youths age 17 and younger.

VCU's women's basketball team has also grown in popularity over the years and attracts about 500 fans to each game played in the Franklin Street Gym on campus. In 1994, VCU was host to the NCAA Women's Final Four. General admission is $5 for adults and $2 for youths ages 17 and younger.

Baseball

VCU's men's baseball team won the CAA regular season title in 1997 and has been ranked as one of the top-25 Division I teams in the country. Several hundred fans attend games at the Diamond on the Boulevard near I-64 and I-95.

Admission is $3 for adults and $2 for youths 17 and younger.

University of Richmond
College Rd. • 289-8388 tickets and information; 289-8363 athletics office

Basketball and football are the main sports played at the University of Richmond in the West End. The football team plays in the Atlantic 10 Football Conference, NCAA Division I-AA. All other teams are in the Colonial Athletic Association, NCAA Division I. Other CAA teams include Virginia Commonwealth University, American University, East Carolina University, George Mason, James Madison, the College of William and Mary, UNC at Wilmington and Old Dominion.

With the exception of football, which UR plays at its stadium near downtown Richmond, all sports are played on campus. There are several ways to get to the campus. Here are two of the easiest. From south side, cross the Huguenot Bridge, turn left onto River Road, then turn right onto College Road. From other locations, take the Glenside Road S. Exit off I-64 to Three Chopt Road. Go east about a half-mile and turn right on Boatwright Drive. It will take you directly to the campus.

Basketball

On any given night, the Richmond Spiders can defeat any team in the country. They have a record of significant wins over nationally ranked teams, including a victory over Syracuse in the 1991 NCAA Tournament. One of the biggest upsets in college basketball, it was the first time a No. 15-seeded team defeated a No. 2-seeded team.

Since 1981, the Spiders have been invited to five NCAA Tournaments, and they reached the Sweet 16 in 1988. They've also logged a number of trips to the NIT. UR players who've joined the NBA include Curtis Blair, John Schweitz and John Newman.

Coached by John Beilein, the Spiders play home games on campus at the Robins Center that has a seating capacity of about 9,000. Games with other Virginia teams and nationally ranked teams have been known to sell out. General admission is $12 for adults and $6 for youths age 17 and younger.

The women's basketball team faces several top-20 teams and has had a string of undefeated seasons in recent years. Games are well-attended by 700 to 1,000 fans. General admission is $5 for adults and $3 for youths age 17 and younger.

Football

UR football games are close-scoring and fun to attend, especially if you arrive early enough for a pregame tailgate party. The most popular games are with the University of Virginia and Virginia Tech.

In the 1980s, the Spiders reached the NCAA I-AA playoffs twice and they had a first-round NFL draft choice — Barry Redden. Redden went on to play with the Los Angeles Rams, the Cleveland Browns and the San Diego Chargers. Another former UR player, Brian Jordan, 1985-88, played with the Atlanta Falcons.

Coached by Jim Reid, who was voted co-coach of the year in 1995, the Spiders play in the Yankee Conference, one of the strongest and most respected Division I-AA conferences in the country. The conference includes Connecticut, Massachusetts, Maine, New Hampshire, Richmond, Rhode Island, Boston, Villanova, Delaware, James Madison, Northeastern and the college of William and Mary.

UR plays home games at the UR Stadium on McCloy Street between downtown Richmond and the university campus. The stadium is the second-largest facility in the Yankee Conference and seats 22,611. You can buy tickets at the gate or in advance. General admission is $12 for adults and $8 for youths 17 and younger. Plenty of parking is available.

Other Sports

Men's soccer games usually draw about 2,000 spectators at the UR Soccer Complex on campus. Since 1995, UR has hosted the NCAA Division I Men's Final Four Soccer Championships at the UR Stadium on McCloy Street in downtown Richmond.

The Spider's baseball team played in the NCAA playoffs in 1995 and 1997. UR games are played on campus, off College Road at Pitt Field.

UR soccer prices for general admission are $4 for adults and $2 for children. Baseball games are free.

Virginia Union University
1500 N. Lombardy St. • 321-2138

At Lombardy Street and Brook Road, close to downtown Richmond, Virginia Union University is a member of the Central Intercollegiate Athletic Association (CIAA), which consists of 12 historically African-American institutions: Bowie, Elizabeth City, Fayetteville, Johnson C. Smith, Livingston, North Carolina Central, Saint Augustine's, Saint Paul's, Shaw, Virginia State, Virginia Union and Winston-Salem.

Virginia Union is primarily known for its basketball and football programs. For information or tickets call the sports information office.

Basketball

Virginia Union has always had one of the best basketball teams in the state. Coached by Dave Robbins, the Panthers are frequently ranked No. 1 in the CIAA and as one of the top-10 teams of NCAA Division II.

Panthers who made it to the professional ranks include Charles Oakley, Terry Davis, A.J. English, Tim Price (Harlem Globe Trotters) and Ben Wallace.

Men's and women's basketball teams play off campus at the Arthur Ashe Center at the corner of Boulevard and Robin Hood Road near the Diamond.

Football

Virginia Union holds the NCAA Division II record for the most consecutive winning seasons. One of the best games of the year is the Gold Bowl Classic, an annual event between the Panthers and their rivals, Norfolk State. All games are played at Hovey Field on campus. Admission to all events is $9 for adults and $5 for students and youths.

Randolph-Macon College
204 Henry St., Ashland • 752-7223

Winning is a tradition at Randolph-Macon College in Ashland, a small school best known for its basketball and football teams. Randolph-Macon also offers men's and women's soccer, baseball, lacrosse, women's basketball and field hockey. All teams play in the Old

---

INSIDERS' TIP

Richmond International Raceway is one of only 16 Winston Cup racetracks in the US, and it's the only race track that runs NASCAR's three major touring divisions — Winston Cup, Grand National and Craftsman Trucks — all on the same weekend.

Arthur Ashe Jr.

For Emily Clore, a 48-year-old former cafeteria worker, "he wasn't Martin Luther King Jr., and he wasn't Malcolm X. But when you saw him, he stood for something. He wasn't always talking, but he always had something to say."

Close-up

For the Reverend Jesse Jackson, president of the Rainbow Coalition, "he turned anger into energy, and stumbling blocks into steppingstones."

They both were talking about Arthur Ashe Jr., who once told an interviewer his life was built "on the values I learned in Richmond. It comes from those role models I came in contact with as a kid." As a tennis legend and as a human rights crusader, Arthur Ashe Jr. was the kind of person all of us would like to be.

He gained fame by winning Wimbledon and the U.S. Open, by being twice-ranked No. 1 in the world, by playing and captaining the U.S. Davis Cup team and, as the late Secretary of Commerce Ron Brown noted, "playing and integrating an utterly white game — and winning." But he gained even greater accolades for his off-court accomplishments and the manner in which he went about them. He raised public consciousness about AIDS, the plight of African-Americans, Haitians and South Africans, and he helped launch an operation called Virginia Heroes in his hometown to try to provide the kind of role models that were so important to him in his formative years.

"The situation concerning African-American males . . . is bleaker than people would imagine," he said. "When I was growing up it was the middle-class Negro community that set the culture. Now it's set by the lower economic level, by the rap music, the way they wear their hats."

Born in Richmond on July 10, 1943, Ashe was four years old when his family moved out of an uncle's home on Brook Road and into a small, one-story house at 1610 Sledd Street on the Brookfield Playground where his father had just been named supervisor. The 18-acre city park was between Chamberlayne Avenue and Brook Road, one block from Virginia Union University. In those days the park was Richmond's largest recreational facility for African-American residents.

"Although Arthur came of age in a segregated society, he had access to something most youngsters, white or black, didn't have: tennis courts right outside his door," says Dr. Francis M. Foster, a retired dentist and one of Richmond's foremost authorities on the history of the city's African-American community.

As an elementary schoolboy, Ashe was already showing great promise as a tennis player. He was enrolled in a junior-devel-

— continued on next page

The Arthur Ashe statue is the most recent addition to Monument Avenue.

Photo: Metro Richmond Convention and Visitors Bureau

opment program sponsored by the American Tennis Association, a tennis organization for African Americans, and at age 10 he was fortunate enough to be taken under the wing of Dr. Robert W. "Whirlwind" Johnson, a Lynchburg dentist who spent his own money coaching and developing Ashe's abilities.

One little-known fact about Ashe is that he also was an outstanding baseball player. "He was a superior ballplayer," Dr. Foster says. "He had the speed of a gazelle and a sharp batting eye."

At Maggie Walker High School, Ashe was "the perfect student, quiet and studious," recalls Roy A. West, former Richmond mayor and at that time a substitute teacher at Maggie Walker. "He paid attention in class. He didn't chitchat with other students. In fact, he didn't say much at all. But when Arthur did speak, you knew this was an intelligent young man."

After his junior year at Maggie Walker, he left his family behind and moved to St. Louis, a tennis hotbed in those days, where he completed high school and pushed ahead with his tennis. He received a scholarship to the University of California, Los Angeles, which then had the preeminent collegiate tennis program in the country. He became UCLA's No. 1 player and the first African-American ever chosen for the U.S. Davis Cup team.

The years that followed tell the story everyone knows: his mercurial rise in the tennis world; bypass heart surgery and his retirement from tennis in the late 1970s; his induction into the International Tennis Hall of Fame in 1985; and his disclosure that he was suffering from AIDS as the result of a tainted blood transfusion during surgery.

The Brookfield Playground and the house on Sledd Street are gone now — the site today of Richmond's main post office. More than 6,000 mourners crowded the nearby Arthur Ashe Jr. Center for his funeral on February 10, 1993, before he was buried in Woodland Cemetery in Richmond's East End.

At the funeral, former New York City Mayor David Dinkins said what was on every mind: "Arthur Ashe was just plain better than most of us."

Dominion Athletic Conference (ODAC) that includes 13 NCAA Division III schools in Virginia and Guilford College in North Carolina.

All sports are played on campus. To get to Randolph-Macon, take the State Route 54 W. Exit off I-95 in Ashland.

Basketball

Coached by Hal Nunnally, the men's basketball team is a top-ranked NCAA Division III team. The yellow jackets have won several Old Dominion Athletic Conference championships and made it to the Final 16 in the NCAA Division III tournament in 1991.

Randolph-Macon joined the ODAC league in 1989, when it switched to the Division III level. All games are played at Crenshaw Gymnasium, with attendance averaging about 600.

Randolph-Macon's women's basketball team has also made it to the final rounds of the NCAA Division III tournament. Games, which usually attract a crowd of between 150 and 300, are played at the Crenshaw Gymnasium. Admission to basketball games is $3 for adults and $2 for students. Children younger than 12 are admitted for free.

Football

To say that football is a big deal here would be an understatement. Randolph-Macon's football team has won more ODAC championships than any other team in the conference. Coached by Joe Riccio, football games usually draw about 2,000 to 2,500 fans, except at the homecoming game and the annual game with Hampton Sydney College when it's not unusual for 5,000 to 6,000 fans to pack the stands.

Randolph-Macon was one of the first schools in the nation to field a competitive football team in 1881. Only 17 schools in the United States had football teams before Randolph-Macon. Fans may remember running back Remon Smith (1984-87), who holds the record as the leading rusher in Virginia collegiate history (4,276 yards). Randolph-Macon plays on Day Field.

Admission is $5 for adults and $2 for students, and free for children younger than 12.

Other Sports

Other popular sports at Randolph-Macon include men's and women's soccer, baseball, lacrosse and women's field hockey. Admission to these games is free.

At our museums and cultural centers, children and adults enjoy intriguing programs as well as hands-on exhibits, not just a lot of dusty artifacts — costumed interpreters and living-history programs bring Richmond's heritage to life.

Attractions and Tours

You'll find an abundance of historical attractions, centuries-old architecture, plantations and battlefields in the Richmond area plus some dynamic family-oriented cultural centers, parks and museums.

Although Richmond is probably best known for its Civil War battlefields and monuments to Confederate heroes on Monument Avenue, the "Capital of the Confederacy" also played an important role in the Revolutionary War and Colonial history. It was at St. John's Church in Church Hill that Patrick Henry gave his famous "Give me liberty or give me death" speech.

At our museums and cultural centers, children and adults enjoy intriguing programs as well as hands-on exhibits, not just a lot of dusty artifacts. On special weekends, costumed interpreters and living-history programs bring Richmond's heritage to life.

There's something here for everyone. We've got walking tours, bus tours and trolley tours. You can stroll through beautiful parks and gardens or ride a world-class roller coaster at Paramount's Kings Dominion Theme Park. You can even go whitewater rafting down the James River.

Locals who think they've seen it all may be surprised by what's new in Richmond. Paramount's Kings Dominion adds exciting new rides, shows and attractions each year. Maymont and the Science Museum of Virginia are adding new exhibit areas, and the "Citie of Henricus" is beginning to take shape. There's even a new do-it-yourself tour and combination ticket for all of the major attractions in the historic downtown area.

If you're here for a visit, we hope you'll enjoy our city as much as we do. If you're a resident and it's been a while since you explored the many attractions offered here, we hope you'll find time to take a fresh look.

To help you get around, this chapter organizes information into the following categories: black history; museums and historic sites; gardens, parks and other outdoor attractions; riverfront attractions; Paramont's Kings Dominion; and tours.

General Information

Richmond Visitors Center
1710 Robin Hood Rd. • 358-5511

This visitors center, next to The Diamond, offers souvenirs and literature on attractions in the area. You also can make reservations at area hotels and choose Richmond postcards from one of the biggest selections in town. Children will enjoy playing on the train and the aviation exhibits at Travelland just outside the center. A video about the area is available for viewing. The center is open Monday through Sunday from 9 AM to 5 PM, with extended evening hours in the summer.

Metropolitan Richmond Convention and Visitors Bureau
6th Street Marketplace, 550 E. Marshall St. • 782-2777

You'll find lots of information, maps and literature here about places to go and things to do in the area. If this location is not convenient for you, try the visitors center on Robin Hood Road (see previous listing). There's also a visitors center at the Richmond International Airport, 236-3260, and a toll-free number for

Richmond-area hotel reservations (800) 444-2777. Discounted rates for lodging the same day are available for walk-in customers only. The same toll-free number offersw an informational packet about Richmond. The center is open Monday through Friday, 8:30 AM to 5 PM.

Ashland/Hanover Visitors Center
112 N. Railroad Ave., Ashland • 752-6766

Friendly counselors at this quaint visitors center inside an old train depot, directly in front of the Henry Clay Inn, are quick to offer information and advice on what to see and do in the Ashland area. Brochures on attractions throughout the Richmond area and maps of the county are also available. You can even board the Amtrak train here. The center has a schedule of stops, but you pay for your ticket after you board the train. The center is open daily from 9 AM to 5 PM.

Bell Tower, Virginia Information Center
Capitol Square, Ninth and Franklin Sts. • 648-3146

Travel counselors at the Bell Tower will provide you with free information about attractions in the area and throughout the state. The center is open Monday through Friday, 10 AM to 4 PM.

Greater Richmond Chamber of Commerce
201 E. Franklin St. • 648-1234

The Chamber of Commerce provides information and literature about the area for new residents. Call for more information.

Black History Attractions

Black History Museum and Cultural Center of Virginia
00 Clay St. • 780-9093

This 19th-century house in Jackson Ward serves as a center for art exhibits, research and other activities related to Virginia's black history and culture. Standing exhibits on Jackson Ward, Second Street and Oliver Hill are

FYI

Unless otherwise noted, the area code for all phone numbers listed in this chapter is 804.

on display, along with changing exhibits about topics such as black inventors. The house was originally built as a residence in 1832. It later served as the Black Public Library and as a high school. The museum sponsors an annual Community Day in August with free admission and musical entertainment in front of the building. Tour guides are available on request. Admission is $2 for adults and $1 for adults older than 55 and children younger than 12. The museum is open Tuesday through Saturday from 11 AM to 4 PM. It's closed on Mondays.

Maggie Walker National Historic Site
110 E. Leigh St. • 771-2017

Maggie Walker was a black woman who rose from poverty and overcame a crippling physical handicap to become a successful banker, newspaper editor and influential civic leader. The daughter of an ex-slave, she founded the St. Luke Penny Bank and was an early advocate of black women's rights. The bank today is known as Consolidated Bank and Trust, the oldest surviving black-operated bank in the country.

Every half hour, park rangers conduct guided tours of the 22-room house in historic Jackson Ward, where the Walker family lived from 1904 to 1934. Built in 1883, the dwelling has been restored and decorated to appear as it did in 1930. The National Park Service operates the site. Groups of ten or more people need to make advance reservations. Parking is available in the neighborhood or at a public lot at Fourth and Leigh streets. A new visitors center with exhibits, a book store and an audiovisual presentation is now open at 600 N. 2nd St. The house is open Wednesday through Sunday from 9 AM to 5 PM. Admission is free.

Museums and Historic Sites

Agecroft Hall
4305 Sulgrave Rd. • 353-4241

This Tudor-style manor house, originally built in the 15th century in Lancashire, En-

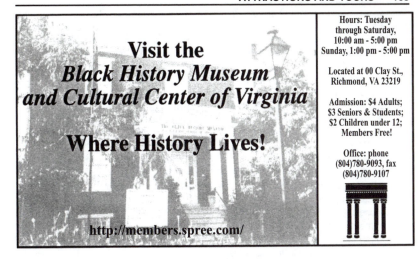
gland, was disassembled and shipped to Richmond in the 1920s to save it from destruction. Period furniture, tapestries, decorative arts and everyday objects of life in 16th- and 17th-century England decorate the interior. Guides offer tours that last about 50 minutes.

"Belly Cheer" is a popular special tour offered daily that includes a discussion of dining and food ways, storage and preparation between 1580 and 1640. Call to find out when the tour is scheduled.

Magnificent gardens surround the hall. You can wander through a garden featuring 17th-century-style plantings, a formal garden, an English Knot Garden, an herb garden, a fragrance garden and a sunken garden, all in a spectacular rolling landscape overlooking the James River. The gardens are especially beautiful from late March until early October. A special spring bulb display with over 5,000 blooms is usually planned for April.

Picnics and pets are not permitted. Admission is $5 for adults; $3 for children ages 6-12; $4.50 for seniors; and children younger than 6 get in free. Admission to the gardens only is half the admission price. If you combine your visit with a trip to the Virginia House next door, you'll receive a combination rate. Group rates are available with advance reservations. Agecroft is open Tuesday through Saturday from 10 AM to 4 PM, and Sunday from 12:30 to 5 PM. It's closed on Mondays.

Beth Ahabah Museum and Archives
1109 W. Franklin St. • 353-2668

This is one of the only Jewish museums in the area. Its archives provide a source for genealogical and historical research on Richmond's Jewish heritage. It also offers changing exhibits on religious and ceremonial objects, holidays and historical events. Trained docents give tours and provide assistance. Parking is available in a lot off Birch Street. Look for the sign. Admission is free with a suggested donation of $3, students and seniors $2. The museum opens Sunday through Thursday at 10 AM and closes at 3 PM. Call for a complete schedule.

Chesterfield County Museum Complex, Chesterfield Historical Society
Chesterfield Courthouse, corner of Krause and Ironbridge Rds. • 748-1026

Take a walking tour of this complex: the Old Courthouse built in 1917; Magnolia Grange, a Federal-style plantation home built in 1822; the Chesterfield County Museum; and the Old Jail. Magnolia Grange and the Chesterfield County Museum charges admission. Entrance to other sites is free or by donation.

Parking is available in front of the Old Court-house and Magnolia Grange. There are several fast-food restaurants nearby, or you can enjoy more relaxed dining at Houlett's Tavern next to Magnolia Grange.

The complex is on Route 10 (Ironbridge Road) at Chesterfield Courthouse near Interstate 95, Route 288 and Chippenham Parkway. Guided tours are available. Library assistants are on duty daily. The buildings are open from 10 AM to 4 PM, Monday through Friday, and from 1 to 4 PM on Sunday.

The Chesterfield County Museum, 6805 W. Krause Road at Chesterfield Courthouse, was built as a replica of the county's Colonial courthouse of 1750. The museum portrays the development of Chesterfield from an agricultural county to a suburban community. Its collections include prehistoric fossils, artifacts from the Indians native to the area, items related to Sir Thomas Dale's English settlement of 1611 and the 18th-century French Hugenot settlers. The museum also presents exhibits portraying the devastation of the Revolutionary and Civil War battles, early schools, churches, a country store, mining and the railroad system. Admission costs $1 for adults, 50¢ for students.

Magnolia Grange, 10020 Ironbridge Road, 796-1479, was named after a circle of magnolia trees that once graced its front lawn. This 1822 Federal-style plantation house was built by William Winfree. Magnolia Grange is noted for its elaborate ceiling medallions and the sophisticated carving on mantels, doorways and windows. It's decorated and furnished according to the style of the 1820s. Tours are offered. Adult admission is $2, seniors $1.50, and students $1.

The Old Courthouse on Ironbridge Road was designed in the Colonial Revival style and was built in 1917 to replace the Colonial Courthouse of 1749. Features include a Roman Doric portico and a domed octagonal belfry. Today it serves as a gift shop and the headquarters of the Chesterfield Historical Society. Visitors may use the research library. A film and changing exhibits on Chesterfield's history are offered for the public. Admission is free.

The Old Jail, also on Ironbridge Road, contains a replica of an old pillory where offenders were exposed to public scorn. Next to the Chesterfield County Museum, the jail was built in 1892 and used for prisoners until 1962. Today it depicts the lives of prisoners during the 1800s and the first half of this century. The Old Jail also presents exhibits of historic police and fire departments. Admission is free.

Edgar Allan Poe Museum
1914-16 E. Main St. • 648-5523

From October 7, 1997, (the anniversary of his death) through January 19, 1998, (his birthday), the Poe Museum celebrates its 75th anniversary with a special exhibit, "In Poe's Own Hand," featuring the first public display of his first edition manuscripts and letters encompassing his entire career. The exhibit will include "Tamerlaine," considered to be the rarest manuscript in American literature, and "Spirits of the Dead," a poem from Alaaraaf.

Each October, the museum sponsors a special Poe Festival with performances, readings and a scholarly symposium at Agecroft Hall. You can also immerse yourself in the macabre world of Poe on Halloween with a candlelight tour of the museum and special readings guaranteed to send shivers down your spine. Special events with 19th-century music, performances, special readings, wine tastings and discussions about 19th-century gardening, medicine and other topics are also offered occasionally throughout the year.

The museum occupies five buildings that open up to enclosed gardens. The Raven Room houses many Poe artifacts. The Old Stone House, built in 1737, is the oldest standing building in the original boundaries of the city. Tours are given every hour. Admission is $6 for adults, $5 for seniors and students. Call for group information. The museum is open Tuesday through Saturday from 10 AM to 5 PM, and Sunday through Monday from noon to 5 PM.

Hanover Courthouse
U.S. 301, Old Court Green • 537-5815

Fifteen miles north of Richmond at Hanover Courthouse, this historic brick courthouse has been in continuous use since it was built in 1735. It was the site of Patrick Henry's first case, Parsons Cause, and is still used today for ceremonial purposes. Free tours are available by appointment only. If you just want to

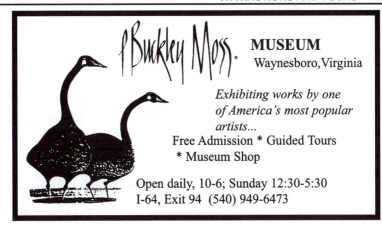

stop by, push a button near the entrance and listen to the recorded message about the history of the building.

Henricus Park/Citie of Henricus
601 Coxendale Rd., Chesterfield County • 706-1340

See the Gardens, Parks and Other Outdoor Attractions section for more information on this historical park.

John Marshall House
818 E. Marshall St. • 648-7998

The great Chief Justice John Marshall built this two-story brick house in downtown Richmond between 1788 and 1790. He lived here until his death in 1835. Now owned by the City of Richmond, the residence has been restored to its original appearance and includes original furnishings and household objects once owned by Marshall. Architecturally, the house combines Federal characteristics with early Georgian elements. Parking is available in metered spaces and nearby public lots. The house is maintained and administered by the Association for the Preservation of Virginia Antiquities. Admission is $3. The house is open from 10 AM to 5 PM, Tuesday through Saturday.

P. Buckley Moss Museum
150 P. Buckley Moss Dr., Waynesboro • (540) 949-6473

Located in Virginia's Shenandoah Valley, the P. Buckley Moss Museum houses a collection of P. Buckley Moss' artwork, spanning the artist's life, including landscapes and some architectural sculptures. This 18,000-square foot building offers resources, exhibitions and programs that examine the artist's cultural and environmental heritage. Guided tours and a museum shop are available. From Richmond, take I-64 W. to Exit 94 and follow the signs. The museum is open Monday through Sunday from 10 AM to 6 PM and on Sundays from 12:30 to 5:30 PM.

Virginia Holocaust Museum
213 Roseneath Rd. • 257-5400

This museum opened in June 1997 as a tribute to Holocaust survivors. Exhibits featuring a family that survived Nazi persecution and immigrated to Richmond, tell the story of the Holocaust and its victims, both the survivors and the deceased. Exhibits and an educational resource center are open to the public Monday through Friday from 9 AM to 5 PM. The museum is open and tours are available on Saturday from 2 to 5 PM, and on Sunday from 12 to 5 PM. Admission is free, but donations are suggested.

Meadow Farm at Crump Park
3400 Mountain Rd., Glen Allen • 672-5100

Open March through early December, Meadow Farm is a 19th-century living-history museum where costumed interpreters re-create life on Dr. John Mosby Sheppard's middle-class farm as it was in the 1860s, just before the outbreak of the Civil War. Unlike many historical attractions, this focuses on the middle class instead of the rich and famous.

You can tour the farmhouse, barn, a 19th-century doctor's office, blacksmith's forge, smokehouse, kitchen, orchard and crop demonstration fields.

Living-history events and reenactments throughout the year create a lot of excitement and activity here on weekends. Events include Sheep to Shawl in April, the Civil War Encampment and Battle in late May, an Old Fashioned Fourth of July, Civil War Days in September, the Harvest Festival in October, and the Yuletide Fest in December.

Formerly the home of Gen. Sheppard Crump, Meadow Farm was donated to Henrico County by his wife, Elizabeth Adam Crump, in 1975.

Changing exhibits focusing on Virginia and Henrico County life are displayed in the orientation center. A video about the farm and a gift shop are also available.

From downtown, take I-95 N. to Interstate 295 W. (Exit 36). Take the Woodman Road S. exit to Mountain Road. Go right and follow the signs. There are plenty of parking spaces. The grounds are open daily most of the year from dawn to dusk. The buildings are open from mid-March through December from noon to 4 PM. The buildings are closed on Monday. Call for information about hours and winter closings. Admission is free.

Money Museum
701 E. Byrd St., Federal Reserve Bank of Richmond • 697-8108

Explore the history of money through items once used for barter such as animal pelts and tobacco, gold and silver bars and certificates. Artifacts related to the production and safekeeping of money are also on display. The museum is on the first floor of the Federal Reserve Bank building and is open Monday through Friday from 9:30 AM to 3:30 PM. It's closed on bank holidays. Admission is free. Appointments are recommended for groups of 20 or more.

Old City Hall
10th and Capitol Sts.

This 1894 Victorian Gothic architectural masterpiece was saved from destruction by the Historic Richmond Foundation. It's now used as an office building. If you are in the area, it's worthwhile to walk through the lobby to see the elaborate interior.

Old Dominion Railway Museum
102 Hull St. • 233-6237

Off the beaten path, near the 14th Street Bridge at the old Hull Street Passenger Station, this museum is housed inside railroad cars while the passenger station is being renovated. You'll find artifacts and photographs related to the history of railroading in Richmond and a small steam locomotive, caboose and baggage car. Guided walking tours of the flood wall are offered on the second Sunday of each month at 2 PM. The museum is open Saturday from 11 AM to 4 PM and Sunday 1 to 4 PM. Tours and admission are free. Group tours are available during the week by appointment.

Children's Museum of Richmond
740 Navy Hill Dr. • 643-KIDO, 788-4949

Kids ages 2 to 12 enjoy coming here to explore and be creative. They can play in a grocery store, doctor's office, ambulance or television news studio. They can try their skills with Computers for Kids, dress in costumes and act out their fantasies on stage. They can even put on a miner's hat and go spelunking in a 40-foot replica of a Virginia limestone cave. In the art studio, children paint, sculpt, make collages and create masterpieces. For more information about the museum, see the listing in the Kidstuff chapter.

The museum is on Navy Hill Drive, formerly known as 6th Street, off Jackson Street near I-95 and Interstate 64 in downtown Richmond. Parking is free. Admission is $3 for children ages 2 through 12, and $4 for adults. Children younger than 2 are admitted free. The museum opens at 9 AM Monday through Friday, at 10 AM on Saturday and at 1 PM on Sunday. It closes at 5 PM during the summer months. The rest of the year, it closes at 1 PM, Tuesday through Friday.

Science Museum of Virginia
2500 W. Broad St. • 367-6552; (800) 659-1727 event line; 36STARS 24-hour skywatch information

The Science Museum of Virginia, in the historic Broad Street Train Station, offers more than 250 hands-on exhibits and participatory programs to encourage visitors to explore the exciting world of science. The museum also offers films projected on a five-story-high domed screen in the Ethyl Corporation IMAX® *Dome* and Planetarium. Planetarium shows are also available. Interactive exhibits feature astronomy, aerospace, chemistry and physics, computers, crystals, electricity and telecommunications. You'll also see one of the world's largest pendulums, suspended from the center of the dome in the rotunda, which demonstrates the rotation of the earth.

In the spring, the museum usually offers a major visiting exhibit such as giant robotic dinosaurs, sea creatures or bears. A variety of special events and activities are offered throughout the year. For more information, see our Kidstuff chapter.

Weekday afternoons and any time in September and January are good times to visit if you want to avoid the crowds. Spring is typically a very busy time with lots of school groups. Allow yourself plenty of time to see everything. You can easily spend half a day here. Lunch is available at the Cosmic Cafe inside the museum. There are several fast-food restaurants nearby, or you can pack a picnic lunch and eat on the grounds. Picnic tables are provided, and there are a few vending machines.

Admission to the exhibit area is $4.50 for seniors, $4 for youths ages 4 to 12 and $5 for adults. With one theater show, admission is $7.50 for seniors, $7 for youths and $8 for adults. The museum opens Monday through Saturday at 9:30 AM, and at 11:30 AM on Sunday. It closes at 5 PM with extended evening hours during the summer. The theater operates on a different schedule. Call for show times.

Scotchtown
Rts. 54 and 685, Hanover County
• 227-3500

One of Virginia's oldest plantations, Scotchtown, was Patrick Henry's home during the Revolutionary War from 1771 to 1778. In western Hanover County about 9 miles west of Ashland, the restored wood-frame Colonial home was built between 1717 and 1719 and is furnished with authentic 18th-century an-

tiques. You can see the kitchen which is in a separate building, the basement of the house that includes a small museum and wine cellar, and the dry well that was used to keep meat and other perishable food fresh. Forty acres of farm and woodland surround the house. Docents conduct tours.

Costumed guides present living history reenactments at special events such as the Scottish Festival and Games in May. Also, during the first full weekend in December, Scotchtown presents candlelight tours of the house, plays and special decorations illustrating Christmas customs of the 18th, 19th and 20th centuries.

This is another great place to take the kids and have a picnic, as some tables and benches are provided. Scotchtown is open April through October. Group tours are available year round. Call for reservations. The Patrick Henry Scotchtown Committee in cooperation with the Association for the Preservation of Virginia Antiquities operates Scotchtown. Scotchtown is open from April through October. It's closed on Mondays and Tuesdays. Hours vary depending on the month. Call for a schedule and admission prices.

St. John's Church
2401 E. Broad St. • 648-5015

Relive Patrick Henry's famous "Give me liberty, or give me death" speech at this historic church in a restored section of Church Hill. The oldest church in the city, St. John's has served a congregation for more than 250 years.

Every Sunday from Memorial Day to Labor Day at 2 PM, actors stage reenactments of the Second Virginia Convention of 1775. The actors portray 11 patriots including George Washington, Thomas Jefferson and, of course, Patrick Henry. All performances are free, but seating is limited, so try to arrive by about 1:30 PM. Costumed interpreters conduct tours and assist visitors.

The graveyard surrounding the church includes the graves of Edgar Allan Poe's mother, George Wythe and several governors. Photographers often find that the sun is a problem since the church faces north; you may want to bring a special lens. Admission is $3 for adults, $2 for seniors, $1 for students ages 7 to 18. Guides offer tours from 10 AM to 3:30 PM Monday through Saturday and on Sunday from

Costumed interpreters are an integral part of many tours throughout Richmond.

3 to 3:30 PM. Ask about Historic Downtown Richmond block tickets for a discount on admission to St. John's Church, the Valentine Museum, the John Marshall House, and the Museum and White House of the Confederacy. See the "Tours" section of the chapter for more information.

State Capitol and Capitol Square
Ninth and Grace Sts. • 698-1788

A free 30-minute tour of the historic capitol building is a favorite among school children and visitors. In the Rotunda you'll see numerous statues, including Virginia's most treasured work of art: the famous statue of George Washington by Jean-Antoine Houdon. Look up, and you'll see the unusual interior dome with skylights that was built about 20 feet below the A-line roof. You'll also see the Old House of Delegates Hall where Aaron Burr was tried for treason in 1807 and the former Senate Chamber where a number of famous paintings are displayed. Built in 1788, the Capitol was the first public building in America built in the Classic Revival style of architecture. Thomas Jefferson influenced the design and secured the services of architect Charles-Louis Clerisseau who modeled the building after the Maison Caree, a Roman Temple built in Nimes, France.

The Executive Mansion, home to Virginia's governors since 1813, is in Capitol Square just east of the Capitol. The Old Bell Tower, built in 1824 for the Virginia Public Guard, is also on the grounds. It's now used as a visitors center. The grounds are always open and include

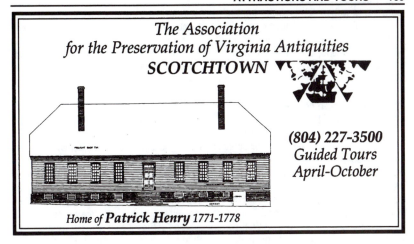

*The Association
for the Preservation of Virginia Antiquities*
SCOTCHTOWN

(804) 227-3500
*Guided Tours
April-October*

Home of **Patrick Henry** *1771-1778*

two spring-fed fountains and numerous statues of famous Virginians. (See our Monuments chapter.) Many people enjoy picnicking here on the grass. During the summer, there's often lunch-hour entertainment in front of the Bell Tower.

If you want to see your representatives at work, visit a session of the General Assembly held for 60 days in even years and for 30 days in odd-numbered years. Sessions begin in mid-January. Space in the galleries limits seating to about 80 to 100 people. To get in, you'll need a free pass from the Capitol hostesses on the second floor in the Rotunda. Just give the pass to the doorman. If the galleries are full, you can watch the sessions on closed-circuit TV in House Room 4 or Senate Room 4. Groups of more than 10 should make a reservation.

Tours are available daily, from 9 AM to 5 PM, March through December, and from 1 to 5 PM on Sundays, December through March.

Tuckahoe Plantation
12601 River Road • 784-5736

Seven miles west of Richmond on River Road you'll find Tuckahoe, considered the finest existing early 18th-century plantation in America. Built by Thomas Randolph in 1712, the grounds include the school where Thomas Jefferson studied.

It's open for tours by appointment only. Admission is $7, or $5.50 for seniors and groups. Admission to the grounds only is $2.

The Valentine Museum
1015 E. Clay St. • 649-0711

This urban-history museum celebrates its centennial year in 1998 and is an excellent place to begin a tour of the city. As the museum of the life and history of Richmond, the Valentine features nationally recognized exhibitions focusing on various aspects of the city's past and its diverse population. A major attraction at the museum is the Valentine's 1812 Wickham House, featuring the nation's only known set of neoclassical wall paintings. Guided tours of the fully restored house are offered hourly, and a museum educator with a rolling history cart filled with hands-on activities gives children a chance to "play with history" in the summer.

The newest exhibit, "From Settlement to Streetcar Suburbs," will open in May 1998 to commemorate the museum's 100th anniversary and showcase its collections, including one of the best costume collections in the nation, examples of decorative arts, industrial arts, paintings, prints, watercolors and photography. The museum also has the most complete library of printed material relating to the city. Changing photo exhibits are displayed several times a year.

In July, the museum throws a block party on Clay Street with live music, food, entertainment, children's activities and street games.

You can enjoy breakfast or lunch in Wickham's Garden Cafe. Free parking is available in a lot behind the museum. Just look for the boot-shaped sign. Group discounts and tours are available. Admission to the house and museum is $5 for adults, $4 for seniors and students, and $3 for children age 7 to 12. Admission is free for children 6 and younger. It's open Monday through Saturday from 10 AM to 5 PM, and Sunday from noon to 5 PM.

Virginia Aviation Museum
5701 Huntsman Rd. • 236-3622

In the Richmond International Airport, this museum, a division of the Science Museum of Virginia, displays an extensive collection of vintage and historically significant aircraft as well as navigation devices and memorabilia dating from 1916 to World War II. You'll also find a World War II diorama with a scale model of ten aerial battles, and exhibits on Women Air Force Service Pilots (WASPS) and Tuskegee Airmen.

In June, the museum presents Flight Day with special activities, planes and children's activities.

Admission to the museum is $5 for adults; $4 for seniors and $3 for children ages 4 to 12. It's open daily from 9:30 AM to 5 PM.

Virginia Fire and Police Museum, Steamer Company No. 5
200 W. Marshall St. • 644-1849

Built in 1849, this is Richmond's only surviving firehouse from the Civil War period, and it's one of the oldest firehouses in the country. The firehouse features Italianate architecture and the museum exhibits hand-drawn, horse-drawn and early motorized firefighting apparatus and equipment dating back to the 1770s, as well as many pieces of police memorabilia. The museum also offers changing exhibits about topics such as famous Richmond fires including the burning of the city in 1865, and the Jefferson Hotel fire, plus interesting and historical aspects of firefighting and police work such as the role of African-Americans on the police force and the use of horses. The museum also maintains a photo and archive collection dating to the mid-19th century.

Best known for its fire safety and injury prevention programs, the museum staff trains more than 100,000 school children in fire safety here each year.

Open Tuesday through Friday from 10 AM to 4 PM, and weekends by appointment only.

Admission is $2 for adults; $1.50 for seniors; $1 for students age 8 to 18; and free for children ages 7 and younger. Police and fire personnel and their families are admitted free. The facility may be rented for parties, meetings and other occasions.

The Museum of Virginia History
428 N. Boulevard • 358-4901

The Museum of Virginia History was built in 1914 as a memorial to Confederate soldiers who died during the Civil War. Today, it houses the world's largest and most comprehensive collection of Virginia history. Here, you can see changing and permanent exhibits depicting and interpreting the state's history.

One of the museum's major exhibits, "The Story of Virginia, the American Experience," will continue to be open until April 1988. It will be expanded and reinterpreted and re-opened in a larger exhibit space in the fall of 1988. Special features of the exhibit include an orientation video narrated by Roger Mudd, drawers for children filled with "please touch" items, George Washington's diary from his first year as President, an 1830s Conestoga wagon and other significant artifacts.

Other long term exhibits include "Arming the Confederacy," the world's largest collection of Confederate-manufactured weaponry and Civil War objects such as rifles, carbines, muskets, pistols, dirks, belt buckles, buttons and more. The museum also has the largest portrait collection in the South, and significant photography archives.

For a full day of art, history and science, combine a visit here with a trip to the Virginia Museum of Fine Arts next door, and the Science Museum of Virginia on nearby W. Broad Street. Parking is available in front of and behind the building or on the street. Admission is $4 for adults, $2 for students and children, $3 for seniors. The museum is open Monday through Saturday from 10 AM to 5 PM, and Sunday from 1 to 5 PM. The library is closed on Sundays.

Virginia House, "An American Country Place"
4301 Sulgrave Rd. • 353-4251

The original materials used to build this beautifully reconstructed English manor home date back to 1124. This castle-like home next to Agecroft Hall in Windsor Farms is furnished with antiques and tapestries. Breathtakingly beautiful gardens slope down toward the river. Owned and operated by the Virginia Historical Society, the house is open daily except Monday. The society usually plans a major spring bulb display for April, and they offer tours.

Admission is $4 for adults, $2 for students and children ages 6 to 12, and $3 for adults older than 55. Admission to the garden is free. It's open Friday through Saturday from 10 AM to 4 PM, and Sunday from 12:30 to 5 PM.

Virginia Museum of Fine Arts
2800 Grove Ave. • 367-0844; 367-0859 tours and group visits

This museum presents a panorama of world art from ancient times to the present and has gained an international reputation for its collections. Outstanding features include one of the nation's leading collections of the art of India, Nepal and Tibet; the Lewis collections of American paintings since World War II; art nouveau and art deco objects; a collection of Easter eggs and objects created by master jeweler Peter Carl Faberg; Goya's portrait of Gen. Nicolas Guye; a rare marble statue of Caligula; Monet's Irises by the Pond; and the Mellon collections of British sporting art and French impressionist and post-impressionist art.

While you're here, you can have lunch in the Arts Cafe or on the patio. And, be sure to browse through the gift shop's extensive selection of gifts, books and crafts. The museum also offers many wonderful programs and classes for all ages. For more information about the museum, see our chapter on The Arts. Admission is free; a $4 donation is suggested. The museum is open Tuesday through Sunday from 11 AM to 5 PM. It's open until 8 PM on Thursdays, and closed on Mondays.

Wilton House Museum
215 S. Wilton Rd. • 282-5936

At this 18th-century plantation house, you can experience the elegance of Colonial architecture and interiors and learn about the daily struggle for survival faced by the forbearers of our country.

Perched on a bluff overlooking the James River, the house is one of the finest examples of the early Georgian style as built in Virginia. The interior paneling is especially noteworthy, and there's a spectacular view of the James River Gorge from the gardens. Bird watchers should keep an eye out for the bald eagles that are frequently sighted here. Since Wilton House is off the beaten path, trained docents conduct tours as visitors arrive so you won't have to wait for a tour. Wilton Road is south of the 5400 block of Cary Street. Admission is $5 for adults, $4 for seniors and students. Children younger than 6 get in free. Group rates are available. The house is open Tuesday through Saturday from 10 AM to 4:30 PM, and Sunday from 1:30 to 4:30 PM.

Gardens, Parks and Other Outdoor Attractions

City Hall Observation Deck
Ninth and Broad Sts. • 780-5990

The top-floor skydeck of City Hall offers one of the best panoramic views of the city and the James River. Perched 19 floors above the ground, the deck is open daily from 9 AM to 8 PM, and it's free.

Farmer's Market
17th and Main Sts.

You'll find pepper strings, onion braids and some of the freshest fruit and produce in town at this colorful, open market in Shockoe Bottom. Local farmers have sold their produce here for more than 200 years. The mar-

---

INSIDERS' TIP

If you're willing to take your chances on getting a last-minute hotel room, reservations and discounts on hotel accommodations in the Richmond area for the same day are available through all of the Richmond-area visitors centers for walk-in customers.

ket is now covered with a roof, and signs marking the historic district have been erected. The market is open every day, except Sunday, all year.

Henricus Park/Citie of Henricus
601 Coxendale Rd., Chesterfield County • 706-1340

Development of the partial reproduction of the Citie of Henricus, a 1600s town on the James River in Chesterfield County, is beginning to take shape. Henricus, now known as Farrar's Island, was established by Sir Thomas Dale in 1611 when the London Company sought a better location than Jamestown for its colony. The second English settlement in America, Henricus was wiped out in 1622 by an Indian massacre. The site now includes a visitors center decorated with 11 flags that have flown over Henricus, a palisade with watchtowers, a storehouse, a necessary building and commemorative monuments. Future development plans include the construction of a replica of what is believed to be the nation's first hospital.

A 2.5-mile round-trip hiking trail through Henricus Historical Park offers spectacular views of the river, and commemorative markers relate interesting tidbits of history. The trail is well-shaded, and there are plenty of benches for resting or picnicking. Visitors may also explore the adjoining Dutch Gap Conservation Area, an 805-acre wildlife area with beaver, deer, wild turkeys and bass fishing. Interpretive hikes are available by appointment. Call 706-1341.

On Citie of Henricus Publick Day, celebrated on the third Sunday in September each year, the park sponsors a historic re-enactment of the lives of the settlers, a 17th-century Church of England morning prayer service, games, food and tours. Old-fashioned games such as hoop-rolling, bowling, stilt-walking and tree-stump checkers take you back to a simpler time. Visitors will also enjoy Indian storytelling and puppet shows, and they can try their skill at historic activities such as candle-making or building a wattle-and-daub hut with a thatched roof.

To get there from Route 10, take Old Stage Road and follow and signs to Dutch Gap Landing at the end of Coxendale Road. Admission is free.

Lewis Ginter Botanical Garden
1800 Lakeside Ave. • 262-9887

Garden and nature lovers will delight at the beauty of this botanical garden where thousands of plant species are artfully arranged across 80 acres to provide spectacular displays throughout the year. Lewis Ginter Botanical Garden is known for its extensive collection of daffodils, daylilies, rhododendrons and azaleas. You'll also enjoy seasonal floral displays and a cottage garden planted with herbs and species roses surrounding Bloemendaal, a charming Victorian manor house that now serves as a visitor center, gift shop and staff office. Originally built in 1888 as a bicycle club, the home was expanded in 1901 and used as a children's hospital until it became a residence in 1906. Major Lewis Ginter's niece, Grace Arents, lived here until she died in 1928.

A major effort to further develop the garden began several years ago and is ongoing. Construction of the Anne Holt Massey Quadrant, a greenhouse complex, is underway, and the E. Claiborne Robins Visitors Center opened in 1999. Other improvements completed during the past few years include a new lake in front of the house that creates a dramatic vista and the Henry M. Flagler Perennial Garden which features three acres of perennials in a garden masterfully choreographed to provide displays of color throughout the year. Visitors will enjoy strolling through the series of garden "rooms" which comprise the Flagler garden. A stone pavilion at one end of the display's central lawn is used for outdoor concerts and performances. The new Lucy Payne Minor

---

INSIDERS' TIP

Take your mother for a stroll through the magnificent gardens of Agecroft Hall and the Virginia House overlooking the James River during the annual Mother's Day Open House. (Admission to the gardens is free.)

Memorial Garden offers a gazebo with a charming display of daffodils, daylilies, a cryptomeria and a study garden of lilies.

Other development efforts include the Martha and Reed West Island Garden in the lagoon in front of the Tea House planted with Venus's flytraps, pitcher and bog plants; and a children's garden area planted with vegetables and flowers from Asia, Africa, and North and South America. Interactive hands-on planting activities and programs are offered.

Long-range plans call for the development of several glass conservatories and houses, a garden, an English woodland garden along the lake and a water garden in and around the lake and lagoon.

Lewis Ginter Botanical Gardens offers a variety of workshops, basic gardening classes, lectures, tours and everything from concerts to camps for kids. Some of the most popular events here include the annual Mother's Day Concert featuring live music, and the garden fair and plant sale held in the fall and spring. The annual Gardenfest of Lights in December offers a serene antidote to the stress of the holiday season.

Surrounded by an Oriental garden, the Japanese-style Lora and Claiborne Robins Tea House (see our Restaurants chapter) serves lunch throughout the year and dinner by reservation during special events. Lunch is also available at the Wheel Club Cafe, April through October.

Allow yourself about an hour for a self-guided tour through the gardens, and wear good walking shoes for grassy and pebbled paths. Maps and information are available at the admissions booth. Guided tours for groups are available in the fall and spring by appointment. General admission costs $5 for adults, $4 for seniors and $3 for children age 2 to 12. Admission is free for members. The house, Tea House, and visitors center may be rented for special occasions. The garden is open from 9 AM to 4 PM Tuesday through Saturday. It stays open until 8 PM on Sundays and Mondays.

Maymont
1700 Hampton St. • 358-7166

With its Romanesque house, arboretum with mature exotic trees, formal Italian garden, Japanese garden, carriage rides, nature center, aviary, native Virginia animal habitats and children's farm, Maymont is without question one of our most favorite places in the city. Established over a century ago, this 100-acre Victorian estate has something that will appeal to everyone.

History, architecture and decorative-art enthusiasts will be impressed by the mansion's original contents. It was once owned by the Dooleys, a wealthy couple that collected objects from all over the world. Guided 30-minute tours of the house are offered in the afternoon until 4:30 PM.

Nature and animal enthusiasts will enjoy the nature center, the children's farm, the bison, whitetail and sika deer, bears, birds of prey, aviary and other wildlife habitats. Arborists, strollers, walkers and picnickers will enjoy the landscaped grounds, walking paths and the variety of beautiful old shade trees.

You can even ride in a turn-of-the-century horse-drawn carriage on weekends from May to November. A ten-minute ride around the Maymont House costs $3 for adults and $2 for children under age 12. Longer carriage rides around the estate may be booked in advance by reservation.

Tram tours of the gardens are also offered on weekends in April and November, and Wednesday through Sunday from May through October. The ride takes about 45 minutes to an hour and costs $2 for adults and $1 for children. Members ride free. Self-guided walking-tour information is available at the gift shop. In addition, the staff offers special garden tours and group tours, but you'll need to make reservations at least two weeks in advance.

Maymont is currently constructing a new nature and visitors center which is expected to open by summer 1999.

Maymont is in the middle of the city on the north bank of the James River, just east of the Boulevard Bridge and south of Byrd Park. If you're interested in the house tour, carriages, Nature Center, arboretum, Italian or Japanese gardens, use the Hampton Street entrance. If you want to see the children's farm and animal habitats, use the Spottswood entrance.

Weather permitting, food and drink concession are open spring, summer and fall. Bicycles, pets, alcohol, kites and automobiles are not allowed in the park. Dress comfortably for walking, as the terrain is hilly and some of the slopes are quite steep.

The grounds are always open from 10 AM to 5 PM. It closes later in the evening from April through October. The mansion, emporium, Nature Center, barn and gift shop are closed on Monday. Admission is free, but a $3 donation is suggested for the house tour. Additional fees are charged for carriage and tram rides. Maymont facilities may be rented for special events, birthday parties and corporate outings.

Three Lakes Nature Center and Aquarium
400 Sausiluta Dr. • 652-FISH, 24-hour info; 261-8230

Three Lakes Nature Center features a 50,000-gallon outdoor aquarium, one of the largest in Central Virginia, a Nature Center and a 127-acre park where plant, fish, bird and animal life abound. You can stroll around a deck and view the aquarium from above, or you can go below for an underwater view of the same kinds of fish that live in the park's lakes, including largemouth bass, bluegill, redear sunfish and black crappie.

The upper level of the Nature Center is filled with special exhibits focusing on the aquarium, lakes, wetlands, animal life and the forest. Visitors learn about the environment and the plants and animals that live here as well as how to maintain and preserve them. Classes, workshops and special programs are also available.

In addition to the Nature Center, this 127-acre park offers fishing, hiking, two picnic shelters, play equipment and an observation deck.

Three Lakes Park is off Wilkinson Road at Sausiluta Drive. Call for more information or to schedule group tours. The nature center is closed on Mondays. The hours vary throughout the year, but it is always open from noon to 5 PM Saturdays and Sundays.

Historic Cemeteries

Hollywood Cemetery
Albemarle and Cherry Sts.

This historic graveyard features numerous statues, monuments and the graves of U.S. Presidents James Monroe and John Tyler, Confederate President Jefferson Davis, Confederate General J.E.B. Stuart and 1,800 Confederate soldiers. Richmond Discoveries offers a guided walking tour here every Sunday. See their listing in this chapter under Tours.

Oakwood Cemetery
3101 Nine Mile Rd.

This is the final burial place for 16,000 Confederate soldiers. It was also the burial site for Union Colonel Ulrich Dahlgren until his father sent President Jefferson Davis $100 in gold to have his son's body sent home for final burial.

Shockoe Cemetery
Hospital St.

This is one of the oldest municipal cemeteries in the nation. Here, you can see the graves of Chief Justice John Marshall, Revolutionary War hero Peter Francisco, Elizabeth Van Lew, a Union spy who lived in Richmond during the Civil War and John and Francis Allan, Edgar Allan Poe's foster parents.

Riverfront Attractions

By the year 2000, San Antonio's River Walk is expected to pale in comparison to what developers have planned for Richmond's Riverfront area and canal walk. A $52 million project to develop 32 acres of the wild and beautiful riverfront along the James River from Fifth to 17th streets, and to restore the Kanawha and Haxall canals and a major turning basin is expected to be completed in the spring of 1999. Bateau rides along the canals are expected to be offered, and the turning

---

INSIDERS' TIP

Experience the thrill of a giant screen format film on the five-story-high domed theater at the Science Museum of Virginia. You'll feel like you've been on a ride at an amusement park.

basin will eventually be surrounded by restaurants, shops and boutiques. Meanwhile, here are some attractions and activities that provide opportunities for visitors to enjoy the scenery, excitement, wildlife and history of the James, from the safety of walkways along the shores or from the vantage point of a canoe, kayak, raft or river boat.

Annabel Lee
4400 E. Main St., Intermediate Terminal
• 644-5700

This 350-passenger paddlewheel river boat replica is the only showboat in town. Departing from the Intermediate Terminal, the Annabel Lee offers dining, entertainment and narrated tours of historical points of interest along the James River east of Richmond. Meals are served buffet-style and two full-service bars are available. The lunch cruise and the dinner cruise travel about 10 miles down river. The trip features live music, entertainment and narrated commentary about the river. On Tuesdays, the plantation-brunch cruise travels about 25 miles and docks at Westover Plantation. (See our write-up in the "Tours" section of this chapter.) The cruise includes tours of the gardens at Westover and full tours of Berkeley and Evelynton plantations. You return by motor coach. During the summer, party cruises are offered some weekend nights from midnight until 2 AM and include appetizers, a DJ or live band and dancing. People usually wear nice-casual to dressy attire for evening cruises. In the afternoons, cruisers dress more casually in sports clothes. Be sure to wear comfortable walking shoes for the plantation cruise and tours.

She sails rain or shine, and reservations are required. To make sure you get a ticket that suits your schedule, call about 30 days in advance. Occasionally you may be able to buy a ticket the day of the cruise if space is available. You may pick up your boarding pass at the ticket booth and begin boarding about 30 minutes before departure time. Free parking is available at the pier. The Annabel Lee has two fully enclosed climate-controlled decks and an open Starlite Deck. Chartered trips are available for weddings, parties, corporate outings, school groups and special events. Ticket prices vary depending on the trip and the meals involved. For lunch, adult tickets begin at $22.95, and children's tickets begin at $10.65. For dinner, adult tickets begin at $29.95, and children's tickets begin at $16.95. Group rates for 24 or more people are available.

Canal Walk
10th and Bank Sts.

This paved walkway along the James River begins at 10th and Bank streets and ends at the James River Plaza. Information provided by historic markers and kiosks tells the history of the riverfront. An additional half-mile riverfront pedestrian path is also available along Tredegar Street from Seventh Street west to the Lee Bridge.

Great Shiplocks Canal Park
Dock and Pear Sts.

This is the site of the lowest of the Kanawha Canal Locks. The stone lock was completed in 1854. An interpretive display provides visitor information.

James River and Kanawha Canal
12th and Byrd Sts.

Conceived by George Washington as a way to open trade with land to the west, the Kanawha Canal was the first commercial canal system in North America. Washington oversaw the initial construction of the project. The canal opened in 1790 between Richmond and Westham. A narrated slide presentation tells the canal's story to visitors.

Richmond Raft Company
4400 E. Main St. • 222-7238;
(800) 540-7238

"Get set to get wet . . . you'll get soaked." That's their slogan, and this is definitely one of the most exciting and fun ways to explore the James River. This full-service outfitter offers various scenic trips on the Falls of the James through the center of the city. It's the only urban whitewater run in the country. You don't have to be experienced — each trip begins with an orientation session and safety instructions. All equipment is provided, and your guide will teach you along the way. Up to six people plus a guide may travel in each raft.

Several trips are available. Richmond Raft

Company offers the Falls of the James paddle raft excursions April through October. The full trip takes about six hours and includes the upper and lower sections of the river. Lunch is provided. The Lower Section is a shorter trip that lasts about three hours and includes the lower section of the river.

Moderate Class IV rapids on these trips always provide exciting moments, but the fastest rides are in the spring when water levels are typically at their highest. The summer months are warmer and more conducive to swimming and sunning along the way, and the fall is the most scenic time.

The Falls of the James and the Lower Section trips are not recommended for children younger than 12. Younger children are encouraged to try the Upper Section trip which involves milder Class I and II rapids, more swimming and scenic rafting. Children must be at least 3 feet tall or weigh at least 60 pounds to participate. This trip lasts about three to four hours and is popular with youth groups and birthday parties. Trip costs range from $35 to $50. Discounts are available for groups of 18 or more. Reservations are required. For weekdays, call about a week in advance. For weekends call about two weeks ahead.

Paramount's Kings Dominion

Rt. 30 and I-95, Doswell • 876-5000

If you love rides and getting wet, this is the place to go. Paramount's Kings Dominion is a 400-acre family entertainment park with seven different theme areas "where the magic of the movies meets the thrills of a lifetime."

The new attraction for 1999 is WaterWorks, a 9-acre addition to the already impressive water park. The two biggest features are Big Wave Bay, a 650,000-gallon wave pool, and Surf City Splash House, a water-powered funhouse for children and adults alike. These two additions complement 15 other attractions at the water park, including slides, tube rides and a river raft ride.

Another new feature at Kings Dominion is Volcano, The Blast Coaster, which debuted at

the end of the 1998 season. The world's fastest suspended roller coaster, Volcano speeds up to 70 miles per hour and faces an 80-foot drop.

Other attractions include Kidzville a town built just for kids. Kidzville features a major new interactive play area, a kiddie coaster and a town square, plus many of the popular Hanna Barbera rides and attractions that visitors have loved for years. At the Kidz Construction Company, kids can scramble through a cement mixer and explore a real dump truck with a web crawl and a cargo of giant suspended balls. They can also twist and slide through a crane tower. Another new attraction here is the Taxi Jam Coaster. Designed to be a child's first coaster, this ride is themed as a mini speed chase with police cars chasing taxis through tunnels.

Thrill seekers won't want to miss the Xtreme Skyflyer and the award-winning roller coaster, The Outer Limits: Flight of Fear. Those daring enough to reserve a flight on the Xtreme Skyflyer are strapped into a flight suit and raised to a height of 152 feet. You pull on a parachute-type ripcord and plummet to the ground in a free fall, then you swoop and soar above the ground reaching speeds of over 60 mph. In the Flight of Fear, you're catapulted in a 24-passenger train to a speed of 53 mph within four seconds. The ride features numerous vertical and horizontal turns in complete darkness.

Nickelodeon Splat City offers wild, messy, hands-on entertainment in a 3-acre area with lots of Green Slime. Everyone can participate in the Mega Mess-a-Mania game show featuring new stunts and challenges from Double Dare, What Would You Do? and other hit Nickelodeon game shows. There's a "Guts"-style obstacle course for kids, a Green Slime maze and a Gak kitchen for making fresh gooey batches of the stuff.

In Wayne's World, an "excellent" theme area, guests can experience the thrilling Hurler roller coaster that exceeds speeds of 50 mph and includes four high-speed turns. Wayne's World visitors will feel like they're actually on the Hollywood set of the Wayne's World films, beginning with a realistic streetscape that recreates Wayne and Garth's hometown and a replica of the set for Wayne's Basement Stu-

Top 10 Attractions in the Richmond Area

1. Paramount's Kings Dominion (more than 2 million)
2. Virginia Museum of Fine Arts (415,145)
3. Maymont (400,000)
4. Science Museum of Virginia (315,544)
5. Virginia State Capitol (164,719)
6. Museum of the Confederacy (70,768)
7. Lewis Ginter Botanical Garden (67,557)
8. Museum of Virginia History/Virginia House (54,843)
9. Three Lakes Nature Center and Aquarium (49,580)
10. Richmond Children's Museum (47,983)

Close-up

(This ranking is based on attendance figures reported by the attractions from January to December 1996. Source: Metro Richmond Convention and Visitors Bureau.)

Photo: Paramount Parks Inc.

Paramount's Kings Dominion is the No. 1 attraction in the area (based on attendance).

dio. There's also Stan Mikita's Restaurant and the Rock Shop music store.

Visitors can also experience the thrill of high-speed professional auto racing at the Days of Thunder racing simulator; dine at Busytown Cafe with characters from Richard Scarry stories; and walk around with movie characters such as Wayne and Garth, Klingons, Vulcans, Romulans and Bajorans, along with Hollywood-style characters and well-known Hanna-Barbera characters.

Throughout the park, you'll find more than 40 rides, including seven world-class roller coasters. Four popular ones are the Shockwave, a stand-up roller coaster; the Anaconda, a looping ride with an underwater tunnel; the Grizzly, a ferocious wooden roller coaster; and the Rebel Yell, a twin-racing roller coaster with one train traveling forward and one train traveling backward. There's also the Scooby Doo Coaster in Hanna-Barbera Land for younger children. Other popular attractions include the White Water Canyon raft ride, the 330-foot replica of the Eiffel Tower and the Hurricane Reef water park with 6 acres of exciting water slides, meandering raft rides, splash areas and wading pools for little ones.

When you need a break from the rides, you can see live performances such as the new Retro-ACTIVE contemporary music/dance spectacular, karaoke performers and animal shows. The park also has evening fireworks shows, musical street parties and concerts.

Arrive early and spend the day. Many people pack a picnic lunch and eat in the park areas just outside the entrance. There's a lot of walking, and it gets hot, so dress comfortably. Season passes for individuals and families are a bargain for locals who like to come here often.

The park is about a 30-minute drive north of Richmond. Look for the well-marked exit off Interstate 95. Discount tickets are offered by

FYI

Unless otherwise noted, the area code for all phone numbers listed in this chapter is 804.

many companies and employers in the area. Just ask at work and watch the ads. Admission is $24.99 for ages 3 to 6; $33.99 for ages 7 and older; and $28.99 for seniors. Children age 2 and younger get in for free. Season passes may be purchased by calling (800) 553-7277.

The park is open daily from Memorial Day weekend through Labor Day. It's open only on weekends from the end of March until Memorial Day, and from Labor Day until October. The park is closed a few days each season for special events, so it's best to call first to make sure it's open the day you plan to visit.

Tours

Plantation Cruise, Annabel Lee
4400 E. Main St. • 644-5700

Combine a cruise on the James River with a visit to the Plantation Row and enjoy dinner or lunch on Richmond's only paddlewheel showboat. The morning cruise includes lunch aboard the Annabel Lee while you cruise down the James for tours of the Westover gardens, and Berkeley and Evelynton plantations. You return to Richmond by motor coach. The evening tour begins with a motor coach ride to Sherwood Forest and Berkeley plantations. Then you'll board the Annabel Lee at Westover, for a return trip dinner cruise back to Richmond. These tours are available only on Tuesdays, April through October. Tickets for lunch are $49.95 for adults, $35 for children under 13. Tickets for dinner are $58.95 for adults and $35 for children under 13.

Historic Downtown Richmond Ticket
1015 E. Clay St., The Valentine Museum • 780-0107

A great bargain for locals and visitors who are in town for more than a day, this block

---

INSIDERS' TIP

Spend an evening listening to free live music during the Innsbrook After Hours outdoor concert series at the Innsbrook Pavilion from April to mid-September.

The third week in October is the ideal time to glimpse the Japanese maple color in the Japanese Garden at Maymont.

ticket includes admission to and information about more than three dozen historic homes, hotels, churches, museums and buildings throughout the historic downtown area. Tickets may be purchased from all three Richmond Visitors Centers, including the Bell Tower at Capitol Square. They're also available from Historic Richmond Tours, the Black History Museum, the Virginia Fire and Police Museum, the John Marshall House, the Library of Virginia's Library Shop, the Museum of the Confederacy, the Valentine Museum, St. John's Church, None Such Place and the Edgar Allan Poe Museum, as well as many area hotels.

Offered for the first time in 1997, this ticket brings together a diverse assortment of historic and interesting sites in Monroe Park, Jackson Ward, Court End, Shockhoe Bottom, Church Hill and the Riverfront. Some charge admission, some are free, some have tours and some don't. Some you may simply want to take note of as you drive or walk by. At others, you'll want to allow an hour or more for tours and exhibit gazing. The ticket also includes a Sunday walking tour offered by Historic Richmond Tours. Call for more information about locations and schedules.

Block tickets cost $15 and are valid for 30 days. Kids under age 6 are admitted free.

Historic Richmond Tours
707-A E. Franklin St. • 780-0107

This tour group offers general and themed walking and riding tours of the city. The "Old Richmond Today" tour is offered daily and includes historic sites and highlights along the Boulevard and Monument Avenue, historic neighborhoods and Capitol Square. The tour lasts about two hours and 15 minutes. They'll pick you up at major hotels and at the Robin Hood Road Visitors Center. Call for reservations. The cost is $16 and $13 for students.

Historic Richmond Tours also offers themed tours including the Civil War Battle-fields, the canal system, historic Church Hill and Hollywood Cemetery. Reservations are required. Step-on guides, meeting and convention services are also available.

Living History Associates
2101 E. Main St. • 788-1493

Skilled interpreters in modern or authentic historical clothing help bring history to life for a variety of tours and events. The staff includes professional historians, teachers, museum staff members, writers, musicians, historical interpreters and others who have a love for history and know how to make it interesting. These are the people you see at special museum events and in advertisements. They offer walking tours, private tours, color guards with fife and drums and other living-history entertainment for schools, special events, children's programs, dinners, lectures and more. Step-on motor coach guide service and other convention and tour services are also available, including arrangements for lodging, meals and transportation. Activities and programs can be custom designed to meet your needs. Make reservations and special requests as far in advance as possible. Location and technical advice for filmmakers is also available.

National Railway Historical Society, Old Dominion Chapter
102 Hull St. • 231-4324

Climb aboard an antique diesel train and take a 17-mile ride on the Buckingham Branch from Dillwyn, Virginia, to the James River at Bremo. Offered only a few times a year on Saturdays in the spring and the fall, the trip takes you through scenic rural countryside and ends on a bridge crossing the James River. The train includes two antique coaches built in the '20s, and two open-air coaches.

There's also a special Santa train ride in December where kids have a chance to talk to the jolly old fella during the trip. About 200 seats are available and they sell out fast, so

---

INSIDERS' TIP

Movies filmed in Richmond include *Day of the Jackal*, *G.I. Jane*, *Kilronan*, *First Kid*, *The Shadow Conspiracy*, *Major Payne*, *Foreign Student*, *Lassie*, *Dave*, *Trading Moms*, *Doc Hollywood*, *Love Field*, *True Colors*, *Toy Soldiers* and *Navy Seals*.

Capital One –
Everything You're
Looking for in a Career...
And More!

Apply Now for:
Front Line Managers
Floor Supervisors

Our Outstanding
Benefits include:

Full medical, eye and dental
coverage from day one

Eligibility for three weeks
of vacation your first full
calendar year

A 401(k) savings plan with
company contributions up
to 9%

A discounted associate stock
purchase plan

Tuition reimbursement
up to 100%

Assistance finding and
paying for day care

A business casual dress code

And much more!

Looking to make a difference?

At Capital One, you can! We're looking for Front Line Managers and Floor
Supervisors with previous management experience who enjoy a fast-paced, high-
tech setting and who seek intellectual and analytical challenges. You should be flexible with proven leadership skills, good interpersonal skills, the ability to meet dead-
lines and manage multiple tasks.

Candidates interested in working in our
Richmond/ West End locations, please
send or fax resume to:
Capital One/Attn: 12037-0210
11011 West Broad Street
Glen Allen, VA 23060
Fax: 804-935-7877

Candidates interested in working in
our Chester office, please send or fax
resume to:
Capital One/Attn: 12040-0177
701 Liberty Way/Chester, VA 23836
Fax: 804-787-7019

Visit our website: www.capitalone.com

Capital One is an equal opportunity employer
committed to diversity in the workplace.
We promote a drug-free work environment.

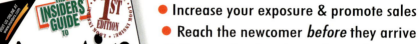

be sure to call at least a month in advance. Tickets are $16 for adults and $9 for children ages 2 to 12. An optional box lunch is available for an additional $6. Trips are sponsored by the Old Dominion Chapter of the National Railway Historical Society. Call for information about upcoming trips and schedules.

Richmond Discoveries Inc.
1701 Williamsburg Rd. • 222-8595

This company offers regularly scheduled guided walking tours of city areas on a variety of themes and custom tours for groups and buses. They specialize in Civil War tours, and guides wear costumes on request.

From March through October, you can join a walking tour of Hollywood Cemetery the first Sunday of each month at 2 PM and every Saturday at 10 AM. There's also a tour themed around the Civil War on Sundays in the spring and fall. Reservations for these tours are not necessary. Call to find out locations and times. Families are encouraged to participate. The cost for adults is $5. There is no charge for children accompanied by an adult.

Richmond Discoveries is the group that sponsors the annual Memorial Day Heritage Weekend and the commemorative parade that goes down Monument Avenue to Hollywood Cemetery.

Winning Tours
1831 Westwood Ave. • 358-6666

This company offers a variety of guide services and tours for groups and individuals. Regular tours are offered each Monday to Williamsburg.

Bus Tours

The following local companies provide charter-group bus service and touring arrangements for attractions in the area and to other nearby destinations.

• James River Bus Company, 915 N. Allen Ave., 321-7661

• Tourtime America, 5115 Commerce Rd., 275-0300

• Virginia Coach Line, 3016 Peebles St., 644-2901

• Winn Bus Lines, 1831 Westwood Avenue, 358-6666

Major Event Facilities

The Richmond Department of Parks and Recreation operates Richmond's Landmark Theater, the Coliseum, Farmer's Market, Richmond Centre for Conventions and Exhibitions and the Arthur Ashe Jr. Athletic Center. Call 780-5733 for more information.

Richmond Coliseum
601 E. Leigh St. • 780-4970

This arena-style facility at Seventh and Leigh streets in downtown seats more than 12,000 spectators and is frequently used for sporting events and music concerts. As home of the Richmond Renegades, the Coliseum's main floor can be converted into an ice rink. Public skating is usually offered following afternoon games.

The Richmond Centre for Conventions and Exhibitions
Fifth and Marshall Sts. • 783-7300

You can rent the entire facility or just a meeting room at the Richmond Centre. The Centre is within walking distance of the Coliseum and major hotels.

Richmond's Landmark Theater
6 N. Laurel St. • 780-4213

In the Fan, Richmond's Landmark Theater, formerly known as The Mosque, seats 3,562 and has one of the most popular stages in the area for music and theatrical performances. It also has a Grand Ballroom and smaller rooms available for rent. The city recently spent about $6 million refurbishing and restoring the auditorium to its original appearance, and it added other improvements including a new sound system, seating and lobby renovations.

Arthur Ashe Jr. Athletic Center
3001 N. Boulevard • 780-6131

This athletic center seats 6,200 spectators and is available for sports events, dances and other functions.

It is not surprising that "On to Richmond!" became the rallying cry of Union troops. One-fourth of the Civil War's battles and 60 percent of its casualties occurred within a 75-mile radius of the city.

The Civil War

Richmond in 1860 was sympathetic to the Confederacy but overwhelmingly opposed to secession. Virginia's governor, a strong Unionist, urged a national convention to calm mounting intersectional animosities. Even the decision by seven Deep South states to leave the Union and the firing on Fort Sumter did not sway Virginia's position. Meeting in Richmond, the Virginia General Assembly issued an invitation to the then 34 states of the Union to attend a peace conference in Washington; simultaneously, a delegation of Virginians was sent to meet with President Lincoln in hopes of averting the looming catastrophe.

But public opinion shifted radically on April 15, 1861, when President Lincoln called for 75,000 volunteers, 8,000 of them from Virginia, to quell the rebellion in the Deep South. Delegates who just a few days earlier had voted 88 to 45 against secession now voted 88 to 55 in favor of it. When a statewide referendum was held on the action the following month, the vote was 4-to-1 for secession, with only four Richmonders voting against it.

Richmond moved quickly to a war footing. It became the principal training, hospital, armament and munitions center for the new Confederacy as well as its capital city. Young men from all over the South came to train under the supervision of Robert E. Lee, a former U.S. Army colonel who had just declined an offer to command the Northern armies, a man who owned not a single slave, but a man who could not turn his back on his native Virginia.

Belle Isle, under today's Lee Bridge, became an overcrowded prison camp for Union enlisted men. A warehouse and ship chandlery at 20th and E. Cary streets was hastily converted into a prison for Federal officers — the infamous Libby Prison. The Tredegar Iron Works at the foot of 7th Street and local arsenals and armories turned out artillery, muskets, ammunition, mines, railroad iron, plate for ironclads and other material needed to wage battle on land and sea.

It is not surprising, then, that "On to Richmond!" became the rallying cry of Union troops, with the city their primary objective for four years, or that one-fourth of the Civil War's battles and 60 percent of its casualties occurred within a 75-mile radius of the city.

Seven military drives were hurled against the beleaguered city. Two, Gen. George McClellan's Peninsula Campaign of 1862 and Gen. Ulysses S. Grant's devastating assault in 1864, brought Union troops within sight of the Capitol. Richmonders became accustomed to the "eternal cannonade" as guns on nearby front lines blasted away night and day.

Richmond-area Civil War battlefields and sites — including Cold Harbor where 7,000 Federal troops fell in a hailstorm of bullets in 30 minutes — abound. A good way to become more familiar with this epic period of Richmond's history is to visit the Chimborazo Visitor Center (on the site of the Civil War's Chimborazo General Hospital, the largest in the world at the time), 3215 E. Broad Street, 226-1981. The center has exhibits, an audiovisual presentation on the battlefields around Richmond, a 30-minute film — *Richmond Remembered* — and battlefield tour maps as well as an audio tape (for rent or purchase) that will lead you on a four-hour tour of area battlefields and parks.

The center is operated by Richmond National Battlefield Park, which contains 10 park units. Each unit of the park is interpreted by National Park Service historical markers, and some sites, such as Fort Harrison and Drewry's Bluff, have short hiking or self-guided trails. Picnic facilities are available at Fort Harrison and at the Cold Harbor Visitor Center.

An essential part of any Civil War tour also is a visit to the Museum of the Confederacy at 12th and E. Clay streets, 649-1861. Read on to our "Civil War Attractions" section in this chapter. Also available for the true Civil War buff is *Insiders' Guide® to the Civil War*. This compact guide will lead you with explicit detail through the War's Eastern Theater — from southern Pennsylvania to western Maryland and throughout Virginia — with tips on shopping, restaurants and accommodations.

Here's an overview of some of the area's most famous Civil War sites listed by chronological significance:

Drewry's Bluff

Federal gun boats, including the ironclad Monitor, were repulsed by Confederate firepower commanding the bluff just below Richmond on May 15, 1862. The fort was never captured during the war.

Seven Pines

It was here, just 7 miles east of Richmond on today's U.S. Highway 60, that Confederate forces under Gen. Joseph E. Johnston assaulted positions of Union forces advancing on the city on May 31, 1862. Johnston was badly wounded.

Chickahominy Bluff

From this vantage point, Gen. Robert E. Lee, who replaced the wounded Johnston, observed Union troop movements prior to what was to become known as the Seven Days Battle in late June 1862. Lee's brilliant strategy and tactics in a series of desperate encounters over the next week forced McClellan's retreat and saved Richmond for the moment. Chickahominy Bluffs National Battlefield Park is along the south bank of the Chickahominy River on U.S. Highway 360.

Beaver Dam Creek

It was here, in a pleasant little creek valley near the intersection of State Route 156 and U.S. Highway 360 (Mechanicsville Turnpike), that the first encounter of the Seven Days Battle took place on June 26, 1862. Confederate troops under Lee's command attempted to break the Union lines by fording the creek and millrace, waist deep in water and under fire from Federal troops on higher ground to the west.

Gaines Mill

It was during the second of the Seven Days, here in the fields around the Watt House, that troops from Texas and Georgia finally broke the strong Union defensive position and sent the Federals retreating across the Chickahominy River. The Watt House today is part of a National Battlefield Park reached on State Route 718 from Route 156.

Savage's Station

Confederate forces here attempted unsuccessfully to disrupt the Union withdrawal toward the James River on June 29. This battle took place almost exactly where Interstate 64 E. crosses Interstate 295 today.

White Oak Swamp

Using artillery, a Union rear guard fought a successful delaying action that allowed the main body of the Union army to move closer to the James and to the protection of Federal gunboats on June 30. This engagement took place near where U.S. 60 crosses I-295 today, just east of the community of Seven Pines.

Malvern Hill

This was the final engagement of the Seven Days Battles. Retreating Union troops under McClellan, with the Confederates in hot pursuit, stopped here to make a stand on July 1, 1862. Confederate troops threw assault after assault up the open slopes of Malvern Hill against massed artillery and infantry fire. All assaults proved futile. According to one Confederate officer: "It was not war. It was murder." McClellan continued to retreat to the safety of Harrison's Landing at Berkeley Plantation and thence to Alexandria.

Berkeley Plantation

During the Peninsula Campaign in 1862 it was at Berkeley Plantation that aerial reconnaissance was first employed: observation balloons used to directed artillery fire. This is the place, also, while it was a Union army base in 1862, that the plaintive notes of "Taps" were composed. Berkeley Plantation is east of Richmond on State Route 5.

FYI

Unless otherwise noted, the area code for all phone numbers listed in this chapter is 804.

Richmond's Battlefields

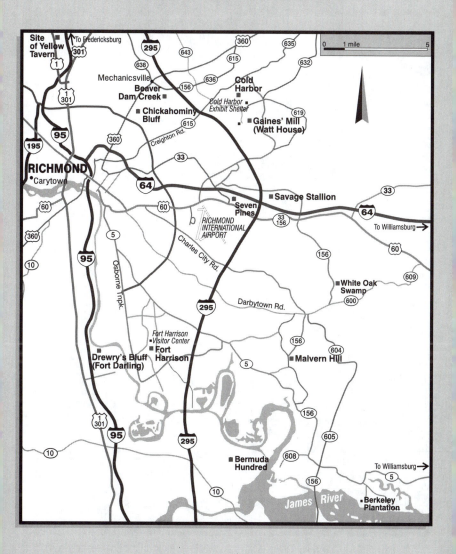

Site of Yellow Tavern

To Fredericksburg

Mechanicsville

Beaver Dam Creek

Chickahominy Bluff

Cold Harbor

Cold Harbor Exhibit Shelter

Gaines' Mill (Watt House)

Creighton Rd.

RICHMOND

Carytown

Seven Pines

Savage Stallion

RICHMOND INTERNATIONAL AIRPORT

To Williamsburg

Charles City Rd.

Osborne Tnpk.

White Oak Swamp

Darbytown Rd.

Fort Harrison Visitor Center

Fort Harrison

Drewry's Bluff (Fort Darling)

Malvern Hill

Bermuda Hundred

To Williamsburg

James River

Berkeley Plantation

0   1 mile   5

Photo: Metro Richmond Convention and Visitors Bureau

Jefferson Davis and his family resided at the White House of the Confederacy during the Civil War.

Yellow Tavern

Two years later, on May 4, 1864, Union forces crossed the Rapidan River and began their final massive assault on Richmond. Confederate cavalry hero J.E.B. Stuart was mortally wounded in fierce fighting on May 11 at Yellow Tavern, almost precisely where Interstates 95 and 295 cross paths between Richmond and Ashland today.

Hanover Junction

Opposing forces met at Hanover Junction, the crossroads of two major Confederate rail supply lines, on May 23.

Haw's Shop

The Union and Confederate cavalry engagement on May 28 here on the grounds of Enon Church was one of the larger cavalry battles of the war.

Cold Harbor

It was here that Confederate troops had dug in, ready for the oncoming Grant. With Lee thus blocking the entrance to Richmond, Grant ordered massive assaults. They were among the most intense of the war. Grant's effort, from May 31 to June 2, was unsuccessful and costly, with thousands of dead and wounded lying unattended for days in a no-man's land before a truce could be arranged. Grant would later call the final assault at Cold Harbor his greatest mistake. But Richmond, again, had been saved. Cold Harbor National Battlefield Park can be reached on Route 156 from U.S. 360.

Howlett Line and Bermuda Hundred Line

Meanwhile, to the south of Richmond at Bermuda Hundred Neck on the James River, a Federal force under Gen. Benjamin Butler had come ashore. Confederate forces built a 3-mile entrenchment line running from the James to the Appomattox River and in May and June 1864 effectively bottled up Butler's army for the remainder of the war.

River Road

Coming through what is today's West End, Union Col. Ulrich Dahlgren led several hundred handpicked cavalrymen down River Road to attack the city in 1864 in an attempt to free prisoners on Belle Isle. He was repelled by the Home Guard on the outskirts of town on what is today's Cary Street. Veering around Richmond, Dahlgren was killed and his men captured when they encountered units of the 9th Virginia Cavalry.

Fort Harrison

To the southeast between Route 5 and the James River, and originally part of the outer ring of defenses around Richmond, Fort Harrison remained in Confederate hands until the latter days of the war. It was finally captured by Grant's troops in actions on September 29 and 30, 1864. Other forts, many within shouting distance of Fort Harrison, managed to ward off the attackers, and Lee made an attempt to recapture some forts in early October.

Richmond would hold out for six more months, until Palm Sunday, April 2, 1865.

It was on that day at St. Paul's Church that Confederate President Jefferson Davis received word that the Union army had breached the main lines at Petersburg, that Lee was retreating toward Danville and that Richmond no longer could be defended.

Confederate warships, riding at anchor in the James River with their magazines loaded, were blown up by their officers. Approximately 900 downtown buildings were burned in the Evacuation Fire after warehouses were set ablaze to keep their contents from falling into enemy hands.

Civil War Attractions

Red, white and blue Civil War Trail signs blaze the route of General Grant's 1864 Campaign Trail, on the back roads of Virginia, from Fredericksburg to Hopewell, and help visitors find sites related to the Civil War. For more information and a map with a listing of sites, call 1-888-CIVIL WAR.

There are self-guided tours through most of the sites, but if you want the inside story and a thorough interpretation, we suggest you contact Richmond Discoveries, 222-8595, a tour company that specializes in Civil War tours. Civil War theme tours are also provided by several other tour organizations. For more information see our Attractions and Tours chapter.

In addition to the following attractions, you may also wish to visit Hollywood Cemetery, Meadow Farm at Crump Park and the Virginia Historical Society.

Museum and White House of the Confederacy
12th and E. Clay Sts. • 649-1861

This museum houses the world's largest collection of Confederate artifacts and documents. You'll be amazed at the extensive collection of Confederate flags, Civil War weapons and the personal effects of military leaders. The museum also offers chronological exhibits documenting the history of the Civil War through battles, leaders and the roles of social groups. On Saturdays, costumed living-history interpreters help bring it all to life.

A new permanent changing exhibit, "The Hope of Eight Million People: The Confederate Soldier" focuses on the war from the soldiers' point of view. Through the display of flags, letters and other artifacts that relate to campfire, religion, recreation and other diversions, the exhibition allows more of the museum's military and flag collection to be on view.

The museum celebrated its 100th anniversary in 1996 with a landmark exhibition, "A Woman's War: Southern Women, Civil War and the Confederate Legacy." The exhibition examines the ways in which the Civil War was extended beyond the battlefields to the homefront. Although the exhibit concentrates on the period of 1860 to 1865, it also gauges the fundamental ways in which the Civil War reshaped women's lives for decades to come. The exhibit is expected to remain open through December 1997.

The restored White House of the Confederacy, home of Jefferson Davis, is next to the museum. Furnishings and decorations vary with the seasons. The home is shown in summer dress from May to mid-September with slipcovers on the furniture and mosquito netting over chandeliers and beds. From Thanksgiving until early January, it's decorated for Christmas. During the summer, living-history interpreters talk to visitors outside the house daily. Guided tours are available.

The Museum presents several special events during the year including a Victorian Bazaar, which focuses on the Victorian period from 1850 to 1900. This is held in the fall at Tredegar Ironworks with entertainment, vendors, and exhibits and demonstrations by educational organizations. There is also a Down Home Family Reunion, an African-American festival, at Abner Clay Park in August.

Admission is $5 for the museum, $5.50 for the White House and $8 for a combination ticket. Senior admission is $4 for the Museum, $4.50 for the White House and $7 for a combination ticket. Student admission is $3 for the museum, $3.50 for the White House tour and $5 for a combination ticket. Children 6 and younger are admitted free. It's open Monday through Saturday from 10 AM to 5 PM, and on Sundays from noon to 5 PM.

Richmond National Battlefield Park
Many locations • 226-1981

The National Park Service protects this site and in doing so preserves the memory of those who fought and died in the Civil War.

The entire national park includes 10 local site areas related to the 1862 and 1864 Civil War battles fought around the city of Richmond. Chickahominy Bluffs, Beaver Dam Creek, Gaines Mill (Watt House) and Malvern Hill are sites of the 1862 Seven Days Battles. Cold Harbor and Fort Harrison represent Ulysses S. Grant's 1864 campaign.

There are two visitor centers and one exhibit shelter. We suggest you start at the Chimborazo Visitor Center for an introduction to the history of the 1862-65 defense of Richmond. Detailed driving tour maps of the battlefields are available. The complete tour of sites involves about a 100-mile drive and will take

---

INSIDERS' TIP

Despite reports to the contrary, fleeing Richmonders only burned the docks and stores of the business district — in a petty game of "If I can't have 'em, you can't either."

one to four hours, depending on how many battlefields you stop to see. The best way to understand the significance of the sites is to spend time walking in the battlefield areas. Admission is free.

Living history programs and reenactments are performed on special occasions to enhance visitors' understanding of the events that took place at these sites. There are also van tours of the battlefields, candlelight walking tours of Fort Harrison, Drewry's Bluff and the Cold Harbor Campaign, weekend walks and talks, and a Junior Ranger program for children ages 6 to 12.

Chimborazo Visitor Center
3215 E. Broad St. • 226-1981

At the site where one of the Confederacy's largest hospitals once stood, visitors can view exhibits, photos, artifacts, maps, a slide program and a film about the battles around Richmond. There is also a battlefield tour on videotape available for rent or sale. The center is open 9 AM to 5 PM daily.

Fort Harrison Visitor Center
Rt. 5 • 226-1981

Exhibits and signs along a self-guided trail through Fort Harrison, which is about 8 miles east of Richmond, provide details of the battle and the fort. Picnic facilities are available. The center is open 9 AM to 5 PM daily.

Cold Harbor Exhibit Shelter
Rt. 156 • 226-1981

The well-preserved trenches along this 1.25-mile tour road are good examples of Civil War field fortifications. A narrated exhibit in the shelter explains the significance of the battle action and strategies. A ranger is available daily to answer questions. Nearby, you'll find the Garthright House that was used as a field hospital and the Watt House that was used as a Union headquarters. Picnic facilities are available.

The shelter, about 10 miles northeast of Richmond, is open from 9 AM to 6 PM daily, and the grounds are generally open from dawn to dusk.

The preservation movement started early enough that today whole city blocks and neighborhoods have been restored, creating a captivating historic ambience.

Historic Preservation

In 1956, plans were on the books to demolish almost all the old buildings in the city of Richmond and replace them with modern, high-rise buildings. However, that same year the Historic Richmond Foundation was established by the Association for the Preservation of Virginia Antiquities (APVA).

Just about every major landmark in the city has been threatened at one time or another, but the preservation movement in Richmond started early enough that today whole city blocks and neighborhoods have been restored, creating a captivating historic ambience.

Thanks largely to the efforts of the Historic Richmond Foundation, the APVA, other preservation groups and concerned individuals, Richmond is one of the few cities that escaped wholesale demolition of its historic buildings during the 1960s. Credit is also due to Mary Wingfield Scott for drawing attention to the need for historic preservation through her lectures and books on Richmond, including *Old Richmond Neighborhoods*.

To the benefit of city government and businesses, historic preservation has proven to be economically profitable as a source of tax revenue and as a major tourism draw.

Preservation began in earnest in 1956, when the Historic Richmond Foundation focused its efforts on saving and restoring the immediate area around St. John's Church in Church Hill. Since the neighborhood had become a rooming-house area, it was difficult to interest people in buying and restoring the property. But the Foundation was able to create interest in restoration by demonstrating what a restored block would look like. By the

mid-1970s, restoration efforts spread to other blocks of Church Hill as people became more interested in returning to the culture of the inner city — a direct reaction to suburban life, evident in cities across the nation.

During the past few decades, Richmonders have become personally involved in historic preservation, and the movement is strongly felt throughout the city. For instance, when Old City Hall was up for sale, there was great fear that it might be destroyed. It took three years and loud citizen protest citywide to save it. Today, it's been completely restored and is used as an office building.

When the city decided to pave Monument Avenue with asphalt, Helen Marie Taylor literally stood in front of a steamroller to prevent it from happening. Following an outpouring of public sentiment, the avenue ultimately was paved with asphalt bricks to retain the original character of the famous street. (The bricks also cost less in the long run than regular asphalt.)

Hundreds of other successful preservation efforts include the establishment of city historic districts and the restoration of Shockoe Slip, Jackson Ward, Monument Avenue, Franklin Street east of Belvidere, the State Capitol, the Ironfronts on Main Street in downtown and the reconstruction of Patrick Henry's birthplace.

Eventually, the restoration of the old National Theatre Building, in the 700 block of E. Broad Street, and other nearby buildings is expected to stimulate further restoration and have a positive effect on the entire street.

There are also times, though, when historic preservation efforts conflict with individual property rights, prompting owners to fight back. Several years ago, in Hanover County, an extensive section of Civil War earthworks on private property was threatened by plans for a new subdivision. Preservationists wanted to save the earthworks, so the county stalled approval of the new development until the situation could be resolved satisfactorily. Unfortunately, the landowner thought that the earthworks were threatening the sale of his property. As a result, he bulldozed over many of the trenches, effectively ending his problem. In the end, the land was sold and only a small portion of the earthworks was saved.

For more information about historic preservation in Richmond, we recommend the book *Old Richmond Today* by Richard Cheek and John G. Zehmer, published by the Historic Richmond Foundation; and *The Architecture of Historic Richmond* by Paul S. Dulaney. Information about historic homes, buildings, museums and neighborhoods is included in these books, as well as in the Attractions and Neighborhoods chapters of this book.

Several of the following organizations play a major role in historic preservation in the metropolitan area. The Valentine Museum, the Museum of the Confederacy, the Virginia Historical Society and other museums and cultural institutions in the area are also actively involved with preservation activities and outreach programs. In addition, there are numerous neighborhood associations that establish and maintain historic districts to help preserve the architectural value and integrity of their properties.

Preservation Organizations

Historic Richmond Foundation
707 E. Franklin St. • 643-7407

The Historic Richmond Foundation was founded in 1956 by the Association for the Preservation of Virginia Antiquities (APVA) to purchase, restore and interest people in saving old buildings. Initial efforts focused on restoring the block of Church Hill around St.

John's Church. The Foundation provides educational services and assistance to people who want to establish historic districts, and it purchases historic property either to save it from destruction or to demonstrate the value of restoration and preservation. Historic Richmond Foundation's activities also include heritage tourism programs and tours. (See our Attractions and Tours chapter for more information.) In addition, the Foundation sponsors the Races at Marengo at historic Marengo estate in New Kent County each spring. Proceeds from the steeplechase races benefit the Foundation. (See our Annual Events chapter.)

FYI

Unless otherwise noted, the area code for all phone numbers listed in this chapter is 804.

Association for the Preservation of Virginia Antiquities
204 W. Franklin St. • 648-1889

This is the local branch of the statewide preservation organization. APVA owns major historic landmarks such as Scotchtown, Marengo and the John House, and maintains them over a long period of time. Call for information about properties or tours.

Chesterfield County Historical Society
Old Chesterfield County Courthouse, 10011 Ironbridge Rd. • 748-1026

Formed in 1981, the Chesterfield County Historical Society has about 1,000 members and operates four historic sites at Chesterfield Courthouse, Museum, Old Jail and Magnolia Grange. The society also manages a gift shop at the museum with items related to Chesterfield and Virginia and has a genealogy committee. The society's photography collection and research library at the courthouse are open to the public. Members publish a journal with scholarly articles about the history of the county. Buildings maintained and operated by the Historical Society are owned by the county.

Virginia Department of Historic Resources
2801 Kensington Ave. • 367-2323

This state agency administers state and federal regulations for historic preservation and maintains archives of historic properties throughout the state including historic districts, individual property and archaeological sites. Anyone interested in looking at the files should call first for an appointment. The department also has a curatorial laboratory and archives collections from sites throughout the state. The staff provides assistance to schools, libraries and museums interested in historic preservation. They also assist people with the establishment of state and federal historic districts and landmarks.

Richmond Commission of Architectural Review
Dept. of Community Development, City Hall, Rm. 510, 900 E. Broad St. • 780-6335

This eight-member commission is appointed by City Council to review exterior changes within the city's old and historic districts including Shockoe Slip, Shockoe Bottom, St. John's Church and Jackson Ward. Four of the members are selected based on recommendations by the local chapter of the American Institute of Architects, the Historic Richmond Foundation, the Association for the Preservation of Virginia Antiquities and the Richmond Association of Realtors. The other members are appointed at-large from the community. Members serve for five years and may be reappointed once. Questions and inquiries should be directed to the Secretary of the Commission at the listed address or telephone number.

Hanover Historical Society
P.O. Box 91, Hanover, VA 23069 • 537-5815

Hanover County's Historical Society has an office and resource center at the Old Jail in Hanover Courthouse on the Green. The society collects historical information and objects related to Hanover County. It published *Old Homes of Hanover County* in 1983 as an outgrowth of a bicentennial project, and recently published another book, *Hanover County, Vir-*

ginia: A Retrospective, that documents the history of Hanover County through local newspaper articles. *A Sketch of the Early History of Hanover County*, also published by the society, documents Hanover County's contributions to the American Revolution. The society has about 300 members.

Hanover Historical Commission
c/o Ashley Neville, Gray & Pape Inc., 1705 E. Main St., Richmond, VA 23223 • 644-0656

The Hanover Historical Commission was established by the county Board of Supervisors in 1988 as a resource committee for the board on historical information. In recent years, the commission established a tourism committee to develop ways to promote historic attractions in the county, and formed a preservation policy committee. It also established a land use and zoning committee to review proposed developments for their impact on historic sites and to advise the planning commission and the Board of Supervisors. A continuing education committee helps inform citizens about county history. The commission functions as an umbrella group for all county historic groups and related organizations. The Board of Supervisors appoints representatives for each of the county's districts. Members serve for one year.

Henrico County Historic Preservation Advisory Committee
History and Historic Preservation Program, Human Services Bldg., Dixon Powers Dr. • 501-5124

Established in 1990, this advisory committee is involved in updating the inventory of county historic sites. The History and Historic Preservation Program staff serves as support to the committee and oversees Meadow Farm, its archives, library and collections. The committee serves as a liaison between the county Board of Supervisors and citizens and con-

INSIDERS' TIP

Scotchtown, in western Hanover County, was Patrick Henry's home during the Revolutionary War from 1771-78 and is one of Virginia's oldest plantations. The restored wood and frame Colonial home was built between 1717 and 1719.

sults with and advises the county manager, the director of recreation and parks and the board of supervisors to identify, interpret, rehabilitate, protect and preserve historic and cultural resources in Henrico County. Committee members are appointed by the board of supervisors from each magisterial district and serve one year. There is also a Henrico County Historical Society. For more information on the society, call 501-5682.

The Trial of Aaron Burr

Andrew Jackson and Washington Irving were among the thousands who converged on Richmond in the summer of 1807, one of the hottest on record, for the treason trial of former Vice President Aaron Burr. Burr was accused of conspiring to establish an independent government west of the Alleghenies, thus threatening dismemberment of the Union.

Jackson, dressed in the attire of a backwoodsman, took to the public green repeatedly to loudly denounce the trial as "political persecution." Irving, then a young correspondent for New York newspapers, sent off dispatches that were highly favorable to the accused. President Thomas Jefferson, bitterly antagonistic to Burr, refused to allow letters in his possession to be used in Burr's defense, claiming executive privilege. Although he finally permitted extracts to be made, echoes of this dispute would be heard almost 170 years later during the Watergate scandals when the Burr case would be cited in the struggle for the Nixon tapes.

Close-up

Hotels and inns in Richmond overflowed — some sleeping three to a bed — and many people camped in covered wagons and tents along the riverbank. The trial was the most important of its kind in American history. It defined the terms of treason in detail for the first time. The trial dichotomized influential and famous individuals as well as political parties and even the executive and judicial branches of government.

Through almost six months, beginning on March 30 when he was brought to Richmond for a preliminary hearing at the Eagle Tavern, the cultured and handsome Burr

Aaron Burr

became a darling of local society. Two men in the bar, apparently impressed with Burr's aristocratic manner, not only signed for his $5,000 bail, but gave him $1,000 to buy a wardrobe to replace the ragged clothes in which he had been arrested near Mobile.

Richmond's hospitality continued through the sessions of the grand jury and the trial itself, all held in the old House Chamber at the State Capitol. Burr became a sought-after guest of prominent Richmond families, and lawyer John Wickham even invited him to a dinner to with Chief Justice John Marshall, the judge who was to preside at Burr's trial. Wickham also invited other friends, some of whom would serve either on the grand or trial juries. Marshall claimed he did not know Burr would be invited, but the situation created quite a stir.

Even after the grand jury returned the indictment for treason on June 24 and although Burr was incarcerated in the city's vermin-infested jail for two nights, Richmond's hospitality continued. He was moved to a brick house at the corner of 9th and Broad streets where he was kept under guard for a period of time. Then he was moved to the newly completed state penitentiary where he enjoyed a three-room suite with callers who every day brought an endless array of delicacies, gifts and messages.

The battle in the courtroom began on August 3. Counsel for the defense included illustrious barristers such as Wickham, Edmund Randolph and colorful Baltimore lawyer Luther Martin (known as "Old Brandy Bottle"). The prosecution included U.S. District Attorney George Hay and William Wirt, author of *The Letters of a British Spy*.

A major event in the whole tableau was the arrival of Gen. James Wilkinson, commander of the United States Army in the West. Although he was described as a "pensioned Spanish spy, confederate with Burr" and as "from the bark to the very core a villain," he was not indicted.

Most people believed Burr was almost certainly guilty of trying to set up some kind of government in the West. But the prosecution's case was torn to shreds when Chief Justice John Marshall ruled that in order to prove guilt it was necessary to show overt acts, with two witnesses present when each act was committed. The prosecution could do no such thing, and the jury on September 1 in an unusual verdict found Burr "not proved guilty . . . by any evidence submitted to us."

Even though Marshall directed the clerk to place the words "Not Guilty" on the record, Burr was not pleased with the less-than-clear-cut outcome. While he went forth a free man, Burr remained under a stigma for the rest of his life.

After the long, hot summer and the heat of the trial, ended, Richmond taverns and inns emptied. Andrew Jackson got back on his horse and left for Tennessee. "Old Brandy Bottle" headed back to Baltimore. And one of the key issues, whether states that had voluntarily entered into a compact could in the same manner withdraw from it, would linger on until it was settled in a clash of arms 50 some years later — an episode in American history in which Richmond again would play a central role.

Five years later Wickham would build a magnificent neoclassical home on East Clay Street, today home of the Valentine Museum.

Where else in the world can you find a collection of memorials to vanquished military leaders in the same country that defeated them?

Monuments

Richmond is often called the City of Monuments and a visit here would not be complete without a tour of the parade of statues on Monument Avenue.

With its tree-lined streets, beautifully landscaped mansions and parklike medians, Monument Avenue is one of the most beautiful streets in the world. From Allen to Belmont avenues, the intersections are adorned with monuments to General Robert E. Lee, Confederate President Jefferson Davis, Commander Matthew Fontaine Maury and Generals Thomas J. "Stonewall" Jackson and James Ewell Brown "J.E.B." Stuart.

The fact that these magnificent monuments to Confederate heroes exist at all is intriguing. Where else in the world can you find a collection of memorials to vanquished military leaders in the same country that defeated them? Their height and grandeur gives them an almost deity-like aura, reflecting the pride and respect Southerners had for these military strategists and the Southern ideals and values they epitomized. The monuments are also recognized as excellent examples of public sculpture.

During the turn of the century, hundreds of people pulled wagons carrying the statues to their present sites, partly because they were so heavy but mostly because they wanted to take part in the special event. A large parade with thousands of Confederate soldiers preceded each unveiling ceremony.

As much as they are a source of pride, the monuments have also been a source of controversy ever since the decision was made to place the first monument, the one to General Robert E. Lee, in the middle of a cow pasture in 1890.

Many residents were unhappy about the decision to place the statue of Lee outside the city limits on donated pasture land instead of in Hollywood Cemetery, Capitol Square or an-other more distinguished area of the city. Imagine how strange it must have been to see the magnificent statue of General Lee guarding an open field in the middle of nowhere. The design of the monument had to be altered because the governor thought it should be at least as high as the monument to George Washington in Capitol Square.

Not everyone was in favor of the monuments. The *Richmond Planet* owner and editor, Councilman John Mitchell Jr., an African American, argued in council and in his paper's editorials against city appropriations for the monument's unveiling. On the day of the unveiling, the paper said the whole proceeding handed down a "legacy of treason and blood."

The monument to General Lee was also controversial in the North where the idea of a monument to a Confederate general created both positive and negative reactions. One Northern newspaper urged Congress to forbid the erection of any more monuments to Confederate heroes and the display of the Confederate flag. Another compared Lee to Benedict Arnold.

Controversy over location continued a few years later in 1894, when the Confederate Soldiers and Sailors Monument was set on Libby Hill instead of at a preferred Monument Avenue site. Organizers of the monument were told that Monument Avenue was "for generals and other important heroes."

In keeping with that concept, the monument to Confederate President Jefferson Davis was erected on Monument Avenue instead of at a site in Monroe Park that Mrs. Davis had selected. The Monument Avenue site also provided a better vista for the monument and further encouraged residential development along Monument Avenue.

Ideas for other monuments have come and gone through the years, including one of a Confederate nurse by Salvador Dali and one honoring Douglas Wilder, the first black governor in the nation. It wasn't until 1996 that the city decided to place another monument on the avenue as a salute to Arthur Ashe Jr., legendary tennis great and human rights ambassador. When the statue was unveiled at the intersection of Roseneath and Monument in July 1996, it was the first new monument placed on the avenue since the monument to Commander Matthew Fontaine Maury was erected in 1929. It is also the first monument on the avenue to honor someone other than a Confederate hero.

The Ashe monument was no exception in the history of controversy that surrounds all the monuments in the area. An international news item, the monument caused quite a stir. Some said Richmond was still fighting the Civil War, some tied it to racial issues, and others said it was much more complicated than that. The African-American community was divided and the white community was divided. There were public hearings, editorials and public-opinion surveys about where it should be located and whether the design by local artist Paul Di Pasquale was suitable. Some wanted to hold an international design competition, but this never materialized, so the DiPasquale statue was constructed and put in place on the avenue.

In addition to the memorials on Monument Avenue, you'll find more than 40 other statues and monuments in streets, parks and cemeteries throughout the Richmond area. Numerous stone markers tell stories of battles won and lost and other important happenings on or near Richmond soil.

Following are a few descriptions and stories related to the monuments. If you're interested in learning more about them, we suggest that you start with a guided bus, trolley or walking tour. (See our Getting Around and Attractions chapters for more information on

these tours.) You may also want to read about the development of the Lost Cause in Charles Wilson's *Baptized in Blood* and Gaines Foster's *Ghosts of the Civil War*, which explains the stages of monument building in the South after the Civil War.

We've included the Monument Avenue monuments in Capitol Square and other interesting and significant monuments around the area.

Monument Avenue

Monument Avenue is famous for its parade of monuments to Confederate heroes including General Robert E. Lee, Commander Matthew Fontaine Maury, Confederate President Jefferson Davis and generals Thomas J. "Stonewall" Jackson and James Ewell Brown "J.E.B." Stuart. All of the monuments are in the middle of intersections, aligned with the center of the parklike medians that divide the avenue. Since Monument Avenue is a busy street, the best way to see the memorials is to park and walk. In July 1996 a monument to Richmond's most famous son, Arthur Ashe Jr., legendary tennis player and human rights ambassador, was erected at the intersection of Roseneath and Monument avenues.

Monuments are listed here as they appear when you travel from east to west on Monument Avenue.

J.E.B. Stuart
Stuart (Lombardy St.) and Monument Aves.

The Stuart Monument and the Davis Monument were unveiled almost simultaneously in 1907, part of a weeklong Confederate reunion attended by about 18,000 veterans. It was not unusual for these ceremonies to receive the entire front page of the newspaper and for 15 or more additional pages to be devoted to related activities and personalities. Stuart was

---

INSIDERS' TIP

Escape the noises of the city at the Richmond Hill Interdenominational Retreat Center, at 2209 E. Grace St. on Church Hill, where two acres of gardens, goldfish, hammocks, benches, chairs, birdhouses and statues await the public, Tuesday through Friday, 8:30 AM to 4 PM. Call 783-7903 for more information.

Photo: Michael Ryan Croxton

For the most part, the city grew around the monuments which helps explain why J.E.B. Stuart looks away from you as you pass by.

quite a ladies' man, and the dashing cavalry-man is portrayed astride his high-stepping horse with a jaunty plume in his hat. Sculptor Fred Moynihan created the approximately 15-foot-tall bronze figure that sits atop a 7-foot granite pedestal.

Robert E. Lee
Allen and Monument Aves.

This monument to Confederate General Robert E. Lee shows Lee on horseback gazing south. Lee's horse, Traveller, was not used for the monument because his appearance was not grand enough. The monument cost $77,000, which was raised through the efforts of the Hollywood Memorial Association and the Lee Monument Association.

After much debate over where to put the statue — Hollywood Cemetery, Libby Hill, Capitol Square, Monroe Park or Gamble's Hill — it was finally decided that it should be placed on donated land at the edge of the city. People weren't happy about putting it outside the city limits in a cow pasture. Until the early 1900s there were only a few buildings on the new Monument Avenue, but eventually, the city grew up around the monuments.

At the request of the governor, French sculptor Jean Antonin Mercie altered the design of the Lee Monument so that it was "not one inch lower" than the statue of George Washington in Capitol Square. The 21-foot-high bronze equestrian figure is mounted on a 40-foot-tall granite pedestal, flanked by two grey marble columns.

When it was erected in 1890, hundreds of citizens pulled wagons carrying the statue to the site where it was assembled. A parade that included 50 Confederate generals, 15,000 Confederate veterans and 10,000 citizens preceded the unveiling.

Jefferson Davis
Davis and Monument Aves.

Erected in 1907 during the same week the Stuart Monument was unveiled, this monument to Confederate President Jefferson Davis was originally planned for a site in Monroe Park selected by Mrs. Davis — the cornerstone had been placed there but was later moved to Monument Avenue. William C. Noland designed the monument, and Edward V. Valentine executed his design. A 7-foot-high bronze figure atop a 12-foot granite pedestal stands in front of another bronze figure, Vindicatrix — an angelic allegorical figure of the South — that is mounted on a 67-foot column. A colonnade of 13 Doric columns encircles the grouping.

Stonewall Jackson
Boulevard and Monument Ave.

The story is that the Confederate veterans in the nearby Old Soldiers Home insisted that since Lee faced the South, Gen. Thomas J. "Stonewall" Jackson should face the North into the eye of the foe. Hence the expression that he faces "defiantly North." A parade that included hundreds of Jackson's soldiers preceded the unveiling of this statue in 1919. William F. Sievers designed the 17-foot-tall bronze equestrian figure that is mounted on a 20-foot granite pedestal.

Matthew Fontaine Maury
Belmont and Monument Aves.

Commander Maury, "the Pathfinder of the Seas," invented the explosive torpedo that wrecked more Northern vessels than any other cause. Erected in 1929, this William F. Sievers creation is an 8-foot-high seated bronze figure of Maury atop a 5-foot granite pedestal arranged in front of an 18-foot-high base that supports a 9-foot-wide bronze globe. At the base of the globe is a depiction of figures tossed by swirling waves, an allegorical tribute to Maury's study of ocean winds and currents. Of all Sievers monuments, this and the Jackson Monument are his favorites.

Arthur Ashe Jr.
Roseneath and Monument Aves.

Designed by local artist Paul Di Pasquale, the sculpture of Arthur Ashe Jr., the legendary tennis great, Richmond native, author and activist is depicted holding a tennis racquet and books, surrounded by children to show his dedication to education. Ashe was the first and only African American to win at Wimbledon. From the design to the location, everything about the monument created controversy with the exception that almost everyone seemed to agree that Richmond should have a prominent monument to Ashe. The Ashe monument was the first monument erected on Monument Avenue since 1929. In July 1996, thousands of people attended the dedication ceremony which was broadcast throughout the world.

Capitol Square

Among the many monuments in Capitol Square are the following:

Harry F. Byrd

Senator Byrd was a United States Senator and Governor of Virginia. Known for his "pay-as-you-go policies" for governmental spending he is depicted carrying the budget in his left hand.

Stonewall Jackson

A group of the Confederate General's admirers commissioned this statue shortly after his death. The state paid for the pedestal and the cost to have it erected.

Dr. Hunter Holmes McGuire

Dr. McGuire was president of the American Medical and American Surgical associations and founder of the University College of Medicine, which later became the Medical College of Virginia.

George Washington

Thomas Crawford's equestrian statue of George Washington was unveiled on the first president's birthday in 1850. Thousands of people hauled the statue from lower Main Street and participated in the event. Although art critics hold different opinions about the quality of Crawford's Washington, they rave over the marble statue of Washington by Jean Antoine Houdon inside the Capitol. Many regard Houdon's work as the most priceless piece of marble in the United States and Virginia's greatest treasure.

Other Monuments in Parks, Cemeteries and Streets

A.P. Hill
Laburnum Ave. and Hermitage Rd.

The efforts of Pegram's Battalion helped

Regarding Confederate Row

Monumental Myths

There's the one about the lady who swore up and down that Lee's horse had come to life. She called the local paper rapt with reports of the bronze steed foaming at the mouth. For many Southerners, this was on par with the weeping Madonna and cause for widespread alert. Feelings were still rather intense at this time in the South. And these

monuments to the great heroes of the Confederacy were indeed much more than metal — as evidenced by an old Tennessee veteran who committed suicide because he was too "enfeebled" to make the Matthew Fontaine Maury statue unveiling.

Luckily investigators made it to the scene before swarms of devotees could start pitching tents around the driveling horse head. And quickly the mystery was put to rest. A honey bee hive was found inside the horses mouth that in the summer heat had apparently begun to froth. While you're in Richmond you may hear the story save the bee hive ending, but you now know better.

What's the Rule?

Then there's the business of the positioning of the Confederate statues. According to whoever sits around and makes such stuff up, the statues facing north are for soldiers that died during the war, and the statues facing south are for soldiers who survived. So much for the Richmonder's ability to read a compass.

Davis and Maury both face east (which isn't an option). And while J.E.B. Stuart's

Photo: Courtesy of Civil War Trails

horse appropriately faces north, he faces east. Stonewall Jackson, who died during the war, does face north even though the sculptor argued that the statue was best viewed if it was faced south. It was only after the tiring insistence of old veterans that Jackson was turned north — not for any particularly attention to war monument tradition, they simply wanted him to keep a close eye on the Yankees.

Facts to Impress Your Friends

Now if you really want to dazzle your friend, stand in front of the Maury statue and prattle on about the allegorical implications of the globed portion (Maury the mariner, Maury the agriculturist, etc.) or just criticize it for looking like a big trophy.

Or, skip down to the Jefferson Davis memorial and dissect it. The figure atop the 60-foot pillar is the spirit of the South, called the "VINDICATRIX" — affectionately known as "Miss Confederacy." If your friend bullishly asks why there are

— continued on next page

The statue of Robert E. Lee has been the subject of speculation and myth.

13 columns in the semicircular colonnade when only 11 states seceded from the Union, smartly reply: "Ahh, but Missouri and Kentucky sent delegates!"

Ooops! The Chisel Slipped!

And it's always nice to know a few sculptor flubs. The horse of such mythic proportions on which Lee rides is not Lee's wartime horse Traveller (trust us).

Jackson's horse, considerably less inspiring than Lee's, is so pathetically gaunt that at the unveiling in 1919 most of the veterans scoffed that it was too skinny to have survived the war. And what do you know . . . the horse wasn't modeled after Jackson's famous mount Little Sorrel, but rather after a local race horse named Superior which the sculptor was able to borrow — probably for cheap.

Lastly, notice the inscription on Jackson's monument: Killed at Chancellorsville. Any Southerner worth his salt knows that Jackson was only wounded at Chancellorsville and died eight days later at Guinea Station — well, you know now.

erect this monument to Confederate Gen. A. P. Hill that was unveiled on Memorial Day, 1892, following an elaborate parade and ceremony. Hill's body was removed later from Hollywood Cemetery and placed under the monument. William Ludwell Sheppard created the 9-foot-high standing figure on a 24-foot pedestal. Major Lewis Ginter donated the land for the monument.

Bojangles
W. Leigh and Price Sts. and Chamberlayne Pkwy.

Bill "Bojangles" Robinson was a famous black tap dancer from Richmond who starred in Broadway productions and motion pictures. His "dance on the stairs" was unique, and he was once named the "outstanding stage and screen star of the year." Erected in 1973 through the efforts of the Astoria Beneficial Club, this was the first monument in Richmond to honor a black citizen. The triangular park where it stands was renamed the Bill "Bojangles" Robinson Square. (Yes, a triangle was named a square.) Robinson paid for a traffic light at the intersection where his statue now stands because there were so many accidents there. Once a millionaire, he gave generously to charities, but when he died there wasn't enough to pay his debts. John Temple Witt created the 9-foot-tall aluminum figure of Bojangles dancing down a flight of steps on a 6-foot-high black marble pedestal.

Carillon, Dogwood Dell
1300 Blanton Ave., Byrd Park

The Carillon is a 240-foot-high bell tower that pays tribute to Virginians who died in World War I. The first-floor gallery is often used for art exhibits, and the tower is sometimes used for climbing and rappelling demonstrations.

Christopher Columbus
Byrd Park, at the south end of the Boulevard

Created by Ferruccio Legnaioli in 1927, this was the first Columbus statue in the South and the first monument in Richmond that was illuminated at night. Virginians of Italian birth sculpted, erected and financed the statue.

Confederate Soldiers Monument
Oakwood Cemetery, east of the Oakwood Ave. entrance

Erected in 1871 by the Oakwood Memorial Association, this granite obelisk on a seven-

INSIDERS' TIP

Although there is no proof that the positions of the monuments were planned this way, the statues of Stuart and Jackson, who both died of battle wounds during the Civil War, face the North, while Lee, who survived the war, faces South.

tiered pyramid base honors the 16,000 Confederate soldiers buried in Oakwood Cemetery.

Confederate Soldiers and Sailors
Libby Park at 29th St. and Libby Terr.

In 1894 William Ludwell Sheppard created this bronze figure that depicts a Confederate soldier standing atop 13 granite cylinders representing the 13 Confederate states. An ornate Corinthian capitol tops the column formed by the cylinders. The stone used in the monument came from granite quarries on the south side of the James River. This monument was denied placement on Monument Avenue, a memorial site reserved "for generals and other important heroes."

Howitzers
Harrison St. at Park and Grove Aves.

Created in 1892 by William Ludwell Sheppard, a former officer in the Howitzers, this monument near the west edge of Virginia Commonwealth University depicts a young artilleryman, "Number One," standing at the piece. The Howitzer Association sponsored the memorial to the cannoneers.

James Netherwood
Oakwood Cemetery, north of the Oakwood Ave. entrance

This is a late 1890s self-portrait of James Netherwood, a local stone carver. He depicted himself with his hat, a worn apron, his carving tools and a stack of granite blocks. The 9-foot-tall granite figure stands above a 20-foot grey marble column reportedly rejected for the Lee monument. A 4-foot-high granite figure of Netherwood's wife, Nancy, is also in the plot.

Light Infantry Blues
6th St. Plaza, 500 block of N. Sixth St.

Erected in 1978 between the Coliseum and 6th Street Marketplace, this 10-foot-high bronze figure depicts a soldier wearing the Blues' uniform with shako hat and feather plume. He stands at parade rest, holding a 1903 Springfield rifle. Light Infantry Blues is a memorial to the National Guard unit of the same name, founded in 1789.

Memory, Virginia War Memorial
U.S. 1 at the north end of the Robert E. Lee Bridge

Memory, a statue honoring Virginian motherhood, is part of the Hall of Memory in the Virginia World War II, Korean and Vietnam War Memorial perched on a bluff high above the James River. In 1956 Leo Friedlander created the 22-foot-high figure of a woman carved from four blocks of Georgia marble. She symbolizes Virginian women as she gazes at the names of more than 11,000 Virginian soldiers who died during the wars engraved on the inside walls of the Shrine of Memory. A gas-fed torch of liberty burns at the base of the statue symbolizing the never-say-die spirit of patriotism. The shrine is a temple-like structure with a wall of columns on one side. Soil samples from American military cemeteries and memorabilia from 200 battlegrounds and battle seas where Americans fought are embedded in the floor. Memory is open daily from 7 AM to 10 PM.

Like everything else in Richmond, the arts community is based on a rich history.

The Arts

Richmond's lively music, arts and theater scene covers a full calendar of symphony, pops, ballet, opera and stage performances, street festivals, outdoor concerts, gallery openings and a week-long summer musicfest.

The city's beginnings as an arts and cultural center didn't happen overnight. Like everything else in Richmond, the arts community is based on a rich history. The city's first theater was built in 1786, and by the mid-1800s only three other cities in the nation could match Richmond's stature as a theatrical mecca. It was during this period that Richmond audiences saw 24 English plays presented for the first time in America. The internationally famous actor Julius Brutus Booth made his U.S. debut here in 1821.

Thomas Sully, the portrait painter, lived and worked in Richmond from 1799 to 1806. The sculpture and painting talents of Edward V. Valentine and William L. Sheppard flourished here in the late 1800s. Richmond also has been the home of such great writers as Edgar Allan Poe and Ellen Glasgow.

One of the interesting footnotes to the city's cultural history is that Allan Hirsh, who grew up in the 800 block of W. Franklin Street, was the composer of the "Boola Boola" song of Yale University.

Today, Richmond is the home of the South's preeminent museum, the Virginia Museum of Fine Arts, and of the internationally traveled Shanghai Quartet. Formed in Shanghai in 1982, the quartet has made its base here with the renowned music department at the University of Richmond since 1988.

To keep up with everything that's going on in Richmond's arts and cultural world, you'll have to become an avid reader of the daily and weekend pages of the *Richmond Times-Dispatch* and of the weekly compendium of events published every Tuesday in *Style Weekly*.

Here are highlights of some of the city's arts organizations and events.

Organizations

Arts Council of Richmond
1401A W. Main St. • 355-7200

The Arts Council of Richmond is a nonprofit organization dedicated to the support, promotion and encouragement of the arts in the metropolitan area. The Arts Council is a great resource of information, and it is the local focal point of the nationwide Business Volunteers for the Arts program. The organization raises its own funds and sponsors exhibitions, including the pacesetting Partners in the Arts arts-education collaborative in public schools and the annual Richmond Children's Festival two-day cultural event for children. The Arts Council also coordinates the Jepson Exhibition Series at the University of Richmond, which is a changing contemporary artist exhibition.

The Richmond Children's Festival, which is the largest of its kind in the United States, is planned around a different international cultural theme each year. It's held every fall at Discovery Park, located next to the Science Museum, and includes singing, dancing, play areas, hands-on art activities and special performances. For more information, see the "Annual Events" chapter.

Downtown Presents . . .
550 E. Marshall St., Ste. 202 • 643-2826

This nonprofit organization sponsors and cosponsors a variety of festivals and events, primarily in the downtown area. Included are

Easter on Parade, Friday Cheers, the Ukrop's/Target Family Jubilee, River City Real Beer Fest, The Big Gig and the Second Street Festival.

One of Greater Richmond's oldest and most popular arts and music festivals is the Family Jubilee. The Arts Council of Richmond originally launched the festival in 1970, but it now is coordinated by Downtown Presents in collaboration with local cultural and civic organizations. The outdoor festival, on a weekend in early June, draws thousands of people to Shockoe Bottom. Local talent is in the spotlight and there's a potpourri of activities for everyone. The River City Real Beer Fest, which takes place at the same time, allows adults to taste ales, lagers and stouts brewed by local microbreweries and food prepared by local chefs. (See our Annual Events chapter for more details.)

Virginians for the Arts
214 N. Jefferson St., Ste. 600 • 783-8140

Virginians for the Arts is a non-profit lobbying organization that has about 600 members throughout the state, including art organizations as well as individuals. Two to three times per year, members receive a newsletter that reports on the group's fundraising efforts. Annually, Virginians for the Arts hosts a reception for legislators. The following day is called Art Advocacy Day, and members go to the Capitol Building and talk to legislators about increasing funding for the arts in Virginia.

Associations

Bon Air Artists Association
15210 Powell Grove Rd., Midlothian 23112 •739-8572

This association sponsors exhibits for its members at a number of local venues, like the James Center and Richmond International Airport. They also lend their support to community events. For the last six years, they have sponsored the Arts at Bellgrade exhibit in Midlothian, attracting artists from outside of town. Proceeds support such charities as the Endowment Fund of the Child Guidance Clinic

and a scholarship fund for an art student at Virginia Commonwealth University. Newsletters are sent monthly to members, who number 100 or more and function as a network for area artists. Those interested in joining should contact Sharon Cresswell, membership chair, at the number and address above.

Richmond Artist Association
P.O. Box 6654, 23230 • 353-5166

The Richmond Artist Association was founded in Richmond in 1955 and today has about 85 members that meet three to four times a year. The group sponsors three exhibits a year and has gallery space at the Shockoe Bottom Art Center for member displays. A quarterly newsletter is sent to all members with a schedules of upcoming events and various points of interest. New members are taken in September by a jury process. Write or call for an application.

Tuckahoe Artist Association
• 288-8843

Formed many years ago to "stimulate interest in the fine arts," this tight-knit group of 50 or so women and men meets once a month, except during summer months, to listen to speakers on subjects like art history, framing, oil painting and the use of color. Each year the group exhibits around the Richmond area, in such places as the James Center atrium, St. Paul's Episcopal Church and Crestar Bank. There are at least four showings a year with a number of member paintings up for sale.

The group also sponsors an annual bus trip to the National Gallery in Washington, D.C. If you're interested in joining, you must get the recommendation of two members. Also, three painting samples will be required for committee approval. Interested parties should call Mrs. Allen Hutcheson at the number above for more information.

Venues

You'll find arts performances scattered throughout the metropolitan area — in down-

FYI

Unless otherwise noted, the area code for all phone numbers listed in this chapter is 804.

Photo: Swift Creek Mill Playhouse

Free music concerts are always just around the corner during The Big Gig.

town piazzas, theaters, restaurants, clubs, concert halls and museums. Some of the main venues for these performances are:

Carpenter Center for the Performing Arts
600 E. Grace St. • 225-9000

The general public, businesses and foundations raised almost $6 million to renovate the old Loew's Theatre for this 2,060-seat performing arts center. Originally opened in 1928, it is an architectural classic of movie palace design, with an interior simulating a Mediterranean courtyard with a starlit sky overhead. Symphony, opera and Broadway shows all play here, and it's a popular place for annual corporate meetings. The center is at the Grace Street entrance of 6th Street Marketplace, and parking is available in decks nearby on Grace Street, 6th Street and in other parking decks within a several-block radius.

Classic Amphitheatre at Strawberry Hill
600 E. Laburnum Ave. • 228-3233

This $2.3 million, 10,000-seat outdoor amphitheater at the State Fairgrounds at Straw-

berry Hill opened in 1992. Its season runs from April to October with country, rock and pop shows. Jimmy Buffett, Travis Tritt, Crosby, Stills & Nash, the Indigo Girls, Dolly Parton, Tina Turner, the Dave Matthews Band, Aerosmith and many others have performed at the amphitheatre.

Richmond Coliseum
601 E. Leigh St.
• 780-4970; 780-4956 events information

With a seating capacity of 13,150, the Richmond Coliseum is the largest indoor entertainment facility in Virginia. It is the big-time, arena-style gathering place for rock, rap and pop concerts. It also hosts sports events, the circus, family shows and ice-skating exhibitions.

Dogwood Dell
Byrd Park • 780-8137 general info, 358-DELL events line

Operated by the Richmond Department of Recreation and Parks, Dogwood Dell is an outdoor amphitheater, sort of a small version of northern Virginia's Wolf Trap. It is the location of the summertime Festival of Arts, among other events and concerts. It is near The Carillon in Byrd Park and seating is on terrace steps and on the lawn.

Richmond's Landmark Theater
6 N. Laurel St. • 780-4213

This 3,565-seat theater dates back to 1927 when its opulent Near Eastern-style structure was built for the Shriners. It was known as "The Mosque" for many years and has been owned by the city since 1939. The name was changed to Richmond's Landmark Theater in 1995 when the building was extensively renovated. It is the home of the 10th-oldest Wurlitzer organ in the United States, and its decor includes five Oriental murals and tiles imported from Spain, Italy and Tunis. It is here that you will find performances by national touring companies and orchestras, plus a wide range of other major events like Garrison Keillor's "American Radio Hour" when it originates from Richmond. Richmond's Landmark Theater is in the VCU area at the corner of W. Main and Laurel streets, and there is a parking deck across the street.

Theater

Greater Richmond's professional-level theater companies stage about 70 shows a year. In addition, there are a number of community and academic theater groups. The telephone numbers listed with each entry will lead you to performance information as well as the ticket office — in many cases, it's one in the same.

Ticket costs vary among the professional theaters, but you can expect to pay betweeen $15 and $35, depending on where you sit and what day you go. Dinner theater tickets are understandably more, but only by about $10. The real deals our found in the community and academic theaters which sometimes offer free performances.

Applause Unlimited
• 264-0299

Applause Unlimited is a puppet, clowning and variety theater group formed in 1993 by master puppeteer Terry Snyder and former Ringling Brothers and Barnum & Bailey circus clown Christopher Hudert. Shows combine puppetry with circus- and vaudeville-style performances. The group has no permanent theater space. It tours within the Henrico County School system and along the East Coast.

Barksdale Theatre
1601 Willow Lawn Dr. • 282-2620

The Barksdale was founded as America's first dinner theater and is the Richmond area's oldest nonprofit theater. For many years it has been known as the "Barksdale Theater at Hanover Tavern" and has been housed in an 18th-century tavern where Patrick Henry once tended bar and where George Washington and Thomas Jefferson stopped during their many travels through the area. In 1996, it moved to its new location in The Shops at Willow Lawn and is now known as the "Barksdale Theater at Willow Lawn." No longer serving dinner, the theater presents a mix of musicals, comedy and dramatic performances. The theater seats up to 234 persons and is open throughout the year.

The Carpenter Center for the Performing Arts
Sixth and Grace Sts. • 225-9000

The Carpenter Center is usually where you'll find national touring companies when they are in town. If this 2,057-seat theater isn't big enough, then performances are scheduled at Richmond's Landmark Theatre with its 3,565 seats. Each season brings about 15 road shows to Richmond. Offerings in recent years have included *Evita*, *Annie*, *Gypsy*, Robert Morse in his one-man play about Truman Capote called *Tru*, *Les Miserables* and *Stomp*. Most road shows are marketed and announced singly except for the "Broadway Under the Stars" series that has included *Funny Girl*, *Kiss of the Spider Woman*, *Man of La Mancha*, *West Side Story* and *Singing in the Rain*.

Chamberlayne Actors Theatre
319 N. Wilkinson Rd. • 262-9760

An all-volunteer group, Chamberlayne Actors Theatre is affiliated with the North Chamberlayne Civic Association and is the oldest independent theatre in Richmond. All auditions are open, and all volunteers are expected to strive for professionalism in their work. The group is dedicated to producing wholesome, family-type light shows four times a year with nine performances of each show. Performances are in the 200-seat North Chamberlayne Civic Association building at 319 N. Wilkinson Road in Henrico County.

Chesterfield Theatre Company
Corner of Shiloh and Entralia Rds., Chester • 748-0698

This is the area's oldest community theater (formerly known as the John Rolfe Players), and it is headquartered in the John Rolfe Playhouse at Shiloh and Centralia roads in Chester. It puts on plays three times a year, in the fall, winter and spring. The company stages its performances in the Chester Middle School auditorium. The company is sponsored partly by the Chesterfield Department of Parks and Recreation.

Encore! Theater
• 257-9773

This nonprofit troupe developed out of the now defunct Rising Sun Repertory Company that was formed in 1985 largely by University of Richmond theater alums. The Encore! Theater group performs year round with a summer touring show, a school-year touring show and its "One Actor Spectacular," which is a series of solo shows focusing on Edgar Allan Poe, Albert Einstein, William Shakespeare, Emily Dickinson and more.

However, Encore! is known mainly for its annual Richmond Shakespeare Festival. The Festival is held at Agecroft Hall, which was disassembled in London and rebuilt in Richmond in 1926. (There's speculation that the original Shakespeare acting troupe performed on the same stage when it was in London.) The Festival lasts through the beginning of the summer with two different plays. If you're available when the Festival is happening, you won't want to miss it.

Experiential Theatre
Windy River Pavilion, Beaver Dam • 741-0377 box office, 741-0408 general information

Year round at this pavilion in Hanover County, the Experiential Theatre acting troupe performs one-act plays and hosts at least one Shakespeare Festival. The Windy River Pavilion seats 150 people, and food and wine are available during the performances. For more information, call the numbers above or write to Hutch Huthinson, 605 Granby Dr., Richmond, VA 23229.

Firehouse Theatre Project
1609 W. Broad St. • 741-0377 box office, 741-0408 general information

Located in the former Engine No. 10 firehouse on Broad Street, this nonprofit troupe produces full-length and one-act contemporary American plays throughout the year, except for during the summer. Classes are available from the group at the black box theatre, which seats 100 and is the only one of its kind in Richmond. For more information, call the numbers above or write to Hutch Huthinson, 605 Granby Dr., Richmond, VA 23229.

Henrico Teen Theatre Company
P.O. Box 27032, Richmond 23273 • 501-5138

Henrico's Division of Recreation and Parks sponsors this group of young actors that makes its home with other county-affiliated theater companies at Rolfe Middle School in Varina, located at 6901 Messer Rd. One play is presented each summer. Teens interested in participating should call the above number.

Henrico Theatre Company
P.O. Box 27032, Richmond 23273 • 501-5138

The Henrico Theatre Company is a volunteer organization sponsored by the Henrico Division of Recreation and Parks. The company opens auditions to anyone who is interested. The group usually presents four major productions a year — Broadway revivals, comedies and an annual one-act showcase featuring winners of its playwriting contest — in the Belmont Park Recreation Center at 1600 Hilliard Road. Call if you're interested in auditioning or would like information on performances.

The Music and Fine Arts Ministry of the West End Assembly of God
401 Parham Rd. • 740-7042

With more than 200 volunteers, this group has managed to produce the biblical blockbuster *The Master's Plan* each Easter since 1986. Only recently, they moved this production from the Carpenter Center to Richmond's Landmark Theater. For over a decade as well, the group has been responsible for Christmas performances in the church sanctuary.

Mystery Dinner Playhouse
9826 Midlothian Tnpk., Best Western Governors Inn • 649-CLUE

If you like audience-involving whodunits, then be sure to head to the dining room of the Best Western Governors Inn, Richmond's murder-mystery dinner theater. Audience members solve a comedy murder mystery while enjoying a delicious four-course dinner. The characters in the show serve your meal, all the while providing clues to help solve the evening's crime. Group discounts are available, and reservations are required.

Randolph-Macon Drama Guild
Theater Dept., Randolph-Macon College, Ashland • 752-4704, 752-7316 box office

This producing organization for Randolph-Macon College in Ashland performs on campus in Blackwell. The guild usually stages four major productions each year.

Richmond Community Theatre and Guild
3003 Collins Rd. • 225-8623

Richmond playwright Marguerita Austin founded this touring, black-experience theater in 1975. Austin remains with the theater today as its writer, and her daughter, Dawnamaria Johnson, directs the plays. The guild performs Austin originals and are featured mostly in local churches.

Richmond Department of Recreation and Parks
900 E. Broad St. • 780-8137

Two plays and one musical are presented each summer in the Festival of Arts at Dogwood Dell in Byrd Park. For more about the Festival, refer to our Annual Events chapter. Springtime productions include dinner-theater presentations at the Carillon in Byrd Park. You can bring your own dinner or get it there. Presentations are under the guidance of the park department's production specialist. Performances are free of charge.

Richmond Theatre Company for Children
111 N. Sixth St. • 644-3444

The Richmond Theatre Company for Children is a nonprofit touring troupe that puts on more than 1,100 performances a year for about 80,000 children in four Mid-Atlantic states and the District of Columbia. It plays day-care centers, festivals and libraries primarily before audiences in the 3 to 8 age group. Occasional performances are open to the ticket-buying public in Richmond.

Richmond Triangle Players
2033 W. Broad St. • 346-8113

Devoted to plays with gay and lesbian themes, this troupe's four-show subscription seasons are staged in a cabaret space at Fielden's, a late-night club at 2033 W. Broad Street, or at Barksdale Theatre, located at 1601 Willow Lawn Dr.

Swift Creek Mill Playhouse
17401 Jefferson Davis Hwy., Colonial Heights • 748-5203

Housed in a 350-year-old grist mill (believed to be the nation's oldest), Swift Creek Mill Playhouse offers a range of theatrical fare. Its musicals are always smash hits. It can be reached directly via U.S. Highway 1 or via Interstate 95 South.

The Playhouse is open year round and has been popular with Richmond theatergoers for many years. Tickets may be purchased for dinner and theater or for the theater only. It also offers a daytime theater series for children. Ask about becoming a season subscriber — it's cheaper.

Theatre at the Bolling-Haxall House
211 E. Franklin St. • 643-2847

This is the resident company of the Woman's Club at its Bolling-Haxall House on Franklin Street. It offers one play in the spring

---

FYI

Unless otherwise noted, the area code for all phone numbers listed in this chapter is 804.

with emphasis on drawing-room comedies and thrillers. Artistic director Robert Watkins stages all plays.

Theatre with Children for Children
Virginia Commonwealth University
• 828-2772

This is the performing arts arm of the Community School of Performing Arts at VCU. Community School pupils, ages 7 to 17, put on annual productions each December at the VCU Performing Arts Center. A series of May performances are given in the VCU Music Center. The company sponsors two touring groups that perform within a 100-mile radius of Richmond and offers a two-week summer theater camp.

Theatre & Company
5104 Richmond Henrico Tnpk. • 329-8006

Actor-director Tony Cosby, the well-known Richmond portrayer of the Rev. Martin Luther King Jr., formed this nonprofit touring company that has presented *King and The Movement*, a play about King, before audiences in Richmond, other Virginia cities and Washington, D.C.

Theatre VCU
Virginia Commonwealth University
• 828-1514

This is the theater company of Virginia Commonwealth University, and it offers undergraduate and graduate programs in theater. Theatre VCU showcases student and faculty work and annually offers four mainstage productions plus "thesis" productions that are usually student-directed. Performances are mostly in the Raymond Hodges Theatre on the VCU Fan District campus.

TheatreVirginia
2800 Grove Ave. • 353-6100

Virginia's flagship professional theater, TheatreVirginia, performs in a 535-seat theater complex within the Virginia Museum of Fine Arts. It is a full member of the League of Resident Theatres and achieved Equity status in 1972. It produces a series of plays in a season that runs from September through June, with each play running for about a one-month period. Productions range from the classics to the contemporary. Subscription packages (including a Flex-Pak that allows theatergoers to pick any three shows they wish from a season) and individual-performance tickets are available.

Dinner is available before the show in the Members Suite for members of the Virginia Museum and for season-ticket holders. Among other educational outreach programs, TheatreVirginia sponsors a statewide playwriting competition, called New Voices for the Theatre. The program includes workshops and readings that are open to Virginia students in grades 5 through 12. Information is disseminated through the local schools but can also be obtained by calling the main office.

Theatre IV
114 W. Broad St. • 344-8040

Theatre IV is based in a two-stage complex at the magnificently renovated Empire Theatre. It offers an Off-Broadway Series as well as a (children's) Family Playhouse and a Theatre Gym series of innovative works produced by guest artists. Its children's touring theater is the second-largest in the nation and reaches an audience of nearly 720,000 in 26 states. Theatre IV was founded in 1975 with a $2,000 nest egg provided by its artistic director Bruce Miller and its managing director Philip Whiteway. It now operates on an annual budget $2.8 million, to include their recent acquisition, the Cincinnati-based ArtReach Touring theater.

The University Players
University of Richmond • 289-8980

Like Theatre VCU, the performances of The University Players at the University of

---

INSIDERS' TIP

The Carytown Gallery Walk is a free, four-block tour of seven art galleries and three restaurants. It's held the first Thursday of every month between 5 and 8 PM.

Richmond add spice and innovation to the city's theater season. The group is an arm of the university's theater department and presents a four-play season in the 500-seat Jepson theater in the George M. Modlin Center for the Arts.

Virginia Union University Players
1500 N. Lombardy St. • 342-1484

This theater group at Virginia Union University presents three plays a year, some in collaboration with the university's music department and with Theatre VCU. The players present productions at various locations.

Music

Each year the Richmond music scene grows larger and more diverse. Credit a recent boom in attractions to the opening of the Modlin Center for the Arts last fall at the University of Richmond. This $22.5 million mega-complex (complete with all-new theaters and galleries plus the remodeled Camp Concert Hall) will offer the region's largest performing art series.

Information on the concert seasons at local colleges and universities is available by calling the University of Richmond at 289-8277; Virginia Commonwealth University at 828-1166, Virginia Union University at 257-5665 and Randolph-Macon College at 752-4721.

Even if money's tight, you're never at a loss for free spring and summer outdoor concerts, such as the Innsbrook After Hours Concert Series, 965-7922, in the New Innsbrook Pavilion off Lakebrook Drive; the GE Financial Assurance Concerts on the Lawn, 281-6699, at Brookfield; Musical Mondays at Maymont, 358-7166; and the Community Pride Culture Series, 222-6484, at the Bill Robinson Playground — plus many more, some to follow in this section and others in our Annual Events chapter.

Photo: Swift Creek Mill Playhouse

This 350-year-old grist mill houses the Swift Creek Mill Playhouse today.

The local churches also have an active concert series beginning in the fall and running through the spring, featuring local, regional and nationally known artists. We mention some churches here, but for convenience, we suggest you call some close to your home and see what they offer.

African-American Heritage Singers
P.O. Box 25714, Richmond 23260
• 783-0904

This professional ensemble of about 14 singers specializes in Southern folk and classical music. It performs locally and around the state. Rehearsals are on Friday evenings at Pace Memorial United Methodist Church, 700 W. Franklin Street.

American Guild of Organists
• 644-0888

The Guild's fall, winter and spring concerts, often including orchestra accompaniment, are performed in area churches.

The Big Gig
550 E. Marshall St., Ste. 202 • 643-2826

The Big Gig, Richmond's Summer Musicfest, is an annual two-week extravaganza consisting of more than 60 daytime and evening concerts held throughout the city. Sponsored by Downtown Presents and the Virginia Union University Department of Music, it is a celebration of music designed to appeal to a broad audience. It takes place in July, and most performances are held outdoors in casual settings such as historic gardens and city parks, inviting audiences to dress comfortably, to relax on blankets or in lawn chairs and to enjoy concerts by renowned musical artists.

Performances range from those by jazz artists Charlie Byrd, Ahmad Jamal and George Shearing, to Mario Bauza's 20-piece Afro-Cuban Orchestra, with some Gilbert and Sullivan and classic Bach on the opposite spectrum. All except five concerts are free of charge. Its ticketed series, called Celebrity Spotlight, has offered performances by Tony Bennett, the Coasters, the Drifters, Emmylou Harris, country singer Kathy Mattea, flutist Herbie Mann and a Scottish concert with pipers and dancers. (See our Annual Events chapter for more information on the Big Gig.)

Chesterfield Community Band
• 744-6528, 796-4723

This 35 to 40-member band rehearses on Monday evenings—during the school year at Manchester Middle School and during the summer at New Covenant Presbyterian Church. A volunteer band, the Chesterfield Community Band was heavily involved in the recent 250th anniversary of Chesterfield County, and it also plays regularly at Maymont's Musical Mondays, the Chesterfield County Fair and retirement homes.

Dixie Land Band
• 730-9146

Depending on the evening and the venue, this fun band is a four- to seven-piece group. It plays all over Richmond, including a monthly show at Legend Brewing Co.

Elbe Musicians
104 Beauregard Ave., Highland Springs, 23075 • 737-1914

This semi-professional band, organized and directed by Andreas Marx, is named after Germany's Elbe River. The group plays traditional polka music from Germany, Austria and Czechoslovakia, as well as a little swing music. Elbe Musicians play regularly at Legend Brewing Co. and Richbrau Brewery with up to 15 musicians at a time.

European Wind Ensemble of Richmond Inc.
104 Beauregard Ave., Highland Springs, 23075 • 737-1914

This volunteer group of about 25 members rehearses on Wednesday evenings at the PBS station in Midlothian. The European Wind Ensemble plays exclusively European band music at about 15 engagements a year, including the Richmond Children's Festival, PBS' Musical Yard Sale, the Richmond Oktoberfest and more.

Fast/Forward
2800 Grove Ave., The Virginia Museum
• 367-8148

Presented by the Virginia Museum of Fine Arts, Fast/Forward offers performances by innovative dancers, choreographers and musicians. If you like the cutting-edge and the experimental, you'll find it in these performances that are staged at the museum from September through May. Tickets are required so call the museum ahead of time.

Friday Cheers
Festival Park (downtown) • 643-2826

Downtown Presents sponsors this series of free Friday evening concerts featuring performances by local and regional pop groups in Nina Abady Festival Park between 6th Street Marketplace and the Coliseum. The weekly outdoor concerts run from May through September. Refreshments are on sale, and the events draw enormous crowds of young people who come to socialize, listen to music and celebrate the workweek's end.

Gellman Room Concerts
101 E. Franklin St. • 780-4740

This concert series, performed in the Gellman Room at the Richmond Public Library, is a fixture on the Richmond scene. The vocal, solo and chamber music concerts are scheduled the second Saturday of each month from October through April. Held in the afternoon, the concerts are free.

Hanover Concert Band
500 S. Center St., Ashland
• 730-9146, 798-6609

This band meets Tuesday evenings at Hanover Arts and Activities Center and plays about 20 performances each year including the Hanover Tomato Festival, the Fourth of July celebrations in Ashland, a Christmas show at Randolph-Macon College and at the Strawberry Faire in Ashland.

Henrico Community Band
P.O. Box 27032, Richmond 23273
• 225-4105

The band room at Tuckahoe Middle School, 9000 Three Chopt Road, echoes with brass, woodwinds and percussion when this community ensemble of about 32 members strikes up for rehearsals on Thursday evenings. It's an all-volunteer group that has a lot of fun.

Jumpin'
2800 Grove Ave., The Virginia Museum
• 367-8148

This popular Thursday evening series in the Virginia Museum of Fine Arts' sculpture garden is a perennial summertime favorite and offers a broad range of music including Cajun, jazz, rhythm and blues and Caribbean. The event is as much social as it is musical, and tickets usually sell out well in advance of each week's event so call the number provided above as soon as you can. The jumpin' starts in late June and lasts through August. (See our Annual Events chapter for a more information on Jumpin'.)

Mary Anne Rennolds Concerts at VCU
922 Park Ave., VCU Performing Arts Center
• 828-6776

Sponsored by the music department at Virginia Commonwealth University, the Mary Anne Rennolds Concerts, named after the wife of the aluminum magnate, bring to Richmond some of the world's finest chamber music. The series includes six concerts annually.

Richmond Choral Society
Reveille United Methodist Church
• 967-9878

The 115-voice Richmond Choral Society was founded in 1946 to perform fine choral music. It presents three concerts a year. A

INSIDERS' TIP

Sold-out performances of The Nutcracker are a big part of the December holiday season, so be sure to get your tickets early.

holiday concert is performed in December, a program of masterworks in early spring and a pops concert in the early summer. Anyone can join, but everyone has to audition first.

Richmond Classical Players
903 Forest Ave. • 288-6056

Specializing in Baroque to contemporary string music, the Richmond Classical Players perform during the winter and spring at Trinity United Methodist Church.

Richmond Concert Band
1506 41st St. West • 230-4356

This is a nonprofit, all-volunteer organization that encourages the appreciation of concert band music and does not require auditions. The band holds rehearsals Tuesday nights at the Tabernacle Baptist Church. The band performs at Dogwood Dell, the State Fair and for special events.

Richmond Jazz Society
P.O. Box 25723, Richmond 23260
• 643-1972

This nonprofit society, dedicated to the preservation and promotion of jazz, presents local and national jazz artists in concert. The society holds monthly meetings that feature guest artists and educators. If you're interested in membership, call the number that's listed above.

Richmond Philharmonic Orchestra
7113 Three Chopt Rd. • 673-4001

The Richmond Philharmonic presents four concerts a year and works to provide local musicians with an opportunity to develop and display their talents in concerts and chamber programs. Inquiries about membership are invited. The group holds rehearsals Monday nights at Ginter Park Presbyterian Church, 3601 Seminary Avenue.

Richmond Pops Band
• 275-5253

Formerly directed by Frank Rowley, who at age 17 played under the direction of John Philip Sousa in a high school band, the Richmond Pops Band is composed of professional and experienced amateur musicians. It offers music from Broadway shows, opera, classical, swing and jazz. In addition to outdoor performances, the band plays a Christmas concert and three other shows at the Jefferson Hotel.

Richmond Symphony
300 W. Franklin St.
• 788-4717, 788-1212 box office

For lovers of classical music, the Richmond Symphony is the biggest game in town. It offers four major series and a number of special programs, in the process offering just about every kind of great music anybody would want. Its Masterworks series hones in on the classics and brings the world's great soloists to the city. Its tremendously successful Champagne Pops series thrills audiences with favorites from Broadway, Hollywood, the realm of popular music and from the best-loved classics. For its All Star Pops series you'll find the Symphony teaming up with the likes of Peter Nero, the Preservation Hall Jazz Band, Roy Clark and Jim Nabors. Its Double Exposure series, launched in 1991-92, is performed at the VCU Performing Arts Center and gives concert-goers an opportunity to meet and talk with featured soloists and performers. If you enjoy great music best when you can wear casual clothes and munch on free pizza, then the Symphony's Kicked Back Classics performances! at the Tredegar Iron Works Gun Foundry, 500 Tredegar Street, are made just for you.

In 1996 The Richmond Symphony, under Music Director George Manahan, received the American Society of Composers, Authors and Publishers Award. This is the fifth time the Symphony has received this national distinction, which recognizes orchestras whose programs demonstrate a strong commitment to the works of 20th-century composers.

Performances run anywhere from $10 to $50, depending on what series you attend and where you sit.

Richmond Symphony Chorus
300 W. Franklin St. • 740-0429

This chorus, conducted by James Erb, performs with the Richmond Symphony and with the Richmond Ballet. The chorus holds auditions in the summer, and rehearsals are Tuesday evenings at Grace Baptist Church in the West End.

2nd Street Festival
Jackson Ward • 643-2826

Second Street north of Broad Street once was the focal point of African-American business and nightlife in Richmond. It is now undergoing a rejuvenation, but the old days are recalled in the annual Second Street Festival sponsored by Downtown Presents every fall in October. Music has always been important to the area; if you like jazz and big band music, this is the place to be. There's always dancing in the streets. (See our Annual Events chapter for more.)

Shanghai Quartet at University of Richmond
Modlin Arts Bldg., Univ. of Richmond
• 289-8277, 289-8980 concert line

Formed in Shanghai in 1982, this internationally acclaimed quartet has been in residence at the University of Richmond since 1989. Its concerts, which provide lovers of great music with a unique opportunity, are performed during the fall and winter months.

Sweet Adalines International
Greater Richmond • 282-SING

This women's group teaches and performs barbershop-style four-part harmony. The Greater Richmond Chapter rehearses Tuesday evenings at Monument Heights Baptist Church at Libbie and Monument avenues.

University of Richmond Music Department
Modlin Arts Bldg.
• 289-8277, 289-8980 concert line

The renowned music department at the University of Richmond offers a full season of other concerts, all free, featuring guest artists and a wide variety of music from September through April. The university's orchestra welcomes community participation.

VCU Community Guitar Ensemble
VCU Recital Hall • 353-3403

This student-community classical guitar group has about 20 players, chosen by audition, and is led by John Patykula. It performs in the Virginia Commonwealth University Music Center at Grove and Harrison avenues two or three times during the school year.

In the summer Guitar and Other Strings series put on at the VCU Performing Arts Center, staged during the Big Gig music festival in July and featuring guitar and other stringed music in styles ranging from classic to folk.

Virginia Choral Ensemble
P.O. Box 24341, 23224 • 275-1322

This urban black ensemble specializes in gospel music and is directed by retired Richmond City School teacher Zeola Heller. The chorus rehearses Thursday evenings at various churches around Richmond. It tours the state and has recorded three albums. Recently, its music was inducted into the Virginia Historical Society's archives. And the group always plans a grand celebration planned for its anniversary on the fourth Sunday in September. 1999 marked its 53rd year of singing.

Virginia Opera
300 W. Franklin St. • 643-6004

One of only two statewide opera companies in the United States and one of the nation's fastest-growing regional companies, the Virginia Opera performs five shows at the Carpenter Center for the Performing Arts each year, often playing to sold-out houses. In a season that runs from October to March, you'll find offerings that range from things like *Othello* and *Figaro* to *Porgy & Bess*. In addition to traditional repertoire, the Virginia Opera is one of a handful of companies in the nation that explores new ground and brings brand-new operas to its audiences.

The Virginians Barbershop Chorus
• 257-9704 info line, 257-7651

Formerly the Tobaccoland Chorus, this 65-member chorus is the Southern Division champion of the Mid-Atlantic District of the International Society for the Preservation and Encouragement of Barbershop Quartet Singing in America. The group gives concerts in Dogwood Dell, performs at Maymont's Christmas festivities, at the Ukrop's/Target Jubilee, in competitions and at conventions, and at benefits and private functions. Rehearsals are Tuesdays evenings at Derbyshire Baptist Church, 8800 Derbyshire Road. New members are welcome.

Vocal Arts Associates/
Opera Theatre
7333 Hermitage Rd. • 266-0548

This group offers training and programs for area singers in opera, recitals, pageants and national auditions. Singers receive lessons, coaching and performance opportunities. The opera theater performs around the city throughout the year.

World Music and Performance
2800 Grove Ave., The Virginia Museum
• 367-8148

Also at the Virginia Museum, this series includes four music and dance performances annually, usually with an ethnic theme.

Dance

If you can think of it, someone in Richmond's probably doing it, from ballet to ethnic dance, modern to square dancing. There's a wealth to choose from, for those who just want to watch and for those who can't help but jump in.

There's the Scottish Country Dancers of Richmond, 740-4404; the Richmond Square and Round Dance Association, 560-4756; U.S. Amateur Ballroom Dancers Association, 276-2049; Richmond Swing Dance Society; Elegba Folklore Society and Virginia Bop. And that's just scratching the surface.

The following is a list of some of the city's larger dance troupes and organizations.

The Concert Ballet of Virginia
11028 Leadbetter Rd., Ashland • 798-0945

The Concert Ballet of Virginia is Richmond's oldest community ballet company. It is based at the Bolling-Haxall House on Franklin Street. It traditionally presents a fall program, a touring Nutcracker, a concert with the Richmond Pops and a spring performance. The dancers number about 65, including 30 members of a junior company. It also has an adjunct company, Concert Ballet Contemporary.

Ezibu Muntu African Dance Co. Inc.
418 E. Main St. • 225-9209

This ensemble of dancers and drummers celebrates the richness of many African cultures through dance, rhythm, rituals and song. The group tours and offers performances, workshops, classes, lectures and demonstrations. The troupe averages two to three public performances per month, including weddings, funerals, rites-of-passage ceremonies, and festivals. Members of the company are chosen by audition.

Fast/Forward
2800 Grove Ave., The Virginia Museum
• 367-8148

This cutting-edge music and dance series presented by the Virginia Museum's 20th-century art department usually includes two dance programs each year.

The Richmond Ballet
614 N. Lombardy St. • 359-0906

The Richmond Ballet is the state ballet of Virginia and is the Commonwealth's only professional ballet company. It produces a full Richmond season — including The Nutcracker, which plays every December to packed houses in an ever-expanding string of evening and matinee performances — and it tours throughout Virginia and the Southeast. The company's expansive repertoire includes works of some of the most influential choreographers of the 20th century, full-length classical ballets and exciting new works by some of today's brightest young choreographers.

The School of the Richmond Ballet, the company's official training affiliate, provides instruction to more than 700 students. Classes in ballet, creative movement and jazz are offered to children, teens and adults. Classes are open to the public. The school can be

---

INSIDERS' TIP

The Richmond arts scene got a real boon in 1996 from the completion of the $22.5 million George M. Modlin Center for the Arts at the University of Richmond.

reached at the same number as the company, see above.

VCU Department of Dance and Choreography
1315 Floyd Ave. • 828-1711

Virginia Commonwealth University's Department of Dance and Choreography annually stages a series of student/faculty dance programs and booked events, usually at the VCU Dance Center.

Museums and Galleries

Looking for an art experience? The best place to start is with the Carytown Gallery Walk. This walking tour, held from 5 PM to 8 PM the first Thursday of every month, takes you from the 3400 block of West Cary Street to the 3100, through seven galleries that offer extended hours and often coordinate art openings to coincide. Refreshments are sometimes provided.

After you get your feel for the variety Richmond has to offer, be sure and visit some of the truly regional galleries, like that of the famed Chesapeake Bay painter, John Barber, at his 5812 Grove Ave. gallery.

The following is a list of the larger and more popular commercial and nonprofit galleries. We've indicated which are commercial in case you are interested in purchasing. Hours always tend to fluctuate and exhibits come and go all too quickly, so call ahead before you visit or look in the *Richmond Times-Dispatch*'s Sunday Entertainment section for current exhibit listings.

The Anderson Gallery
907 W. Franklin St. • 828-1522

The Anderson Gallery is Virginia's Museum of Contemporary Art. It is on the campus of Virginia Commonwealth University, which has one of the largest art schools in the nation. The gallery (actually eight separate galleries over three floors) exhibits the work of regional, national and international artists and gives visitors an inside look into work being done by VCU students and faculty. Admission to exhibits and lectures is free.

Artspace
6 E. Broad St. • 782-8672

This nonprofit co-op gallery has evolved into a focal point for area art — especially figurative work and cosmic themes — that is both thoughtful and challenging. Most shows combine two or three artists whose works deal with similar themes. Artspace hosts performance art, including poetry, plays and dance, on the weekends.

Cudahy's Gallery
1314 E. Cary St. • 782-1776

Cudahy's, a commercial gallery, features three floors of paintings, prints and crafts. Most of the artists have Virginia roots, but the gallery often expands to include talent from the mid-Atlantic and southeastern parts of the nation. The gallery also operates a portrait service and exhibits samples of work by dozens of portrait painters who work on commission.

Elegba Folklore Society Cultural Center
101 E. Broad St. • 644-3900

Photography and art exhibitions with an African-American perspective are featured here throughout the year, along with other cultural events, programs, workshops and festivals.

Eric Schindler Gallery
2305 E. Broad St. • 644-5005

One of Richmond's oldest art enclaves, the Eric Schindler Gallery, a commercial gallery, is in the historic district of Church Hill and carries an eclectic mixture of wares. Along with paintings by Parks Duffey of life in the Caribbean done in 1989 and work by other artists, you'll find 16th-century engravings, reproductions of 18th-century architectural prints, old books and even pieces of historic memorabilia.

INSIDERS' TIP

For scheduling information on fine arts and cultural events, you can call Artsline, a 24-hour service of WCVE-FM. The phone number is 345-ARTS.

Gallery 5800
5800 Grove Ave. • 285-0774

This commercial gallery specializes in local and national artists who use a wide variety of mediums. It has monthly exhibits that are sometimes organized around a them, specifically local artist Lynn Blackmore's worldwide travels. Gallery 5800 is amid The Shops on the Avenues at Libbie and Grove avenues in the West End.

Lora Robins Gallery of Designs from Nature
University of Richmond • 289-8237

Displays here sparkle with gems, jewels, minerals, seashells and corals, fossils and cultural artifacts. Larger items include a 1,700-pound amethyst geode, a giant, man-eating clamshell from Australia's Great Barrier Reef and a three-foot-high alabaster model of the Taj Mahal. The gallery, as its brochure says, is designed to "create an awareness, appreciation and understanding of the handicraft of nature." This it does, in room after room. The Lora Robins Gallery is a gem of a museum that has received too little attention for too long.

Marsh Art Gallery
Modlin Center for the Arts,
University of Richmond • 289-8276

In faculty size and student enrollment, the University of Richmond's art department is small compared with VCU's, but the Marsh Art Gallery nevertheless takes very seriously its mission to show a wide range of significant art. Its exhibition program grows more ambitious every year and focuses, one at a time, on prominent artists. Founded in 1968, the *Richmond Times Dispatch* recently called it, "the best place in Richmond to see contemporary art."

Reynolds Gallery
1514 W. Main St. • 355-6553

The Reynolds Gallery exhibits works by nationally known artists from New York along with major works by regional artists from Virginia and Washington, D.C. Included in the gallery are works on paper, watercolors, sculpture and furniture. This gallery has become one of the city's premiere commercial galleries.

1708 Gallery
103 E. Broad St. • 643-7829

This nonprofit contemporary art gallery is artist-owned. The opening receptions at 1708 are the Richmond art scene's "in" spot. They're usually held on the first Friday in the month. Community outreach includes "Art Pros" mentorships and "Gallery in the Schools." Volunteer involvement is welcomed.

Shockoe Bottom Arts Center
2001 E. Grace St. • 643-7959

Want to observe artists at work? If so, then Shockoe Bottom Arts Center, a commercial studio, invites you to tour its studio spaces for more than 50 artists working in a variety of styles and media. The Center also holds monthly juried exhibitions, plus frequent demonstrations, lectures and special events.

Uptown Gallery
1305 W. Main St. • 353-8343

Here you'll find the work of 30 artists who not only produce the art but staff the gallery. The group works in a diversity of styles and media including oil, acrylic, watercolor, pastel, pen and ink, charcoal, collage, stone, metal, clay and photography. Art classes and workshops are offered. Artist members of this commercial gallery include well-known local names.

The Virginia Museum of Fine Arts
2800 Grove Ave. • 367-0844

When *Vanity Fair* wrote up the opening of the Virginia Museum's new 90,000-square-foot West Wing in the mid-1980s, the magazine's "Best Fetes" column noted the presence of pop artist Andy Warhol, writer Tom Wolfe and well-known artists such as Julian Schnabel, Richard Estes and George Segal. The event was covered by French, Italian, British, German and U.S. network television. All of this perhaps gives some indication of the reputation The Virginia Museum of Fine Arts has attained. It is unequaled in the South, and it is without question the star in Richmond's cultural crown.

Its permanent collections range from the opulent art of the Czars and the works of old masters to one of the greatest assemblages of American 20th-century decorative art and the nation's finest collection of art of Tibet, Nepal and India. If you have even just a remote interest in art, the Virginia Museum of Fine Arts should be number one on your list.

Other Venues

In addition, you'll find exhibitions in a variety of other places. These include shows by area art clubs and artists in the small gallery just off the main lobby of the Crestar Bank at 10th and Main streets, shows featuring area art and photography at the Jewish Community Center at 5403 Monument Avenue, exhibitions of folk art at the Meadow Farm Museum in Henrico County, exhibitions in the first- and second-floor galleries at the Richmond Public Library at 101 E. Franklin Street, and exhibitions by Virginia artists in the second-floor lobby of the NationsBank Center at 12th and Main streets, in the James Center I lobby at 901 E. Cary Street, in the lobbies of the WRIC-TV building in Arboretum Place, and occasionally at the Virginia Eye Institute on the north end of the Huguenot Bridge.

Crafts

There are more than 200 craft, hobby and special interest groups in the Richmond area ranging from the Needlepoint Guild and the Bonsai Society to the Richmond Craftsman's Guild and the Weavers Society. You can find a listing of many of these organizations in the "Discover Richmond" section published in a Sunday edition of the *Richmond Times-Dispatch* in early August. The section can be purchased separately at the front desk of the newspaper office at 333 E. Grace Street.

Arts In The Park
1112 Sunset Ave., Byrd Park • 353-8198

Arts In The Park, held the first weekend in May in Byrd Park, is the largest outdoor arts and crafts show on the East Coast. The nationally known arts show, now in its third decade, is sponsored by the Carillon Civic Association and draws artists and craftspeople from 38 states. Admission is free, and there is free parking at the nearby University of Richmond Stadium with free shuttle bus service to and from the stadium. More than 100,000 people turn out for the show each year. It's a must on any art lover's calendar. (See our Annual Events chapter for more.)

. . . But Is It Art?
3031 W. Cary St. • 278-9112

A group of fairly young craft artists has opened this commercial gallery as a cooperative effort. A suite of small rooms displays their works.

Barksdale Theatre presents musicals, comedies and dramas
throughout the year.

Elegba Folklore Society
101 E. Broad St. • 644-3900

Across the street from the Richmond Public Library and next door to the Linden Row Inn, this craft shop features a collection of contemporary artwork, hand crafts, original cards, and familiar and exotic gift items. See the write-up for the Society in the "Galleries" section of this chapter.

The Hand Workshop Inc./Virginia Center for the Craft Arts
1812 W. Main St. • 353-0094

The Hand Workshop is a nonprofit center for the visual arts. Since 1962 it has offered art classes for children, teenagers and adults and art exhibitions by prominent regional and national artists. Classes and workshops cover a wide spectrum from pottery and metalworking to printmaking and sculpture.

The Hand Workshop also sponsors the annual Richmond Craft and Design Show, featuring selected artists from across the United States. Individual and household memberships are available and include discounts on activities. It has partnership programs with local public schools and offers scholarships to talented teens.

Writer's Groups

Richmond has a great literary heritage going back to the days of Edgar Allan Poe. While many Richmond writers prefer to work on their own, others find support and encouragement by becoming affiliated with various writers' groups and clubs.

The Hand Workshop Inc.
1812 W. Main St. • 353-0094

The Hand Workshop offers workshops in both novel and poetry writing. (For more information, see the "Crafts" section of this chapter and the Kidstuff chapter.)

The National League of American Pen Women
• 744-8229

This association of professional women in the creative arts (including writers, artists, poets and musicians) meets six times a year. Industry authorities are frequent guests at these meetings. Every two years the league sponsors a writers' conference and an art show. Members receive a bi-monthly newsletter updating them on member honors and upcoming events. Those interested in joining are encouraged to call.

New Virginia Review Inc.
1306 E. Cary St. • 782-1043

New Virginia Review is a statewide non-profit organization dedicated to encouraging writers and readers of contemporary literature in Virginia. Programs include a book and author tour, a writing contest, fellowship residencies for writers at the Virginia Center for Creative Arts, a newsletter and an annual anthology. Poetry, fiction and essays are eligible for consideration for publication in its *New Virginia Review* magazine, which is printed three times a year and is available in bookstores or by subscription.

The Virginia Writers Club
1205 E. Main St. • 648-0357

Founded in 1918, this 400-member club is clearly the largest writer's group in the area, with six chapters located throughout the state, and ostensibly the best venue to network. Writers in all fields are welcome to join, including published and non-published writers. The club has a speakers bureau and sponsors seminars on topics, such as, "How to get published" and "How to get an agent." Four to five meetings are held each year and are generally advertised in the *Richmond Times Dispatch*.

With chapters throughout the state, members are invited to attend any chapter meeting they like at any time. All members receive a newsletter five times a year offering chapter news, how-to information and spotlights on members who have published recently. The club also offers a mentoring program for less experienced writers. Dues are $25 per year.

Alternative Film

Some of the most thought-provoking and unusual films in town are shown at local universities. Schedules of upcoming films are available by calling the numbers listed. (Feature-film movie theaters are listed in our Nightlife chapter.)

International Film Festival
University of Richmond • 289-8860

Alternative films are also shown at the University of Richmond in the Adams Auditorium of the Boatwright Memorial Library at the Festival, which happens twice a year. Admission is free. All foreign-language films are shown with English subtitles.

James River Festival of the Moving Image
Virginia Commonwealth University
• 355-1383

The annual James River Festival of the Moving Image offers screenings, seminars and juried competitions in film and video every April at Virginia Commonwealth University. These showings and events are open to the public. VCU also presents an annual French Film Festival in the spring at Byrd Theater.

Whatever type of music you prefer, you'll hear it at the BIG Gig.

Annual Events

Richmonders turn out in great numbers for events, parades and festivals, especially the Richmond Children's Festival, Strawberry Hill Races, Camptown Races, June Jubilee, the BIG Gig, the State Fair, the International Food Festival and the Jaycee's Christmas Parade.

We love an excuse to party, and we have a festival for everything, especially food. There's a tomato festival, a pork festival, a watermelon festival, oyster festivals, Virginia food festivals, Greek food festivals, and international food festivals.

We have described many of our popular events throughout the book, but to help you put it all together, here's a month-by-month rundown of our major events.

January

Bassarama
600 E. Laburnum Ave., Strawberry Hill
• **228-3200**

This three-day weekend exhibition features bass-fishing demonstrations and seminars by world-famous fishermen. You'll see how lures and fishing techniques actually work in the "hog trough," a clear-sided tractor trailer full of water, bass and underwater structures that simulates actual fishing conditions. A special area for kids features a trout-fishing pond, and numerous exhibitors sell boats, bait, rods and reels and every imaginable fishing-related item.

Community Learning Week
• **321-5374**

Community Learning Week, in mid-January, is the nation's only weeklong series of events, conferences and workshops built around the life and philosophy of the Rev. Dr. Martin Luther King Jr. More than 75 business, civic and social organizations sponsor it.

February

Maymont Flower and Garden Show
Fifth and Marshall Sts., Richmond Centre
• **358-7166**

In midwinter, the Maymont Flower and Garden Show offers a refreshing preview of spring. Held each February at the Richmond Centre in downtown Richmond, this four-day event is Virginia's largest flower and garden show and one of the top garden shows on the East Coast. You can stroll through uniquely designed blooming indoor landscapes featuring tens of thousands of trees, flowers and shrubs. Full-size ponds, gazebos, fountains and garden statuary are also displayed, and landscape designers and contractors are available to answer your questions. You'll find every imaginable flower or garden-related item on display or for sale including lights, furniture, ornaments, baskets, handcrafts, flags, sculpture, flowerpots, books, tools and more. Numerous gardening and horticultural associations and organizations have exhibits, and well-known speakers discuss educational topics. Although the show is open from morning until night, the best time to go to avoid the crowds is around 5 PM. Proceeds benefit the Maymont Foundation.

Richmond Academy of Medicine Auxiliary Antique Show
2500 W. Broad St., Science Museum
• **367-6552**

This week-long event brings together some of the top antique dealers from Virginia and surrounding states in the intriguing spaces of the Science Museum of Virginia, the former Broad Street Train Station. Open to the public, the event's proceeds are used to support local charities selected each year by the Richmond Academy of Medicine Auxiliary.

March

Bay Days
2500 W. Broad St., Science Museum
• 367-6552

Experience the sights, sounds, crafts and culture of the Chesapeake Bay. Touch a sea creature, view regional art, tap your toes to a sea chantey, try out tasty bay treats and delight in many crafts and craftsmen. Bay Days is included with museum admission.

Bizarre Bazaar Spring Market
Fifth and Marshall Sts., Richmond Centre
• 673-7015

This popular weekend craft show features nationally known crafters and artists exhibiting their spring and summer novelties and gift items.

CAA Men's Basketball Tournament
601 E. Leigh St., Richmond Coliseum
• 780-4970, 262-8100

State college basketball rivals compete annually in this well-attended, end-of-the-season basketball tournament at the Richmond Coliseum. Colonial Athletic Association teams include American University, East Carolina University, George Mason, James Madison, Old Dominion University, William and Mary, University of North Carolina at Wilmington, University of Richmond and Virginia Commonwealth University.

Children's Book Festival
Various locations • 355-7200

This popular festival, held each year, promotes children's interest in reading. The event begins with a family breakfast and features children's book sales, storytellers, costumed characters and family activities. It's held at local schools, but the location changes each year. Area schools distribute information about the event.

Chili Cook-Off
3001 N. Boulevard, The Diamond parking lot • 756-6426

Sample some of the best chili you'll ever eat, and cast your vote for your favorite at this popular gastronomical event that takes place the last Saturday in March. Live entertainment, music and exhibits by selected community organizations add to the activity. Admission is about $5. There is an additional charge for food.

St. Patrick's Day Parade
W. Broad St. • 965-2339

Celebrate the wearin' o' the green at this fun-to-watch parade held on the Saturday closest to St. Patrick's Day each year. The parade starts at West Broad Street and Horsepen Road and proceeds east to Willow Lawn Shopping Center. You'll see every baton twirler in Richmond, several high school bands, horses, corporate floats and Shriners. There's also a two-mile race. Be sure to bring lawn chairs and blankets to stake your spot on the side of the road.

Virginia-Carolina Craftsmen's Spring Classic
600 E. Laburnum St., Strawberry Hill
• 228-3200

Hundreds of craftsmen from Virginia, North Carolina and surrounding states participate in this major show that offers almost every craft item imaginable. Many people buy tickets for the entire weekend event so they can see it all. Daily admission varies, call for cost.

April

Easter on Parade
The Fan • 643-2826

Several blocks of Monument Avenue in the Fan District are sectioned off for this old-fashioned Easter parade among the monuments. If you like people-watching, you don't want to miss this one. Join the crowd, stroll down the avenue and enjoy the sights and entertainment. The porches of elegant mansions become stages for some of the area's best jazz, bluegrass and Dixieland musicians, while roving characters and performers provide delightful entertainment everywhere you look. Special activities, including carousel and Ferris wheel rides, face-painting, bonnet-decorating and more make the event a kids' favorite. Be sure to bring your camera for the annual bonnet contest usually held in front of the Davis monument. Pets and coolers are not allowed.

Revelers fill Monument Avenue for Easter on Parade.

Event maps are available from food vendors and the information booth. The event is free, but the food costs a small fortune.

Family Easter
Maymont • 358-7166

This delightful, but crowded event offers visitors a chance to enjoy Maymont walking tours, nature center, farm and carriage rides, plus live music and fun holiday activities for the whole family. Everyone will enjoy the popular egg hunts, rolls, tosses and races as well as the giant straw maze. There's also "The Best Bonnet Contest," pony rides, puppet shows and craft activities for the whole family. There is no admission fee and most of the activities are free. For more information about Maymont, see the description and directions on how to get there in our Attractions chapter. It's one of the best places to go in the city anytime!

Herbs Galore
Maymont • 358-7166

Bring a friend and learn more about herbs and herb gardens at this weekend event held each spring. Talk to expert gardeners and buy some unusual herbs for your own garden. Admission is free to the event, but there is a fee for the seminars. See our Attractions chapter

for directions and more information about Maymont.

Easter Egg Hunt
Poor Farm Park, Highway 54, Ashland, and Pole Green Park, Pole Green Rd., Mechanicsville • 798-8062

Sponsored by the Hanover County Department of Parks and Recreation, this event draws thousands of community members. The day begins at 10 AM at Poor Farm Park with the Easter Bunny and music. Divided into age groups, children hunt for Easter eggs, specifically those with prize dots on them. It lasts about two hours. The event is repeated at 1 PM at Pole Green Park. Admission is free.

Historic Garden Week in Virginia
12 E. Franklin St. • 644-7776, 643-7141

The last full week in April, hundreds of private homes and gardens throughout the state are open for tours as part of Historic Garden Week, sponsored by the Garden Club of Virginia. In the Richmond area, about 15 to 20 homes are open each year for about three days during the tour period. Co-sponsored by the Historic Richmond Foundation, this tour marks the only time many homes and shrines, including Westover Plantation, are open to the public. Proceeds are used to help restore historic grounds and gardens throughout the state. A guidebook with information about tour locations and schedules is available February 1 from the Garden Club of Virginia. The guidebook also includes information about other historic landmarks and shrines in the state. Call one of the numbers above to obtain a guidebook.

Admission usually ranges from about $12 to $20 for block tours. Admission to individual homes is about $2 to $5.

Southern Women's Show
600 Laburnum Ave., Strawberry Hill
• (800) 849-0248

Each spring, the Southern Women's Show arrives at the State Fairgrounds on Strawberry Hill with four days of learning, shopping and tasting. Don't miss this chance to see fashion shows, hear expert financial advice, visit boutiques, attend educational seminars and discover art and home decorating ideas and techniques. You can even have a professional makeover and a quick health check. Admission is about $6.

Strawberry Hill Races
600 E. Laburnum Ave., Strawberry Hill
• 228-3200

This steeplechase is one of the biggest annual events in the area and has become Richmond's rite of spring. Proceeds benefit local charities. The Richmond Symphony was selected to be the lead benefactor in 1993, replacing the Historic Richmond Foundation, which benefited from the races for more than a decade. The Symphony uses the proceeds to expand its youth and school programs throughout Virginia.

Held in April, the races are preceded by balls, carriage parades and parties. The day of the races, people hold elaborate themed tailgate parties, and many dress in fashions or costumes to complement their party themes. It's a big reunion for locals, and you'll see just about everything from sunbathers guzzling beer to Rolls Royces and people dressed in top hats and tails sipping French champagne. Be sure to walk around the infield to see it all. Prizes are awarded for the best tailgate parties. Call in advance to reserve a space or to enter the tailgate competition. Tickets cost about $16 in advance, $25 at the gate.

May

Arts in the Park
1112 Sunset Ave., Byrd Park • 353-8198

If you like parks, crowds, arts and crafts, you'll like this free event held each year in Byrd Park. More than 100 selected exhibitors and artists from all over the country offer unusual and hard-to-find items.

Camptown Races
Graymont Park, Ashland • 752-6678

Some of the fastest horses in the area sprint around Hanover County's Graymont Park at Camptown Races, Virginia's only flat-track horse racing event. A variety of races around the ½-mile oval track are open to thoroughbreds, Arabians and quarter horses. Graymont is about 2 miles north of Ashland off U.S. Highway 1 on State Route 641.

Children's activities are offered, and the event is fun for families and tailgaters. Prizes are awarded for the best parties. Proceeds benefit various charitable and civic projects in Hanover County. Call to reserve a spot. Admission is $12 a person in advance; $15 at the gate.

INSIDERS' TIP

Batter up! The World's Largest Softball Tournament featuring more than 400 teams from the U.S., Iceland and Canada is usually held on Memorial Day weekend at more than 72 locations around the area. A home-run hitting contest kicks it off in Glen Allen on Friday. Games begin at 8 AM and usually last until about 10 PM. Call 266-8317 for more information.

Harness Racing Season
Colonial Downs, New Kent • 966-7223

The 30-day standardbred, harness racing schedule begins at the end of May at Virginia's only pari-mutuel betting race track. General admission is $2, not including a program or parking.

Mother's Day Open Houses
Agecroft Hall • 353-4241
Lewis Ginter Botanical Garden • 262-9887

Agecroft Hall and the Lewis Ginter Botanical Garden have special activities each year to celebrate Mother's Day, including garden tours and outdoor concerts. For more information about these places, see our Attractions chapter.

River City Real Beer Fest
Farmers' Market in Shockoe Bottom • 643-2826

Co-sponsored by Downtown Presents and the Mid-Atlantic Association of Craft Breweries, this two-day festival features more than 40 different types of beer brewed by more than 20 breweries and delicious food to go with it. Purchase the required mug for $3 and pay a small fee for the samples of your choice. Along with the tastings, there are free seminars for anyone who would like to drink smarter. Experts are available to discuss topics such as different beer styles, brewing processes and the craft beer industry. The festival stage features live music all weekend, and you can shop for a variety of beer-related paraphernalia and brewing supplies. The festival is open Saturday from noon until 9 PM, and Sunday from 1 to 6 PM.

Scottish Festival and Games
Scotchtown • 227-3500

At Scotchtown, the Revolutionary War home of Patrick Henry, hundreds of Scottish and Irish descendants celebrate their heritage with old-fashioned games and clan competitions at the Scotchtown Festival. Numerous exhibitors offer Scottish and Irish clothing, accessories, books, plants and food. Participants come here from all parts of the United States. Scotchtown is just west of Ashland off State Route 50. For more information about Scotchtown, see the description in our Attractions chapter.

Winston Cup Race Weekend
Richmond International Raceway
• 345-RACE

The Pontiac Excitement 400/Hardee's Fried Chicken Challenge 250 draws more than 60,000 spectators for this major NASCAR event. The raceway becomes a city within a city with campers, trailers and race fans from all over the country who want to watch famous drivers speed around the ¾-mile track at speeds of faster than 200 mph. Tickets for the Winston Cup race start at about $70 and sell out fast, so buy yours early. Tickets for other races are about half that and can be purchased at the gate.

June

All-American Soap Box Derby
740 Navy Hill Rd., Children's Museum of Richmond • 358-6878

Every spring, about 60 kids race down 10th Street at about 25 mph to see who will go to the national Soap Box Derby championships in Ohio. The event is surrounded with art activities, games, a safety fair and entertainment such as in-line skate-team demonstrations. Participants may receive help from their parents. Kits are available from the museum. Registration begins as early as February.

Ashland Strawberry Faire
Randolph-Macon College • 752-6766

Strawberry shortcakes, pie-eating contests and other strawberry-related activities are the focus for this sprawling fair held each year on the campus of Randolph-Macon College in Ashland. Hundreds of craftsmen, businesses and community organizations set up exhibits and demonstrations, and a variety of performances featuring local entertainers and school groups are offered. Children's games and contests round out the family-oriented activities. Admission is free.

Festival of the Arts
Dogwood Dell/Carillon, 1300 Blanton Ave., Byrd Park • 780-8137

Free concerts, dances and theatric performances are offered at this multi-tiered, grassy outdoor amphitheater for several weeks each summer during the Festival of the Arts. Bring a picnic supper, a blanket or lawn chairs and relax under the evening stars. You'll see everything from rock 'n' roll to classical ballet. It's great family entertainment. Once you get to the park at Boulevard and Idlewood Avenues, just head for the Carillon, a 240-foot Georgian bell tower that pays tribute to Virginians who died in World War I. There's room for about 3,000 people, but come early to get the best seats and room for your spread. Admission is free.

Greek Festival
Greek Orthodox Cathedral, 30 Malvern Ave. • 355-3687

This popular food festival, which takes place the weekend after Memorial Day, features delicious Greek food, entertainment and cultural activities. It's the largest of its kind in the country and draws 35,000 people over a four-day period. The Cathedral has a membership of about 2,500 communicants.

Jumpin'
2800 Grove Ave., Virginia Museum of Fine Arts • 367-8148

Each year during June, July and August, the Virginia Museum of Fine Arts offers a Thursday evening outdoor music series in the sculpture garden. A summertime favorite, the series offers a broad spectrum of music including Cajun, jazz, rhythm and blues and Caribbean. Tickets usually sell out well in advance. Call the museum for a schedule and ticket information. See our Attractions chapter for more information about the museum.

Photo: The Arts Council of Richmond

The Richmond Children's Festival features an international cultural theme each year.

Spring N2 Summer10 and Scooper Bowl
2500 W. Broad St., Science Museum
 • **367-6552**

Celebrate summer fun in this science festival featuring music, food, educational demonstrations, children's activities and entertainment for all ages and "all you can eat" Breyers ice cream. One charge includes ice cream, the event and museum exhibits.

Ukrop's/Target Family Jubilee
Brown's Island • 643-2826

Sponsored by Ukrop's and Target, this one-day event is filled with food, music and hands-on activities that are fun for the whole family. Admission is free. Look for details in the daily newspaper.

July

The BIG Gig, Richmond's International Festival of Music
Various locations • 643-2826

Whatever type of music you prefer, you'll hear it at the BIG Gig, Richmond's International Festival of Music. As many as 50 free concerts are offered at the Nina Abady Festival Park, the Carpenter Center and at nontraditional venues such as office buildings, shopping centers, city parks and gardens. A brochure with a complete schedule is available in May Call Downtown Presents, 643-2826, for a free copy.

Hanover Tomato Festival
5501 Mechanicsville Tnpk., Battlefield Park Elementary School • 798-8062

Hanover County's celebrated tomatoes are the focus of this annual event featuring BLT sandwiches, tomato fritters and fresh tomatoes. Sponsored by the Black Creek Fire Department on a Saturday near the Fourth of July, this festival attracts thousands of people.

Activities include live music, tomato-eating contests, a parade, crafts, demonstrations and games. Admission is free.

Fourth of July Celebrations
Various locations

The most popular Fourth of July fireworks display is at the Diamond, 359-4444, immediately after the Richmond Braves ballgame. Buy your tickets early because they usually sell out. You can also celebrate the Fourth at a number of other places in the area including the Chesterfield Fairgrounds, 748-1623, Meadow Farm, 672-5100, and Innsbrook, 965-7922. Admission fees vary.

Musical Mondays
Maymont • 358-7166

Enjoy the soul-stirring music of Richmond's best community bands while you picnic or just relax on the spacious grounds of Maymont. Offered every Monday night for several weeks beginning in mid-July and running through August, this event is reminiscent of the days when people were entertained on summer evenings by bands playing at the village green. Admission is free. For more information about Maymont, see our Attractions chapter.

August

Carytown Watermelon Festival
Cary St., Carytown • 359-4645; 353-1525

About nine blocks of Cary Street are closed for this friendly street party sponsored by the Carytown Merchants Association. Stroll down the middle of the street and enjoy a slice of watermelon, samples of food from area restaurants, exhibits, sidewalk sales and live entertainment. It's a great chance to see old friends and do some people-watching. There is no admission fee. Always on Sunday, it runs from 10 AM to 6 PM.

INSIDERS' TIP

You'll find a variety of free concerts offered almost every week during the summer: "Musical Mondays at Maymont" and "Friday Cheers" at the Nina Abady Park downtown as well as "Fridays at Sunset" at Kanawha Plaza.

Virginia Food Festival
600 E. Laburnum Ave., Strawberry Hill
• 643-3555, 228-3200

Sample the best foods in Virginia from Chesapeake Bay blue crabs and oysters to beef, pork and native Virginia wine, plus everything in between. Tickets are $20 a person for this popular one-day event.

September

Civil War Days Re-enactment
Meadow Farm • 672-5100

Living history re-enactments of Civil War days on a middle-class farm are offered during a weekend in September at Meadow Farm. Re-enactors present a variety of activities such as blacksmithing demonstrations, tours of the doctor's office and house, and interpretive dramas. It's fun and educational for the entire family. For more information about Meadow Farm, see the description in the Attractions and Tours chapter. Admission is free.

Fall Garden Fair and Plant Sale
Lewis Ginter Botanical Garden • 262-9887

Stroll through the Lewis Ginter Botanical Garden with about 10,000 other gardening enthusiasts while you shop for plants and gardening accessories from hundreds of vendors scattered throughout the grounds. In particular, you'll find a great selection of herbs, daylilies and trees. The event is free with admission to the Garden. For more information, see our Attractions and Tours chapter.

Henricus Publick Days
Henricus Historical Park • 748-1161

On Citie of Henricus Publick Day, celebrated on the third Sunday in September each year, the park sponsors a re-enactment of the lives of the settlers, a 17th-century Church of England morning prayer service, games, food and tours. The event features old-fashioned games such as hoop-rolling, bowling, stilt-walking, tree-stump checkers and a variety of other hands-on historical activities such as candle-making and storytelling.

Sir Thomas Dale established Henricus as the second English settlement in 1611 when the London Company sought a better location than Jamestown for its colony. It includes the site of what is believed to be the first hospital in America. Admission to the event and the park is free. For more information about Henricus, see our Attractions and Tours chapter.

Exxon NASCAR Select Battery 400 Race Weekend
Richmond International Raceway
• 345-RACE

The Miller Genuine Draft 400/Autolite Platinum 200 NASCAR Race Weekend draws more than 60,000 spectators. The raceway becomes a mini-city with campers, trailers and race fans from all over the country who've come to watch famous drivers speed around the ¾-mile track at speeds of faster than 200 mph. Tickets sell out fast, so buy yours early. Reserved seats are $70 and $75.

State Fair of Virginia
600 E. Laburnum Ave., Strawberry Hill
• 228-3200

Every September the State Fair returns with something for everyone. There are craft displays, blue-ribbon winners, livestock displays and demonstrations, midway rides and games, Italian sausages and corn dogs, big-name entertainment shows, magic shows, side shows, a circus and lots and lots of exhibits by companies and organizations from all over the state. Many employers and companies offer discount tickets for the weeklong event. Ask at work or watch the ads. Advance tickets cost $12.

INSIDERS' TIP

Finding a place to park for some of the most popular annual events can be frustrating unless you plan ahead. Practice your parallel parking, allow plenty of time to find a spot on the street, and be prepared to walk several city blocks to reach your destination.

Thoroughbred Horse Racing Season
Colonial Downs, New Kent • 966-7223

And they're off! Cross your fingers and place your bets for the start of the 25-day thoroughbred horse racing season at the new Colonial Downs race track in New Kent County. Races are scheduled Friday through Tuesday. General admission is $2, not including parking or a program. See the Spectator Sports chapter for more information.

October

2nd Street Festival
2nd Street • 643-2826

This two-day festival on Richmond's historic 2nd Street celebrates the culture and heritage of Richmond's African-American community and serves as a reunion for many who have lived and worked here or frequented the area. You'll find jazz, ragtime, gospel and music from

The Hanover Tomato

Sometime around the middle of June, when the local news media starts running prime-time feature stories about how the Hanover tomato crop is growing, you start to get the feeling that this is not an ordinary tomato.

For as long as anyone can remember, the Hanover tomato, grown in the eastern part of the county it's named after, has been the queen of local produce. Many locals won't buy any other type of tomato, and some people drive in from out-of-state to buy several pounds of them.

Bursting with juicy, vine-ripened flavor, the lush red fruit wins taste test after taste test. But no one has ever been able to explain why they're so good. Some say the magic is in the dirt — sandy, loamy, coastal-plain soil — but this same type of soil is found in the surrounding counties where the tomatoes just aren't as good. People have even tried transplanting tomato plants from Hanover into similar soil to no avail. Any way you slice it, the Hanover grown tomato is still the best.

Hanover tomatoes are some of the first to hit the market. You'll find them at grocery stores and produce stands around the Fourth of July, and you'll find over a hundred bushels of them at the annual Hanover Tomato Festival attended by over 10,000 people each July at Battlefield Park Elementary School in Mechanicsville. (The festival is written up in this chapter.)

Sponsored by the Black Creek Volunteer Fire Department, the Ashland/Hanover Chamber of Commerce and the Hanover Herald Progress, the event features the Little Miss Hanover Tomato Festival contest, live entertainment, crafts, community booths, and of course BLTs,

— continued on next page

The Hanover tomato is the queen of produce in the Richmond area.

Photo: Herald-Progress Newspaper

fried green tomatoes, tomato and mayonnaise sandwiches, tomato pie and other tomato-inspired food items.

Peppered with truck farms (the local description for produce farms) Hanover County has a strong agricultural heritage that goes beyond its famous tomatoes. Conditions are also excellent for growing other fruits and vegetables such as corn, sweet potatoes, green peas, onions, lettuce, asparagus, spinach, cabbage, broccoli, okra, lima beans, green beans, parsnips, melons, eggplant, radishes, peppers, strawberries and blackberries. Delicious though they may be, none of these other fruits or vegetables have challenged the tomato as the queen of Hanover produce.

1920 through 1950. The festival also has dramatic performances, children's activities, dancing in the street and soul food such as chitlins, pigs' feet, fish, fried chicken, collard greens and more. Vendors sell clothing, jewelry, prints and other wares. Admission is free.

Autumn Harvest Grand Illumination Parade
W. Broad St. • 266-6808

One of the oldest parades in Richmond, the Autumn Harvest Grand Illumination Parade starts in the evening and travels from Willow Lawn Shopping Center down Broad Street to the Virginia Department of Motor Vehicles. It includes local high school bands, local personalities, Shriners and illuminated floats. It used to be called The Tobacco Festival Parade.

Harvest Festival in Shockoe Slip
Cary St. • 782-9431

Sponsored by the Shockoe Slip Merchants Association, this street party offers Richmonders of all ages a chance to parade their costumes and participate in a variety of fall and Halloween activities. Shockoe Slip is on Cary Street from 12th to 14th streets. Admission is free.

Heritage Faire
Poor Farm Park, Highway 54, Ashland • 798-8062

This event, sponsored by the Hanover County Department of Parks and Recreation, draws thousands of community members and about 100 exhibitors. The day is filled with an abundance of activities, including carriage rides, children's games and craft demonstrations. Ethnic exhibits, such as Native American, Mountain Men and Scottish American demonstrations, are a big part as well. Admission is free.

Festival 1893
Maymont • 358-7166

Every October, Richmonders celebrate the first year that Maymont's original owners, Major James and Sally Dooley, lived at Maymont. The couple stayed there and created gardens, walkways and more until the grounds were donated to the city of Richmond in 1925, upon Sally Dooley's death. The highlights of Festival 1893 is a decorated-carriage parade that ends at Maymont, children's games and a cake walk. Admission is free.

Richmond Children's Festival
Discovery Park, 2500 W. Broad St. • 355-7200

This delightful outdoor festival celebrates children and the arts. The weekend event held at Discovery Park features music, drama and other professional performances, plus crafts, roving entertainers and food. The activities are usually themed around a different culture each year. Thousands of families attend. Admission is free.

INSIDERS' TIP

Before you visit one of the attractions in the area, be sure to call ahead to find out about their hours. Many locations are closed on Mondays, and quite a few offer extended hours during the summer.

November

Ashland-Hanover Olde Time Holiday Parade
Ashland • 752-6766

This is a small-town Christmas parade with a lot of enthusiasm. It starts west of town on State Route 54, heads east, crosses U.S. Highway 1 and ends at the Ashland-Hanover Shopping Center. Call for more details.

Crestar Richmond Marathon
• 285-9495

This is the area's biggest sporting event with about 3,000 runners, joggers and wheelchair racers entered for the full 26.2-mile marathon, the 13.1-mile half-marathon or the 5-mile race. It's a sanctioned race, but it's probably more of a social event as thousands of spectators turn out to cheer their friends and neighbors. A variety of activities near the start and finish at 6th and Broad streets add to the festivities. For more information, see the description in our Spectator Sports chapter.

The First Thanksgiving
Berkeley Plantation, 12602 Harrison Landing Rd., Charles City County • 829-6018

Spend the day at this beautiful plantation on the James River and watch an outdoor drama commemorating the events of the first official Thanksgiving celebration held in this country. It wasn't at Plymouth, it was here. You'll enjoy living-history performances, dancing and demonstrations by representatives from local Indian tribes and live musical entertainment. You'll also find Southern-style food and an arts and craft show featuring some of the finest artisans in the area. The celebration is held the first Saturday in November. Admission to the event includes a tour of the plantation house and gardens. See our Daytrips chapter for more information about Berkeley Plantation.

Great American Indian Pow Wow
3000 Mechanicsville Tnpk., The Showplace • 225-8877

This is an authentic Native-American Pow Wow open to the public. The first one in 1991 was so successful that organizers decided to make it an annual event. You'll see Native American dancing, costumes, craft-making and competitions. Admission fees vary.

Joy from the World
2500 W. Broad St., Science Museum • 367-6552

Beautifully decorated exhibits and trees from more than 25 countries and cultures create a magic atmosphere that lasts from the end of November through early January. In December, traditional crafts, songs, foods, music and workshops fill the Science Museum with an international air. All exhibits and events are included with museum admission unless otherwise noted.

Model Railroad Show and Swap Meet
5701 Huntsman Rd. • 236-3622; 367-6552

The Model Railroad Show brings together railroad enthusiasts, vendors and rooms full of working train displays. Relive your childhood and introduce your family to the world of model railroading. Z, N, HO, S, O and O Standard gauge trains travel through detailed dioramas and layouts. Lots of memorabilia and information add to the day's fun. The show is included with museum admission.

Urbanna Oyster Festival
Urbanna • (804) 758-5540

We're cheating on this one because it's not a Richmond-area event, but since so many Richmonders go to this festival, we thought it should be included. In fact, this festival is so popular that the water pipes under the streets broke from the weight of the crowd several years ago. (It's more spread out now and not as crowded as it used to be.)

This festival is held the first weekend in November every year. Oyster fans will find raw, steamed and roasted oysters, oyster stew, oyster fritters and fried oysters. If you don't like oysters, the crab cake and soft-shell crab sandwiches are good bets, and there's lots of other food to eat. You'll also find an art show, crafts, a few amusement rides and tours of tall ships docked in the harbor. The Saturday afternoon parade features numerous high school bands, Shriners and literally every fire department within driving distance (you won't believe the sirens!).

Try to get there before 9 AM on Saturday if you want to park anywhere close to the festivities. Visit on Friday to avoid the crowds and miss the parade. Admission is free.

Virginia-Carolina Craftsmen's Christmas Classic
600 E. Laburnum Ave., Strawberry Hill • 228-3200

Hundreds of craftspeople from Virginia and surrounding states offer unique hand-crafted Christmas gifts, accessories and more at this annual weekend event. You'll find thousands of folksy gift items and decorations made of wood, pottery, glass, tin and fabrics.

December

Bizarre Bazaar
600 E. Laburnum Ave., Strawberry Hill • 228-3200

Nearly 300 juried exhibitors and nationally known artists display everything from boutique and designer accessories to crafts, gifts and gourmet foods.

Capital City Kwanza Festival
Richmond Centre • 266-5428

African dance, music and performances surround this celebration of Kwanza, an African harvest festival.

Christmas Open Houses

Most of the attractions and several historic homes are decorated for the holidays and offer free Open Houses and holiday activities during December. These include the Executive Mansion in Capital Square, 786-2220; Agecroft Hall, 353-4241; Court End locations, 649-0711; Scotchtown, 227-3500; Lewis Ginter Botanical Garden, 262-9887; Wilton House, 282-5936; Hanover Courthouse, 537-5815;

Magnolia Grange, 796-1479; and Meadow Farm, 672-5100. See our Attractions and Tours chapter for more information on the individual sites.

Gardenfest of Lights
1800 Lakeside Ave., Lewis Ginter Botanical Garden • 262-9887

Recapture the magic and peacefulness of the holiday season at the Lewis Ginter Botanical Garden with an evening stroll through the mystical lighting effects throughout the grounds from 5:30 to 9 PM. The Bloemendaal House is also beautifully decorated with natural materials and garlands. Regular admission prices are charged. See our Attractions chapter for more information about the Lewis Ginter Botanical Garden.

Grand Illumination
901 E. Cary St., James Center • 344-3232

Celebrate the beginning of the Christmas season at this spirit-filled community event in downtown Richmond, and watch with thousands of people as the Christmas lights and the reindeer display at the James Center are lit for the first time. Choral presentations by area high schools, horse-drawn wagon rides, children's activities and street performers surround the event.

Holiday House Tours

Various homes including historic mansions and restored town houses are decorated and open for tour during the holidays on the Downtown Richmond House Tour, 648-7998; the Fan District House Tour, 344-7998; the Church Hill House Tour, 643-3643; and Ashland's Tour of Homes, 798-2728. Call in advance for locations and ticket information.

Jaycees Christmas Parade
Broad St., Downtown • 644-9607

This is a big parade with giant balloon characters, famous personalities, Santa and hundreds of bands, floats, twirlers and pa-

---

INSIDERS' TIP

The anything-goes bonnet contest at Easter on Parade, Richmond's signature Easter event held on Monument Avenue, brings out some of the silliest bonnets and outfits in town.

rade units. The Richmond Jaycees sponsor the parade that starts at the Virginia Department of Motor Vehicles on Broad Street and ends at the Richmond Coliseum on Seventh Street. The streets along the route are lined with people about five deep on each side. Get there at least 30 minutes before the parade starts for a good spot, and bring chairs and blankets. The schedule and parade route are detailed in the *Richmond Times-Dispatch* before the event. The parade lasts about two hours.

Tackiest Christmas Decorations Tour
Numerous locations

Every year, some holiday enthusiasts go to extremes, decorating their homes with so many lights that they have to generate their own electricity. You have to wonder where they store all the plastic trains, carolers, candy canes and Santas for the rest of the year. Watch the *Richmond Times-Dispatch* for a description and map of the tour. Some of the homes are so popular, you actually have to wait in traffic to see them. Others have so much to see, you'll want to park and walk around for a closer look.

Victorian Christmas
Maymont • 358-7166

Previously called the Christmas Open House, this December event includes Maymont house tours, carriage rides, a visit from Father Christmas, caroling, a wreath sale and more. Admission is free.

A number of wineries and vineyards within driving distance of Richmond are open for tours or festivals with an abundance of special activities in October, Virginia Wine Month.

Daytrips

Richmond's central location makes it an ideal starting point for daytrips. You can drive to nearly every part of the state within a few hours. To the east, you can visit Virginia Beach, the Chesapeake Bay, Colonial Williamsburg, Jamestown, Yorktown, the Eastern Shore and the James River Plantations. To the west, you'll find the Shenandoah Valley, the Blue Ridge Mountains, the heart of Virginia's wine country, and Jefferson's Monticello. To the north is a wealth of cultural activities and attractions in Washington, D.C., and Fredericksburg. To the south, are Civil War sites and more than 250 years of history in Petersburg. The Eastern Shore and the Highlands of southwest Virginia offer an abundance of wildlife, natural areas and recreational opportunities, but you'll need to allow more than a day for a trip.

Virginia is so rich with a variety of attractions and scenic places, we can't possibly cover them all here. To help you plan your daytrips, we suggest you refer to the *Insiders' Guides® to Williamsburg*, *Virginia Beach*, *Washington D.C.*, the *Chesapeake Bay*, the *Blue Ridge* and *The Insiders' Guide® to the Civil War in the Eastern Theater*. A complete list of titles and information about how to order them is included in the back of this book. In this section we've included other destinations that may not be included in other Insiders Guides®.

For general information and maps, start with Virginia Tourism Corp., 901 E. Byrd St., 786-4484.

Plantations

Several Colonial plantations on the James River, southeast of Richmond on State Route 5 in Charles City County, are historically and architecturally interesting, with beautiful views of the river from artistically landscaped lawns and gardens.

From Richmond you can drive to most of them in about 30 minutes or you can see them from the river the way the colonists did on The Annabel Lee paddlewheel riverboat on a cruise that departs from Richmond. There's more information about the Annabel Lee's Plantation Cruise in the Attractions and Tours chapter. A block ticket is also available if you plan to visit several plantations. As a general rule, you'll find that most of those listed here are open daily year round from about 9 AM to 5 PM. You'll probably find that you'll want to spend an hour or two a each plantation. Tours are usually offered continuously throughout the day. Hours and days of operation may vary depending on the season. Call for current schedules.

Lunch and dinner are offered at two excellent restaurants in the area. Indian Fields Tavern, 9220 John Tyler Highway, 829-5004, is housed in an old restored farmhouse surrounded by beautiful countryside. The cuisine features fresh ingredients including Virginia hams and Chesapeake seafood. For a more historic ambiance, critically acclaimed colonial dining is available at the Coach House Tavern, 12602 Harrison Landing Rd., 829-6003, in a restored outbuilding at Berkeley Plantation near the manor house. Lunch is served by costumed staff daily; dinner is by reservation. See our Restaurants chapter for more information.

Many of the plantations have facilities that may be rented for weddings, corporate outings, receptions and other social activities. Those that do are noted. A few are also bed and breakfast inns.

Belle Air
11800 John Tyler Hwy. • 829-2431

Built in 1670, this plantation features original heartpine timbers and America's finest Jacobean stairway. The landscaped grounds overlook expansive rolling farmland. It's open to the public only during Historic Garden Week in April. During other times, group tours are available by advance reservation. Belle Air is also available for small weddings and parties, and has a bed and breakfast for honeymoon guests.

Berkeley Plantation
12602 Harrison Landing Rd. • 829-6018

Built in 1726 by Benjamin Harrison IV, Berkeley is the oldest three-story brick home in Virginia. Harrison's son, the second owner of the plantation, was a signer of the Declaration of Independence and a governor of Virginia three times. William Henry Harrison, the ninth president of the United States, and Benjamin Harrison, the 23rd president, are descendants of Benjamin Harrison IV.

Berkeley was also the site of America's first Thanksgiving in 1619. A festival commemorating the event is held here each year during the first Sunday in November. Formal, terraced boxwood gardens and lawns extend over a quarter of a mile from the house to the James River. Tours are offered. Near the manor house, the acclaimed Coach House Tavern, which we've described in the "Plantation"-section introduction, serves lunch daily and dinner by reservation. The grounds and fish house may be rented for functions.

Edgewood
4800 John Tyler Hwy. • 829-2962

This 1849 Gothic Revival mansion is open for tours and also serves as a bed and breakfast inn. The house features six bedrooms filled with antiques, a freestanding spiral staircase in the grand hall and 10 fireplaces. The grounds include a grist mill built in 1725. According to legend, you can still hear the footsteps of a woman who once lived here as she searches for her lover who never returned from the war. Reservations are required for tours and rooms. Edgewood can be rented for special occasions, Victorian tea party luncheons, weddings and other events.

Evelynton
6701 John Tyler Hwy. • 829-5075

Evelynton was the home of Edmund Ruffin who is credited with firing the first shot of the Civil War at Fort Sumter. It's been the home of the Ruffin family since 1847. The property was originally part of Westover Plantation, and the house features examples of decorative arts from the great houses of Virginia. The house and gardens are open for tours and are available for catered occasions such as weddings, receptions and corporate meetings. There's also a gift shop. Call for information.

North Bend Plantation
12200 Weyanoke Rd., Charles City • 829-5176

Built in 1819, North Bend Plantation is one of the oldest bed and breakfast buildings in the area. About a mile off State Route 5 on Weyanoke Road, the Greek Revival plantation house is on the National Register of Historic Landmarks and is also a designated Virginia Historic Landmark. Ridgely and George Copeland are the third generation of the family to own the home, and they still cultivate the plantation's 250 acres. In 1864, Union General Phil Sheridan used North Bend as his Civil War headquarters. Union breastworks still exist on the grounds. Special possessions displayed to visitors include a fine collection of old and rare books, colonial antiques from related early James River plantation families and an antique doll collection. North Bend is also available for weddings and receptions.

Piney Grove at Southall's Plantation
16920 Southall Planation Ln. • 829-2480

A rare example of the Tidewater log architectural style, Piney Grove was built in 1800 by Furnea Southall, and now serves as a bed and breakfast. The grounds feature gardens and a nature trail. Rooms are tastefully appointed with working fireplaces and antiques that reflect the history of the plantation. After a busy day of sightseeing, relax with a mint julep and wake up to a plantation-style breakfast.

Sherwood Forest
14501 John Tyler Hwy. • 829-5377

Built in 1730, this 300-foot-long frame house looks similar to the way it appeared in 1845 when it was renovated by former President John Tyler. The home was also owned by President William Henry Harrison. Original

18th-century furnishings throughout the house include heirlooms of the Tyler family, descendants of whom still live here. A 12-acre garden features more than 80 varieties of century-old trees. Refreshments and mansion or garden tours are available. The grounds may be rented for special occasions.

Shirley
501 Shirley Plantation Rd. • 829-5121

Founded in 1613, Shirley is the oldest plantation in Virginia and has been the home of the Hill-Carter family for 10 generations. Anne Hill Carter, mother of Gen. Robert E. Lee, was born and married here, and Lee received part of his schooling here. The mansion was completed in 1738 and appears for the most part in its original state. An architectural treasure, the mansion features a three-story circular staircase with no visible means of support, carved walnut staircases, superb paneling and elegant carved detailing. A number of brick outbuildings — including a two-story kitchen, laundry house and two barns — form a Queen Anne forecourt. Other structures include a stable, smokehouse and dove cote. The 10th generation of the original family now oversees the farm and house. Tours are offered daily, except on Christmas and Thanksgiving.

Westover
7000 Westover Rd. • 829-2882

Built in 1730, Westover is one of the finest examples of Georgian architecture in America. This was the home of William Byrd II, the founder of Richmond and Petersburg. It's known for its superb proportions and early 18th-century gates. Overlooking the James River, the grounds are open daily. Group tours of the house and grounds are available by reservation. The house is closed except during Historic Garden Week.

Wineries

The winemaking industry in Virginia has experienced a revival since the 1960s that has made it the 11th-largest wine producer in the country. There are six designated grape-growing regions and about 50 wineries, most of which are concentrated in the Shenandoah Valley, Charlottesville, Middleburg, Front Royal/The Plains and Southwest Virginia. The most popular Virginia wines include Chardonnay, Riesling and Cabernet Sauvignon and Merlot. Seyval and Vidal are popular French hybrids. For a free list of Virginia's wineries write: Virginia Wine Marketing Program, Virginia Department of Agriculture and Consumer Services, Division of Marketing, P.O. Box 1163, Richmond 23209; or call 1-800-828-4637.

A number of wineries and vineyards within driving distance of Richmond are open for tours or festivals with an abundance of special activities in October, Virginia Wine Month. Road signs with a grape cluster design are posted within a ten-mile radius of each winery. To get you started, we've provided descriptions of a few of the most unique and popular wineries within an hour or two of Richmond. Generally speaking, they're usually open from about 10 AM to 5 PM daily. Call for specific hours.

Afton Mountain Vineyards
234 Vineyard Ln., Afton • (540) 456-8667

Taste the wines and tour the man-made aging cave in the midst of the beautiful Blue Ridge Mountains. At this winery, grapes are picked by hand and a gravity-flow processing system is used to move the grapes through the wine-making process without pumps. The cave provides ideal conditions for storage. The winery is closed on Tuesdays.

Barboursville Vineyards & Historic Ruins
17655 Winery Rd., Barboursville • (540) 832-3824

With over 125 acres in vineyards, Barboursville is one of the single largest vineyard and estate producers on the East Coast, and it was the first Virginia winery devoted exclusively to European varietals. Dr. Gianni Zonin, who owns the vineyard as well as Italy's largest private winery and a number of historic vineyards, was attracted to Barboursville because the climate, landscape and soil conditions are similar to those in Tuscany.

Along with a tour of the winery, visitors may also tour the remains of a mansion built by Thomas Jefferson for Governor Barbour. The ruins and the Tuscan Room are popular settings for romantic weddings.

It takes about 30 minutes to get to Barboursville from Charlottesville. Drive north on Route 250 to Route 20 North. Following Route 20, you'll start to see signs for the vineyard and tours. From Richmond take U.S. Highway 33 West to Route 20 South where you'll begin to see the signs.

Chateau Morrisette
Winery Rd., Floyd • (540) 593-2865

Known for its food and flowers, as well as its award-winning wines, Chateau Morrisette offers tours of the winery that is housed in a charming native stone and wood building. Outdoor patios and gardens offer views of the Blue Ridge Mountains and the Rock Castle Gorge Wilderness Area. An annual event here is the Black Dog Jazz Concerts held the second Saturday of the month, June through October, from noon to 5 PM.

Ingleside Plantation Vineyards
5872 Leedstown Rd., Oak Grove
• (804) 224-8687

Ingleside is the only vineyard in Virginia where the visitors can arrive by boat. Located in the Northern Neck region, Ingleside is directly between the Potomac River and the Rappahannock River a few miles east of Fredericksburg. Since it was established in 1834, the plantation has served as a boys' school, a Civil War garrison, a courthouse and a dairy.

The winery offers tours, a tasting room, a museum with artifacts from Native American tribes and a gift shop. About 50 acres are planted, and the winery is best known for its sparkling wines. Special events include Barrel Tastings in the spring and fall, Jazz in the Courtyard in June and a Holiday Open House. There's also a Seafood Extravaganza in September.

Oakencroft Vineyard & Winery
1486 Oakencroft Lane • (804) 296-4188

The fact that each of its vintages has been a medal winner sets Oakencroft apart from other Virginia wineries. Located in the Monticello region, just 3.5 miles from Charlottesville, it's also memorable for its idyllic country farm setting with gorgeous views of the Blue Ridge Mountains and a picturesque lake. The tasting room is filled with antiques.

Special events here include a Spring Fiesta, July 4th Blues Concert, Harvest Fest and Holiday Open House. Tours and tastings are offered throughout the year, on a seasonal schedule. Be sure to call first to get the current hours.

The Oasis Winery
14141 Hume Rd. • (540) 635-7627

This internationally acclaimed winery near the Skyline Drive maintains over 100 acres of vineyards and has some of the oldest plantings of Cabernet Sauvignon and Chardonnay in the state. It's also the state's largest producer of sparkling wine. You can tour the two-story underground winery, enjoy a gourmet meal in the cafe, picnic beside the lake or smoke a cigar on the Oasis Cigar Patio.

Piedmont Vineyards & Winery
2546D Halfway Rd., Middleburg
• (540) 687-5528

Enjoy picnicking, wine tasting and winery tours here in the heart of northern Virginia's hunt country. The winery is located at Waverly, a pre-Revolutionary War farm, with a house that dates back to the early 17th century. The winery also plays host to private parties, weddings and receptions.

Prince Michel & Rapidan River Vineyards
HCR 4 Box 77, Rt. 29 South, Leon
• (540) 547-3707, (800) 869-8242

Just south of Culpeper, this French Provencial winery with over 150 acres of vineyards, features a restaurant with classic French cuisine, and an extensive wine museum where you'll see antique winemaking equipment and rare bottles. There's also an audiovisual presentation about the history and development of viticulture. The self-guided tour of their 150,000 gallon capacity winery includes stainless steel fermenting tanks and a traditional barrel room.

The Williamsburg Winery, Ltd. and Gabriel Archer Tavern
5800 Wessex Hundred, Williamsburg
• (757) 229-0999

Noted for having the state's largest barrel cellar, the Williamsburg Winery is housed in a

Photo: Metro Richmond Convention and Visitors Bureau

The original house at Evelynton Plantation was burned during the Civil War.

17th-century-style farmhouse on a 320-acre farm, just three miles from Williamsburg. Best known for its Chardonnay, the winery includes a 17th-century-style tasting room, and a museum with related antiques and an extensive collection of bottles. Visitors can enjoy fine foods and wine in the relaxing old European atmosphere at the Gabriel Archer Tavern, located on the grounds near the winery. Both Winery and Tavern are closed on Mondays.

Windy River Winery
20268 Teman Rd., Beaverdam • (804) 449-6996

This winery celebrated its first release in April 1997 and is only about 30 minutes north of downtown Richmond. Overlooking the North Anna River, the winery has 8 acres of vineyards on rolling hills in historic Hanover County. Tastings and tours are offered daily.

Fredericksburg

About an hour north of Richmond, straight up Interstate 95, is the small southern town of Fredericksburg. Founded in the early 1700s as a tobacco port on the Rappahannock River, Fredericksburg offers a view of colonial, Revolutionary War and Civil War history. This was the home of George Washington, and the site of several significant Civil War battles at Chancellorsville, the Wilderness and the Spotsylvania Court House.

There are several self-guided walking tours of historic neighborhoods, and during the spring and summer you won't want to miss the excitement of the Renaissance Faire. For shopping, Old Town Fredericksburg offers several blocks of antique stores, restaurants and specialty shops filled with historic memorabilia, folk art and crafts. For dining, you'll find everything from grill-style cafes and mom and pop delis to sophisticated bistros with French, Mediterranean or Sicillian cuisine, all in the Old Town area. View the menus at the Visitors Center and take your pick. Or, for an informal family meal, pack a picnic and sup beside the Rappahannock River or at a battlefield park. You can even get a box lunch or sandwiches to-go at places such as Chez V or Olde Towne Wine and Cheese. Look for a great spot near Chatham or The Copper Shop. For a more traditional meal with a historic ambience, try the Kenmore Inn in the elegant parlors of this 18th century brick house.

Some of the most visited places here include:

Visitors Center
706 Caroline St. • (800) 678-4748

Most people begin their visit here at the Fredericksburg Visitors Center in the center of Old Town where friendly travel counselors are more than willing to help you plan your day with maps, brochures, sample menus and a free parking pass. You can also see a 13-minute video tape to help you get oriented. Be sure to ask about the Hospitality Pass and Pick Four, two block ticket options that offer great deals on admission prices. The Hospitality Pass includes admission to seven attractions and costs $19.75 for adults and $7 for students. The Pick Four includes four attractions of your choice and costs $13.75 for adults and $5.50 for students.

Belmont / The Gari Melchers Estate and Memorial Gallery
224 Washington St. • (540) 654-1015

This estate was owned by renowned American artist Gari Melchers. The stone studio overlooking the Rappahanock River contains a selection of Melchers' works, and the house is furnished with items collected by the Melchers. The Marguerite Stroh Visitor Center here includes a museum shop, orientation theater, and Stafford County history and visitor's center. Admission is $4 for adults and $1 for students. It's open daily.

Fredericksburg Area Museum and Cultural Center
907 Princess Anne St. • (540) 371-3037

This museum provides an overview of the city from prehistoric times through Indian and Colonial settlement, the Revolutionary War, the Civil War, to the early 20th century. There are six permanent exhibit galleries. Admission is about $4 for adults and $1 for students. It's open daily. Discounts are offered to groups and AAA members.

Fredericksburg/Spotsylvania National Military Park, Chancellorsville Battlefield Visitor Center
Rt. 3 West • (540) 786-2880
Fredericksburg Battlefield Visitor Center
1013 Lafayette Blvd. • (540) 373-6122

Begin your self-guided tour of Civil War battlefields at the Fredericksburg Battlefield Visitor Center, then visit other battlefields in Spotsylvania County where most of the fighting occurred. In the Battle of Fredericksburg at Marye's Heights and Chatham, General Robert E. Lee won a decisive victory over Union forces commanded by General Ambrose E. Burnside. Later battles here at Chancellorsville, the Wilderness, and Spotsylvania Courthouse were more costly to the South in manpower and resources.

Park historians are on duty daily at both the Fredericksburg and the Chancellorsville Battlefield Visitor Centers. Wayside exhibits, exhibit shelters, interpretive trails and historic buildings help retrace the history of the Civil War in this area. Maps and directions are available from the Visitor Centers. The battlefields are open daily until dusk. Admission is free.

The Hugh Mercer Apothecary Shop
1020 Caroline St. • (540) 373-3362

This 18th-century physician's office offers a vivid living-history interpretation of Colonial medical practices. Admission is $4 for adults and $1.50 for students. It's open daily.

The James Monroe Museum and Memorial Library
908 Charles St. • (540) 654-1043

This museum showcases many of the personal possessions, furnishings and papers of

---

INSIDERS' TIP

Virginia has eight underground caverns including Luray Caverns, the East Coast's largest show cave, and Skyline Caverns, the only place in the world where anthodites, delicate white spiked flowers, are found.

America's fifth president and his wife, Elizabeth. Admission is $4 for adults and $1 for students. It's open daily.

Kenmore
1201 Washington Ave. • (540) 373-3381

This plantation, home of Fielding and Betty Washington Lewis, the only sister of George Washington, was constructed just before the Revolutionary War, and was oft-visited by George Washington. It was blasted with cannon fire during the Civil War and used as a hospital during the Battle of Chancellorsville. Kenmore's restored gardens now spread over a city block. It's open daily March through December and weekends in January and February. Admission is $6 for adults and $3 for students. Family and group rates are available.

The Mary Washington House
1200 Charles St. • (540) 373-1569

George Washington purchased this house for his mother, Mary Ball Washington, and she lived here for the last 17 years of her life. You'll find many of Mrs. Washington's favorite possessions and a picturesque English-style flower garden. The house and gardens are open daily for tours. Admission is $3 for adults and $1 for students.

Renaissance Faire
**1175 Kings Highway, Sherwood Forest
• (540) 371-3999**

If you're feeling adventurous, plan a visit in the spring and summer when the Renaissance Faire is in town (April-June). Each weekend, costumed characters bring a renaissance village and seven stages to life with jousting matches, knights in armor, jesters, pageantry and all sorts of merrymakers. Feast on hearty food and drink and enjoy the artistry of fine crafts created as you watch. Admission is $11 for adults, $5.50 for children ages 6-12. A Queen's Pass is a season's pass that sells for $30.

The Rising Sun Tavern
1304 Caroline St. • (540) 371-1494

Built in the 18th century by George Washington's youngest brother Charles, the Rising Sun offers a taste of old-time tavern life. You'll be greeted by a costumed hostess or "tavern wench," and invited to hear a lively interpretation of the tavern's story. The tavern is decorated with period furnishings. Visitors can sip spiced tea and see "man-sized" checkers made from a whale's backbone. Admission is $4 for adults and $1.50 for students.

Charlottesville

A little over an hour northwest of Richmond along Interstate 64, situated at the foothills of the Blue Ridge Mountains in the heart of Virginia's wine country, is the city of Charlottesville. Founded in 1762 as the county seat to Albemarle and named in honor of King George III's wife Charlotte, Charlottesville (then, some 50-acres large) was staked-off on a hilltop overlooking the Rivanna River. Today, eight annexations later, the city is independent of its mother county Albemarle, fully incorporated and thriving with a land area of some 10 square miles. But not lost in all this growth is the city's charm, perhaps best evidenced by the downtown area.

In 1976 Charlottesville's business district got a long awaited facelift. A pedestrian mall, the Downtown Mall, was designed for the city's Main Street; and over the years it has grown to include a convention center and ice-skating rink at the western terminus and a newly completed amphitheater at the eastern end. Along the tree-lined walk of what used to be a car-jammed thoroughfare, you'll find a string of restaurants, retail stores, galleries, coffee houses, ice-cream shops, bookstores, outdoor cafes and a movie theater. Closer to the University of Virginia is the Corner: a collection of student shops, cafes, bookstores and night spots. This area is always teeming with students.

In terms of good food, you're sure to be pleased with most any eatery you patronize in Charlottesville — and there are a number to chose from — but there are a few particularly good ones worth mentioning. For some fine dining, try the popular but rather highbrow Boar's Head Inn and Sports Club, (804) 296-2181. Or there's the C & O Restaurant, a good example of the best of both worlds with an upstairs dining room for the more formal affair and a bistro located downstairs for the casual crowd: (804) 971-7044. A visit to Charlottesville would feel hollow to most Insiders without grabbing a Gus Burger at the White Spot, (804) 295-9899, or some bagels and a caesar salad from Bodo's Bagels Bakery, (804) 293-6021; both on the Corner.

Barboursville Vineyards
17655 Winery Rd., Barboursville
• (540) 832-3824

Virginia has nearly 50 farm and estate wineries, and within a small radius of Charlottesville you'll find at least a dozen — most open for touring and taste sampling. In keeping with the Jefferson theme, we recommend visiting the Barboursville Vineyards. See the section on Wineries in this chapter for a full description.

Charlottesville/Albemarle Convention Center and Visitors Bureau
(804) 977-1783; (804) 293-6789

For more information on places to visit and things to do in Charlottesville, contact the Charlottesville/Albemarle Convention Center and Visitors Bureau or pick up a copy of the *Insiders' Guide® to Virginia's Blue Ridge.* But here are some places you shouldn't miss.

Monticello
Rt. 53 East, Charlottesville
• (804) 984-9822

Monticello, the home of Thomas Jefferson, is about 70 miles west of Richmond and only minutes from Charlottesville. The tour of this Jefferson-designed architectural treasure is interesting to school-age children and adults. Many of Jefferson's novel household inventions are on display, and the house affords an interesting glimpse into the private life of one of the country's most influential characters. The gardens are filled with an amazing variety of herbs, flowers, trees, fruits, vegetables and other plants; and the garden tour offers stunning views of the mountains and countryside.

Start your visit at the Thomas Jefferson Visitors Center. If you hit the right season, be-

tween April and October, you can enjoy a visit to the Thomas Jefferson Center for Historic Plants' Garden Shop, located in the tent at the Shuttle Station. The shop offers plants and seeds and books for sale. Since the majority of seeds and plants come directly from the Center's greenhouses, they make terrific heirlooms.

To get to Monticello, take Exit 121 off I-64, turn south (left) on Route 20 and follow the signs for Monticello. Children six and younger are free; six to 11, $5; 12 and older, $9. Picnic facilities are available.

Also of interest and close by to Monticello are Ash Lawn (home of President James Monroe), (804) 293-9539, and the Michie Tavern (pronounced "mickey" — before someone corrects you), (804) 977-1234.

FYI

Unless otherwise noted, the area code for all phone numbers listed in this chapter is 804.

University of Virginia
McMurmic Rd., Miller Hall, Charlottesville
• (804) 982-3200

This is indeed Jefferson country, and what would a visit to Charlottesville be without a tour of Mr. Jefferson's University. The University of Virginia, with little dispute, is an architectural marvel. The first college "campus," this was Jefferson's last and most public experiment in architecture. He personally supervised its early rise in 1817 from a "disused cornfield rising high and dry by itself" to what would become a textbook landscape of harmonious forms. When construction began, there were "no obstructions in the way of trees or bushes," said Jefferson, so he immediately set out with ten men and garden spades to grade the Lawn. His vision was an "academic village," whereby living and learning were married in form. With the Rotunda, then the library, serving as the academic centerpiece, the professors, students and classrooms were intermingled along the edges of the lawn. You can walk the grounds yourself, but to best appreciate Jefferson's achievement (and to catch the Pavilion gardens), we suggest you take the free guided tour offered by the University year round. Tours meet at the Rotunda entrance facing the lawn every hour between 10 AM and 4 PM (except during the school's three-week holiday break spanning December and January.)

Petersburg

Just 22 minutes south of Richmond along the Appomattox River, the historic city of Petersburg is rich with Civil War history. The city endured a 10-month siege, the longest of any American city. Prior to the Civil War it had the largest free-black population of any other city in the nation and residents enjoyed a better lifestyle than people in most of the other industrialized cities in the South. Life before and during the Civil War is documented at the Siege Museum and at the Petersburg National Battlefield Park.

Aside from Civil War history, you'll also find one of the nation's best collections of antebellum buildings, tobacco warehouses and early 19th-century storefronts as well as an abundance of antique galleries, boutiques, craft shops, restaurants and sidewalk cafes in Olde Towne Petersburg. There's also a flea market every weekend in the old railroad station.

For something to eat, try the restaurants in Olde Towne, including Alexander's (Greek and Italian cuisine), Portabella (intimate/Italian-inspired cuisine), the Farmers Market (American cuisine), Leonardo's (deli & more), and The Dixie, a local favorite with everything from hot dogs to meat loaf and mashed potatoes.

Visitors Center
425 Cockade Alley, Old Towne
• 733-2400, (800) 368-3595

Travel counselors at the Visitors Center in the restored McIlwaine House built in 1915 will help you plan your visit. It's open daily, and there are plenty of parking spaces.

1817 Farmers Bank
19 Bollingbrook St. • 733-2400

This is one of the oldest bank buildings in the country. The second floor was used as the residence of the cashier and his family. Visitors can see a heavy old safe which is lowered through the floor to a vault at night. It's open April through September, Friday through Monday, from 9 AM to 5 PM. Admission is $3 for adults, $2 for students ages 7-12 as well as seniors.

Centre Hill Mansion
1 Centre Hill Ct. • 733-2400

Filled with decorative arts, this Federal-style mansion was built in 1823 by the Bolling family. Ornate woodwork and plaster motifs reflect the grandeur of the time. The interior was later redesigned in the Greek Revival style. In the basement, visitors will see part of a tunnel that once connected the house to the river. It's open daily from 10 AM to 5 PM. Tours are offered every hour on the half hour. Admission is $3 for adults and $2 for students and seniors.

Civil War Trails
Lee's Retreat • (800) 6-RETREAT

Civil War Trail road signs blaze the route Lee took during his retreat from Petersburg to Appomattox. About 20 stops along the scenic backroads help tell the story of General Lee's 100-mile forced march, the devastating hardships and the surrender at Appomattox. Maps for this drving tour are available on request.

First Baptist Church
236 Harrison St. • 732-2841

Recognized as the earliest organized black church in America, the First Baptist Church was organized in 1774. Petersburg's first black high school opened here in 1870. Guided tours are available for groups.

Gillfield Baptist Church
209 Perry St. • 732-3565

The second-oldest black congregation in Petersburg and one of the oldest in the country, Gillfield Baptist Church celebrated it's 200th anniversary in 1997. The church maintains the oldest church records in the nation, and visitors can see the exhibits document-

INSIDERS' TIP

Humpback Bridge, three miles east of Covington, Va., is the only surviving curved-span covered bridge in the country.

ing the history of the congregation in the Heritage Room. Guided tours are available by appointment.

Old Blandford Church
319 S. Crater Rd. • 733-2400

Built in 1735, Blandford Church is famous for its 15 magnificent Tiffany windows created by Louis Comfort Tiffany and donated by the Confederate states in honor of their dead. There's also a graveyard where more than 30,000 Confederate soldiers are buried. The church is open daily from 10 AM to 5 PM. Tours are offered every 30 minutes. Admission is $3 for adults, $2 for students and seniors.

Pamplin Historical Park & The National Museum of the Civil War Soldier
6125 Boydton Plank Rd. • 861-2408

For more history after you've seen the national parks, visit America's newest and most innovative Civil War historical park, just south of Petersburg. Pamplin is a 363-acre park that features the very interactive National Museum of the Civil War Soldier, Tudor Hall, a military encampment similar to the one originally on the site, Battlefield Center, a restaurant, picnic facilities and museum store. Admission is $10, senior citizens $9, and ages 6-11 $5. Group rates are available. It's open every day from 9 AM to 5 PM, except Thanksgiving, Christmas and New Year's Day.

Petersburg National Battlefield Park
1539 Hickory Hill Rd. • 732-3531

This national park includes the site of the Battle of the Crater and a map presentation showing troop movements during six major battles. The City Point Unit of the battlefield has wayside exhibits and features Gen. Ulysses S. Grant's winter headquarters. The Five Forks Unit shows where Grant's forces captured Petersburg's railroad lines, a week before Gen. Lee surrendered his troops at Appomattox.

The Siege Museum
15 W. Bank St. • 733-2400

In the historic Exchange Building, built in 1839, the Siege Museum tells the story of how the people of Petersburg experienced and overcame the devastation of war, and of a time when a chicken cost $50. It's open daily from 10 AM to 5 PM. Admission is $3 for adults, $2 for students.

Trapezium House
244 N. Market St. • 733-2400

Built in 1815, this unique house has no right angles. Perhaps that's because the original owner Charles O'Hara was told that evil spirits could not dwell in houses without parallel walls. Then again, the lot has odd angles, too. It's open April through September, from 10 AM to 5 PM. Tours are offered every hour on the half hour. Admission is $3 for adults, $2 for students and seniors.

U.S. Quartermaster Museum
Bldg. 5218, Avenue A, Fort Lee • 734-4203

You'll see military artifacts here that date back to the Revolutionary War, including uniforms, weapons and Patton's jeep. It's open until 5 PM, Tuesday through Sunday. It's closed on Monday. Opening hours vary, call in advance. Admission is free.

U.S. Slo-pitch (Softball) Hall of Fame
3935 S. Crater Rd. • 732-4099

The exhibits here pay tribute to the people, champions, history and traditions of slo-pitch, one of America's most popular sports. It's open Monday through Sunday until 4 PM. Admission for adults is $2, students age 10 and over $1, and children younger than 10 are admitted free.

Violet Bank Museum
326 Royal Oak Ave. • 520-9395

Just across the bridge from the Petersburg Visitors Center, at the top of the bluff in Colonial Heights, is the highstyle Federal home built in 1815, that Lee used for his headquarters during the Seige of Petersburg in 1864. It now serves as a historical house museum with military artifacts from the war as well as domestic items and furnishings. It's open Tuesday through Saturday from 10 AM to 5 PM and from 1 to 6 PM on Sunday. Admission is free.

Virginia Motorsports Park
U.S. 1, Dinwiddie • 732-RACE

Just south of Petersburg, the Virginia Motorsports Park offers NHRA drag racing. Call for a schedule of events.

The "Rivah" and the Bay

For most established Richmonders, the river and the Bay are always calling, whether it's for rockfishing in deep December or tubing in early spring. But come June, what were silent whispers become deafening yalps. With about ten rivers and the largest, most productive estuary in North America in our back yard, it's hard to imagine ignoring the water's call — why try?

Going to the "rivah" (localese for just about anything with a current and fish) is a summer tradition. Many families have vacation homes on the James, Potomac, Rappahannock, York, Mattaponi, Pamunkey, Piankatank, Chickahominy or Wicomico rivers. In fact, it's not unusual for several generations of relatives to share in the ownership of a single river cottage and gather there for family reunions.

Most of these vacation getaways are tucked in quiet river communities where you provide your own entertainment and feast on Chesapeake Bay blue crabs, oysters, rockfish and Southern-fried hush puppies. You can go fishing, crabbing, boating, sailing or skiing. Or, you can spend a lazy day on a breezy porch with a good book or a deck of cards. If you swim, be forewarned, especially after a long summer drought, we have a healthy supply of stinging nettles. If you find these minor pests particularly gruesome (say, you're allergic), stick to the freshwater creeks or stay upriver where the water is less brackish. Stinging nettles avoid fresh water.

You'll find hundreds of popular places all along the rivers and by the Bay. If you're not lucky enough to have your own cottage, you can rent one. Just ask around or look for the ads in the newspaper. The *Richmond Times-Dispatch* is good place to start, but just about any of the papers will do. If you're just looking for a place to drop a boat or a jet ski, most river towns of any real size have a public landing or at least a marina where you might have to pay a dollar or two ramp fee. Frequent boaters can rent slips or trailer spots.

For a more in-depth look at Virginia's river country, you might want to look at *The Insiders' Guide® to Virginia's Chesapeake Bay*. There you'll find an excellent breakdown of the Tidewater region.

Some of our favorite places include Lanexa, Coles Point, Gloucester Point, Smith Point, Kilmarnock, Irvington, Windmill Point, Deltaville, Gwynn's Island, Mathews, Colonial Beach, Sandy Point, Sting Ray Point, Urbanna and Wicomico Church. Here are two specific trips to give you a good introduction.

Rappahannock River Cruise
Tappahannock • (804) 453-2628

Located only an hour away from the center of Richmond in the charming riverside community of Tappahannock is the cruise boat Capt. Thomas. This narrated river cruise begins with a two-hour ride along the virtually unspoiled shores of the Rappahannock River. You'll be treated to multiple species of waterfowl, including the bald eagle and osprey.

The cruise makes one stop at the Ingleside Plantation Winery where you'll tour of one Virginia's premier farm wineries and sample a few of their unique varieties. A buffet is available at the winery, but you may choose to bring your own lunch.

The cruise departs Hoskins Creek in Tappahannock at 10 AM and returns at 4 PM. With an enclosed, heated and air conditioned cabin, the Capt. Thomas runs rain or shine from May through October (except Mondays). Snacks are available on board. Reservations are necessary.

To get there, take Route 360 East from Richmond for approximately 45 miles into the town of Tappahannock. The dock and parking lot are to the right, just before the Hoskins Creek bridge.

While you're in Tappahannock, you'll want to visit some of the many antique and unique gift shops, particularly the Nadji Nook on Queen Street and Riverside Accents on Route 17. As for restaurants, Tappahannock's biggest draw is clearly Lowery's Seafood Restaurant, (804) 443-4314, located on Route 17. Run by the Lowery family since 1938, this restaurant offers an extensive and reasonably priced menu. Be sure to try the soft shell crabs (when in season), and black-eyed peas and

Take a stroll on the paths that wind through Maymont's flower beds and feast your eyes.

stewed tomatoes. For a less formal lunch on the town's historic Prince Street, try the Rivahside Cafe, (804) 443-2333 and its mouthwatering eclair cake.

Reedville

As you drive down Reedville's Main Street, which ends abruptly at water, it feels like you're approaching the end of the world. And to crack open a map, it looks like it too. Situated at the very tip of the Northern Neck (the finger of land between the Rappahannock and Potomac Rivers), Reedville dangles like a fruit from a lofty bough over the vastness of the Chesapeake Bay. But what seems like the end of the line was once, surprisingly enough, the richest town per capita in the United States. Reedville's golden age, at the turn of the century, came from their menhaden fishing industry and is evidenced by the great Victorian mansions which line Main Street, most of which are now bed and breakfasts. Reedville still reigns as the center of the largest fishing industry in the U.S. While in town you'll want to visit the Reedville Fisherman's Museum, (804) 453-6529, which houses a collection of artifacts and historical material from the town's menhaden industry, past to present. And for some great seafood (offering take-out as well), stop by Elijah's Restaurant, (804) 453-3621 — named after Elijah Reedville, the town's founder.

Reedville is also the port of call for two cruise boats which shuttle people daily to Tangier Island and Smith Island. Both of these islands sit isolated in the middle of the Bay about 12 miles off shore and seven miles from one another. Primarily quaint fishing villages, these islands and their inhabitants get a lot of attention from linguists. Most of the island dwellers share the same last names, names which date back on these islands to the 17th and 18th centuries. Studies have actually been done on their speech patterns, which are considered to be the closest relatives to the Elizabethan dialect — yes, even closer than the British.

The Smith Island Cruise departs from the KOA Kampground aboard the 150 passenger Capt. Evans at 10 AM and returns by 3:45 PM. Reservations are required so call ahead to (804) 453-3430. The cost is $19.50 for adults and $9.75 for children ages 3–12. The Tangier Island Cruise leaves from its dock on Cockrell Creek aboard the Chesapeake Breeze at 10 AM and returns by 3:45 PM. Reservations are also required, (804) 453-2628. The cost is $20. Both cruises run May to October.

Reedville is indeed a rare find — that is, if you can find it. You don't want to venture into this region without a good map — and make sure it's a recent one. These roads are confusing enough to natives. The easiest way takes about two hours. From Richmond follow Route 360 East. This will take you through Tappahannock and across the Rappahannock River. Reedville is actually the dead end of Route 360, but don't think it's a nice straight shot. Watch for route signs. The Tangier Island Cruise has you veer right on to Route 646 off Route 360 at Lillian (3 miles past Route 200 is another name for Lillian). Follow Route 646 to Route 656 and follow the signs to the dock. To get to the Smith Island Cruise, pass through Lillian on Route 360 and go left on Route 652 (Sunnybank Road). Go 2 miles to Route 650 (Campground Road) where you should see signs for the campground and cruise.

The Blue Ridge

Just one hour west of Richmond, you can drive along the highest crests of the Blue Ridge Mountains and enjoy majestic vistas and valley overlooks on Skyline Drive and the Blue Ridge Parkway. The drive is always beautiful, but the best time to go is in the fall when the

---

INSIDERS' TIP

Civil War Trail road signs mark the route of the 1862 "Peninsula Campaign" in the Tidewater area between the York and James rivers, Lee's "1864 Campaign" against Grant, and "Lee's Retreat" from Petersburg to Appomattox. For maps and brochures with points of interest, call 1-888 CIVIL WAR.

colors of the leaves are at their peak. To get here, take I-64 West from Richmond and proceed west past Charlottesville to the Afton-Waynesboro exit at U.S. Highway 250. You'll find yourself at the confluence of Skyline Drive and the Parkway.

If you love the outdoors and beautiful scenery, you'll want to come here often. You can hike, fish, camp and picnic. There are also eight caverns open for tours including the Endless, Luray, Grand, Skyline, Massanutten, Shenandoah, Natural Bridge and Dixie caverns. Call the Virginia Tourism Development Group, 786-4484, for specific information. If skiing is your thing, don't expect the Swiss Alps but there are a number of fine ski resorts: Bryce (540) 856-2121; Massanutten (800) 207-MASS; Wintergreen (800) 325-2200; and the Homestead (540) 839-1766.

Other points of interest include the Apple Blossoms Festival in Winchester, Virginia, the Museum of Frontier Culture in Staunton, and the annual Jousting Tournament at Mt. Solon. Contact the Virginia Tourism Development Group, 786-4484, for more information, or pick up a copy of the *Insiders' Guide® to Virginia's Blue Ridge*.

Natural Bridge

To have one of the seven natural wonders of the world only two hours west of you in Lexington, Kentucky, makes it a must-see. Natural Bridge is a geologic formation that spans a 200-feet-deep mountain gorge. This rock bridge (besides serving as a bridge) has served to inspire painters and photographers from around the world and has made the surrounding area a world-renown nature retreat. Today it boasts the Cedar Creek Nature Trail, nearby Natural Bridge Caverns and hotel accommodations for the many visitors drawn to the majesty of the bridge and its environs.

A 45-minute narrated sound and light show is presented nightly at sunset beneath the Bridge and features the music of Verdi,

Rossini, Debussy, Wagner, and Liszt. Natural Bridge Caverns hosts a 45-minute guided tour that descends 34 stories into the striking underground landscape of the East Coast's deepest commercial cavern. The Natural Bridge and Cedar Creek Trail open year-round at 8 AM and close at dark, after the light and sound show. The caverns are open 10 AM to 5 PM. Natural Bridge is located on Route 11 at Route 130, just south of historic Lexington and I-64.

Walton's Mountain Museum

6484 Rockfish River Rd., Schuyler
• (804) 831-2000

Waltons fans rejoice! On October 24, 1992, the Walton's Mountain Museum officially opened its doors to the nearly 6,000 fans outside champing at the bit. In on the celebration were the show's creator Earl Hamner, his brothers and sisters, several of the shows writers and producers and numerous cast members. Never has the tiny town of Schuyler, where Hamner was reared, population 400, received such attention.

For years tourists have driven by the old white house where the famous television show's creator Earl Hamner spent his youth (the house is much like the one used in the actual television show), but now visitors can visit the Walton's Mountain Museum, housed a stone's throw away in the Schuyler Community Center (Hamner's old school). In the museum you'll find painstakingly recreated sets from the television show, copies of scripts and a video documentary of interviews with Hamner and cast members. Visitors can shop in Ike Godsey's store which features over 600 items, many made by local craftspeople.

The Museum is open daily from the first Saturday in March through the last Sunday in November. Visiting hours are from 10 AM to 4

INSIDERS' TIP

The first bourbon whiskey in America was distilled at Berkeley Plantation. Berkeley was also where "Taps" was composed while Civil War Union soldiers were encamped there.

PM. Admission is $5 ($4 for seniors older than 65 and members of groups of 20 or more). Children 12 and younger are admitted free of charge.

From Richmond, take I-64 West to Charlottesville and Route 29. Schuyler is between Charlottesville and Lynchburg, a few miles off of Route 29.

From the city to the suburbs to the rural countryside, it's a metropolitan area that's rich with a diversity of neighborhoods that have their own personalities and traditions.

Neighborhoods and Real Estate

Richmond has all the cultural amenities and attractions of a growing metropolitan area, yet it also has the charm and intimacy of a small town. From the city to the suburbs to the rural countryside, it's a metropolitan area that's rich with a diversity of neighborhoods that have their own personalities and traditions. That might be why so many people who live here never move away, and why so many families think it's a great place to live.

You'll find historic Antebellum and turn-of-the-century homes, plus contemporary, colonial, lakefront, riverfront and golf course homes, multimillion-dollar estates and working farms. You'll also find a lot of involved people. Many neighborhoods have active community associations that organize Neighborhood Watch programs, sponsor social activities and unite over zoning issues.

Richmond also enjoys a renewed interest in city living, and we're very proud of our restored neighborhoods near downtown. There has already been a great deal of renovation in the Fan and Church Hill. Renovation efforts are also under way in Jackson Ward, Oregon Hill, Shockoe Slip and Shockoe Bottom.

To help you get your bearings, we've organized information in this section to correspond with the way Insiders talk about the area — by neighborhoods and sections of town. If you're interested in buying property, see the "Real Estate" section in this chapter for information about how the metropolitan Richmond area is divided into numbered real estate sections.

Historic City Neighborhoods

The Fan

This historic neighborhood just west of downtown derives its name from the way the streets fan out from Monroe Park at Belvidere Street to the Boulevard. The Fan includes the famous Monument Avenue with its gracious mansions that sell for as much as $1 million or more, and turn-of-the-century town houses that range upwards in price from $75,000 to about $250,000, depending on size, location and how much renovation has been done. Fan renovation efforts became popular in the 1960s, and most of the homes here have been at least partially renovated. You'll also find a number of apartments and duplexes for rent, and two high-rise apartment buildings, The Berkshire and River Towers, in the downtown area near the Fan.

Tree-lined parks and streets, beautifully landscaped courtyards, rooftop gardens, cobblestone alleys, brick sidewalks and numerous neighborhood restaurants and pubs

---

INSIDERS' TIP

It has long been a popular myth that Richmond, like Rome, was built on seven hills. Charles Dickens, on a visit to Richmond, counted eight. We can name eleven easily.

add to the charm of the area. It's also just minutes away from many of Richmond's historic and cultural attractions and parks.

Most of the people who live here enjoy a casual, active lifestyle. Residents include students and faculty from nearby Virginia Commonwealth University as well as families, singles and professionals from diverse social, economic and ethnic backgrounds.

Church Hill

Overlooking Shockoe Bottom, Shockoe Slip and downtown, Church Hill is Richmond's first historic district and includes St. John's Church where Patrick Henry made his famous liberty speech. The area around the church is the oldest intact residential district in the city. The "Hill" was Richmond's main residential section for the middle and upper class for more than 100 years. Then, it gradually declined as the city moved west following the railroads and the trolley system.

Most of the homes here are two- or three-story brick town houses in a variety of styles, including Federal, Greek Revival, Italianate, Second Empire, Queen Anne and Colonial Revival.

Several parks offer attractive green spaces, and thanks to the hilly location, many homes have views of the river or city skyline. Gas street lamps and brick sidewalks add to the historic ambiance. The Christmas season brings neighbors together with a candlelight walk and caroling, the Christmas Ball and the house tour.

Homes that need renovation range from about $50,000 to more than $100,000. Renovated homes cost from about $110,000 to more than $300,000. Homes nearby range from gutted frame houses at bargain prices to fully renovated homes for $130,000.

FYI

Unless otherwise noted, the area code for all phone numbers listed in this chapter is 804.

Oregon Hill

Next to the Fan, Oregon Hill has relatively smaller town houses that range price from about $35,000 to more than $100,000, depending on the amount of renovation needed. Hollywood Cemetery and the James River Park surround two sides of this small neighborhood that was originally known as Sydney. Early residents of Oregon Hill usually worked at nearby foundries, armories and mills.

Today, you'll find a lively mix of families, students and urbanites from a variety of backgrounds and cultures who like to fix up old homes.

Jackson Ward

In the heart of downtown, north of Broad Street, Jackson Ward includes historic 2nd Street, the Maggie Walker House and the Bojangles Statue. The Richmond Coliseum and 6th Street Marketplace are nearby. The neighborhood has a variety of 19th- and early 20th-century urban row houses that range in price from $35,000 to about $150,000, depending on how much renovation is needed or has been done. A majority of the city's cast-iron porches are in this neighborhood, reflecting the influence of the European craftspeople who once lived here.

Shockoe Slip/ Shockoe Bottom

Just east of downtown near the river, Shockoe Slip was once the commercial center of Richmond. This quaint area features brick sidewalks, a few cobblestone streets, restaurants, shops, hotels, nightlife and apartments

---

INSIDERS' TIP

Oregon Hill was so named because the people who lived there thought it was so far from the center of town that it was like moving to the Oregon Territory.

in renovated 19th-century warehouses and buildings.

Shockoe Bottom is down the hill from the Slip. This trendy neighborhood near Dock Street is the hottest nightclub section in town and includes the colorful and historic Farmers Market and the Edgar Allan Poe Museum. It's the home of art studios, galleries, apartments and restaurants, all housed in renovated and readapted buildings, including the Market Slip apartment complex across from the Farmers Market.

Tobacco Row

The Tobacco Row project east of downtown comprises about 15 city blocks between 22nd and Pear Streets along the James River. In the early to mid-1900s, there was a concentration of manufacturers in this area, and the architectural styles range from the 1840s to the 1930s. Several old warehouse buildings have been renovated and transformed into apartment houses where monthly rent averages around $600. Development began in the mid-1980s. The first phase included more than 2 million square feet of office, retail and residential space. Tobacco Row is considered to be one of the country's most ambitious redevelopment projects and is the single largest economic recovery tax-act project in the United States.

West End

Sometimes called the "fashionable" or "trendy" West End, this area is generally thought of as the area that stretches west from the Boulevard and includes part of Richmond and part of Henrico County. The area between the Boulevard and Thompson Street is called West of the Boulevard; the area west of Parham Road is the Far West End.

The elite Country Club of Virginia, the University of Richmond and the exclusive neighborhoods of Windsor Farms, Westhampton and Westmoreland Place lend prestige to the area. River Road, with its stately old homes overlooking the river, adds an air of charming elegance, while the boutiques and shops of

Carytown offer a unique shopping experience comparable to what you might find in D.C.'s Georgetown.

Windsor Farms stretches from Portland Place to Locke Lane and from Cary Street to the James River. It includes some of the area's most beautiful homes and two of Richmond's most significant historical attractions, Agecroft Hall and the Virginia House. Many of the estate homes here have spectacular views of the James River and are worth millions of dollars. Other homes in this planned community vary in size and feature Georgian-style architecture. The streets circle outward from the Grace Baptist Church and the common area in the center of the neighborhood. Originally, Windsor Farms was the 500-acre estate of Thomas C. Williams Jr. Designed to resemble an English village, it was subdivided in 1926, and was a prime element in the westward development of the city as the affluent sought larger plots of land.

Other relatively newer communities here include Lockgreen on the James River near Windsor Farms and Kanawha Trace, perched on a bluff overlooking the river near Maymont. Kanawha Trace features contemporary condominiums and affordable town houses. Lockgreen offers a collection of luxurious town houses and single-family residences off Old Locke Lane in a variety of prices ranging up to several million dollars.

West Enders enjoy convenient access to gourmet restaurants, such as duJour, and several fashionable shopping areas — Regency Square, The Shops at Libbie and Grove, and River Road Shopping Center. Henrico County schools and a number of private schools in the area are considered excellent. Numerous churches and two of the best hospitals in the area, St. Mary's and Henrico Doctors Hospital, serve the West End's residents.

Far West End

People mean many different things when they say the Far West End. We think it means the rapidly growing suburban area of Henrico County west of Parham Road. New developments include Foxhall, Morgan Run, Wyndham (a golf course community), Wellesley with lakeside, single-family homes and town house communities, the "dream houses" of Windsor on the James, off scenic River Road, and family-oriented developments, such as Rockstone, Northbrooke and Riverlake Colony.

There's also a proliferation of apartment complexes and condominium homes here with monthly rents ranging upward from about $450 a month.

Residents enjoy the lake, playing fields, soccer, hiking, jogging at Deep Run Park and excellent educational opportunities at reputable public and private schools in the area. There are hundreds of subdivisions, townhouse communities and apartment complexes throughout the West End and the Far West End, with homes that start around $80,000 and range upward to a million dollars. Home and condominium architectural styles include Cape Cod, Colonial, Victorian, contemporary, transitional and Georgian.

Northside

Northside usually refers to the area of the city north of Broad Street where you'll find the State Fairgrounds, The Diamond, the Arthur Ashe Center, Bryan Park, the A.P. Hill Monument, Virginia Union University, Presbyterian School of Christian Education, and the Union Theological Seminary. Old established neighborhoods, such as Ginter Park, Bellevue and Highland Park, help define the diversity of the residents who live here.

Ginter Park, developed by Maj. Lewis Ginter in 1892, was one of the first planned communities in the area. A designated historical area, Ginter Park includes restored Victorian-style homes and turn-of-the-century mansions ranging from about $100,000 to more than $300,000. According to local legend, Maj. Ginter wanted to develop a neighborhood on the north side of Richmond so that the sun would not be in his eyes going to or from work.

Bellevue is another old established neighborhood with an arched entrance-way off Hermitage Road that features spacious homes built in the 1920s and 1930s for people with large families. The neighborhood extends to Brook Road where residents swap stories at the local drugstore.

Highland Park is an old community, just south of the State Fairgrounds and the Richmond International Raceway, with unrestored turn-of-the-century houses. Efforts to restore the neighborhood are under way.

Northern Henrico County

Northern Henrico County is a growing suburban and rural area that includes Glen Allen, Lakeside, Dumbarton, Chamber-layne Farms and Chamberlayne Heights neighborhoods. Interstates 295, 95 and 64 provide fast, convenient access to any destination in the metropolitan area.

Glen Allen, an old rural community enjoying rapid growth, includes a variety of single-family homes ranging in price from about $100,000 to more than $200,000. This is the area that includes the Innsbrook residential and office park development, historic Meadow Farm and Crump Park, the Crossings Golf Course and Virginia Center Commons shopping mall.

New developments in this area include Mountain Glen, Meadow Farms, Lexington and Cameron Crossings, a condominium community.

Closer to Richmond, Lakeside and Dumbarton are established Northside neighborhoods with economically priced single-family residences and apartment complexes and numerous small businesses. Bryan Park is famous for its azalea displays; the Lewis Ginter Botanical Gardens, Belmont Golf Course and Jefferson Lakeside Country Club are focal points of this area. Homes range from about $50,000 to more than $100,000.

Chamberlayne Farms and Chamber-layne Heights were two of Richmond's first middle-class suburban neighborhoods that began developing in the mid-'50s. Homes here are priced from about $90,000 to $145,000.

East End

Eastern Henrico County is usually referred to as the East End and includes the Highland Springs, Sandston and Varina areas near the Richmond International Airport and the Richmond Industrial Park. With the opening of the White Oak Semiconductor Plant of Motorola-Siemens on the Elko tract, and the expansion of the Richmond International Airport, this area is expected to undergo a period of significant growth and change. A number of commercial warehouses and light industrial parks also have developed here recently.

The East End offers economical housing in a rural, suburban setting. Prices range from $35,000 up to $300,000. Some of the new developments include Cedar Fork Estates, Fairfield Woods, Foxboro Downs, Oak Glen, Wynfield, Deep Run Ridge, Elko Station and White Oak Hills.

Residents have convenient access to Dorey Park, a popular recreational area with a fishing lake, playing fields, picnic areas, tennis courts and trails. The Glenwood Country Club is also nearby.

South Side

South Side includes everything on the south side of the James River — South Richmond as well as Powhatan and Chesterfield counties.

People who live in South Side have access to downtown and areas north of the river via the Powhite Parkway Bridge, Edward Willey Memorial Bridge, Huguenot Bridge, Nickel Bridge, Robert E. Lee Bridge, Manchester Bridge and the I-95 bridge. The Chippenham Parkway Connector and a sophisticated system of roads keeps traffic moving quickly and smoothly most of the time to destinations throughout the metropolitan area.

South Richmond

In South Richmond, you'll find major sections of the James River Park System, beautiful old Forest Hill Park, Willow Oaks Country Club and the established neighborhoods of Westover Hills, Stratford Hills and Forest Hill. South Side is also home to McGuire Veterans Hospital, Philip Morris (one of the world's largest cigarette manufacturers) and Deepwater Terminal, the Port of Richmond.

There are homes for every budget and lifestyle here, including the Bluffs at Stony Point condominium community and the prestigious cliffside homes that wind along Riverside Drive high above the James River.

Chesterfield County

Chesterfield is the largest county in the metropolitan area and is still experiencing rapid growth. It's saturated with new developments and subdivisions and miles of shopping centers and office complexes along Midlothian Turnpike (U.S. Highway 60).

Residents enjoy an excellent county school system that is expanding as fast as it can to catch up with the growth. There are also numerous recreational opportunities and parks, including Pocahontas State Park and Rockwood Park. Chesterfield is the home of several commercial parks including the Arboretum, Center Pointe, the Commonwealth Center, the Acropolis, Moorefield and Waterford.

Shoppers will find a large selection of stores at Cloverleaf Mall and Chesterfield Towne Center, the largest mall in the area. Sycamore Square offers unusual boutiques and great restaurants in a village setting. People who live in Chesterfield County receive excellent medical care at Chippenham Hospital.

Historic Bon Air and the award-winning communities of Brandermill and Woodlake are among the best-known Chesterfield neighborhoods. Salisbury and River's Bend on the James are two other talked-about communities known for their luxury homes and excellent golf courses.

Bon Air, the "good air" community, got its name years ago when Richmonders used to travel here by train to stay in their summer or weekend homes to escape the coal smoke in the city. Some of the old Victorian inns are still standing, and the neighborhood features a variety of Victorian-style homes, especially along Buford Road. This old established community is just across the Huguenot Bridge from the West End.

Chester is another established community that developed just before the Civil War as a popular summer resort for Richmonders. According to legend, after the Civil War, treasure hunters from the North rushed to Chester to look for $800,000 in military money that a general supposedly buried here. The treasure has yet to be found. The older sections of Chester are known for their quiet village character. Home prices here range from about $100,000 to $150,000. Winfree's Village is one of the newest developments with homes starting around $110,000. You'll also find the lakefront, golf course community of Chesdin Landing with homes ranging from $300,000 to more than $1,500,000. In most of the newer developments prices begin around $200,000.

Brandermill and Woodlake, developed by East West Partners of Virginia, are planned communities in the western part of the county surrounding Swift Creek Reservoir. Their designs are very similar. Brandermill is the oldest and includes cluster homes, condominiums, golf course homes and lakefront homes. It's a complete community with shops, restaurants, tennis courts, waterfront parks, boat landings, jogging and walking trails, fishing docks, swimming and windsurfing. Residents also enjoy the amenities of the Brandermill Inn and Conference Center. Together the communities have more than 5,500 homes that vary in style from Colonial to contemporary and in price from $90,000 to more than $500,000. Thanks to the new Powhite Extension and Route 288, people who live here can drive to downtown or the West End in about 20 minutes.

The Salisbury community in the western part of the county is built around the 40-acre lake and the Salisbury Country Club, which has one of the best golf courses in the area. Estate homes surround the site of the country home where Patrick Henry lived while he was governor of Virginia. Salisbury was one of the first coal-mining communities in the country. Most of the homes in the community are Colonials. Townhouses that back up to the golf course are among the newest additions.

River's Bend on the James was the first planned community in Chesterfield County to be built on the James River. Luxury homes here range from about $160,000 to $1 million. A challenging 18-hole PGA golf course with beautiful views of the river is a focal point of this new community.

Birkdale is another Chesterfield County golf course community still under development, and Foxcroft, in the western part of the county, offers Victorian, traditional and transitional homes ranging from $150,000 to more than $300,000.

Other neighborhoods with new homes ranging upwards from $100,000 include the lakefront community of Paget, LakePointe town homes, Bayhill Pointe, Bermuda Orchard, Pheasant Run and Hampton Park with it's old-fashioned sidewalks and street lamps. Other neighborhoods with new homes ranging from $200,000 to $500,000 include Windsor Farms, Summerford, Wellington Farms and The Highlands, a new golf course community.

Hanover County

Hanover County offers world-famous tomatoes and relaxed "country" living in an area that's rich with Civil War battlefields and history. It's the second-largest county in the metropolitan area, but it has the fewest people, and most of them would like to keep it that way. They unite frequently over zoning issues and oppose any development that doesn't adhere to a comprehensive plan.

The county is usually divided into sections referred to as eastern Hanover, Hanover Courthouse, and western Hanover.

Eastern Hanover

In eastern Hanover just off U.S. Highway 360, you'll find the town of Mechanicsville, with its landmark windmill bank building and proliferation of independent, family owned businesses. Cherrydale is an older established neighborhood here, and Battlefield Green is a popular new one with condominiums and single-family homes. Pebble Creek is another new community that offers a variety of home sizes and plans.

The nearby Cold Harbor area is included in the Richmond National Battlefield Park System and is famous for its battlefields and Civil War sites. There's a variety of housing and subdivisions throughout the area.

Still farther east is the area known as Old Church, named after an Anglican church established in 1718. The old Immanuel Episcopal Church on Route 606, built in 1853, is the successor to the first church building. This rural area includes several historic estates and plantations and contemporary new homes on the Pamunkey River. People who live out here think nothing of driving 10 or more miles to the nearest country store. There are numerous farms but only a few planned neighborhoods such as Pine Knoll and Sinclair Manor. Lake Idylwilde, featuring 10-acre lots on a wooded lake, Old Church Place and Pamunkey River Farms are some of the newest neighborhoods. The Mattaponi and Pamunkey Indian reservations are nearby.

Hanover Courthouse

North on U.S. Highway 301 is the Hanover Courthouse area, named after the historic Hanover Courthouse built in 1735. This is the center of the county government; it's also the site of the historic Hanover Tavern.

Richmond Newspapers' production facility and Hanover Airport, a popular take-off site for hot-air balloons, are nearby in the Atlee-Elmont area. On a pleasant day, it's not unusual to see several hot-air balloons drifting above the fields and trees.

Kings Charter was the first planned community in this area and has received several design awards. It features a variety of homes centered around a restored historic mansion that now serves as a community building. There are two lakes, a country club, tennis courts, jogging and bike trails and a fitness center. Ash Creek is one of the newest developments with homes ranging from $130,000 to $275,000. Other new developments include Ash Creek, Berkeley Forest, Lee's Crossing, Magnolia Ridge, Milestone and Parson's Cause, which is being developed around the site of Patrick Henry's birthplace.

INSIDERS' TIP

Greater Richmond's curbside recycling program serves more than 195,000 households in seven localities. For recycling options in your area, call the Central Virginia Waste Management Authority at 359-8413. It's a minor hassle that does a world of good.

The Houndstooth Cafe and Thyme and Sage are popular area restaurants. Antiques shops abound on U.S. 301, and Virginia Center Commons is the nearest and newest place to shop.

Western Hanover

Western Hanover includes Montpelier and Beaverdam. It's mostly rural and very scenic with views of the South Anna and North Anna rivers. Overhill Lake is a popular recreation and swimming area, and the Up and Away Dude Ranch is the site of many outdoor picnics and barbecues.

Ashland

Popularly known as "the center of the universe," Ashland is the home of Randolph-Macon College, founded in 1830. Residents love the small college-town atmosphere and beautiful 18th-century Victorian homes with their wraparound porches and generous lawns.

Bounded by suburban and rural areas in Hanover County, Ashland is close to Scotchtown, the pre-Revolutionary home of Patrick Henry, the Ashland Berry Farm, Paramount's Kings Dominion amusement park and the historic Hanover Tavern. The Smokey Pig, the Ironhorse and Homemades By Suzanne are popular restaurants in the area.

River Run, an established development next to the Hanover Country Club, offers 90 heavily wooded homesites overlooking rolling fairways and beautiful greens. River Run is one of the few areas in western Hanover County offering public utilities.

Ashland was originally developed as a summer community for workers of the Richmond, Fredericksburg and Potomac Railroad. A commuter rail line connecting Ashland to Richmond opened around 1900 but was discontinued in the 1930s.

People who live here tend to be very active in local politics and are doing a good job of balancing the small-town character of the area with growth and development.

Neighboring Areas

Many people who work in Richmond live in Goochland, Powhatan, King William and New Kent counties. If you don't mind a 30- to 60-minute commute to downtown Richmond, these rural areas offer quiet, relaxed country living and more home for your dollar.

Powhatan County is just south of the James River and west of Chesterfield County. Beautiful plantation homes and historic churches, some of which date back to the 1700s, reflect Powhatan's rich heritage.

King William Woods and Country Town were among Powhatan's first subdivisions to offer new homes and 1-acre, zoned-residential lots. Newer developments such as Shadow Creek, Sherwood and Norwood Creek, offer building sites between 1 and 3 acres along scenic Huguenot Trail, which follows the James River along State Route 711. The Greywalls community is nestled amid horse farms, James River plantations and the private Foundry Golf Club. Another residential option for the golf enthusiast is Chatsworth at Millquarter, which fronts the public Millquarter Golf Course.

Recreational opportunities abound in Powhatan. County residents and neighbors frequent the boat landings and the wildlife preserve. On any given weekend you'll find families fishing, power boating and canoeing around Watkins and Maidens landings on the James River. The Appomattox River is another recreational mecca.

With the opening of Colonial Downs parimutuel race track and the development of new golf courses such as Royal New Kent, nominated for the best new golf course in the country, New Kent County is poised for a period of explosive growth. Existing homes range in price from $20,000 to $200,000. New developments here with homes up to

---

INSIDERS' TIP

King of sausage and country/western singer Jimmy Dean lives on the north side of the James River in Henrico County.

$150,000, include Brookewood Manor, Quinton Estates, Ranch Acres and The Woods at Five Lakes.

South of Richmond is the Tri-Cities area, which includes Hopewell, a scenic town overlooking the James and Appomattox rivers, Colonial Heights and Petersburg, small cities on the Appomattox River.

Petersburg is the largest of these cities and has many historic and Civil War attractions and restored areas. Fort Lee is here, so many area residents are involved with the military. Virginia State University is nearby in Ettrick, and there are historic plantations on both sides of the James River on state routes 5 and 10. Southpark Mall, one of the largest and most beautiful shopping malls in the area, has spectacular holiday exhibits that attract people from throughout the Richmond area as well as shoppers from out of state. There's more information about Petersburg in our chapter on Daytrips.

Real Estate

A national study of more than 70 metropolitan areas by E&Y Kenneth Leventhal Real Estate Group ranked Greater Richmond among the 10 most affordable housing markets in the nation. *Kiplinger's Personal Finance* magazine ranks Richmond as the most promising place in the nation to buy a home. The average sale price of a home in the Greater Richmond area is $133,058, according to the Multiple Listing Service, and apartment rents range anywhere from $400 to $1,500 per month depending on size and location.

All of this means you can live comfortably in Richmond without spending an arm and a leg. And the lifestyle options are wide-ranging. Whether it's in-town and urban or suburban or rural, the chances are very good that you'll be able to find a neighborhood and an architectural style that meets your desires and needs. Downtown living is on the upswing, so if you like the center-city way of life you should check out the possibilities.

Annual events such as the HomeSights home show, the Parade of Homes and the Homearama are good ways to get a sampling of what's available.

To make the search for your home or apart-ment a little easier, metropolitan Richmond is divided into numbered real estate areas. The numerical designations of these areas are used by the Multiple Listing Service and in most real estate advertising.

The simplest way to understand how this numbering system works is to remember that Area 10 covers the center city, including the downtown business district, The Fan and Church Hill. From here, everything spreads out in quadrants. Zones in the 20s (such as areas 20, 22 and 24) are to the west, zones in the 30s are to the north, zones in the 40s are to the east, and zones in the 50s and 60s are across the James River to the south.

This chapter includes some names, addresses and phone numbers of people who can help you get settled in, whether you want to rent or buy. Space does not permit a complete listing of services, so you may want to talk things over with friends or coworkers before picking up the phone.

Relocation Services

Relocation specialists can do a lot to smooth your move to or around the Richmond area, especially if yours is a two wage-earner or a single-parent household where time is at a premium. Some local specialists in relocation include:

Bowers, Nelms, Fonville, Long & Foster Relocation Service Center
2800 Buford Rd., Ste. 101
• **272-2800, (800) 446-6009**

The Relocation Division of Bowers, Nelms & Fonville offers a full range of services tailored to meet the individual needs and interests of individuals and corporations considering a move to or from the Richmond area. The professionals at BNFL&F can assist you with finding the right real estate agent. Call their toll free number and ask for a Relocation Coordinator. The relocation team can assist temporary housing for corporate moves. Tours are provided as well.

The BNFL&F Relocation staff provides in-house training to its agents, so their agents know about the most recent happenings in the relocation market.

Napier-Old Colony Relocation Center
13356 Midlothian Tnpk., Midlothian
• **794-4531**

With 35 years of experience in real estate, Napier-Old Colony Realtors is well aware of the special needs of newcomers to the Richmond area. Its Relocation Center works diligently to tailor services to each individual family so that moves will be as worry-free as possible. Working with corporate clients of transferees referred through the Cendant Homequity Relocation Network, Napier-Old Colony's Relocation Center provides pre-move counseling and hotel reservations in addition to area and neighborhood tours. The service also provides information on schools, mortgages, neighborhoods, taxes, cost of living and special interests to all clients. Through the Places Rated Almanac computer program, transferees may compare Richmond with their present location. The Relocation Center's goal is to make a new town feel like home.

Richmond Relocation Services Inc.
412 Libbie Ave. • **282-7200**

Richmond Relocation Services and its residential real estate division, Virginia Properties, provides destination and residential real estate services to incoming transferees. It provides full-day tours of city and county neighborhoods, career counseling for spouses, schooling information for children, tax planning, community networking and legal assistance. As an independent resource, it works to address individual needs in a way that enhances employer-employee relationships. Through Virginia Properties it helps transferees purchase a home, find a rental home or arrange a temporary living situation.

Virginia Landmark Relocation Services
1801 Libbie Ave. • **285-3935**

Richmond has been Virginia Landmark's hometown for more than 30 years, and its relocation services staff works with both individuals and corporations. It offers a highly individualized approach as it works to help newcomers get plugged in to the community based on their special interests. Virginia Landmark begins with advance personal contact to dis-

cuss plans for the initial visit. A relocation agent prepares individualized information packages and arranges a specialized orientation tour that can encompass everything from the arts to community organizations. It helps with the housing search, appointments with mortgage lenders and with recommendations on professionals whose services may be needed in connection with the move. Lunch is delivered on moving day, and Virginia Landmark hosts informal gatherings for newcomers to enhance their knowledge of the city after the move.

Virginia Realty & Relocation
6726 Patterson Ave.
• **282-4031, (800) 633-6643**

Virginia Realty & Relocation provides complete residential relocation services to the individual and corporate transferee. Its standard relocation services include spousal career assistance, public and private school information, home buying counsel, personalized tours of the Richmond area, moving company discounts and buyer representation, all free of charge. Virginia Realty & Relocation's realtors are experienced and accommodating.

Temporary Housing

Some temporary housing options are described in the "Corporate Apartments" section of our Accommodations chapter and also under the Apartment Property Managers section that follows. Costs for temporary housing are generally going to be less than that of an average hotel, unless you choose to scale up. Here are some companies who can take care of all of the details for you.

Wynne Residential Suites
2251 Dabney Rd.
• **359-8534, (800) 338-8534**

Wynne Residential Suites is a specialist in corporate relocation and temporary housing. Its accommodations provide furniture and accessories (such as television, pots and pans, towels and sheets), and it will take care of services such as utilities, telephone, cable television, and even maid service if you want it. Cost is less than that of an average hotel room. Time limitations may apply to certain apartments.

King Properties Inc.
4825 Radford Ave.
• **353-1122, (800) 457-1007**

King Properties has three locations with one-, two- and three-bedroom furnished suites with phone, cable television, pool, tennis. Suites include kitchens. Minimum stay is seven days.

ExecuStay by Marriott
565-B Southlake Blvd.
• **272-6155, (800) 705-7829**

ExecuStay offers fully furnished apartments complete with housewares, utilities, cable TV, maid service, social activities, pools and fitness centers. Minimum lease term is 30 days.

Renting a Home or an Apartment

A wide variety of home and apartment rental options is available in the Richmond area, and you should have no problem finding a place that suits your lifestyle. As you look around, be sure to get answers to the following questions.

1. Does the rental rate include utilities, especially those needed for heat and electricity? Some landlords include utilities such as gas for cooking and heating as part of the rent package; others do not. It can make a big difference.

2. How large a deposit is required? Usually this is a month's rent, but it can be as low as $200.

3. Are there any fees or charges for various expenses that are not refundable?

4. If you have a pet, will the landlord permit the kind of pet you have and, if so, is any extra fee or deposit required?

5. If you should need to move out early because of a job offer in another city or as a result of a change in marital status, can you sublease or transfer the lease to another tenant?

The landlord determines how long the lease will run. Usually it is for one year, but some offer six-month and even month-to-month leases. Most leases require you to notify the landlord 30 to 90 days in advance if you want to terminate; otherwise, most leases automatically renew for another term. Read your lease carefully before you sign it. This is the time to resolve questions and, if mutually agreeable, to modify or add clauses to the lease. Remember that the lease is a legal document, so treat it accordingly. A properly executed lease is for your protection as well as the landlord's.

Some of the best rentals are never advertised. These are the apartments and homes that have so much appeal that they are literally passed from friend to friend. The best way to find places like this is through networking with business associates and friends.

While you're waiting for your connections to come through, we've provided a list of publications and services that'll give you a sense of what's out there — and, who knows, that might have just the right place.

A Rental Solution
P.O. Box 28188, Richmond, VA 23228
• **559-7933, (888) 905-7368**

A Rental Solution offers free customized rental relocation services, including apartments, corporate housing, roommates and more in Richmond, Petersburg, Henrico, Hanover and Chesterfield. With the information clients provide, a relocation counselor prepares a customized relocation package that includes information about apartment pricing, availability, amenities, floor plans and pictures. The services can be used via the Internet, fax, mail or telephone.

Apartment Showcase
10810 Hasty Ln., Ste. 205 • 745-1088

Published four times a year, *Apartment Showcase* contains helpful locator maps and color photos of apartment complexes and amenities. The booklet is divided into separate sections for different parts of town, and it

INSIDERS' TIP

Stonewall Court in the West End owns bragging rights to the oldest civic association in the Richmond area.

contains information on corporate and short-term rentals. Like other publications listed here, Apartment Showcase is available free of charge at various locations like Ukrop's, Wal-Mart, Food Lion and most local malls.

Around the James
8513 Oakview Ave.
• 553-1017, (800) 899-1285

This is a free service that provides fully furnished corporate apartments all around the metropolitan area. If you tell Around the James what you're looking for, they'll find it for you and make sure everything—linens, utilities, furniture, and more—is ready for your moving day.

Apartment Guide
8002 Discovery Dr., Ste. 311 • 288-9238

This is a handy pocket-size guide that can be picked up for free at 7-Eleven stores and a wide variety of other locations. It is divided by geographical parts of the city. One nice thing about this guide is that it provides rental rates in most cases.

Apartment Information Center
5500 Pony Farm Dr. • 329-6666,
(800) 542-3276 in Va., (800) 368-7669
outside Va.

General Services Corporation's (GSC's) Apartment Information Center will provide assistance in culling through the GSC listings. They deal primarily in apartment communities as opposed to random apartments throughout the Greater Richmond area. They can be reached at the above telephone numbers.

Newspaper Classified Ads

The classified advertising columns of area newspapers are good places to find that one-of-a-kind rental. Apartment and home rental ads appear daily in the *Richmond Times-Dispatch*, and the newspaper carries apartment ads in great abundance on Sunday. *Style Weekly*, available free at restaurants, bookstores and curb-side, is often the best place to look for the really nifty rentals. It's published every Tuesday, and copies go fast. If you're looking for a rental in Ashland or in one of the counties, you also should keep an eye on weekly newspapers serving those areas.

Seniors Housing & Services Guide
10810 Hasty Ln., Ste. 205 • 745-1088

Published quarterly, the *Seniors Housing & Services Guide* provides maps, color photos and plenty of information about Richmond's senior living community. The guide includes the nuts and bolts on independent and assisted living as well as continuing- and specialty-care communities in the metropolitan area. *Seniors Housing & Services Guide* is available for free at Ukrop's, Wal-Mart, Food Lion and most local malls.

Apartment Property Management Companies

Some of the larger apartment communities in the metropolitan area are managed by the following firms. Management of apartment communities can change from one firm to another, but this is the way things stood at the time of this writing.

Avalon Bay Communities
2807 N. Parham Rd. • 270-9884

Apartment communities managed by Avalon are new and upscale and include, Avalon Woods in Richmond and Avalon at the Boulders on South Side.

Colony Management Corporation
8814 Fargo Rd. • 282-2900

Colony offers townhouse-style apartments in the Far West End, on the North Side and south of the James. Many offer tennis courts, clubhouses, swimming pools and fitness facilities. Apartment sizes range from efficiencies to three bedrooms. Corporate and short-term leases are available.

EWN Properties Inc.
901 Moorefield Park Dr.
• 330-7966, (800) 926-5563

Apartments and apartment homes managed by EWN Properties are new and state-of-the-art with a wide variety of amenities. They come in sizes ranging from one to three bedrooms and are designed for upscale living. Locations are on the North Side near Virginia Center Commons, in the West End, in the East End and in Chesterfield. EWN's properties include communities such as The Meadows (West End), Cross Creek (Chesterfield), Mill Trace (Mechanicsville) and The Timbers (Bon Air).

General Services Corp. (GSC)
5500 Pony Farm Dr. • 329-6666

GSC, "The Apartment People," manages 14 apartment communities that offer a wide choice of locations in the West End, Chesterfield County and on the North Side. Most have swimming pools and athletic and fitness facilities. One has a nine-hole putting green and six lighted tennis courts. Many have social programs. Gas utilities are included for heat, hot water and cooking. GSC publishes a Richmond-area *Apartment Locator* which can be picked up free of charge at many locations. The *Apartment Locator* contains descriptions of residences and a map of GSC apartment locations.

Great Atlantic Real Estate
5001 W. Broad St. • 285-7567

Crater Square in Petersburg and Courthouse Square in the West End are just two of the properties managed by Great Atlantic. Crater Square has a pool and offers one-, two- and three-bedroom garden style apartments. Courthouse Square has both town house and garden style apartments. Great Atlantic also manages units in Ashland.

Grubb (Ellis)-Harrison & Bates
830 E. Main St. • 788-1000

Harrison & Bates is one of the premiere real estate firms in Richmond, and it handles top-flight properties all over town.

King Properties Inc.
4825 Radford Ave. • 353-1122

Representing nine apartment communities, King Properties offers more than 50 floor plans ranging from one-bedroom and one-bedroom/ loft arrangements to three-bedroom layouts. Apartment locations are in the West End and

south of the James. Short-term corporate and guest apartment leases are available at three locations.

McCormack Baron Management Services Inc.
2 S. 25th St. • 649-1850

These are the people who handle the leasing of Tobacco Row. In the Shockoe Bottom area and just to the east of the city's financial district, Tobacco Row covers 15 blocks of old tobacco factories along the James River and is the largest historic renovation project in the nation. Apartments include many amenities. Some have fireplaces, and there is a swimming pool.

Morton G. Thalhimer Oncore International
1313 E. Main St. • 648-5881

One of Richmond's major real estate sales and management firms, Morton G. Thalhimer Oncore International offers apartments ranging from The Berkshire, a downtown luxury highrise, to those in the West End.

Management Services Corp.
826 Cabell Ave.
• 747-6968

Harbor Village, managed by MSC, offers two-bedroom, two-bath apartments and is in the far West End. The lush landscaping, lighted tennis courts, sand volleyball court and other amenities are its big draws.

Mark Merhige Real Estate, Brokerage & Development Inc.
1555 E. Main St. • 780-3140

Mark Merhige has specialized in the development and rehabilitation of historic properties since 1986 including five Shockoe Slip/ Shockoe Bottom apartment properties: Shockoe Hearth, the Wm. Hill Building, Jackson Warehouse, Pine Alley, and the Cornerstone Building.

INSIDERS' TIP

Financier Patricia Kluge is a primary backer for Hampton Park, an old-fashioned neighborhood in Chesterfield County, with sidewalks, street lamps and front porches.

The Poe Truth

One of America's most well-known poets, Edgar Allan Poe spent his boyhood in Richmond. He came here with his mother, Elizabeth Arnold Poe, an actress who appeared at the Richmond Theatre. In 1811, when Poe was just 2 years old, she died at age 24 from fevers. After her death, Poe went to live with Frances and John Allan. He took Allan as his middle name, but rarely used it. He usually signed his name Edgar A. Poe.

Poe spent his life creating more than 200 poems, short stories and other writings, but "The Raven," the hair-raising poem that made him famous, gave him a reputation as a fine writer.

First published over 150 years ago on January 29, 1845 by the New York weekly *The Evening Mirror*, "The Raven" was introduced by the newspaper as "the most effective single example of 'fugitive poetry' ever published in this country, and unsurpassed in English poetry for subtle conception, masterly ingenuity of versification, and consistent sustaining of imaginative lift and 'pokerishness'" (which meant something like spooky). "The Raven" was an immediate success and brought Poe national and even international acclaim.

Close-up

His first journalistic job was editing the *Southern Literary Messenger* at 15th and Main streets in Richmond. A stinging critic and master storyteller, Poe's name soon became a household word. People knew who Poe was and knew about his black bird. Children followed him down the street quoting "nevermore," "nevermore."

It is said that he enjoyed the attention and the publicity but didn't care much about money. His work was art for art's sake, and he lived most of his life in poverty. He was paid $15 for "The Raven," a fair price at the time, but without the copyright protection

Photo: The Poe Museum

Edgar Allan Poe's spirit is still alive in the many Richmond buildings he spent time in.

writers enjoy today, he received nothing for the numerous reprints, parodies, imitations, songs or pictorial representations it inspired.

Poe was ahead of his time. He was also a binge drinker, a problem that contributed to a fallacious image of the poet. After Poe died in 1849 at the age of 40, he was maligned by critics who exaggerated the negative aspects of his work and his life. Even today, the idea of Poe as a drug addict, drunkard and manic depressive is entrenched. The Poe Museum pledges to rid their many visitors of their misconceptions of the great writer.

The French poet Charles Baudelaire translated many of Poe's works and helped to change Poe's reputation. Today, some critics say that Poe was a meticulous writer who could not have produced the work he did if he were in a chronic disturbed or drugged state. His many accomplishments show him to be one of America's finest and most influential writers — he created the modern detective story, helped develop science fiction as we know it today and set the standards for literary criticism in 19th-century America.

His writings include: "The Fall of the House of Usher," "The Pit and the Pendulum," "The Black Cat," "Eureka," "The Tell-Tale Heart," "Tamerlane and Other Poems," "The Gold Bug," "The Murders in Rue Morgue" and "Ligeia," a short story he considered his best.

The spirit of Poet is all over Richmond. The following is a list of spots that the Poe buff won't want to miss.

Edgar Allan Poe Museum
1916 East Main St. • 648-5523

Where better to start: the Old Stone House. Yep, it's old — in fact, one of the oldest structures in the city, circa 1737. But nope, Poe didn't live here. There's a good chance he never stepped foot in it. About the closest scholars can put him to the house is in the facing street. In 1824, at the age of 15, Poe stood as a member of an honorary military guard escorting the Marquis de Lafayette to a dinner at the Old Stone House.

Monumental Church
1224 E. Broad St.

This is the site of the old Richmond Theatre where Poe's mother gave her last performance in October of 1811 as the Countess Winstersen in "The Stranger." She then fell ill due to "fevers" and died that December. Three weeks later the theater burned to the ground, killing 74 people including the governor. Soon thereafter the present church was erected over the site. Moneys were raised through the sale of pews. Poe's foster father John Allan, who would later attend the church, bought pew number 80. The church no longer has services and is open to the public.

The Elmira Royster Shelton House
2407 East Grace St. (private residence)

Elmira Royster Shelton, in a full-circle twist of fate, managed to be Poe's first and last love. As teenagers they were secretly engaged — "secretly" because Elmira's parents disapproved of Poe, most likely because his mother was an actress. Poe left his fiance to attend the University of Virginia. By the time he got back for Christmas, Elmira had left Richmond and become engaged to a Mr. Shelton. It appears that Elmira's parents had intercepted Poe's letters from school, forcing Elmira to believe Poe had forgotten about her. But 23 years later, in 1849, while on a lecture circuit stop in Richmond, Poe rekindled his affair with the then-widowed Elmira.

He was often seen frequenting her home on East Grace. Reports vary, but it seems

— continued on next page

that when Poe left Elmira that September on a boat for Baltimore, he intended to marry her. But mysteriously, Poe vanished for six days only to resurface half-dazed in a Baltimore tavern wearing soiled clothes that weren't even his. He died four days later in the Washington Medical College hospital.

Talavera
2315 West Grace St. (private residence)

Reports place Poe here on September 26, 1849, his last night in Richmond before heading out to Baltimore. During his final stay in Richmond, the late summer and early fall of 1849, Poe had been a frequent visitor of Talavera, at that time the farmhouse of the Talley family, situated in what was then the suburbs of Richmond. Poe was particularly acquainted with Susan Archer Talley, with whom he discussed "The Raven" (which Miss Talley boldly insisted was flawed) and the "Poetic Principle."

On their last visit together, Miss Talley recalled Poe's excitement over his renewed affections with Elmira. She would much later write of his departure: "After a few steps he paused, turned, and again lifted his hat in a last adieu. At that moment a brilliant meteor appeared in the sky directly over his head, and vanished." Poe would die a week later.

Other Sites

Much of Poe's Richmond is gone, but we're lucky enough to know where most of the buildings that he knew best were located. A few sites worth mention follow. The Ellis & Allan Mercantile Store (northeast corner of 13th and Main) was Poe's foster father John Allan's store and the place where Poe first lived (above the store) after being taken in by the Allans. The Southern Literary Messenger Building (southeast corner of 15th and Main) was the three-story building where as the Messenger's associate editor Poe first made a name for himself. Poe boarded with Virginia Clemm and her mother "Muddie" at the Yarrington Boardinghouse (12th and Bank, across from the Capitol Square) while he worked at the Messenger; it's also the place where Poe and Virginia Clemm were married. Moldavia (southeast corner of 5th and Main) is the mansion John Allan landed after inheriting the fortune of his uncle William Galt in 1825; Poe was only here briefly before leaving for the University of Virginia in 1826.

If you're looking for the players in Poe's life-drama, they're resting about the city. Poe's mother was interred in the churchyard at St. John's Church. Her tombstone is, however, a twentieth-century addition and regretfully only marks the general area where she was buried. Also buried at St. John's is Poe's boss Thomas W. White, founder of the *Southern Literary Messenger*. Venturing to the north side of the city, to Shockoe Hill Cemetery, you'll find Poe's foster parents, John and Francis Allan; Poe's "Helen," Jane Craig Stanard; and Elmira Royster Shelton, Poe's first and last love.

Sentinel
3512 Corum Dr., #512 • 527-1496

Sentinel's West End apartment community is new and offers one- and two-bedroom units. There is a swimming pool as well as a wide range of athletic and fitness amenities. Some units have fireplaces and/or balconies.

Trammell Crow Inc.
3301 Copper Mill Trace • 747-8181

If you're looking for a West End location with vaulted ceilings, fireplace, racquetball court, tennis court and two swimming pools, then Copper Springs managed by Trammell Crow will be just the right place.

United Dominion Realty Trust
10 S. Sixth St. • 780-2691

United Dominion manages a variety of affordably priced apartments and apartment townhouses in the West End and on the North Side and South Side. Amenities vary from location to location but include swimming pools, play areas for children and fully furnished guest apartments for friends and family.

Wilton Companies
9101 Patterson Ave. • 740-7192

Wilton Companies offers homestyle living at affordable prices in its 17 different apartment communities in the West End Apartments. Apartment townhouses range in size from one bedroom to three bedrooms. Amenities include swimming pools and play areas for children.

Buying a Home in Richmond

There are about eight basic steps to buying a house in Richmond. If all goes well, this is how it works:

1. With the help of an agent, the buyer signs a sales contract that is submitted to the seller with a good faith deposit. The deposit is usually held by the selling broker until closing, when it is credited to the sale price of the house. In Richmond, the usual contingencies in a contract include inspections of the property, the ability to secure financing and the sale of the buyer's present home. In 1993 it became law that the seller must provide the buyer at the time of contract signing either a disclosure statement regarding the seller's knowledge of existing problems with the property or a disclaimer statement signed by both parties that the property is being sold "as is."

2. The sales contract is accepted and signed by the buyer. From this point on, the average closing time is 60 to 90 days.

3. The buyer submits a mortgage application that includes a detailed financial statement. The lender orders an appraisal of the property, a credit report and verifications of employment and of the source of funds for the down payment. The lender asks for a check at this time to cover costs of the credit report and the appraisal.

4. The lender receives the credit report and appraisal; the mortgage application is approved; a loan commitment is issued to the purchaser; and the closing package usually is sent to the buyer's attorney who will handle the closing.

5. The buyer's attorney orders a title examination and survey, title insurance and usually the homeowners insurance policy.

6. About a week before closing, the buyer and seller notify utility companies of change of ownership.

7. Closing is usually held at the office of the buyer's attorney. The closing represents the transfer of title. The buyer checks with their attorney's office several days before closing to find out the amount of the cashiers check needed at closing to cover the balance of the down payment, closing costs and escrow items.

8. Immediately after closing, the attorney records the transaction at the appropriate courthouse, and the buyer receives the keys. The buyer takes possession.

Publications you may find helpful in your search for a new home include:

Metro Real Estate
333 E. Franklin St. • 649-6348

Published by Richmond Newspapers Inc., this tabloid-format magazine is issued monthly and distributed with home-delivered editions of the *Richmond Times-Dispatch* on the first Saturday of every month. It also is available at about 150 rack locations throughout the metro area. It contains photographs of homes for sale and stories about residential communities, home builders and real estate professionals.

Harmon Homes
Richmond Edition • (800) 955-5516

This publication, available free at many locations, contains residential listing offered by real estate firms in the area. It is published every two weeks by Harmon Publishing.

Homes & Land — Richmond
2711 Buford Rd. • 272-0776

Magazine sized in format, with more than 100 pages, this nifty full-color showcase of offerings by area Realtors is published every month and can be picked up free of charge at boxes throughout the city and suburbs. For high-dollar home seekers it contains a special "Estates & Homes" section.

Realtors

There are about 4,000 licensed real estate agents in the Richmond *Multiple Listing Service* directory. A number have earned the status of Realtor through extensive professional training and adherence to a strict code of ethics. These professionals can be identified by the gold "R" lapel pin and by the symbol when it is used on business cards and stationery.

One of the most far-reaching changes in services provided by Richmond real estate firms in recent years has been the introduction of the "buyer's agent." Traditionally, a real estate agent has fiduciary responsibility to the seller. Now more and more firms have agents who can be engaged to look out for the interests of the buyer and to negotiate on the buyer's behalf. Their fee is a percentage of the sale price. If this kind of service is of value to you, be sure to ask about it.

The real estate firms selected for this guide are recognized as some of the best. There are others in town who are excellent, but space does not permit a complete listing. The Yellow Pages are a good reference for all of the firms in town, and a complete listing of RAR members is available from the Richmond Association of Realtors (RAR) at 5002 Monument Ave., 358-5358.

Bowers, Nelms, Fonville, Long & Foster
4435 Waterfront Dr., Innsbrook
• **346-4411, (800) 446-6009**

BNF is the second-largest independent residential real estate firm in the nation and the largest residential real estate firm in Richmond. With more than 400 associates in Richmond and 16 strategically located offices, it covers the whole metropolitan area and offers a complete range of services. If you're looking for home and don't know which of the 400 agents to call, BNFL&F's Homefinding Coun-

selors will match you with an agent. It also has an office in Kilmarnock that specializes in river property in the Northern Neck area.

Century 21 — Old Richmond Realty Ltd.
910 Parham Rd.
• **741-4090, (800) 472-3344**

This firm is one of the largest Century 21 franchises in the area and is hooked into Century 21's nationwide referral network. It is involved in in-town and suburban residential sales throughout the metropolitan area, from starter homes to more expensive property. It also handles sales of the new modular homes that are available in many attractive styles and that can cut construction time in half.

Century 21 — Signature Realty
2800 Buford Rd. • **330-4222,**
(800) 989-RELO relocation services

This firm, in the heart of Bon Air, provides full-service residential real estate services. Its sales associates are experienced in residential resale, new construction, financing and relocation.

Coldwell Banker — Goode & Company
2820 Waterford Lake Dr.
• **744-1494, (800) 359-3537**

This firm specializes in residential property south of the James River, although its listings include attractive city and country property throughout the metropolitan area. It also offers high-quality new homes beginning in the $80s and running up to those of more than 4,000 square feet. In addition to residential sales and new home construction, the firm offers commercial services.

Coldwell Banker — Vaughan and Company Inc.
9701 Gayton Rd. • **740-6683**

Vaughan and Company specializes in the

INSIDERS' TIP

The "Citie of Henricus," now part of a park in Chesterfield County, was the second English settlement in Virginia. It was settled in 1611 by Sir Thomas Dale when the London Company sought a better location than Jamestown for its colony.

West End, although you will find property in Chesterfield, Powhatan and Hanover counties and on Richmond's North Side among its listings. New homes account for a large part of their business.

The Covington Company
5809 York Rd. • 288-8317

The Covington Company has residential specialists ready to provide service to people relocating within the Richmond area as well as those coming to Richmond from other places. Experience, sensitivity to personal needs and knowledge of the local residential market give Covington the ability to serve needs of both buyers and sellers.

C. Porter Vaughan Inc.
9201 Forest Hill Ave.
• 320-9661, (800) 228-9199

This sizable firm is a member of the All Points Relocation Service. Its total range of real estate services includes residential property, site development and property management. It is the developer of the prestigious Salisbury subdivision.

East West Realty
14700 Village Square Pl., Midlothian
• 739-3800

A full-service firm, East West Realty specializes in residential real estate in Chesterfield County. East West Realty is an affiliate of East West Partners of Virginia. The developer of the nationally recognized lakefront communities of Woodlake and Brandermill, East West Realty represents homes and homesites in the award-winning planned communities of Rivers Bend, Foxcroft, Woodlake and Brandermill. Homes in these communities range in price from $90,000 to $500,000, offering a great selection of new and resale homes in styles that range from traditional to contemporary.

ERA — Woody Hogg & Associates
7284 Hanover Green Dr. • 559-4644
1360 E. Parham Rd. • 262-7371

With an office in Mechanicsville and another in the West End, Woody, Hogg & Associates is a full-service residential real estate firm.

Highlands Realty
8400 Highland Glen Dr., Chesterfield
• 748-7361

Highlands Realty is the place to call for information about The Highlands, a 2,500-acre planned community near Chesterfield Courthouse with large lots, a lake and a golf course. Homes range from $180,000 to over $700,000.

Hometown Realty
7240 Lee Davis Rd., Mechanicsville
• 730-7195
9568 Kings Charter Dr., Ashland
• 550-1900

Hometown Realty specializes in resales as well as new construction. It currently represents 10 subdivisions in Hanover County, with homes ranging from the $90,000 to $300,000. Both the Mechanicsville and Ashland offices cover the Greater Richmond area. In addition, the firm has an office in Tappahannock that covers the Northern Neck area. Together, the offices offer the services of 60 agents.

Joyner & Co.
2727 Enterprise Pkwy. • 270-9440

Joyner & Co. offers relocation services and can help you get set up in a home either within the metro area or on a farm in a nearby rural location.

Metropolitan Real Estate Inc.
1791 Cambridge Dr. • 741-4108

In the West End of Richmond, Metropolitan Real Estate Inc. specializes in new home real estate. Metropolitan represents the communities of FoxHall, Royal Oaks and Riverlake Colony with properties from $280,000.

Napier-Old Colony Realtors
13356 Midlothian Tnpk. • 794-4531

One of the area's largest real estate firms, Napier-Old Colony has served the needs of the Richmond community for about 40 years. Its original offices were in Northern Chesterfield County. There are now offices conveniently north and south of the James River to better serve the entire metropolitan area.

Napier-Old Colony offers homes in a wide variety of styles and price ranges. In addition to traditional brokerage services, Napier has buyer brokerage services available. Specializing in relocation services, Napier works with many local corporations and is the exclusive representative of Cendant Homequity, the nation's oldest and largest relocation company. Additional services include in-house mortgage origination through Cendant US Mortgage and custom home design and construction through Napier Signature Homes.

Neville C. Johnson Inc.
4905 Radford Ave. • 355-7981

Neville C. Johnson in the late 1950s pioneered the designation "The Fan" for the neighborhood stretching from Harrison Street to the Boulevard. Before that, property in the area was advertised simply as townhouses. The firm, with offices in the West End, today specializes in residential properties ranging in value from $150,000 to $1 million and in property management. It has expanded beyond its original Fan District base and now also is active in the Near West End, the Far West End and south of the James. It also handles some country property. It has a referral setup.

Proctor Realty Company Inc.
6726 Patterson Ave. • 282-3136

Founded in 1949, Proctor Realty has an excellent reputation. With 20 sales associates, the firm has been recognized as one of Richmond's most productive real estate companies on a per-agent basis. Its seasoned personnel are knowledgeable about the whole Richmond area. In addition to residential, farm and land sales, Proctor Realty has a commercial division and an affiliate relocation company, Virginia Relocation.

Prudential Slater James River Realtors
8900 Three Chopt Rd.
• 288-8351, (800) 637-2341

This is a large firm that is involved in residential and commercial sales and also offers property management and relocation services. It has offices in the West End and in Chesterfield and Hanover counties and, in addition to sales of existing property, represents builders of new homes.

Prudential Savage & Company Realtors
9321 Midlothian Tnpk. • 560-ROCK

Prudential Savage & Company Realtors has been a major factor in the residential real estate market south of the James River since 1977. A good way to check out what's available in the Richmond area is to visit the firm's Home Information Center in Chesterfield Towne Center (379-6585).

RE/MAX Commonwealth
7201 Glen Forest Dr. • 288-5000
3434 Lauderdale Dr. • 360-5200
1520 Huguenot Rd. • 794-2150

This RE/MAX firm was formerly known to Richmonders as Brooks & Innes. Both, RE/MAX offices specialize in residential property, farms and property management. It offers a complete range of real estate services.

Simmons-Baker Realty
605 Research Rd. • 794-9488

Simmons-Baker represents more than a dozen subdivisions in Chesterfield, the West End and Hanover County. Homes in these communities are of colonial design and are known for their excellent construction and competitive pricing within the $90,000 to $125,000 range. The firm offers a total range of real estate services including property sales, property development and property management. It is the exclusive listing agent for Emerald Homes.

Virginia Landmark Corporation
1801 Libbie Ave. • 285-3935

Virginia Landmark is a member of Christie's Great Estates and has been an important player in the Richmond real estate market since the early 1960s. Its residential arm handles sales throughout the city, and the firm has been involved in the development of single-family subdivisions as well as condominium construction and conversion. It assists corporations in selling houses of employees transferred out of the Richmond area.

Virginia Properties
412 Libbie Ave. • 282-7300

The exclusive Richmond-area affiliate of Sothebys International Realty, Virginia Properties specializes in residential real estate, historic properties, farms and estates. The Relocation Center of Virginia Properties has broad experience handling individual and corporate transfers, and its Timely Solutions division concentrates on the downsizing and retirement market. Virginia Properties is a charter member of the National Trust for Historic Preservation's Historic Real Estate Program.

Newcomers Clubs

A good way to meet people is through hobby and special interest groups. A list of these groups is published in the annual, early August "Discover Richmond" section of the *Richmond Times-Dispatch* (single copies of this section are on sale throughout the year at the newspaper's front desk at 333 E. Franklin Street).

In addition, two organizations are open to anyone who has moved to the Richmond area within the past two years: the Newcomers Club of Richmond, Margaret Potter at 285-2205 or Dorothy Harrison at 740-2720; and the New Virginians Club, Connie Peck at 762-4774. There also are neighborhood newcomer organizations such as the Chesterfield Welcome League, Jan Grant at 744-6715.

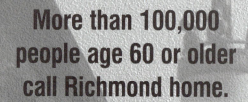

More than 100,000 people age 60 or older call Richmond home.

Retirement

Richmond appeals to many retirees because it's big enough to offer cultural activities, educational opportunities and second careers, yet small enough to allow for relatively stress-free transportation. Retirees are also attracted to the area's central location—it's a short trip from here to nearby tourist destinations such as Williamsburg, Washington, D.C., the Shenandoah Valley, the Chesapeake Bay, beaches and rivers.

More than 100,000 people age 60 or older call Richmond home. Most are from the area or have family or friends who live here. As the area's senior population increases, Richmond retirees will be able to choose from a more housing options and services than ever before.

To help seniors maintain an active and independent lifestyle, many retirement homes and communities in the Richmond area offer assisted living arrangements that allow residents to live independently, participate in activity programs and take advantage of housekeeping, grounds maintenance, transportation, meals and personal services, as needed.

For those who don't want to join a retirement community, an increasing number of organizations offer a variety of home, health and personal services for seniors who live at home but are unable to live independently.

For retirees who like being homeowners but don't want all the work and worry, at least one development—Summer Hill at Stony Point—provides homeowners security and maintenance services in a neighborhood that offers the fellowship, programs and services of a typical retirement community.

In the Richmond area, you'll also find numerous programs, clubs, support groups, publications and organized activities for seniors, including trips, golf groups, athletic competitions, walking clubs and dances. In this section, we've provided a sampling of some of the innovative and reputable retirement communities and organizations. This chapter does not include information on nursing homes. For information about programs, services and other housing options, we suggest that you start with the Capital Area Agency on Aging.

Organizations

Capital Area Agency on Aging
24 E. Cary St. • 343-3000

This private, nonprofit organization is part of a nationwide system developed as a result of the Older Americans Act and administered by the Virginia Department for the Aging. It's a great place to start when you need information about senior clubs, housing, home equity conversion, long-term care, social security, services and opportunities in the Richmond area for people age 60 and older. If the staff can't help you directly, they'll put you in touch with someone who can. In addition to its role as an information clearinghouse, the agency also provides some direct services, such as a job referrals and meals programs. Other services include health insurance counseling, resource coordination, money management, homecare and a newsletter for seniors. Services are free, but donations are accepted.

City and County Recreation and Parks Departments
900 E. Broad St., Richmond • 780-5733
6801 Wagners Way, Chesterfield County • 748-1623
200 Berkley St., Hanover County • 798-8062
8600 Dixon Powers Dr., Henrico County • 672-5100

The recreation and parks departments of Richmond and each of the surrounding counties sponsor a variety of senior recreation programs and activities, including walking clubs, arts and crafts, gardening classes and trips. Contact the nearest office for details.

Virginia Association of Area Agencies on Aging
530 E. Main St. • 644-2804

This not-for-profit agency has two main programs. First, the Long-Term Care Ombudsman Program takes and investigates the concerns and complaints of senior residents who are receiving long-term care in Richmond. Second, Operation Restore Trust is a program designed to combat Medicare and Medicaid fraud.

Virginia Department for the Aging
1600 Forest Ave., Suite 102 • 662-9333 Long-term Care Ombudsman Office

The Virginia Department for the Aging works primarily with transportation and in-home meals and services as well as with statewide policy and legislation concerning tax-relief, healthcare and transportation issues involving elderly people. Most of the department's services are provided through the Capital Area Agency on Aging; however, the department's staff provides free, confidential counseling and complaint resolution regarding long-term care options.

Services

Canterbury Club
1600 Westbrook Ave. • 261-5287

During the past few years, what began as a home meal-delivery service has grown into a full-service club that provides almost any type of assistance that elderly people need to maintain independent living in their own homes. But it's not just for seniors, younger people can use it, too. Operated by Westminster Canterbury, the Canterbury Club offers minor exterior home repairs, lawn and garden maintenance, home healthcare, nursing assistance, transportation, companions, personal care services, financial services, gift buying and more.

You can request services or order meals as often as you need them, on a regular or temporary basis. Meals are prepared by the Canterbury kitchen, then delivered to your home, frozen and ready for cooking in the microwave. It's an ideal solution for people who are recuperating from a hospital stay or as a backup for caregivers who are going on vacation and need help taking care of an older relative or friend. Some business people also use the service to help feed their families if they have to travel out of town.

ElderHomes Corp.
110 Giant Dr., Suite C • 233-2827

This service group is a community development corporation, a non-profit organization that provides assistance to elderly people with home maintenance and rehabilitation issues.

Foundation for Senior Independence
113 Granite Springs Rd. • 674-8886

The Foundation teaches computer classes to seniors. Two week-long courses are offered—basic and advanced. Each class, which lasts about one week, costs $100.

Meals on Wheels
1600 Willow Lawn Dr. • 673-5035

All meals are delivered by volunteers to anyone over age 18 who is unable to shop for food or prepare meals for themselves and who has no other reliable means of obtaining daily meals. A hot mid-day meal and a cold snack are available during the week, and frozen meals are provided for weekends. The deliv-

FYI

Unless otherwise noted, the area code for all phone numbers listed in this chapter is 804.

INSIDERS' TIP

Two area publications devoted to senior issues are: *Mature Life*, a bimonthly publication published by the Capital Area Agency on Aging, and *Prime Living*, a special section in the Monday edition of the *Richmond Times-Dispatch*.

ery area includes Richmond, and parts of Chesterfield, Henrico and Hanover counties. Prices are based on ability to pay. To begin service, you need to submit an application at least 24 hours in advance.

Mature Options
8100 Three Chopt Rd., Ste. 144 • 282-0753
Owned by Norah Knutsen, an experienced Gerontological Clinical Nurse Specialist, Mature Options assists older adults and their families with the selection and management of long-term care services best suited to their individual needs. The staff works closely with clients to explore a full range of options from in-home assistance or adult day care to assisted living arrangements or institutional care.

PrimeDynamics
9506 Bonnie Dale Rd. • 935-6800
PrimeDynamics is three companies in one. First, it publishes books for the elderly, focusing on setting up to thrive throughout aging by discussing housing, finances and spirituality. Second, the West End company hosts seminars about the same topics. And third, PrimeDynamics offers one-on-one workshops that focus on financial planning and more.

Virginia Properties Relocation Center
412 Libbie Ave. • 282-7300
To help meet the special needs of people

who are selling their homes to move to a retirement setting or a smaller home, Virginia Properties offers a program known as Timely Solutions. The program includes free consultation on insurance, landscape and interior design, and step-by-step guidance for moving. Professional services regarding legal considerations, taxes, financial issues, repairs and estate sales are also available at discounted rates. A Personal Move coordinator works with each homeowner to arrange all the details and provides guidance throughout the process. The cost is $20 per hour.

Health and Wellness Programs

Bon Secours Richmond VIVA
1300 Westwood Ave. • 915-8345
Designed for people age 50 and older, this health and wellness program helps members attain a healthier, safer and more active lifestyle. Members are entitled to free health screenings and education, discounts on exercise, leisure and travel programs and health-related items and services. VIVA is sponsored by the Bon Secours–Richmond Hospitals including St. Mary's, Stuart Circle, Richmond Community and Memorial Regional. The fee for a lifetime membership is $15 per person or $25 per couple.

Senior Friends at Columbia Hospitals
1602 Skipwith Rd. • 330-4000

Anyone age 50 or older may participate in this health club for seniors. Health screening, newsletters, education programs, exercise classes, and travel, fitness and pharmacy discounts are available for members. Senior Friends is sponsored by Columbia Hospitals in the Richmond area including Johnston Willis, Chippenham, Henrico Doctors, Retreat and the Hanover Outpatient Center. Membership is $15 for one year, $25 for two years and $25 for a couple for one year.

Retirement Communities

The group of people age 60-plus is the fastest growing population in Richmond as well as other parts of the country. Because there are far too many Retirement Communities to list them all, we suggest looking through the phone book as well as checking out *Senior Housing & Services Guide* for the community that suits you best. The latter is a quarterly publication that provides maps, color photos and lots of information about Richmond's senior living community. The guide includes the nuts and bolts on independent and assisted living as well as continuing- and specialty-care communities in the metropolitan area.

Beaufont Towers Retirement Community
7015 Carnation St. • 320-1412

Beaufont Towers is an established retirement community in Southside Richmond. This gracious four-story brick building offers 176 apartments—studios and one- or two-bedroom units. Home to about 200 residents, Beaufont Towers offers independent living, assisted living and a special needs wing for residents with Alzheimer's and dementia.

Residents enjoy services that include professional management, maintenance and nursing services, wellness programs, meals served in elegant dining rooms, housekeeping and linen service, and scheduled transportation for shopping and medical appointments.

A full-time activities director keeps residents busy with a calendar packed with arts and crafts, religious services, exercise, trips, bridge games and more. Other amenities include a library, a convenience store, a chapel, a parlor, solariums, a grand gazebo, gardening areas and a beauty and barber shop.

A unique affiliation with the neighboring Beaufont Healthcare Center enables Beaufont Towers to offer residents total care without the burden of an additional fee. Residents receive priority admission to the healthcare center, should they ever require a more skilled level of care.

Monthly rates range from $1,310 to $2,075 depending on the level of care, size of apartment and number of occupants.

Bon Secours Retirement Community at Ironbridge
6701 Ironbridge Pkwy., Chester • 748-7000

Specifically designed for seniors who do not want to live alone or who require some assistance with daily living activities, this community offers a friendly, elegant and secure environment filled with Southern hospitality.

Residents may choose studio apartments, one-bedroom suites, private or semiprivate rooms. Facilities include a library, activity and exercise rooms, lounges, and beauty and barber shops. Services include meals, housekeeping, laundry, emergency medical call systems, safety and security systems, scheduled transportation and 24-hour, full-service personal care. A full-time social director coordinates activities.

No entrance fees are required. Monthly rates range from $1,845 to $2,525 for unfurnished, single-occupancy apartments. The monthly fee includes utilities, all meals, housekeeping, laundry and more. Furnished apartments and rooms are also available.

Brandermill Woods
14311 Brandermill Woods Tr. • 744-1173

This retirement community opened in 1986 and leases single-story cluster homes with attached garages and apartments to energetic couples who are typically in their early 70s. All levels of care and a full range of services are available as residents' needs change. There are two three-story apartment buildings, cluster homes, a clubhouse, a healthcare complex and a nursing home. The healthcare com-

plex includes assisted-living apartments and a 60-bed, licensed nursing home. On about 40 acres, this community adjoins the larger residential community of Brandermill.

Residents enjoy an intergenerational mix of people in the neighborhood. The natural country setting is excellent for bird watching and leisurely strolls. A walking path around the lake makes for an especially relaxing yet stimulating jaunt. Membership to the Brandermill Country Club is available.

Services include security guards, medical alert buttons, up-and-about buttons, exterior and interior maintenance, transportation, planned excursions, exercise and activity programs. The average rent is about $2,000 per month for two people in a two-bedroom home. All utilities, housekeeping and some meals are included.

Braxton Retirement Community
Lakemere Dr. at Ironbridge Rd. • 275-2689

About 5 miles from the courthouse area in Chesterfield County, Braxton Retirement Community offers home ownership without the hassle or worries of maintenance or security. This 43-acre community features sidewalks, street lamps, a computerized security gate and a clubhouse with a library, kitchen, exercise room, media room and meeting room. About 70 single-family homes have been built since development began in 1992. When the community is completed, there will be about 130

homes on 0.33-acre parcels of mostly open land. All homes are built by owner and developer W.S. Carnes, a Richmond area builder for more than 40 years.

Designed for active retirees, the community offers convenient and easy access to the Richmond area via Chippenham Parkway and Route 10. Residents also enjoy walking trails and a fishing pond. Social and recreational activities are planned and coordinated by the homeowners. No healthcare or other services are offered, but a list of providers is available.

Each resident has an access code that allows them to pass through the community's computerized security gate. Visitors use a phone at the gate to call residents, who open the gate via a remote telephone code.

Homes may be built for $167,000 or more, depending on design and square footage. Homes range in size from 1,400 square feet to 2,500 square feet and feature quality construction using your plans or spec plans offered by the community. You must be at least 55 to live here. There is an annual $125 community fee.

The Guardian Place
1620 N. Hamilton St. • 355-3013

Designed exclusively for seniors age 62 or older with moderate incomes, The Guardian Place features state-of-the-art accommodations for the elderly. The modern four-story brick building opened in 1994 with 120 independent living apartments. Future expansion is planned. Studios and one- or two-bedroom apartments are available.

Developed by United Methodist Family Services, the Guardian Place was the first retirement home in Virginia that was financed with tax credits. Residents' annual income must not exceed an amount set annually by the Virginia Housing and Development Authority (VHDA).

The Guardian Place provides a community room, library, beauty shop and courtesy transportation for residents. A resident manager is available 24 hours a day, and each apartment has emergency call buttons. Residents enjoy spacious grounds, garden plots, potluck dinners, luncheons, bridge parties and crafts classes. They also have convenient access to public transportation, shopping and nearby cultural attractions and colleges. Some residents are still employed or work as volunteers. There is no entrance fee. Monthly rates range from $515 to $725, including utilities.

Ginter Hall West
12411 Gayton Rd. • 741-9494

In a quiet residential area in the West End, Ginter Hall West provides personal assisted-living care for senior citizens. Constructed in 1987, the brick facility includes 128 rooms with the capacity for 236 residents. Services include 24-hour personal care, meals, activity programs, religious services, housekeeping, laundry, an emergency call system and a beauty salon/barber shop.

Ginter Hall West also provides a respite program to assist families with daily caregiving tasks. Stays may last two or more weeks. Respite Care residents receive the same services and amenities offered to permanent residents.

Monthly rates range from about $2,000 to $3,300, depending on the size of the apartment and number of occupants. Daily rates are also available. There is no entrance fee.

The Hermitage
1600 Westwood Ave. • 355-5721

Owned by Virginia United Methodist Homes Inc., the Hermitage is an established continuing-care retirement community on the edge of Ginter Park. The Georgian-style mansion was originally built as a private residence in 1911. Residential wings were added after it opened as a retirement home in 1949, and the 82-bed healthcare center was added in 1978. About 250 people of all faiths live here. One-, two- and three-room apartments are available for independent living. Assisted-living apartments are also available, and a special Alzheimer's care center recently opened. Situated on seven acres of beautifully landscaped lawns, the Hermitage provides a full range of support services, a beauty shop, a chapel and a sundry store. Residents are very active in creative arts, music and religious activities and enjoy the attention of an active group of volunteers.

There is an entrance fee. Monthly rates start at $1,855 for one person, and include meals, housekeeping, transportation, activities and other support services. Life care plans are also available.

The Hermitage at Cedarfield
2300 Cedarfield Parkway • 967-9000

Cedarfield's small-town environment offers a safety net of care and support for retired couples and individuals of all ages. Built on 75 acres of rolling countryside, Cedarfield offers 226 apartments, 85 cottages, 42 assisted living apartments, 23 Alzheimer's rooms, and a 60-bed healthcare center. More than 20 different floor plans are available. Meal plans are flexible, and residents enjoy a putting green, tennis courts, walking paths, indoor swimming, and shops, and have access to banks, pharmacy, deli, library, fellowship hall and chapel. A full-time activities director provides a full schedule of activities. Cedarfield offers a full continuum of service including independent living, assisted living, licensed short-term and long-term nursing, therapy services and recuperative care.

There is an entrance fee, and monthly rates for apartments are $1,536 to $3,101, depending on number of occupants. Monthly rates for cottages range from $2,765 to $3,421.

Imperial Plaza
1717 Bellevue Ave. • 264-1380

This retirement community near Bryan Park has it all—shopping, dining, a 278-seat theater, a post office, a beauty shop and a bank.

In fact, since over 1,100 people live here, it even has its own voting precinct.

Everything here is housed in one complex with enclosed walkways, so you don't have to venture outside in bad weather or go up or down any steps. There are three nine-story brick buildings and one 13-story building in a parklike setting on 30 wooded acres. More than 800 independent living units from one-bedroom apartments to two-bedroom penthouses are leased on a yearly basis. An additional 152 assisted living apartments opened recently.

A full range of support services, transportation, security and emergency pulls are available. For those who need a little extra help, meals and personal services are provided to residents in their private apartments in the Assisted Living Center, where there are licensed practical nurses on duty 24 hours a day.

Built in the late 1960s, the buildings were recently renovated, and new carpeting and appliances installed.

A full-time activities coordinator keeps residents busy with song and dance shows, gardening, art classes, bus tours, shopping excursions, church services, bridge, pool, horseshoes, bingo and committee work.

Monthly rents range from about $590 to $1,655 with additional charges for optional services.

Lakewood Manor
Baptist Retirement Community, 1900 Lauderdale Dr. • 740-2900

This campus-style, life-care community operated by Virginia Baptist Homes Inc. is in the West End on more than 50 wooded acres. It's home to about 400 people of all faiths who are typically in their late 70s and 80s. There are five three-story apartment buildings, a new three-story assisted-living building, a healthcare center and a community center, all connected by covered walkways.

Residents choose from a variety of floor plans and apartment sizes. Dining service is provided, or residents may prepare their own meals; all apartments have kitchens.

A full range of security and support services are available. Lakewood Manor also provides a bank, a convenience store, a beauty and barber shop, a woodworking shop, gardening areas, a billiards room and a library. People who live here like to travel and participate in many cultural, social and religious activities.

The healthcare center provides physical, speech and rehabilitative therapy, care for temporary illnesses, recuperation from hospitalization and long-term nursing care.

There is an entrance fee, and monthly fees range from $1,410 to $1,962 per month.

Manorhouse
3000 Skipwith Rd. • 270-3990
2800 Polo Pkwy., Midlothian • 379-2800

Both the West End and South Side Manorhouse Assisted Living Retirement Communities provide security, peace of mind and comprehensive, 24-hour personal-care services. Residents enjoy 24-hour emergency call systems, closed circuit television and fire resistant construction.

Standard amenities include personal-care assistance, housekeeping and maintenance, laundry service and scheduled transportation for shopping, doctor visits and worship services. Daily meals are prepared by a licensed dietician and served restaurant-style. A full-time activities director coordinates social and recreational programs. Guest meals, room service, dry cleaning service and short-term respite care are also available.

Monthly rates range from about $2,080 to $2,595 for an unfurnished unit depending on the size and number of occupants. Furnished units are also available. Daily rates are available for respite care. There is no entrance fee.

Our Lady of Hope Health Center
13700 N. Gayton Rd. • 360-1960

Open since January 1996, Our Lady of Hope Health Center offers assisted living, nursing home services and an Alzheimer's Unit in a rural setting in the far West End. Situated on eight acres, the two-story brick building includes an assisted-living center on the first floor with 34 studio and one-bedroom apartments.

Services include assistance with personal care, 24-hour nursing as needed, dining room meals, housekeeping, laundry services and an emergency call and security system. Residents enjoy a full schedule of activities, arts and crafts, gardening, transportation, wellness programs and a beauty and barber shop. Pastoral counseling and physical, occupational and speech therapy are also available. The facility includes a chapel, library, multipurpose room, sun porch and solariums.

A nonprofit nondenominational retirement community, Our Lady of Hope Health Center is sponsored by the Catholic Diocese of Richmond and managed by Coordinated Services Management Inc. There are no entrance fees.

St. Mary's Woods
1257 Marywood Ln. • 741-8624

In the West End across from Gayton Shopping Center, St. Mary's Woods is a nonprofit retirement community sponsored by the Catholic Diocese of Virginia. Residents live in studio, one- or two-bedroom apartments with kitchens and patios or bay windows.

The community provides security and a full range of other services. Facilities include a medical/outpatient clinic, a beauty and barber shop, a dining room, a library, a chapel, a whirlpool, a large multipurpose room, activity rooms and a craft room equipped with a ceramic kiln.

Assisted-living residents enjoy the same apartment selection and amenities with the addition of special services. The staff includes a full-time registered nurse and 24-hour nursing assistance.

Residents can participate in exercise programs, art and religion classes and community service projects. They can play bingo and bridge and go to movies.

INSIDERS' TIP

Summerhill at Stony Point is the first retirement community in the area where you can own your own home and still receive the support and amenities of a retirement community.

"I like all the tradition here.

Mom likes all the new ideas."

Our new health services include special care neighborhoods in assisted living and health care, and more private rooms in the Via Health Care Center. Focusing on creative, structured resident programs, we value our fifty-year tradition of building relationships with residents and families. For the best of yesterday and today, call 804-355-5721.

A licensed facility of
Virginia United Methodist Homes, Inc.

THE HERMITAGE

1600 Westwood Ave.
Richmond, VA 23227
www.hermitage-vumh.com

EQUAL HOUSING
OPPORTUNITY

Monthly rates range from $1,355 to $2,677 and include services, utilities and meals. There are no entrance fees.

Summerhill at Stony Point
9250 Forest Hill Ave. • 320-8312

This was the first and may be the only retirement community in the area where you can buy a home. To live here, you must be at least 55 years old and capable of living independently. Situated on 19 partly wooded acres beside a lake, Summerhill at Stony Point is within walking distance of the Stony Point Shopping Center. Arranged in a village setting, 88 homes are available with one, two or three bedrooms. All of the homes are one story, with brick or vinyl siding and cedar-shake roofs. Some are lakefront. There is also a lodge with a private dining hall, exercise room, library, activity room and common area.

The scenery is beautiful, and it's not unusual to see residents and their grandchildren fishing for bream and bass in the lake. Known as a place to hear live music, the community sponsors concerts at the lodge.

The community is affiliated with Bon Secours Richmond Health System and provides a full range of support services including a full-time activity coordinator, wellness and fitness programs, security, emergency medical call buttons, exterior home maintenance and grounds upkeep, trash pickup, transportation, emergency response, meals and home healthcare alternatives. Prices range from $110,000 to $225,000.

HCR Manorcare Health Services
2125 Hilliard Rd. • 266-9666

HCR Manorcare offers assisted living in a gracious, upscale environment. People who live here are usually surviving spouses in their 80s or 90s. Located in the Lakeside area, across from the Lewis Ginter Botanical Garden, the two-story brick home includes 52 units. A full range of support services are provided, including meals, an activities program, a beauty shop, exercise equipment and an emergency call system. Residents enjoy shopping, movies, music programs, bridge, games and a variety of other activities.

There is no entrance fee, and monthly rates start at $2,160, depending on the size of the apartment and the number of occupants.

The Virginian
300 Twinridge Ln. • 330-4252

Between Bon Air and Midlothian Turnpike in Chesterfield County, The Virginian offers 117 one- or two-bedroom apartments or studios for people age 55 or older who are capable of living independently. Most apartments have patios or balconies. Facilities include craft and multipurpose rooms, billiards, a library, a chapel, a big-screen TV, a lounge and an exercise room. Services include meals, transportation, housekeeping, planned activities and an emergency alert system.

Monthly rates range from about $1,000 to $2,000 and include utilities, meals, transportation and housekeeping.

Westminster Canterbury
1600 Westbrook Ave. • 264-6000

There is usually a waiting list of people who want to live in this life-care community, so many retirees make plans to move here many years in advance. Sponsored by the Presbyterian and Episcopal churches, this is the only retirement community in Richmond accredited by the American Association of Homes and Services for the Aged (AAHSA).

Westminster Canterbury opened in 1975 and offers 341 independent-living apartments, 96 assisted-living apartments and 150 private rooms in the healthcare center. Individual cottages for independent living are also available through The Glebe, an organization of Westminster Canterbury that offers individual cottages, with separate rates and contracts for services.

Residents here enjoy the truly intergenerational atmosphere created by the highly rated on-site child development center. Some residents volunteer to hold babies and read or play with the preschoolers. Those who don't participate as volunteers enjoy seeing the youngsters strolling the grounds and using the pool and other facilities.

Services and facilities at Westminster Canterbury include a new computer center, heated indoor pool and fitness center, a coffee shop, a laundry room, banking, a beauty and barber

Working Together To Care For You

St. Mary's Woods Retirement Community and Our Lady of Hope Health Center are located in two beautiful residential settings in Richmond's West End. Sponsored by the Catholic Diocese of Richmond, both communities are non-profit and non-denominational. A full CONTINUUM OF CARE is offered between St. Mary's Woods and Our Lady of Hope Health Center with NO ENTRANCE FEES and a PRIORITY ADMISSION exchange.

St. Mary's Woods Retirement Community

1257 Marywood Lane
Richmond, VA 23229
Independent Living and
Assisted Living Services
in an apartment setting.
804-741-8624

Our Lady of Hope Health Center

13700 North Gayton road
Richmond VA 23233
Three levels of specialized care: Assisted Living Center
Nursing Center
The Christopher Center—designed especially for Alzheimer's and Dementia residents.
804-360-1960

EQUAL HOUSING OPPORTUNITY

shop, a gift shop, catering, transportation, valet service, a pharmacy, physical therapy, doctors' and dentists' office, a clinic, a library and a chapel.

There are several contractual options, and entrance fees may be required. Monthly rates start at $1,303 and range, depending on the size of the apartment, services and number of occupants.

The William Byrd Apartment Homes
2501 W. Broad St. • 359-5200

Designed for people age 62 or older with moderate incomes, this retirement community was financed through the tax credit program and offers independent living in the historic William Byrd Hotel across from the Science Museum of Virginia.

Renovated and readapted in 1996, the old hotel now includes 107 one-bedroom apartments and activity areas on the first floor. A designated Virginia historic landmark, the original marble floors, staircase and woodwork have been restored, and the common areas are decorated in the style of the mid- to late-1920s.

Conveniently located near downtown Richmond, the William Byrd is on the bus line, and residents are within walking distance of the Senior Center of Richmond on Monument Avenue, and nearby grocery stores, pharmacies, banks, museums and cultural activities.

Services include an optional meal plan, laundry, home healthcare visits, 24 hour pull-cord emergency service and 24 hour attendant-controlled entry and security.

One-year leases are available. Monthly rates range from $475 to $575. Utilities are included.

Health magazine has named Richmond as No. 1 in the nation based on opportunities for a combination of healthy lifestyle and first-class medical care.

Healthcare

Richmond is a pace-setting medical community and home to the fourth-largest university-affiliated teaching hospital in the nation. Its medical researchers are the lead players in a national study of childhood cancer, it is a focal point of genetic research, and it is the national headquarters of the United Network of Organ Sharing that links transplant centers, organ procurement organizations and laboratories across the United States.

The American Medical Association has designated Greater Richmond as a Prime Medical Center and *Health* magazine has named the city as No. 1 in the nation based on opportunities for a combination of healthy lifestyle and first-class medical care.

The city is emerging as a hub of biomedical firms and is the home of the Center for Innovative Technology's Biotechnology Institute where work is underway on everything from curing sleep disorders to running clinical trials of a vaccine to prevent tooth decay. A new 20-acre, $180 million, 1.5-million-square-foot Virginia Biotechnology Research Park opened in 1995 in downtown Richmond. Now fully complete, it houses the state forensic and medical examiner's offices and employs as many as 3,000 scientific and support personnel. The park is adjacent to Virginia Commonwealth University's Medical College of Virginia, one of the top-ranked medical schools in sponsored biomed research. Already more than 50 biotech companies have been attracted to the Richmond area and a Virginia Biotechnology Association has been formed.

Richmond surgeons pioneered heart and kidney transplants, and many of the transplantation procedures used today were perfected at the Medical College of Virginia many years ago. Gerontology professionals seek the latest information on aging through the Medical College of Virginia's Geriatric Education Center, which offers live, interactive teleconferences throughout the world.

Hospitals

Among the medical resources available to Richmond area residents are 12 acute-care and nine specialty hospitals.

Charter Westbrook Behavioral Health System
1500 Westbrook Ave. • 266-9671

This private psychiatric and chemical-dependency treatment facility for children, adolescents and adults is affiliated with Charter Medical Corporation and is Virginia's largest private psychiatric hospital. The 210-bed facility provides free 24-hour assessments, referring patients to an appropriate program and physician. Community education programs are sponsored all year, and a speakers bureau is available to groups. It also operates a counseling center in Fredericksburg.

Children's Hospital
2924 Brook Rd. • 321-7474

Private, nonprofit Children's Hospital offers specialized inpatient and outpatient services for children and young adults from birth to age 21. Medical-surgical specialties include developmental pediatrics, allergy, anesthesiology, cardiology, dentistry, endocrinology, gastroenterology, neurology, neurosurgery, physical medicine and rehabilitation, ophthalmology, oral surgery, orthopedic surgery, otolaryngology, plastic surgery, radiology, rheumatology and urology. In addition, the hospital offers special therapy and support services including career development, child-adolescent psychology, education, child-life activities, nutrition counseling, occupational and physical therapies, social services and speech pathology-audiology. Recently established, the Neurosciences Center for Children provides specialists from Children's Hospital and the Medical College of Virginia to treat a variety of neurological problems. The Motion Analysis Laboratory at Children's Hospital is one of only a few of such facilities on the East Coast and is designed to provide help for individuals with functional problems. Adding to their full range of services, Children's Hospital offers limited therapy services and specialty programs in the West End and South Richmond.

Chippenham Medical Center
7101 Jahnke Rd. • 320-3911

South of the James River, Chippenham Medical Center is Central Virginia's largest private, comprehensive healthcare facility with 466 beds. Special units include the Virginia Heart Center, Cancer Treatment Center, Chest Pain and Emergency Room, Women's Medical Center, Central Virginia Laser Center, Sleep Disorders Center, Sports Medicine and Occupational Health Center and Diabetes Treatment Center. Chippenham also operates Tucker Pavilion, a 113-bed substance abuse and mental-health facility that provides numerous treatment options for adults and adolescents. Its Fast Track Emergency Room is designed to separate those with minor medical needs from acutely ill patients. The hospital is owned by Columbia/HCA Healthcare Corp.

HealthSouth Medical Center
7700 Parham Rd. • 747-5600, 747-5757 Dial-a-Nurse

HealthSouth, once known to Richmonders as St. Luke's, is a 200-bed hospital in the West End. The medical center offers excellent acute-care services in most medical and surgical areas and specializes in oncology, orthopedics and sports medicine. In addition, it houses both inpatient and outpatient physical rehabilitation facilities and the Virginia Center for Pain Man-

FYI

Unless otherwise noted, the area code for all phone numbers listed in this chapter is 804.

agement. The medical center's free Dial-a-Nurse service enables people to call and speak with a nurse who will answer questions, send information or make a referral to a doctor.

Henrico Doctors' Hospital
1602 Skipwith Rd. • 289-4500

This popular 340-bed West End hospital is a comprehensive facility and has been recognized as one of "America's best heart hospitals" by a book of the same name. It has also been recognized for excellence in cardiac surgery by the *Wall Street Journal* and the *Consumers Guide to Hospitals*. Its Women's Pavilion offers obstetrics, infertility treatment, newborn and pediatric intensive care and pediatrics. Its Virginia Transplant Center handles heart, liver and kidney transplants. The hospital's Virginia Laser Center was the first hospital in the state to perform innovative laser surgeries, including laproscopic vagotomy, a laser treatment of stomach ulcers. The mid-1990s saw the addition of an expanded Pediatrics Center (with a pediatrics emergency room), a Joint Replacement Center, a Chest Pain Center and an Orthopedic/Neurological Unit. The hospital is affiliated with Columbia/HCA Healthcare Corp.

Johnston-Willis Hospital
1401 Johnston-Willis Dr. • 330-2000

Chesterfield County's only hospital, this 282-bed acute-care facility has the latest in laser and diagnostic technology. Its reputation has attracted top specialists, and it has 11 service centers that work together to promote faster and safer recovery. These include the Center for Outpatient Surgery, Physical Rehabilitation Services, the Center for Work Re-Entry, Home Therapies, the Healthy Weigh Weight-Loss Program, Physician and Fertility Referral, Pediatrics and the hospital's own Sports and Fitness Center. The hospital also has a 24-hour, full-service emergency center as well as cancer, heart, diabetic and women's-

INSIDERS' TIP

Plans are underway in Henricus Park to build a replica of what is believed to be the nation's first hospital.

health centers. A wing provides private, home-like Family-Centered Single-Room Maternity Care that allows husband/family overnight stays. The hospital is owned by Columbia/HCA Healthcare Corp.

McGuire Veterans Affairs Medical Center
1201 Broad Rock Blvd. • 675-5000

This is one of the largest healthcare facilities in the Richmond area and is the leader in VA hospitals. Named after the local physician who originated the concept of free care for veterans after the Civil War, Hunter Holmes McGuire, the hospital has been serving veterans since 1946. The original facility was replaced about a decade ago by a new $116 million, 814-bed hospital that features a wide range of services. Strongly affiliated with Medical College of Virginia Hospitals, it houses one of the largest transplant centers in the nation. Its 120-bed spinal cord injury center has received widespread acclaim. The hospital's other special units include a hospice and a nursing home. There are also units for surgical and intensive care, coronary care and drug and alcohol dependency treatment.

Medical College of Virginia Hospitals
401 N. 12th St. • 828-9000

Nationally renowned for its emergency medical facilities and Level I trauma center, Medical College of Virginia Hospitals of Virginia Commonwealth University is the only local hospital listed in the book *The Best Hospitals in America*. Its heart transplant program was one of the first two in the nation to be certified by Medicare. Surgeons at the hospital today also perform liver, kidney, heart-lung, pancreas, bone marrow, corneal, bone and tissue transplants. Its Massey Cancer Center, a regional referral center for the state, is in the vanguard of cancer research, exploring tumor immunology, anticancer drug therapy and childhood cancer. Neonatal intensive care and research into infant health problems are among specialized programs at the Children's Medical Center. The first civilian burn unit in the country was opened here, and the hospitals are the site of one of a handful of federally funded geriatric education and psychiatric cen-

ters in the country. With 903 beds, 92 outpatient clinics and four family counseling centers, Medical College of Virginia Hospitals is a formidable asset for the city.

Capitol Medical Center
701 W. Grace St. • 775-4100

Capitol Medical Center has 180 beds, all in private rooms at semiprivate rates. It is the only general medical-surgical hospital in the Richmond area where you will find this kind of a deal. The hospital is in the VCU area and has a 24-hour emergency room. In addition to medical and surgical services, intensive care and outpatient surgery, Capitol specializes in occupational medicine and psychiatric and neurological care.

HealthSouth Rehabilitation Hospital of Virginia
5700 Fitzhugh Ave. • 288-5700

The specialized, multidisciplinary team here provides advanced care to patients with a variety of diagnoses, such as amputation, arthritis, chronic pain, joint replacement, strokes, brain injury, joint replacement, strokes, brain injury, spinal cord injury, pulmonary, speech and hearing impairment and work-related injury.

This 40-bed inpatient hospital offers spacious patient and group therapy rooms, as well as a large gym and swimming pool, beautifully landscaped courtyards and a community dinning room. "Dedicated to rebuilding lives, one day at a time," the hospital offers rehabilitation programs designed to meet individualized needs.

Retreat Hospital
2621 Grove Ave. • 254-5100

In the Fan District near the Virginia Museum, Retreat traces its roots to the days when it was the first hospital in Richmond. Always known for a high level of personal care, the 227-bed hospital has in recent years made substantial investments in new technology and facilities. It has a 24-hour emergency center and offers a full range of inpatient and outpatient medical and surgical services. The hospital, affiliated with Columbia/HCA Healthcare Corp., provides a variety of acute services, including cardiac care (with open-heart facilities), orthopedics, endoscopy, pulmonary medicine, neurology, oncology and women's and senior services. Services include pain management, plastic surgery, endoscopy, MRI, CT scans, X-rays, cardiac rehabilitation and lab testing. It serves Hanover County with an outpatient surgical center in Mechanicsville at 7016 Lee Park Road, 730-9000.

Richmond Community Hospital
1500 N. 28th St. • 225-1700

This is the only acute care hospital on the city's east side. Besides general medical-surgical patients and an expanding outpatient ambulatory service, the 104-bed hospital operates a 24-hour Urgent Care Center and treats heart conditions and other serious medical or surgical complications. Its psychiatric unit specializes in treatment of adult patients with chronic or acute mental disorders. The hospital is affiliated with Bon Secours-Richmond Health Corp.

Richmond Eye and Ear Hospital
1001 E. Marshall St. • 775-4500, 775-4527
Specialist Connection

As Richmond's only specialty-care surgical hospital, Richmond Eye and Ear Hospital is the leading provider of microsurgery of the eye, ear, nose and throat as well as of oral, plastic and reconstructive surgery. The Joint Commission for Accreditation of Healthcare Organizations awarded the hospital with "Accreditation with Commendation" for 1995-1998. It has been ranked as one of the top hospitals in central region for efficiency and productivity by the Virginia Health Services Cost Review Council. The hospital's Virginia Center for Cosmetic and Reconstructive Surgery offers free educational consultations. The Specialist Connection is the hospital's physician referral program. Free educational pamphlets are available on numerous specialty-care topics. Richmond Eye and Ear Hospital has the most complete inventory of state-of-

the-art ophthalmology equipment and services in the region.

Memorial Regional Medical Center
8260 Atlee Rd., Mechanicsville • 254-6000

Formerly known as Richmond Memorial Hospital, Memorial Regional Medical Center opened its doors to patients on May 30, 1998. The first acute-care hospital in Hanover County, this 225-bed facility is designed around a healthcare delivery concept called "family-centered care." It's located near the intersection of Atlee and Meadowbridge Roads at Hanover Medical Park.

The hospital offers the full spectrum of healthcare services for families, including acute care, ambulatory services, obstetrics and a 24-hour emergency room. Other outpatient services available at Hanover Medical Park include diagnostics and treatment, physical rehabilitation (owned and operated by Sheltering Arms Physical Rehabilitation Hospital), radiation therapy, urology and physician practices, including primary care and sub-specialties.

Memorial Regional Medical Center is affiliated with Bon Secours–Richmond Health Corp.

St. Mary's Hospital
5801 Bremo Rd. • 285-2011

In the West End, St. Mary's is housed in impressive facilities at Monument Avenue and Bremo Road. It has 391 beds and an active emergency room (including a Children's Emergency Center), and it provides a broad array of services. These include coronary, intensive and medical-surgical care, a comprehensive cancer program, hospice, total joint replacement, psychiatric care, sleep disorders and women's services. Its nursery and maternity New Life Center is a popular place, and the hospital has a neonatal and pediatric intensive care unit. St. Mary's is the home of the Virginia Kidney Stone Center. It offers home

---

INSIDERS' TIP

A good way to get rid of the winter blahs and improve your psychological health in February is to take in the Maymont Flower and Garden Show at Richmond Centre.

healthcare and ambulatory surgery, and it has introduced a new bedside registration program. The hospital is affiliated with Bon Secours-Richmond Health Corp.

Sheltering Arms Physical Rehabilitation Hospital
1311 Palmyra Ave. • 342-4100

Sheltering Arms, a private, nonprofit institution, provides the state's most comprehensive physical rehabilitation services. With the area's only therapeutic heated swimming pool, Sheltering Arms offers a therapeutic heated swimming pool, with memberships available to anyone with a disability. Outpatient programs are offered to individuals with brain injury, stroke, spinal cord injury, arthritis, amputation, neuromuscular disorders such as Multiple Sclerosis Post-Polio Syndrome and Parkinson's Disease. Specialty outpatient clinics are provided for treatment of sports and orthopedic injuries. Day rehabilitation and back-to-work programs are offered at the newest Sheltering Arms' facility at St. Mary's Hospital, 288-1545. Day rehab and outpatient physical therapy are offered at Hanover Medical Park, 730-0196 and 730-0175, respectively. Sheltering Arms has an inpatient facility for more severe cases and it's adjoined with Memorial Regional Medical Center. It has 40 beds and can be reached at 764-7054.

Stuart Circle Hospital
413 Stuart Cir. • 358-7051,
359-WELL Call-for-Health line

In the Fan District at the intersection of Monument Avenue and Lombardy Street, this 153-bed general medical-surgical hospital offers a full range of advanced services. Special services include chemical dependency treatment, intensive care, coronary care, cardiac services, a women's unit, accredited mammography services, occupational medicine, orthopedics including sports medicine, home health and surgical services including laproscopy and laser surgery. Stuart Circle was the first hospital in Virginia to open a chest pain center as part of its 24-hour emergency room.

If you are looking for a doctor or if you have medical questions, you can dial its Call For Health line and get answers from regis-

tered nurses. The hospital is affiliated with Bon Secours–Richmond Health Corp.

Tucker Psychiatric Pavilion
7101 Jahnke Rd. at Chippenham Pkwy.
• 323-8695

This 113-bed psychiatric and chemical-dependency treatment facility is affiliated with Chippenham Medical Center. Tucker's professional staff provides a wide range of services to adolescents and adults. Treatment settings include inpatient, partial hospitalization and intensive outpatient programs.

Virginia Heart Institute
205 N. Hamilton St. • 359-9265

The Virginia Heart Institute was established in 1972 as the first outpatient cardiac hospital in the United States to provide ambulatory cardiac catheterization. Medical advances in early identification of coronary disease led the Virginia Heart Institute to the development of a cardiac rehabilitation program in 1976 for patients with prior coronary angiography. In order to treat heart disease in its early stages, the Virginia Heart Institute recommends a complete heart screening with its state-of-the-art equipment and techniques for individuals 35 years of age and older. If a patient is diagnosed with heart disease, the Virginia Heart Institute offers a treatment and monitoring program and aids the patient in resuming a normal, healthier lifestyle. Common treatment includes drug therapy which may eliminate the need for cardiac surgery.

Virginia Treatment Center for Children
515 N. 10th St. • 828-3129

Formerly affiliated with the state mental health department, this public psychiatric hospital for adolescents and children is now part of the Department of Psychiatry of the Medical College of Virginia Hospitals. With a wide range of services, the center provides inpatient hospitalization and partial hospitalization programs. The hospital is unusual in that it reaches out to serve Virginia's mental health system with training opportunities, public education, technical assistance and consultation rooted in its 30 years of experience with young Virginians and their families. In 1990 it was the only psychiatric hospital in Virginia rated among the top 10 percent nationally, and in 1992 the hospital won a national award from the American Psychiatric Association.

West End Behavioral Healthcare System

12800 West Creek Pkwy. • 784-2200

West End Behavioral Healthcare System, formerly known as Psychiatric Institute of Richmond, has an 84-bed facility in the West Creek section of western Henrico County, across from the future Motorola site. The full-service facility offers outpatient, day treatment and brief-stay acute services for adolescents. It also offers 24-hour assessment and referral services. Its innovative psychiatric and substance-abuse treatment alternatives are designed to meet the challenges of today's lifestyles.

911

Dialing 911 will put you in touch with an enhanced emergency communications network that serves Richmond and the counties of Chesterfield, Goochland, Hanover, Henrico and Powhatan. The system can identify the address from which you are calling and is designed to take care of emergency, fire, police and rescue calls. If you need emergency medical transportation you also can call 911, but you should call a rescue squad or ambulance services' business telephone number if your need is simply for routine transportation to or from a hospital. If you call 911 in a nonemergency you are subject to a fine.

Walk-in Medical Centers

Like metropolitan areas across the nation, Richmond has a number of walk-in family medical centers. Most are open every day for extended hours, and no appointment is necessary.

Chester Family Medcare
12900 Jefferson Davis Hwy., Chester
• 796-2373

Patient First
2205 N. Parham Rd. • 346-8083
2300 E. Parham Rd. • 346-9018
11020 Hull Street Rd. • 346-8707
8110 Midlothian Tnpk. • 965-9175
12101 Chalkley Rd., Chester • 965-9066
12 N. Thompson St. • 965-0079
3370 Pump Rd. • 965-5535

Urgent Care
400 Ste. A Glenside Drive at Staples Mill Rd. • 262-4763

Nonprofit Health Services

There are many health organizations, clinics and services that are publicly funded or are supported by private contributions. Many charge patients on a sliding scale based on their ability to pay. Some of these organizations and services are listed below.

Fan Free Clinic
1010 N. Thompson St.
• 358-8538, 358-6343

Instructive Visiting Nurse Association
908 N. Thompson St. • 355-7100

McGuire Veterans Affairs Medical Center Outpatient Clinic
1201 Broad Rock Blvd. • 675-5000

Memorial Guild Guidance Clinic
2319 E. Broad St. • 649-1605

Richmond Area High Blood Pressure Center
1200 W. Cary St. • 359-9375

INSIDERS' TIP

The stature of Richmond's medical community has been nationally recognized since the mid-1800s. The U.S. Medical Association held its annual convention here in 1852.

Richmond AIDS Information Network
1010 N. Thompson St.
• 358-AIDS, 358-6343

Richmond Medical Center for Women
118 N. Boulevard • 359-5066

VCU/MCV A. D. Williams Clinic
1200 E. Marshall St. • 828-3780

VCU Psychological Services Center
806 W. Franklin St. • 828-8069

Virginia League for Planned Parenthood
Tower Bldg. • 355-4358

Health Departments

You're likely to have a health clinic within minutes of wherever you live in Richmond. These clinics provide a variety of medical and educational services, including prenatal care, family planning and immunizations. Most clinics are general service clinics but some specialize in mental health and women's health

(they are so noted). Though government funded and operated, these clinics will charge for their services — with the exception of childhood immunizations which are free — but don't let that discourage you from seeking them out, since patients are billed on an ability-to-pay basis.

Certain clinics allow walk-ins on certain days, but it's always best to call and make an appointment, or at least see when walk-in days are being held. The following is a list of clinics throughout the Greater Richmond area.

Richmond

South Richmond Health Center
4730 Southside Plaza • 780-2642

Calhoun Health Center
426 Calhoun St. • 780-4588

This facility performs immunizations and focuses on nursing case management.

Chest and STD Clinic
500 N. 10th St. • 780-6855

The Clinic focuses on chest diseases, communicable diseases and sexually transmitted diseases.

A shady spot is a great beginning to a relaxing afternoon.

Family & Child Health Program
900 E. Marshall St. • 646-3337

This is a good number to call if you're interested in preventive care. The professionals here will teach you how to get and stay healthy.

Richmond Behavioral Health Authority
107 S. 5th St. • 819-4000

This is a good source for help and information with regard to substance abuse, mental health and retardation. The department does not treat patients but rather evaluates interested parties and can refer them to the appropriate treatment centers.

Henrico County

Henrico County Health Department
8600 Dixon Powers Dr. • 672-4651

Henrico Mental Health Center
10299 Woodman Rd.
• 261-8500, 261-8484 24-hour number

Chesterfield County

Chesterfield County Health Department
9501 Lucy Corr Dr. • 748-1691, 768-7202 mental health center

Hanover County

Hanover County Health Department and Mental Health Center
12312 Washington Hwy., Ashland
• 752-4313 health department; 752-4200 mental health and crisis center

Referral Services

Physicians

Bell Atlantic's *Greater Richmond Yellow Pages* carries more than 75 pages of listings of physicians, almost twice as many pages as

it devotes to lawyers. If you don't have friends, relatives or business associates who can recommend a physician, there are a number of referral services and organizations in town ready to help you. Referral services are free.

In addition, many hospitals will have their own physician referral service. You might want to check with the hospital nearest you. At the end of this section, we've listed a few of the larger hospital-operated services.

Richmond Academy of Medicine
• 643-6631

This referral service lists more than 1,200 physicians and specialists who are members of the Academy. The service will provide the names of three physicians, based on your description of your needs.

Columbia/HCA Physician Referral Service
• 330-4000, (800) 888-DOCS

Columbia/HCA offers information on physicians affiliated with Columbia/HCA Healthcare Corp. The Columbia/HCA hospital affiliates are Chippenham Medical Center, Hanover Outpatient Center, Johnston-Willis Hospital, Henrico Doctors' Hospital and Retreat Hospital.

Medical College of Virginia Hospitals
• (800) 762-6161

Medical College of Virginia Hospitals has an in-house physician-referral service that you can call for information about the many services provided by MCV Hospitals.

Bon Secours Referral Service
• 270-DRDR; (800) 468-0199

A service of St. Mary's Hospital, more than 1,200 physicians in Central Virginia and Tidewater are listed with them.

Charter-Westbrook Hospital
• 261-7121

HealthSouth Medical Center
• 747-5679

Richmond Community Hospital
• 281-8520

Richmond Eye and Ear Hospital
• 775-4527

Memorial Regional Medical Center
• 270-3737

St. Mary's Hospital
• 270-3737

Stuart Circle Hospital
• 281-8520

Virginia Center for Plastic and Reconstructive Surgery
• 775-4526

Dentists

Richmond Dental Society
• 379-2534

If you're looking for a dentist in the area, your best bet is to call the Richmond Dental Society. This is the American Dental Association's local chapter. They will provide referrals based on your geographic location within the metropolitan area or on your need for a specialist.

Chiropractors

Virginia Chiropractic Association
• 344-1565

If you're looking for a chiropractor, this service can help put you in touch with the one best suited for you. Almost 260 chiropractic doctors are listed with this association.

Alternative/ Holistic Healthcare

With regard to alternative and holistic healthcare options, Richmond is teeming with providers; however, there is no clearinghouse organization to direct you to, nor are there currently any publications. Since most alternative/holistic practitioners work alone, out of their house or a single office or through a shop, it's difficult to keep tabs on their movements.

For starters, you can look in the phone book under "Holistic Medicine." It's best to first decide which modality you'd like to pursue, perhaps discussing your options with a physician or friends. Everything from acupressure and reflexology to homeopaths and herb treatment can be found in Richmond; unfortunately, you need to know what you want, otherwise its a maze.

On occasion, practitioners will advertise in some of the local magazines, such as *Style Weekly*, but don't bet on it. Most of their advertising is done by word-of-mouth; it's far more practical, and needless to say, profitable. Though there are a few alternative healthcare bookstores in the area, they hardly reflect the scope of what's available; instead, they tend to focus on the modalities in which they specialize (in other words, focusing on the practitioners whom they have on board). Toll-free numbers are available for most modalities. You might want to consult a local bookstore for a guide, such as *Alternative Medicine: A Definitive Guide*, compiled by The Burton Goldberg Group. It'll put you in touch with a provider in the area.

Numbers to Call

In the event of an emergency, here is a quick reference to some of the more frequented helplines.

Emergency (requiring ambulance, police or fire department)	911
AIDS Hotline	358-AIDS
Child Abuse Hotline	(800) 552-7096
Crisis Pregnancy Center	353-2320
Emergency Shelter	Families, 782-9276; Men, 788-0880; Women, 278-8700

Missing Children Information	(800) 822-4453
National Sexually Transmitted Disease Hotline	(800) 227-8922
Poison Control Center	828-9123
Psychiatric Crisis/Substance Abuse Hotline	780-8003
Youth Emergency Shelter (ages 12-17)	740-7322
YWCA Women's Advocacy Program	796-3066
(Crisis intervention for raped and battered women)	

An extensive list of telephone numbers of agencies and organizations offering support and counseling services in the Richmond area is carried under Community Service Numbers in the front of the white pages of the local telephone book. Here are just a few.

Al-Anon (for families of alcoholics)	353-4885
Alateen (for children of alcoholics)	353-4885
Alcoholics Anonymous	355-1212
Alzheimer's Association	320-HOPE
Anonymous HIV Testing & Counseling	828-2210
American Red Cross	780-2250
Big Brothers/Big Sisters Services Inc.	282-0856
Capital Area Agency on Aging	343-3000
Deaf and Hard of Hearing Community Counseling	762-9671
Grief Resource Center	360-2884
Learning Disabilities Council	748-5012
Leukemia Society	673-8855
Meals on Wheels	673-5035
Mothers Against Drunk Driving (MADD)	278-9063

Travellers Aid Society of Virginia		643-0279
United Way Services Referral		275-2000
Widowed Persons Support Group		288-4474
YWCA Women's Hotline:	Richmond shelter	643-0888
	Chesterfield shelter	796-3066

Blessed by a high degree of business and parental involvement, area schools maintain high standards of quality and have a national reputation for developing innovative programs.

Schools and Child Care

Excellent public schools and numerous private schools offer a variety of educational choices for residents of the Greater Richmond area. Blessed by a high degree of business and parental involvement, area schools maintain high standards of quality and have a national reputation for developing innovative programs.

Ongoing, cooperative efforts among the schools also benefit the entire metropolitan area. For example, five area school systems share the resources and programs of the locally funded Mathematics-Science Center; Thomas Jefferson High School is a regional Governor's School; Henrico televises classes to more than 30 school divisions throughout the state; and students throughout the area have access to the MCI Hotline, staffed by teachers who help with homework assignments. Area schools also participate in a Cultural Relations Fellowship Program, an exchange program between local students and German students that gives them an opportunity to live, work and attend school in a foreign country.

Each county and the City of Richmond has its own unique school system. All of them offer federally funded preschool programs such as Early Childhood Special Education, Title I and Head Start. In addition, they also all offer special educations for students with special needs and learning disabilities. An overview of each school system is included in this chapter followed by a sampling of private schools and child-care providers in the area.

Public Schools

City Schools

Richmond School System
301 N. Ninth St. • 780-7710

Amid the challenges facing most urban school systems, Richmond has gained a reputation for its diversity of award-winning programs for gifted and talented students, advanced-placement studies, technical and vocational schools, and magnet and model schools.

The system serves more than 28,000 students and operates 35 elementary schools, 10 middle schools, nine high schools, four exceptional education facilities, three vocational educational schools and a nationally recognized arts and humanities center.

Beginning with early childhood and continuing through adult education, Richmond's public schools offer expansive instructional programs and a variety of learning environments to meet the needs of all students, regardless of age or ability. Exemplary schools based on model and magnet instructional themes exist at all grade levels. Richmond's public schools are recognized nationally for programs in early childhood, exceptional and vocational education. Both students and faculty have earned regional, state and national honors.

Richmond City School Board

The Richmond City School Board is an elected body responsible for setting policy and ensuring that the school system follows state and federal guidelines. Nine members serve two-year terms. Meetings are held twice a month in the board room on the 17th floor of City Hall. The school board invites citizens to air their views during a 30-minute public information period at each meeting. If you wish to speak, you must register by 10 AM on the day before the meeting. Certain guidelines and restrictions apply to speakers. For more information, call 780-7716.

Enrollment

Some elementary and middle schools have open enrollment policies, but students who live in a school's attendance zone are usually given first priority for enrollment.

At the magnet high schools the first priority is given to students who live in the school's residential area. If a student wishes to attend a magnet program outside their residential area, they must apply to the school.

To apply for a magnet or a model school, parents and their children must first choose which learning environment will best meet their needs and interests. Model elementary schools are divided into three attendance zones to provide parents with a choice of programs. Call or visit the school of your choice and ask for details.

Students entering school for the first time, or those new to the division, must provide the following information at the time of registration: birth certificate, immunization record, Social Security number, proof of address with recent utility bills and a recently completed physical examination report. For further details, call Pupil Placement at 780-7811.

Gifted Students

Richmond Public Schools provide accelerated learning environments for students in kindergarten through 12th grade. Academically advanced secondary students may enroll in advanced placement or honors classes in all subject areas. High school-age students identified as academically gifted or potentially gifted may choose to attend alternative high school programs at Richmond Community High or Open High. For more information, call 780-7805.

FYI

Unless otherwise noted, the area code for all phone numbers listed in this chapter is 804.

Exceptional Education Programs

Students with special needs between the ages of 2 and 22 are provided with classroom environments ranging from resource rooms to special schools that best meet their needs. Richmond's exceptional education program includes nationally recognized facilities such as and a speech center and classes for hearing-impaired students.

The school system includes a vocational program for trainable mentally retarded and severely handicapped students. The program is community-based and includes hands-on vocational training for students at local businesses and public workplaces. For more information, call 780-7312.

Richmond Technical Center

Since opening in 1968, the Richmond Technical Center has been one of the state's premiere regional vocational education centers, serving Richmond and the counties of Charles City, Hanover, King William and New

INSIDERS' TIP

The Richmond Public Schools Harp Ensemble is one of only a few of its kind in the nation. Recently, the ensemble was selected as one of only 17 groups from the U.S. to perform at the London Parade Festival.

Kent. Instructors teach more than 20 technical, trade and business courses to prepare students for entry-level jobs. An evening program for adults is also available.

The center offers flexible hours, after-school courses and site-based instruction. Courses include computer-assisted drafting and design, pre-engineering and management information technology, masonry, cabinetmaking, carpentry, electrical trades, printing, commercial art, auto mechanics, autobody repair, graphics communication, cosmetology, practical nursing, commercial foods, machine trades, welding and electronics.

Arts and Humanities Center

In the Mosby Building at 1002 Mosby Street, the Arts and Humanities Center provides specialists who serve as resource teachers in all areas of the arts. As part of the Artists in the Schools and Writers in the Schools programs, the center also sponsors visual artists, quilters, sculptors, painters, potters and other artists who visit middle and high school art classes to discuss their techniques, philosophies and education.

Volunteers in Public Schools

Richmond also has an especially successful Volunteers in Public Schools program that attracts more than 5,000 volunteers a year from all walks of life who serve as lunch buddies, mentors and tutors. To find out more about volunteering, call 780-7711 or 780-7649.

School-Business Partnership

This program links schools with area corporations to provide students with academic and cultural enrichment activities and organizations. It motivates them to stay in school, expands their knowledge of career options and provides mentors and role models to help build students' self-esteem.

Several hundred businesses, including large corporations, government agencies and small businesses participate in the program. For more information, call 780-7711 or 780-7649.

Kindergarten and Elementary Schools

The elementary education program is de-signed to strengthen students' academics, enrich their cultural experiences and build their self-esteem. Emphasis is placed on reading and communication skills, mathematics and number concepts and an understanding of history and how it shaped the present. The average student/teacher ratio in the elementary schools is 21-to-1.

There are 35 elementary schools, including 12 model schools listed below, which offer a thematic-based instructional approach. Interested students must apply for admission to their schools. Gifted and talented students are challenged through the SPACE (Special Program for Academic and Creative Excellence). For more information contact the executive director of school support, 780-7777 or 780-7788, or call the following model elementary schools:

• Bellevue Model School, 2301 E. Grace St., 780-4417, provides academic enrichment through the visual and performing arts.

• Blackwell Model School, 1600 Everett St., 780-5078, is a family and community education center.

• John B. Cary Model School, 3021 Maplewood Ave., 780-6252, provides quality education.

• J.B. Fisher Model School, 3701 Garden Rd., 327-5612, specializes in critical and creative thinking.

• William Fox Model School, 2300 Hanover Ave., 780-6259, specializes in creative and innovative thinking.

• Ginter Park Model School, 3817 Chamberlayne Ave., 780-8193, focuses on international studies.

• Mary Munford Model School, 211 Westmoreland Ave., 780-6267, also focuses on international studies.

• Southampton Model School, 3333 Cheverly Rd., 320-2434, specializes in environmental science.

• Swansboro Model School, 3160 Midlothian Tnpk., 780-5030, focuses on creative writing.

• Westover Hills Model School, 1211 Jahnke Rd., 780-5002, focuses on communications and technology.

• Whitcomb Court Model School, 2100 Sussex St., 780-4318, specializes in technology.

• Woodville Model School, 2000 N. 28th Street, 780-4821, focuses on the performing and visual arts.

Middle Schools

For students in the 6th through 8th grades, the middle school curriculum is designed to help students master basic skills, understand concepts and problem-solving and explore various electives such as foreign languages, computer technology, fine arts and vocational education. The student/teacher ratio in Richmond city middle schools is 22-to-1.

State-designated vanguard, model and theme-based schools offer instruction in areas such as creative arts, academic enrichment, international studies and technology to provide middle school students with a range of educational settings. All schools offer an academic core of communicative arts, mathematics, science and social studies.

Programs for gifted and talented students, extracurricular opportunities, mentorships and partnership initiatives with area corporations and universities, and activities designed to promote self-esteem and healthy lifestyles are an integral part of the middle school curriculum.

High Schools

Students in the 9th through 12th grades can participate in college preparatory, vocational and technical training, and work-study programs. For advanced students, an honors program offers the opportunity to take a number of college-level courses while still in high school. In 1998, Richmond City seniors earned nearly $14.1 million in scholarships, grants and aid, and almost 80 percent of graduates plan to pursue advanced education.

Richmond offers a variety of high school settings including alternative schools for academically gifted and talented students, one of the nation's few public military high schools, a regional Governor's School, plus magnet programs in teacher training, life sciences, international studies, business enterprise systems, the arts, math, science and technology, and vocational/technical studies. The student/teacher ratio in the high schools is 22-to-1.

The following is a list of the model high schools:

• Armstrong Professional Development Teacher Academy, 1611 N. 31st St., 780-4017, is a joint effort with Richmond Public Schools, the University of Richmond, Virginia Commonwealth University, Virginia State University and Virginia Union University. Students who want to teach observe classrooms and implement innovative instructional approaches designed to meet the needs of urban students.

• Franklin Military, 1611 N. 31st St., 780-8526, is the first and one of the few public military schools in the country.

• Huguenot Life Sciences, 7945 Forest Hill Ave., 320-7967, prepares students for both entry-level careers and higher education in the health professions. Members of healthcare organizations and medical and dental societies provide assistance as program consultants and guest lecturers.

• Thomas Jefferson International and Governmental Studies, 4100 W. Grace St., 780-6028, offers international and governmental studies, concentrating in areas such as International Business and Technology, Diplomacy and Governmental Relations and International Cultures and Law.

• John F. Kennedy Math, Science and Computer Technology, 2300 Cool Ln., 780-4449, offers pre-engineering and pretechnical sequences. Courses include computer-assisted design (CAD) and programming, biology, chemistry, physics and accelerated math courses.

• John Marshall Business Enterprise Systems, 4225 Old Brook Rd., 780-6052, teaches students skills in business management, information systems, business writing and

---

INSIDERS' TIP

In Richmond, the Binford Model Middle School which specializes in international education, world languages and 21st-century careers has built such a strong reputation for excellence, that the school has a waiting list of over 200 students who want to attend school there.

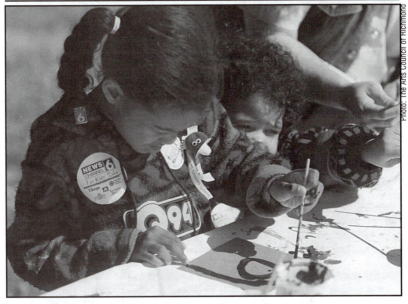

Partners in the Arts, organized by the Arts Council of Richmond, brings arts education into public schools.

speaking and economics. Courses are offered in computer concepts, business communications, marketing, international business information systems and financial management. Local businesses provide resources, mentoring and shadowing experiences.

• Open High, 600 S. Pine St., 780-4661, engages students in college preparatory course work at various locations throughout the community. The school emphasizes independent thinking and community involvement. Internships, university study and mentorships are part of the unique individualized curriculum.

• Richmond Community, 5800 Patterson Ave., 285-1015, instructs students in a college preparatory curriculum that features advanced placement courses and "minimesters," which provide students with opportunities to combine study and travel, and enroll in classes at area universities.

• George Wythe High School for the Arts, 4314 Crutchfield St., 780-5037, opened in 1990 as the area's only public high school program for students interested in studying the visual and performing arts. The school offers courses

in theater, dance, drama, visual arts and arts technology. Practicing artists visit the school regularly to provide demonstrations and master classes, and to offer career guidance. The school system's Arts and Humanities Center is here.

Adult Education

Richmond offers adult education courses during the day at the Adult Learning Center on Leigh Street. The popular evening programs are offered primarily at John Marshall High School and at the Richmond Technical Center. Adult programs are open to all city residents.

County Schools

Chesterfield County

Chesterfield County School System
9900 Krause Rd. • 748-1405

Chesterfield County operates the largest school system in the Richmond area and one of the largest in Virginia. The county serves more than 51,000 students, a number that grows by about a thousand a year. Chesterfield has 59 schools, including the Chesterfield Career Development Center, 9 high schools, 11 middle schools, 36 ele-mentary schools and two alternative schools. Two new schools are planned for the future, including the new Matoaca high school and one elementary school.

Chesterfield schools enjoy a reputation for excellence and have been named for several years by "SchoolMatch" as among ten percent of the nation's schools that have "what parents want." The criteria for this selection include rigorous academics, low student/ teacher ratios, and above-average expenditures in instruction and library/media services.

About 75 percent of its students go on to colleges or technical schools. Chesterfield County students also consistently score higher than the state average on standardized tests, including the SAT. Statistics on test scores and other measurements are available on request.

The school system strives to maintain high academic standards in a safe and respectful environment for learning and promotes community involvement, continuing improvement and use of new technology.

A Curriculum Council and subject-area curriculum committees, which include parents and community members, guide these efforts. School councils, as well as active PTAs and advisory groups, provide additional community involvement and decision making at the individual school level.

Chesterfield County School Board

The first elected school board in Chesterfield County took office in January 1996. The five-member board represents the five county magisterial districts and serves the community as a whole. Members serve four-year terms.

The school board meets twice a month except in July, August, November and December when it meets once. Unless otherwise announced, meetings are usually held in the county administration public meeting room, 9901 Lori Road, in the Courthouse complex. They are open to the public unless otherwise specified by law. You may also see the meetings on a live broadcast aired on Comcast Channel 6.

Public participation is encouraged at every level in the school system. The School Board policy manual and School Board meeting agendas are available for inspection at each school and the School Administration Building, 9900 Krause Rd.

Enrollment

Transfer students should register during school office hours at the school they will attend. For attendance zone information, call 748-1666. Proof of county residency is required, and it's helpful to bring a report card from the previous school. The Chesterfield school will request a transfer of records from the previous school.

Each student enrolling in a Virginia public school for the first time must provide a birth certificate, Social Security number and a medical record of immunizations. Elementary students must also have a physical examination within 12 months of the beginning of the school year

Gifted Education

The county provides services for students identified as gifted at their home schools or through center-based programs at several county schools including Henning Elementary School, Marguerite F. Christian Elementary School and Manchester Middle School. There is also a special mathematics and science program at Clover Hill High School for selected county students. Honors and advanced-placement courses are offered to secondary students. Chesterfield also implemented the international Baccalaureate program at two high schools. And students can participate in two Governor's schools—the Governor's School for International Study in Richmond and the Appomattox Governor's School for Art and Technology in Petersburg.

Special Education

The county provides a full range of special-education programs for students with special needs from birth through age 21. Programs and services are for students who are learning disabled, emotionally disturbed, mentally retarded, multi-handicapped, visually impaired, hearing impaired, and speech and language impaired.

Chesterfield County Career Development Center

The center offers more than 20 career programs including computer information systems, electronics, manufacturing laboratory and licensed practical nursing. The county's Second School Day program offers high school credit courses at night at the center. For more information, call 780-6260.

Business and Industry Partnerships

Communities in Schools supports alternative education at all school levels to help prevent students from dropping out of school. Students may work toward receiving a high school diploma at several locations.

Elementary and Middle Schools

Children must be 5 years old by September 30 of the school year to enroll in kindergarten. A full-day kindergarten program is offered. Chesterfield also offers a preschool program for children with disabilities who must be 2 years old by September 30.

Elementary schools include grades K through 5, and the student/teacher ratio is 24-to-1. Middle schools include grades 6 through 8, and the student/teacher ratio is 22-to-1.

High School

All high schools operate on a seven-period alternating block class schedule similar to a college schedule where students take most of their classes in longer blocks of time on alternating days. Through an agreement with John Tyler Community College, students may receive both high school and college credit in certain courses while still in high school. The student/teaacher ratio is 21-to-1.

Adult Education

More than 200 adult-education courses are offered and serve about 3,000 residents each year. English as a Second Language programs are provided at several schools in the county with a steadily increasing number of students representing more than 20 languages.

Hanover County

Hanover County School System
200 Berkley St., Ashland • 752-6000

Hanover County is enjoying a growing reputation for excellent schools and innovative programs including School Renewal, a school-based management program that provides continuous improvement in school climate, planning, curriculum and instruction, staff development and communication.

Hanover County Public Schools received the prestigious Award for Continuing Excellence (ACE) in 1997, at the Virginia Forum of Excellence, in recognition of the school system's efforts to continue its cycle of improvement and track results. Hanover Schools is the first school system and the first public sector organization to receive this award. (All past awards have gone to private organizations.)

Students in Hanover County consistently score above state and national averages on standardized tests. About 84 percent of the students plan to continue their education after high school.

Schools, students and teachers are frequently recognized throughout the state for excellence. Liberty Middle School and Beaverdam Elementary School were recently recognized as Blue Ribbon Schools by the U.S. Department of Education. The national Blue Ribbon Schools program selects schools based on their leadership, teaching environment, curriculum and instruction, community and parental support, and organizational vitality.

Special enrichment programs in Hanover County include an Artist-in-Residence and Writer-in-Residence. Students explore mathematics and science topics at the Mathematics-Science Center, a resource shared by schools in the metropolitan area. They also participate in the annual Festival of the Arts and Sciences each spring and numerous competitions such as Odyssey of the Mind, Young Authors, a county spelling bee, the Metro Science Fair and Virginia Junior Academy of Sciences.

Hanover County operates 12 elementary schools, three middle schools and three high schools. The middle and high schools were recently expanded and renovated. Pole Green Elementary School is expected to open in the fall of 2000 to accommodate growth.

Hanover County School Board

A school-board member from each of Hanover's seven magisterial districts is appointed to a four-year term by the board of supervisors.

Monthly meetings are held at 7:30 PM on the second Tuesday of each month in the school board office at 200 Berkley Street in Ashland. The public is encouraged to attend meetings and participate

The school board appoints the Superintendent, who acts as the chief administrator and executive officer of county schools.

Enrollment

Contact the Hanover County School Administration Office at 365-4500 for enrollment information.

Classroom Snapshot

All Hanover County schools, K through 12, offer parents a unique voice-mail communication system called "Classroom Snapshot" that enables them to listen to a message recorded by their child's teacher, 24 hours a day. The message summarizes the day's activities, explains homework assignments and includes announcements. Parents can also listen to messages from the principal, general school information and school menus. Hanover schools were the first in Virginia to use this type of voice-mail communication system.

Gifted and Talented

This program serves about 2,000 students who are identified as gifted and talented. Elementary students receive differentiated classroom instruction and enrichment programs.

They also participate in a resource program provided by full-time specialists in gifted and talented education. Middle schools are served by full-time specialists, and gifted and talented resources and seminars are offered as electives to 6th through 8th grade students. In secondary schools, academically gifted students are encouraged to enroll in advanced courses. Students talented in art, creative writing and music are encouraged to enroll in elective courses in their talent areas.

Each high school has a specialist who coordinates enrichment activities. Mentorships are available, and rising juniors and seniors may be selected to participate in the Governor's School for the Gifted, a four-week summer program at area colleges and universities. Seniors are encouraged to apply and participate in the Emerging Leaders program. Offered in partnership with the University of Richmond Jepson School of Leadership, the program includes a summer institute at the university and follow-up seminars during the school year.

A gifted and talented program advisory committee composed of parents, teachers, administrators, students and community representatives is appointed by the school board and meets quarterly. Parents are invited to attend orientation meetings and countywide workshops and seminars. They also receive school-based and county newsletters. For more information, call 365-4554.

Special Education Programs

Hanover County provides special-education and related services to all children with disabilities from birth through age 21. For more information, call 365-4500.

Vocational/Technical Education

Students are encouraged by the school to plan a program of studies within an occupational theme such as business/finance, marketing, engineering/technology, health/human services, agriculture/natural resources and fine arts/media. Juniors and seniors may enroll in selected technical courses at Richmond Technical Center and J. Sargeant Reynolds Community College. Classes taken at J. Sargeant Reynolds Community College earn both high school and college credit. Tech Prep Programs and Youth Apprenticeships with area businesses are also available. For more information, call 365-4646.

Adopt-a-School Partners in Education Programs

Hanover has partnerships with more than 100 area businesses, agencies and civic associations that share resources, personnel and services with the school. In return, schools provide businesses with the use of school facilities, equipment and student decorative projects.

In the Effective Communication for Employment program, more than 92 representatives from area businesses teach 10th and 11th grade students job-seeking and performance skills such as telephone etiquette, interviewing and how to complete applications.

Elementary Schools

The curriculum for kindergarten through 5th grade provides varied educational experiences for students to develop their maximum physical, social, emotional and cognitive potential through programs in language arts, mathematics, social studies, health, science, physical education, art and music. All classes are equipped with computers.

Middle Schools

Students in grades 6 through 8 take a rigorous academic curriculum that includes language arts, mathematics, science, social studies and health/physical education. An alternate day block schedule provides options for students to select art, band, chorus, forensics, gifted/talented resource, computer concepts, technology, teen living, theater arts and structured science research.

Individual needs are met through a Gifted/Talented Program, the Special Education Program and tutorial assistance. Unique features of the curriculum include accelerated-learning opportunities for students to receive high school credit in mathematics and foreign languages. Students must meet a keyboarding requirement by passing a semester course or by passing a proficiency test in keyboarding prior to grade 9. Each grade level contains faculty serving on interdisciplinary teams led by a senior teacher who serves as the

Photo: City of Richmond Parks, Recreation and Community Facilities

Parks and Recreation departments offer after-school programs in everything from martial arts to ballet.

curriculum and instructional leader/coordinator for the grade.

High Schools

Students in grades 9 through 12 may select courses from a comprehensive menu which encourages the development of academic and technical skills. Graduation requirements include proficiency in keyboarding and computer applications as well as four units in history and the social sciences. In addition, students may take advantage of dual-enrollment college courses at J. Sargeant Reynolds Community College, Randolph Macon College or Virginia Commonwealth University.

High school students have opportunities to participate in a variety of special programs including the Model U.N.; the Stock Market competition sponsored by Virginia Commonwealth University; internships with the school system's Channel 36; Youth Symphony; Olympics of the Mind; the Governor's Foreign Language Academies; and the National U.S. Constitution competition, "We the People." In addition, in partnership with the University of Richmond, students may participate in the Emerging Leaders program to develop their potential and explore leadership applications.

Adult Education

The Adult Education Department offers preparatory classes for the General Educational Development (GED) exam, Adult Basic Education (ABE), adult literacy, courses for high school credit and classes for enrichment and skills improvement, including basic and advnaced computer. For more information, call 365-4538.

Henrico County

Henrico County School System
3820 Nine Mile Rd. • 652-3600

One of the state's largest school systems, Henrico County serves nearly 39,000 students, and has always had a strong academic program. About 85 percent of Henrico's graduates continue their education after high school. About a fourth of the students earn a "B" average or better, and about half of the students earn advanced-studies diplomas. Henrico County Public Schools operates 39 elementary schools,

nine middle schools, eight high schools, two technical centers and one adult education facility.

Henrico County Public Schools serve nearly 40,000 students. The system operates 59 schools and has more than 2,400 teachers. In 1997-98, the Nuckols Farm Elementary School opened in the Three Chopt District; the L.Douglas Wilder Middle School opened in the Fairfield District in the spring of 1998.

Five computers in each first through fifth grade classroom greet elementary students thanks to a $10 million computer initiative put in place by the school system during the 1995-96 school year. That addition of 3,500 computers more than doubled the number of computers in the system. To ensure continuity for students as they progress, Henrico has funded a $15.4 million secondary technology initiative to place five computers in each sixth-grade classroom as well as computer networks and at least one mulitmedia computer in every middle and high school classroom.

Recently developed high school specialty centers offer concentrated studies in specific areas including alternative studies; engineering, design and future transportation; the arts; foreign-language immersion; science, mathematics and technology; humanities; communications; leadership, government and global economics; and the international baccalaureate.

Henrico County schools, students and programs have earned state and national recognition. The U.S. Department of Education has recognized seven Henrico schools as national Blue Ribbon schools, including Douglas Freeman High School, Hermitage High School, Godwin High School, Brookland Middle School, Longan Elementary School, Tuckahoe Middle School and Baker Elementary School.

Outstanding and new programs include the aviation program; Japanese taught from Henrico's television studio and broadcast all over the country; Ameurop Cultural Relations Program, a Peer Advisor program; and a vocational program in which students build houses to sell. Also, Springfield Park Elementary School offers a German/English International Program.

Enrollment in Henrico's specialty centers

continues to grow. Each high school is home to at least one of the specialty centers, which offer choices to students who are highly motivated in a particular subject area. Specialty centers include the Center for the International Center for Communications at Varina High School; the Center for Leadership, Government and Global Economics at Freeman High School; the Center for Foreign Language Immersion at Tucker High School; the Center for Science, Mathematics and Technology at Godwin High School; the Center for Engineering, Design and Future Transportation at Highland Springs High School, the Center for Diversified Studies at Virginia Randolph Community High School; and the Center for the Arts at Henrico High School. Moody Middle School offers the first middle school specialty center, the Center for the International Baccalaureate. Students must apply to the specialty centers to be considered for enrollment.

Business and community involvement is encouraged through the Lay Advisory Committee, Community Council Program, Golden Age Program and a number of advisory committees. The Henrico Education Foundation was established in 1991 and is led by area business people to provide opportunities for students and teachers beyond those available in the school system.

Henrico County School Board

A school board member from each of Hanover's seven magisterial districts is elected to a four-year term. Monthly meetings are held at 7:30 PM on the fourth Tuesday of the each month in the Glen Echo Auditorium, 3810 Nine Mile Road in eastern Henrico. The public is encouraged to attend meetings and participate.

Enrollment

General information about Henrico schools is available from the public information office, 652-3726. To find out which school your child will attend, call the research and planning office, 652-3830. Then, contact the principal at the school. If you are transferring from another school division, you will need to provide a birth certificate, proof of residency, an immunization record, Social Security number,

withdrawal papers from the last school attended and a copy of the last report card. The new school will send for a transcript of records. Kindergarten registration is held each spring on publicized dates.

Gifted Program

Students in kindergarten through the 12th grade who are identified as gifted may participate in a variety of academic, creative and community programs. For more information, call 652-3790.

Special Education

Henrico offers special education programs to children from ages 2 to 21. Programs are designed to meet individual handicapping conditions through the development of an individual educational program. Whenever possible, students attend regular classrooms. A Parent Resource Center, 343-6523, at the Math and Science Center provides information and training for parents of special-education students. For more information, call 652-3801.

Technical Education

Vocational-education students choose from a variety of opportunities. They may build houses or fly airplanes, or they may choose to take courses in marketing, home economics, business, agriculture, health occupations, technology or trade and industrial education. Students attend a half-day at their home school and a half-day at either the Hermitage or the Highland Springs Technical Centers. Through the Ameurop Cultural Relations Program, vocational-education students may spend 10-week apprenticeships in West Germany.

School-Business Partnerships

In this partnership program, businesses and schools sign an agreement to share resources. For more information, call 652-3858.

Kindergarten and Elementary Schools

Elementary schools include kindergarten through the 5th grade. An integrated curriculum helps students understand how different areas of study relate while reinforcing the importance of language and communication skills. Weekly art and music instruction as well as physical fitness classes are included as part of the regular elementary program.

Henrico offers a Head Start program at several elementary schools, a Chapter 1 program, and remedial and tutorial assistance programs, including PRIME. The county also offers the English as a Second Language program.

Middle Schools

Academic requirements in middle school (6th through 8th grades) include English, mathematics, science and social studies. Students may also choose exploratory subjects. Henrico middle schools provide a gradual transition from elementary school to high school as courses become more difficult and demands on students become greater. The middle schools are currently being restructured with community and parent feedback.

An alternative middle school in the former Mount Vernon Baptist Church on W. Broad Street near Parham Road is an option for students who are not meeting expectations in regular classroom settings or who need special disciplinary or academic attention. Students at the alternative middle school must adhere to a dress code and develop a strong work ethic, responsibility and respect for others.

High Schools

The curriculum for the 9th through 12th grades includes college preparatory, work/study programs, and vocational and technical training that provide entry-level job skills. Five foreign languages are taught including Japanese. Honors and advanced placement courses are offered for students who demonstrate the ability and desire for in-depth study.

The Virginia E. Randolph Community High School offers an alternative approach to earning a diploma for students who are not performing to their potential.

Adult Education

This program offers adults three ways to complete high school: General Educational Development classes and testing, an External Diploma program and an Adult High School program. English as a Second Language is also available to adults. Henrico also offers dozens of special-interest courses such as furniture upholstering, boating, marketing, management, investment and real estate classes and seminars. A schedule of classes is mailed to county residents twice a year.

An adult education center in Highland Springs includes administrative offices, classrooms and laboratories. Through the Golden Age Program, senior citizens age 60 and older do not have to pay tuition for adult education classes; they also receive free admission to school athletic events and musical productions. For more information, call 328-4095.

Private Schools

Private schools in the city of Richmond and surrounding areas offer a variety of traditional curricula as well as ungraded and other nontraditional learning environments. Some schools have special programs for gifted students or learning-disabled and emotionally disturbed students. Day care and before- and after-school care are also available through some of the schools. Tuition fees vary widely.

Private schools in Virginia have their own accreditation system that is overseen by the Virginia Council for Private Education. Schools that receive VCPE accreditation are recognized by the State Department of Education.

If you're interested in enrolling your child in a private school, the Virginia Association of Independent Schools suggests that you begin your search in the fall a year before you want your child to be enrolled and look for a school with a mission that matches your vision of what you want for your child. Ask for catalogues and contact the admissions office to schedule an interview. You should also visit the school when it's in session. Tours, class visits and informal meetings with students, faculty and administrators are generally available.

Here's a sampling of the private schools in the area. Please note that schools with religious affiliations generally accept students from other religious backgrounds. This list is not meant to be all-inclusive, but is sufficiently comprehensive to start you out well on your search.

All Saints Catholic School
3418 Noble Ave. • 329-7524

About 230 students are enrolled in this coed school which was established in the 1920s as St. Paul's and St. Gertrude's. The schools were combined under the All Saints name about 15 years ago. Instruction is offered for preschool through 8th grade. There is also an after-school program.

Benedictine High School
304 N. Sheppard St. • 355-8679

Benedictine Monks run this boys-only Catholic school that offers college preparatory instruction from 9th through 12th grade. The school enrolls about 290 students. The student body is diverse and represents a variety of neighborhoods, faiths and ethnic groups. JROTC is required of all students to promote citizenship and leadership.

Blessed Sacrement-Huguenot
2501 Academy Rd. • 598-4211

Blessed Sacrement-Huguenot is a coeducational, college-preparatory, nonsectarian, independent school with a Learning Skills Program for college-bound students. This Powhatan County school opened in 1959 and currently enrolls approximately 400 students in preschool through grade 12. Transportation is provided for some areas. Discounts are available if more than one child per family is enrolled.

Collegiate Schools
N. Mooreland Rd. • 741-9722

This college preparatory school in the far West End offers instruction for kindergarten through 12th grade. Class sizes are small and the average student/teacher ratio is about 15-to-1. About 1,500 students are enrolled. An after-school program is available daily until 6 PM. The school is open year round. Some need-based financial assistance is available.

Fork Union Military Academy
Fork Union • (804) 842-3212

Though not in Richmond proper, this private boys' school has been educating Richmond youths since 1898, so it deserves a spot here. Fork Union is about 50 miles west of Richmond and is a nonprofit institution affiliated with the Baptist General Association of Virginia. It is a college preparatory school with more than 95 percent of its graduates going on to higher education. Comprised of a junior school for grades 6 through 8, and an upper school for 9th through 12th graders, and one year of post-graduation study. The Academy uses a basic military system to promote structure and organization for its students. The present student body has boys from 35 states and 15 countries.

Good Shepherd Episcopal School
4207 Forest Hill Ave. • 231-1452

This coed school enrolls about 175 students in prekindergarten through grade 7. Children age 3 and older are admitted. Extended day care from 7 AM until 6 PM is available. Classes are small, and the teacher-student ratio is about 1-to-10.

Hanover Academy
115 Frances Rd., Ashland • 798-8413

This school serves about 120 students in preschool through the 7th grade. Established in 1959, the school offers a 1-to-15 teacher-student ratio. All teachers are state-certified.

Landmark Christian School
4000 Creighton Rd. • 644-5550

This school was established in the 1960s and offers kindergarten for 4- and 5-year-olds and instruction for 1st through 12th grade. About 300 students are enrolled. Transportation is available. Discounts are available if more than one child in a family is enrolled.

Liberty Christian School
8094 Liberty Cir., Mechanicsville
• 746-3062

About 165 students are enrolled here in preschool through 5th grade. Discounts are available if more than one child in a family is enrolled. This school was established in 1961, and limits class size to 20.

Richmond Montessori School
499 Parham Rd. • 741-0040

About 270 students from ages 2½ to 14 attend this school's ungraded, individualized alternative education program. An extended school-day program is available year round.

Rudlin Torah Academy
6801 Patterson Ave.
• **288-7610**

This coed school teaches secular and Judaic studies and enrolls about 155 students in kindergarten through 8th grade. Some tuition assistance is available. Full-day kindergarten is offered. Established in 1966, the school is known for its individualized, nurturing approach to education. Classes are small, with a teacher-student ratio of about 1-to-12.

St. Andrew's School
227 S. Cherry St. • 648-4545

About 100 students in kindergarten through 5th grade attend this school. Established in 1894, the school has an open enrollment policy and there is no tuition fee. The teacher/student ratio is about 1 to 17. Originally, the school was built to serve children living in Oregon Hill, but today children from all over the metropolitan area attend school here. The school operates on an endowment.

St. Benedict School
3100 Grove Ave. • 254-8850

About 225 students in kindergarten through 8th grade attend this Catholic school where the environment is highly structured. Catholic families receive discounts if more than one child in a family is enrolled. After-school care is available.

St. Bridget's School
6011 York Rd. • 288-1994

About 480 students in kindergarten through 8th grade attend this coed Catholic school. Catholic families receive discounts if more than one child in a family is enrolled. After-school care is also available for grades 1 through 5.

St. Catherine's School
6001 Grove Ave. • 288-2804

Established in 1890, this is one of the oldest private schools in Richmond. About 725 students attend this girls-only, independent college preparatory Episcopal school for grades junior kindergarten through 12. Each

year, 100 percent of the school's graduates go on to college. An optional residential boarding program is offered for grades 9 through 12. Day care is available for students in grades JK through 7. Advanced-placement courses and extracurricular sports and arts programs are also available. Courses for grades 9 through 12 are coordinated with St. Christopher's.

St. Christopher's School
711 St. Christopher's Rd. • 282-3185

About 820 students attend this boys-only, independent college preparatory Episcopal school for junior kindergarten through grade 12. The high school division is coordinated with St. Catherine's School. Day care is available for students in grades JK through 7. Established in 1911, 100 percent of the school's graduates continue their studies in college. The teacher/student ratio is about 1 to 8.

Saint Gertrude High School
3215 Stuart Ave. • 358-9114

About 275 students are enrolled in this girls-only Catholic school for grades 9 through 12. The school emphasizes college preparation and offers many honors and advanced placement courses. Established in 1922, the teacher-student ratio here is about 1-to-9.

St. Michael's Episcopal School
8706 Quaker Ln. • 272-3514

This coed school was established in 1957, and offers a traditional teaching environment. About 370 students are enrolled in kindergarten through 8th grade. The teacher-student ratio is about 1-to-10.

The Steward School
11600 Gayton Rd. • 740-3394

This coed college preparatory school enrolls about 285 students from kindergarten through grade 12. This is a small school with an average teacher-student ratio of about 1-to-12. Established in 1972, 100 percent of the graduates go on to college. Before- and after-school care is available.

Stony Point School
3400 Stony Point Rd. • 272-1341

About 100 students in junior kindergarten

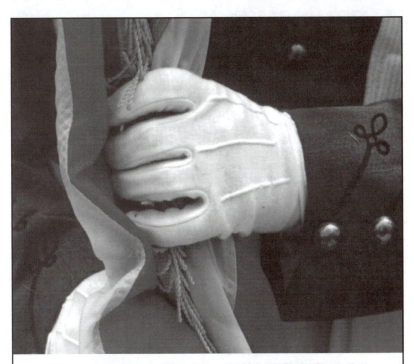

TO IMPROVE AMERICAN EDUCATION, THE GOVERNMENT PROPOSED "GOALS 2000" HERE, "GOALS 1898" WORKS JUST FINE.

Our mission is to prepare young men for college, not a career in the military. But it's really amazing what a uniform, teamwork, self-discipline and exposure to Christian ethics can do. To learn more about how our middle, upper and postgraduate college preparatory programs change boys' lives, write to:

Director of Admissions,
Fork Union Military Academy,
P.O. Box IG-1
Fork Union, Virginia 23055
1-800-GO-2-FUMA
www.fuma.org

We will teach your son that respecting rules is important. But respecting oneself is essential.

FORK UNION MILITARY ACADEMY

through 8th grade attend this coed school. Classes are small, with one teacher for about every 10 students. Discounts are available for families who have more than one child enrolled in the school.

Trinity Episcopal School
3850 Pittaway Dr. • 272-5864

About 340 students in grades 8 through 12 attend this coed college preparatory day school. Established in 1972, the teacher-student ratio is about 1-to-12, and nearly 100 percent of the graduates continue their education in college.

Private Special Education Programs

Dooley School
8000 Brook Rd. • 262-1663

Dooley School at St. Joseph's Villa provides alternative and special education for exceptional adolescents ages 6 through 19 who are emotionally disturbed, learning disabled, mentally retarded or behaviorally disordered. Day and residential programs are available. Students are ususally referred through schools, courts or social services, but private placement is accepted.

New Community School
4211 Hermitage Rd. • 266-2494

About 70 students with dyslexia learning disability are enrolled here in grades 6 through 12. Established in 1971, the school offers a college preparatory program and a low teacher-student ratio.

Riverside School
2110 McRae Rd., Bon Air • 320-3465

About 50 students are enrolled in this nonsectarian school for children in grades 1 through 8 with language learning disabilities, especially dyslexia. One-on-one tutoring sessions are provided daily, and the student/

teacher ratio is very low. The school was established in 1974.

Zipstar
700 E. Franklin St. • 775-0660

Students can now learn anytime, anywhere with the help of Zipstar, a relatively new company that offers middle and high school classes via the Internet. Open since 1998, Zipstar offers the core courses: English, math, science and social studies. Repeatedly failing a course, travel plans during summer school, or a variety of reasons lead students to Zipstar— "it fits the needs of a lot of people," owners say. The courses, which are self-paced, cost $250 apiece. Zipstar has certified teachers, the courses are based on Virginia standards of learning, and all area schools districts accept the credits. Because of so many requests, Zipstar is planning to launch Gradstar, a program for adults who need high school diplomas or GEDs.

Educational Organizations

Virginia Association of Independent Schools
8001 Franklin Farms Dr. • 282-3592

This statewide organization, established in 1973, provides its members with a school-evaluation and accreditation process recognized by the Virginia Department of Education, professional development opportunities, professional services and networks and comparative surveys on member-school operations. VAIS also monitors state and federal legislation. About 72 independent schools are members of VAIS. Member schools must have been in operation for at least five years and have an accredited academic program at least through the 2nd grade.

Virginia Council for Private Education
8001 Franklin Farms Dr. • 282-3594

VCPE was organized in 1974 as a Virginia

INSIDERS' TIP

Tuition costs at private schools in the Richmond area range from about $1,300 to over $9,000 a year per student.

affiliate of the National Council for American Private Education (CAPE). It's comprised of more than 12 different associations, and each represents academic institutions. All VCPE members must be not-for-profit and have a racially nondiscriminatory enrollment policy. VCPE acts as a liaison to the State Department of Education and the State Board of Education, and provides an accrediting process for members. Call for information about accredited private schools.

Child Care

If you have children, you'll probably need to find a good source for child care whether you're working full-time, part-time, at home, or just need a break.

As in most metropolitan areas, there are a number of options to consider before you decide what type of child-care service is best for your situation. There are home-based child-care providers, child-care centers, church and community organization services, employer-based child care, au pairs, nannies and live-in caregivers.

If you prefer a family setting for your child, and you want a home-based child-care provider, we recommend that you talk to other mothers, child-care centers and people at community organizations and churches for information about reputable caregivers in your area. You can also check the ads in the *Richmond Times-Dispatch* and county weeklies or use the assistance of a child-care referral service that keeps lists of caregivers who have vacancies. The weekly cost for full-time care is about $50 to $100. Hourly rates start at about $2. Infant care costs more than care for toddlers and preschoolers.

The Virginia Department of Social Services can provide you with a list of licensed home day-care providers, but there are many excellent home-based caregivers who do not have licenses. There are many licensing requirements, but basically, caregivers who keep fewer than six children do not need a license.

The Department of Social Services can also provide you with a list of licensed day-care centers. Usually, day-care centers provide care for children ages 2 through 12. Most of the centers require that children be potty-trained before they are accepted. (You'll find that most day care for infants is provided by individuals; fewer than 20 percent of the centers offer infant care.) Rates range from about $56 to $125 a week, depending on the age of the child.

Before- and after-school care is available through many day-care centers, the YMCA, home-based caregivers and some area schools.

There are also caregivers who will come to your home and do light housekeeping. You'll find these individuals through personal referrals and newspaper ads. Rates start at about $40 a day.

You may also want to consider a nanny. There are several nanny referral services in the area which we list in this chapter. Weekly rates range from about $200 to $400.

If you need day care on a part-time basis or just occasionally, many churches in the area sponsor Mothers' Morning Out Programs. These typically operate as parent-cooperative efforts, with minimal or no fees. Some of the schools in the area also offer day-care services as part of home economics or vocational training courses to give students an opportunity to work with children. The YMCA, recreation centers, churches and other community centers may also be good sources for other temporary or short-term care such as after-school care.

Virginia Department of Social Services, Licensing Division
Wythe Building, 1604 Santa Rosa Rd.
• **662-9773**

The state Department of Social Services serves as a regulatory and licensing agency for child-care centers and providers. The department provides lists of licensed centers and family home-care providers in the Richmond area.

The department also maintains records on religiously exempt facilities and investigates complaints about regulated facilities. The department will provide some information about the number and type of complaints filed against providers, centers and exempt facilities.

Division of Family Services Child Day Care Programs Unit
730 E. Broad St. • 662-9773

Part of the Department of Social Services, this program area assesses the availability and affordability of child care, especially for at-risk 4-year-olds and other at-risk preschoolers. The program also administers federal grants including subsidies for programs like Head Start.

Information on Head Start programs for at-risk preschoolers is available through Virginia Commonwealth University School of Social Work or area schools. Call the VCU School of Social Work at 828-8200 for more information.

Research and Referral Services

KidCare
5001 W. Broad St. • 649-0219

This child-care referral service for the Richmond area was established in 1986 by the Memorial Child Guidance Clinic. KidCare maintains a list of about 500 day-care providers and 450 day-care centers with information about locations, fees, schools and services. The staff can provide information about providers who are equipped to take care of children with special needs.

In addition, KidCare provides training courses in safety, child development, and parenting. The staff also helps individuals set up home child-care services.

Providers pay a small fee to be listed, and parents pay about $15 for each zip-code area listing of providers. Lists include licensed and registered providers, day-care centers, and most of the church-exempt providers. Some employers offer the referral service as an employee benefit.

KidCare also offers child-care training. Students learn CPR, first aid, child safety, child development, creative play and learning, child health, child education and cognitive learning as well as professionalism and interpersonal communication skills. Instructors include KidCare staff members and other child-care professionals in the area. Workshops are also offered on evenings and weekends. Call the school for enrollment information.

Nannies by KidCare
5001 W. Broad St. • 282-6085

This service provides referrals for full-time, part-time and live-in nannies for permanent or temporary situations. About 125 nannies are placed in permanent situations each year.

Nannies listed with the service must provide character and child-care references in addition to any mothering experience they may have had. The agency checks providers' child-abuse, criminal and driving records, provides an employment verification check and requests medical and health information. The staff also conducts personal interviews that include child-care scenario questions about nutrition, discipline, play and emergency care.

Families pay a one-time, nonrefundable $75 retaining fee, plus a $550 placement fee for full-time nannies, a $350 placement fee for part-time nannies, a $700 fee for live-in nannies and a $250 fee for summer nannies. Families receive a complimentary booklet on interviewing, hiring and keeping a nanny. It also includes tax information, sample contracts and problem-solving advice. Placement usually takes an average of four to six weeks. Salaries average about $300 a week or $7 an hour.

Christian Nannies
530 E. Main St.
• 649-8268

This service provides referrals for nannies in the Richmond area who demonstrate Christian values to the children they care for, regardless of denomination. Nannies are available to work on a live-in, full-time, part-time, summer-only or temporary basis.

The agency conducts a screening process that includes a statement of health, referrals, DMV, employment verification and criminal-record checks. The staff also conducts an extensive interview and provides drug screening and AIDS tests on request. Red Cross classes and courses in parenting, child care and safety are offered as well.

The agency lists an average of 150 nannies actively seeking positions. Placement fees vary — a part-time nanny is $290, full-time is

$575 and live-in is $750. The average placement time takes about four to six weeks.

Care "4" Kids
530 E. Main St. • 649-8804

Care "4" Kids is a nonprofit organization that provides referrals for family day-care providers, special schools and day-care centers. Child-care training, CPR, first aid, and educational classes are also offered for parents and providers.

The staff visits each provider who is registered and conducts medical, DMV and criminal checks. Referrals are free. Providers are screened in advance, so referral lists include only providers with vacancies who are interested in caring for additional children.

Registered providers may join the Neighbor-to-Neighbor program which provides networking opportunities, health insurance, bulk buying power, memberships to discount clubs and social activities such as Easter egg hunts and holiday parties for providers, children and parents.

Care "4" Kids also offers a consultation service for businesses that want to start an in-house day-care service for their employees and a contractual service to help businesses assist their employees with day-care issues.

The Nanny Connection
7261 Beach Rd. • 796-3004

This company provides a complete range of in-home child-care service, nannies, parent helpers and sitters for live-in, full-time or part-time work. They also provide overnight, emergency and sick child care. They even provide babysitters or nannies for out-of-town hotel guests. Established in 1987, this is Richmond's first and oldest nanny service.

The agency verifies and talks to references, conducts personal interviews, checks criminal records, child-abuse histories and driving records. Nannies must also be CPR certified and have at least a high school education and a minimum of three years experience in child

care or an educational background in early childhood. They must also be at least 21 years of age.

Placement fees vary depending on the type of service you need from about $895 for a live-in nanny to $675 for a full-time nanny to $400 for a part-time nanny. Part-time nannies are usually paid $7 to $10 per hour, and full-time experienced nannies earn about $250 to $400 a week. Placement usually takes about four to six weeks.

AuPairCare
• (800)4AuPair

Headquartered in San Francisco, this company provides European nannies to families around the country. The women and men are between the ages of 18 and 25 and are thoroughly interviewed and screened by the company. While living with the family as a family member, participating in everyday events, the au pair provides a maximum of 45 hours per week of child care. The cultural exchange aspect of the program is a wonderful advantage of this type of care, according to families who currently participate. The au pairs are in the country on a 13-month visa and are overseen while here by a community coordinator who provides emotional and practical support for both the au pair and the family. Cost, regardless of the number of children you have, averages $208 a week.

Stony Point Learning Center
3039 Stony Point Rd. • 323-1234
2920 Pump Rd. • 360-4141 (Children's Castle)
8006 Discovery Dr. • 282-1033 (Tree Tops)

This nationally accredited preschool and child-care center emphasizes social and emotional growth for the children who attend. Your infants and toddlers can partake in both before- and after-school programs as well as on a full- or part-time basis. And now Stony Point and its two sister facilities have a summer camp program, so children can attend year round.

The institutions of higher learning in Richmond are an enormous cultural and educational resource for the community and provide broad opportunities for continuing education for residents.

Colleges and Universities

Richmond is home to one of the top-ranked and most heavily endowed private universities in the nation, to one of the country's most historic African-American universities and to one of the nation's top public research universities.

All told, there are 10 institutions of higher learning in the Greater Richmond area. They are an enormous cultural and educational resource for the community and provide broad opportunities for continuing education for residents.

The following information is brief, especially in terms of available continuing education opportunities. For more detailed information, call the phone numbers listed. For information on the various spectator sports associated with many of these institutions, see our Spectator Sports chapter.

Randolph-Macon College
204 Patrick St., Ashland • 752-7305

Randolph-Macon, with an enrollment of about 1,100, is a private, coeducational liberal arts college located in the attractive little town of Ashland. It is among a select group of only 10 percent of colleges and universities with a Phi Beta Kappa chapter. It ranks as a Liberal Arts I institution in a Carnegie Commission study along with colleges and universities such as Amherst, Williams, Smith, Wellesley, Swarthmore, Davidson and Oberlin.

The college offers 30 major areas of study, including arts management, biology, chemistry, the classics, computer science, business/economics, English, environmental science, fine arts, French, German, history, international studies, mathematics, philosophy, physics, political science, psychology, religious studies, romance languages, sociology and Spanish.

Since its founding in 1830, Randolph-Macon College has been recognized nationally for its challenging liberal-arts and sciences curriculum. A higher percentage of Randolph-Macon graduates have gone on to earn their Ph.D.s than that of any other private college in Virginia. Thirty percent of their graduates go directly on to graduate school. Particular strengths are in the natural and physical sciences and premedical studies. Study-abroad programs are also available to eight countries.

University of Richmond
off Three Chopt Rd. • 289-8000

For a number of years the University of Richmond, one of the nation's most heavily endowed private universities, has ranked among "America's Best Colleges" in the annual list compiled by *U.S. News & World Report*. For three consecutive years it also placed

---

INSIDERS' TIP

Five buildings at Virginia Union University are National Historic Landmarks. Its Belgian Building once was a part of the 1939 New York World's Fair. Its newest building is the $6.6 million L. Douglas Wilder Library and Learning Resources Center.

second in the South with a 95.9 out of 100 rating. A guidebook written several years ago by Princeton University students ranked the University of Richmond's campus as one of the five most beautiful in the nation. Collegiate Gothic architecture predominates. The guidebook also concluded that UR's students are America's second best-looking!

Founded in 1830 by Virginia Baptists, the university is coeducational and enrolls about 2,900 full-time undergraduate students and about 1500 full-time graduate and law students from 40 states and 17 foreign countries. Thirty-five percent of the freshmen rank in the top 10 percent of their respective secondary school classes.

In the West End on a 350-acre campus that includes a 10-acre lake, the University of Richmond includes Richmond College, the residential college for undergraduate men in liberal arts and sciences, and Westhampton College, the residential college for undergraduate women in liberal arts and sciences. It also includes the E. Claiborne Robins School of Business, with its Richard S. Reynolds graduate division, the T.C. Williams School of Law, a graduate school for arts and sciences and the School of Continuing Studies which includes the summer and evening schools and continuing education programs.

The university's Jepson School of Leadership Studies is the first in the nation to offer a bachelor's degree in this important field.

An executive master of business administration degree program is designed for those who wish to pursue part-time academic study of management and who already hold baccalaureate degrees and management positions. Its Women's Resource Center involves more than 6,000 men and women in self-improvement classes, life-planning seminars, support groups and job and career counseling. Evening classes are offered for four majors, and noncredit classes are offered in a variety of fields.

FYI

Unless otherwise noted, the area code for all phone numbers listed in this chapter is 804.

Virginia Commonwealth University
821 W. Franklin St. • 828-1349
1101 E. Marshall St. (MCV) • 828-9800

Virginia Commonwealth University, in center city, is the state's largest urban university (22,000 students). It is one of the nation's top public research universities and has one of the nation's largest evening school programs. It offers 136 degree and certificate programs, including many that are not available at any other institution in Virginia. About 80 percent of faculty members hold the highest degree in their field.

The university has two campuses: the academic campus in the Fan District and the Medical College of Virginia campus, or east campus, downtown. The university is coeducational, state-supported and traces its history back to the founding of the Medical College of Virginia in 1838.

VCU's east campus is the site of the Medical College of Virginia Hospitals, one of the largest and most active university-affiliated healthcare centers in the United States. This campus houses the schools of allied health professions, dentistry, medicine, nursing, pharmacy and basic sciences. All of this makes VCU one of only 20 universities in the nation with a school in every health-related discipline.

The academic campus is the home of the colleges and schools of the arts, business, education, engineering, humanities and sciences and social work. The School of the Arts is one of the largest in the nation. The School of Business is one of only three in the nation with a chair in real estate, and the Management Center offers more than 200 programs a year for private industry and government.

VCU also offers opportunities for study abroad through its Center for International Programs, 828-6584.

INSIDERS' TIP

New opportunities in engineering studies will be available at Virginia Commonwealth University's new $20 million engineering school.

University of Richmond students have been attending classes in Ryland Hall since 1914.

Virginia State University
20708 4th Ave., Petersburg • 524-5902

Founded in 1882 as the first public comprehensive institution of higher learning for blacks in the nation, Virginia State University (VSU) has since grown to over 4,000 students strong, representing close to 40 states and nearly 20 foreign countries. VSU is located in Chesterfield County at Ettrick, on a bluff overlooking the Appomattox River and the historic city of Petersburg.

VSU offers close to 50 academic major in four schools: Agriculture, Science and Technology; Business; Liberal Arts and Education; and Graduate Studies and Continuing Education. Programs awarded specialized accreditation include commercial art and design, dietetics, education, engineering technology, music and social work.

The university is home to the 1995 and 1996 CIAA Champion Trojan Football Team as well as the acclaimed VSU Gospel Chorale, named best in the nation in 1996 and

1997. VSU is one of Virginia's two land-grant institutions and operates a 416-acre agricultural research and demonstration facility a mile from its 236-acre, tree-lined campus. A leader in agricultural research and diversification, VSU was awarded $200,000 by Gov. Allen in June 1997 to assist black farmers across Virginia.

With a great deal invested in capital improvements, VSU's campus is rife with activity. A new baseball field just opened in the spring of 1997; and the 1997-98 school year will see a new Cooperative Extension building, a new music building and a new wing for the School of Business.

Virginia Union University
1500 N. Lombardy St. • 257-5600

Virginia Union University is among the nation's finest traditionally African-American institutions of higher learning and has been a powerful force in shaping the history of Richmond. In the process it has educated many of the city's and the state's leaders, such as former Virginia governor Douglas Wilder.

It offers 22 undergraduate liberal arts and business majors as well as graduate degrees in theology. Majors with the highest enrollment are business, criminal justice, teacher education, and history/political science.

Its core liberal arts curricula is augmented by specialized programs such as a dual-degree engineering program in conjunction with the University of Michigan, the University of Iowa and Howard University in Washington, D.C.; and a joint-degree program in law with St. John's University School of Law in New York.

The Sydney Lewis School of Business Administration at Virginia Union offers undergraduate degrees in business, with majors in accounting, business administration and business education.

Virginia Union attracts students from all over the United States and from abroad, and its undergraduate student body of about 1,500 students represents 28 states and eight foreign countries.

Community Colleges

J. Sargeant Reynolds Community College
1651 E. Parham Rd. • 371-3000

Sargeant Reynolds Community College enrolls about 11,500 students on three campuses: downtown at 700 E. Jackson Street; in Henrico County on Parham Road, 1 mile west Interstate 95; and in Goochland County on State Route 6 near the courthouse.

The college is the third largest in the Virginia Community College System and offers college transfer classes as well as more than 60 career-oriented programs. Developmental studies in math and English are offered to those who are not yet qualified to enroll in a program.

A specialty of the downtown campus near the Medical College of Virginia is health-career training. Popular programs at the Parham Road campus are those in engineering and electronics. Agricultural and automotive/diesel programs have the heaviest student involvement at the western campus.

Both the Parham Road and downtown campuses offer free career counseling and placement offices that are open to the public. Programs to help women enter or return to the job market and independent-study classes are also offered. At the downtown campus, the Center for the Deaf helps deaf and hard-of-hearing students enter the educational programs of the college.

Studies can lead to an Associate in Applied Science degree or certificate, an Associate of Arts or Science degree in liberal arts, engineering or science, or certification in areas including computer technology and hotel and restaurant management.

In addition to the main telephone number listed above, the downtown campus can be reached directly at 786-6791, the Parham Road campus at 371-3270, and the western campus at 371-3667.

John Tyler Community College
13101 Jefferson Davis Hwy. • 796-4000

John Tyler Community College enrolls about 6,000 students annually in credit courses at three locations: the Chester Campus, the Midlothian Campus and the Fort Lee Center.

Studies at John Tyler lead to associate in applied science degrees, associate degrees in arts and sciences for transfer, and certificates and career studies certificates in vocational and technical subjects. The community college offers studies in college prerequisite skills, continuing-education courses, and noncredit recreational and personal-interest courses. In addition, Tech Prep programs are offered through linkages with area high schools.

The most sought-after curricula are liberal arts for transfer to four-year colleges and universities, business management and administration, computer information systems, electronics, nursing, physical therapist assistant and police science.

The Extended Learning Institute allows students to study independently under the tutelage of a faculty member. John Tyler's Weekend College allows eligible students to pursue an associate degree through an innovative program designed to meet the needs of adult learners. The college's Business, Industry and Government Services Center offers an

extensive array of professional development courses and seminars tailored to the needs of individuals, organizations and businesses. Courses and seminars cover topics such as computer software programs, office management, supervisory skills and total quality management.

In addition to the phone number listed above for the Chester campus, the Midlothian campus can be reached at 378-3446 and the Fort Lee Center can be reached at 861-2762.

Theological Studies

Baptist Theological Seminary at Richmond
3400 Brook Rd. • 355-8135

Baptist Theological Seminary at Richmond (BTSR), established in 1991–92, is supported by The Baptist General Association of Virginia, the Cooperative Baptist Fellowship and by Baptist churches and organizations. Fully accredited by the Association of Theological Schools, it prepares men and women for ca-

reers in churches and other organizations and offers the Master of Divinity, a three-year basic preparatory degree for a variety of fields of ministry; the Master of Divinity/Master of Arts in conjunction with the Presbyterian School of Christian Education; the Master of Divinity/ Master of Social Work in cooperation with the VCU School of Social Work; and the Doctor of Ministry, a three-year, post-Master Divinity degree for people working full-time in ministry.

BTSR participates with three other local institutions in the Richmond Theological Consortium: Union Theological Seminary, Presbyterian School of Christian Education and Virginia Union University's School of Theology.

Union Theological Seminary-Presbyterian School of Christian Education
3401 Brook Rd. • 355-0671

These two schools were recently united by the federation of seminary, founded in 1812, and the school of Christian Education, founded in 1914. The Union Theological Seminary-Presbyterian School of Christian Education (UTS-PSCE) occupies a 50-acre campus in Ginter Park, a historic residential area in Richmond's north side. UTS-PSCE prepares men and women for pastoral and educational ministries in the Christian church.

The seminary is recognized for its vigorous academic program and its pioneering work in the field education and student-in-ministry experiences. Its excellent library of about 250,000 volumes and its audiovisual, closed-circuit television and other electric teaching aids provide special learning opportunities.

UTS-PSCE offers 10 degree programs: Master of Divinity, Master of Arts (Christian Education), a duel degree combining both those programs (M.A./M. Div.), Master of Theology, Doctor of Philosophy and Doctor of Education as well as two dual-degree programs are offered with VCU: M.S./M. Div. in Criminal Justice; and M.S.W./M.A. in Christian Education. UTS-PSCE has about 330 students and is a member of the Richmond Theological Consortium which also includes the Baptist Theological Seminary at Richmond, the School of Theological Seminary at Richmond and the School of Theology of Virginia Union University.

Regional Centers of Other Colleges and Universities

Bluefield College Division of Adult and Continuing Education
306 Turner Rd, Ste. 6 • 276-3788

In response to the needs of the working adult, Bluefield College opened its Division of Adult and Continuing Education (D.A.C.E.), hoping to offer to adults, even full-time working adults, an opportunity to complete or continue their college education without stopping everything. Bluefield College offers its students fully accredited associate and baccalaureate degrees in a variety of majors. The D.A.C.E.

has 17 locations outside of its central base in Bluefield, Virginia.

Classes generally meet only one evening a week. With appropriate prior college credits and/or prior experience, most majors can be completed in about 15 months. Three fields of study are offered for degrees in Bachelor of Arts or Sciences: Organizational Management and Development, Administration of Justice and Christian Ministries.

Adults with a minimum age of 25, two years of work experience and 54 hours of college credit from an accredited institution may qualify for admission. For information about an introductory meeting, call the number above.

Mary Baldwin College, Richmond Regional Center
1801 Libbie Ave. • 282-9111

Mary Baldwin's Richmond Regional Center offers a nonresidential, nontraditional Adult Degree Program designed for working men and women who wish to earn a bachelor of arts degree. Advanced credit may be given for life and work experience. More than 20 majors in the liberal arts are offered, including healthcare administration and business administration. A Master of Arts in teaching also is available. Group courses meet in the evenings or on Saturdays. Students may also engage in individual, directed study.

Old Dominion University — TELETECHNET
Library of Virginia • 800 E. Broad St.
• (800) 968-2638
John Tyler Community College
• 13101 Jefferson Davis Hwy. • (800) 968-2638
J. Sargeant Reynolds Community College
• 1651 E. Parham Rd. • (800) 968-2638

Old Dominion University has established TELETECHNET in partnership with community colleges, military installations and corporations throughout Virginia. TELETECHNET is a statewide system utilizing an interactive satellite broadcast link to deliver baccalaureate and master's degree programs to over 25 sites across Virginia.

Students complete their first two years of college through their local community college or other institution and ultimately receive their degree from Old Dominion University. The program is designed for part-time attendance, catering to the nontraditional student who may be working full-time and carrying other responsibilities.

In the Richmond area, TELETECHNET offers over 15 baccalaureate degrees and four post-baccalaureate degree programs, as well as other opportunities for individuals to enroll in courses for personal satisfaction. Three sites serve the Richmond area: on the Parham Road campus of J. Sargeant Reynolds Community College, the Library of Virginia in downtown Richmond and on the Chester campus of John Tyler Community College.

University of Virginia, Richmond Center
7740 Shrader Rd., Ste. E • 662-7464

The Richmond Center is operated by the Division of Continuing Education of the University of Virginia, Charlottesville. It offers a variety of credit and noncredit courses, seminars and custom-designed programs, on a contractual basis, to meet specific needs of organizations. Included in the center's portfolio are a recorded program for attorney certification; teacher-recertification training; seven master's degree programs in engineering; a 30-hour certificate in human resources; a small-business management series; a Leadership Colloquium for Women; and programs on management, environmental health, leadership, foreign culture and languages, publishing and communications. A course is provided for teacher recertification and engineers preparing to take the state examination. The center also provides contract courses to businesses, associations, health organizations and other interested groups.

Averett College, Richmond Campus
7501 Boulders View Dr., Ste. 110
• 330-7407

Averett College brings Richmond a unique approach to continuing education designed to meet the needs of the working adult. The college offers evening classes for undergraduates and graduate degrees in business administration at two Richmond-area locations as well as multiple company on-site programs. Degree concentrations are in management, accounting, finance and strategic planning. Classes meet one night per week and are coupled with weekly study-team meetings. Founded in 1859, Averett College has main campuses in Danville, Vienna, Richmond, Tidewater and Raleigh, North Carolina. Richmond-area campuses are in The Boulders, off Midlothian Turnpike, and in the West End at Parham Road and Interstate 64.

In addition to thoroughly covering the arts and cultural scene, *Style Weekly* explores, analyzes and dissects all the things that make Richmond tick and sometimes the things that keep it from ticking.

Media

Richmond is part of the magnificent Southern journalistic tradition that has produced some of the country's greatest editors, reporters and television commentators. It also is the home of Media General, a diversified communications company with major interests in metropolitan newspapers, weekly newspapers, broadcast and cable television, newsprint production and other operations in the United States and Mexico.

The city in recent years remained one of only a few in the nation with both morning and afternoon dailies. That all changed in 1992 when the afternoon *Richmond News Leader* was combined with the morning *Richmond Times-Dispatch*. It was on the *News Leader*'s pages that editorial writers Douglas Southall Freeman and James Jackson Kilpatrick and editorial cartoonist Jeff MacNelly first gained national attention, and it was as a reporter on the *News Leader* that television commentator Roger Mudd got his start. The *Times-Dispatch* editorial page was edited for many years by Pulitzer Prize-winning editor and historian Virginius Dabney. Paul Duke, originator and former host of PBS's "Washington Week in Review," is a native Richmonder and cut his teeth here with The Associated Press. ABC network weatherman Spencer Christian's first television job was here in Richmond.

One of the first African-American newspapers published in the United States was *The Richmond Planet*. *The Planet* gained national prominence from 1884 to 1929, during the time it was edited by the illustrious John R. Mitchell Jr. He fought courageously and indefatigably against Jim Crow laws and was responsible for forming the Mechanics Savings Bank of Richmond in 1902. The newspaper was sold in 1938 to Baltimore interests and at that time was renamed the *Richmond Afro-American* and

The Richmond Planet. The newspaper, a trusted friend of the African-American community, continued in publication for more than 100 years, until it discontinued publication in February 1996.

If you're a trading-card collector, you'll be interested to know that two national catalogues — *Tuff Stuff*, covering trading cards and sports collectibles, and *Tuff Stuff's Collect!*, covering entertainment collectibles, — are published in Richmond and distributed nationally. The same offices publish *Beans & Bears!*, a guide to beanbag and teddy bear collectibles.

In this chapter, we've provided the Richmonder's essentials media resources — newspapers, some specialized publications, local magazines, and lists of the local TV and radio stations.

Local Newspapers

Richmond Times-Dispatch
333 E. Franklin St. • 649-6000

The *Times-Dispatch* is published daily and has a Sunday circulation of almost 250,000 copies. The newspaper has correspondents and bureaus throughout Virginia and a bureau in Washington, D.C. Its coverage of local and state political, business, sports, and general news is extensive. It publishes weekly "PLUS" community news sections for Chesterfield, Henrico and Hanover counties and the Tri-Cities. On Mondays it carries an expanded business section called "Metro Business," and each Thursday it publishes a "Weekend" section devoted to upcoming cultural and arts programs and special events. On Saturdays, the *Greensection* insert provides a week-long schedule of TV and movie listings. You can also find this information in the paper's daily "Entertainment Flair" section.

Richmond Free Press
101 W. Broad St. • 644-0496

The *Richmond Free Press* is the city's newest African-American-owned newspaper. The weekly was launched by a group of influential local citizens in 1992 and is dedicated to high-quality coverage of local events and "issues that confront the African-American community." The full-size format newspaper has a circulation of about 28,000. It is published and distributed at about 300 outlets on Thursday.

The Voice
416 N. Second St. • 644-9060

This weekly African-American-owned tabloid is published on Wednesdays. Covering general news but concentrating on economic development and human interest features, *The Voice* is distributed free of charge in Richmond and seven Southside Virginia counties and has a circulation of about 44,000.

Goochland Gazette
3052 River Rd. W., Goochland • 556-3135

Distributed on Thursdays, this weekly has a "paid circulation" of about 3,000. It serves the "horse country" of Goochland County, just to the west of the metro area, where many Richmond business executives live.

Herald-Progress
11293 Air Park Rd., Ashland • 798-9031

This lively semiweekly, published every Monday and Thursday, covers Hanover County and has a paid circulation of about 8,000. It usually consists of two sections and often has special sections.

Mechanicsville Local
P.O. Box 1118, Mechanicsville, Va.
• 746-1235

Published weekly, the *Mechanicsville Local* has a circulation of about 21,000 copies and is mailed free of charge to households in the 23111 and 23116 ZIP code areas of eastern Hanover County. It is distributed on Wednesdays.

The Village Mill
3001 E. Boundary Terr.
• 744-1035

Published by the Brandermill Community Association, this full-size newspaper covers community news and serves the neighborhoods and businesses of Brandermill. It is published monthly and has a circulation of about 4,200 copies.

Out-of-Town Newspapers

The most extensive variety of out-of-town newspapers (about 60, United States and foreign) is available at Books A Million, 9131 Midlothian Turnpike, 272-1792. The Barnes & Noble Store in the Shops at Willow Lawn shopping center carries Sunday editions of many newspapers from major cities in the United States and abroad. The *New York Times*, *The Washington Times*, *The Washington Post* and *The Wall Street Journal* are available at street-corner vending machines, which are plentiful, especially downtown. These newspapers are also sold at the Jefferson, Hyatt, Marriott and Omni hotels, at the State Capitol, at the Riverfront Plaza Sundry Shop and at certain chain drugstores and 7-Elevens. The Norfolk newspaper, *The Virginian-Pilot* also is available at some of these locations and in vending machines.

Specialized Publications

Catholic Virginian
14 N. Laurel St. • 358-3625

This is the newspaper of the Catholic Diocese of Richmond. It is published biweekly on Mondays and is mailed to 66,000 homes.

Family Style
1118 W. Main St. • 358-0825

Family Style is a full-size tabloid focused on the art of parenting in Richmond. Published monthly, it offers parents a calendar of family-related events, tips on disciplining children, seasonal craft ideas, and more. Distributed free of charge around Richmond with its sister publication, *Style Weekly*.

Fifty-Plus
1510 Willow Lawn Dr., Ste. 203
• **673-5203**

Published monthly, *Fifty-Plus* is a tabloid-size newspaper geared to the 50-and-over crowd in the Richmond metropolitan area. More than 30,000 copies are distributed free of charge to 350 locations around town. Subscriptions are available for $15 per year.

Focus
P.O. Box 36480, Richmond, VA 23235
• **560-1898**

According to its tagline, *Focus* is "Richmond's Eye on Entertainment." With a concentration on music, this tabloid gives Richmonders the scoop on upcoming events. *Focus* is distributed free to local bookstores, coffee houses, and grocery stores every other month.

Good News Herald
1522 Rogers St. • 780-0021

"Our editorial policy is to herald nothing but good news," says the masthead, "to spotlight positive citizen role models." Content features community personalities and is heavy on church news. Presses run nearly 9,000 copies, about once a month. It's distributed in 86 churches around Richmond.

Good News Publications
4202 Park Place Ct., Ste. F • 527-8384

Good News Publications issues free glossy publications with good news about schools, localities and neighborhoods. *The Far West End Press*, with a circulation of about 22,000 copies and *Henrico County Leader*, with a circulation of about 20,000 copies.

Home Style
1118 W. Main St. • 358-0825

Published monthly, *Home Style* is "Richmond's resource for home and garden." The full-size tabloid offers its readers gardening tips, decorating ideas, a peak inside some of Richmond's finest homes and more. Dis-

tributed free of charge around Richmond with its sister publication, *Style Weekly*.

Innsbrook Today
4600 Cox Rd., Ste. 101, Glen Allen
• **346-3088**

Published monthly, this magazine covers Innsbrook and Deep Run area news. It has 60,000-plus West End readers and is hand-delivered to every office and business in the area as well as to every home in Innsbrook's five neighborhoods.

Inside Business
1113 W. Main St. • 358-5500

A premium-quality business tabloid, *Inside Business* is published weekly by Landmark Communications Inc. It is mailed free of charge to 20,000 business owners. It contains feature-length articles, news briefs and an opinion page. Subscriptions are available free of charge.

Jewish News
212 N. Gaskins Rd. • 740-2000

This weekly is received by about 5,000 families on Fridays. It covers local Jewish events and Israeli and international Jewish topics.

Mature Life
24 E. Cary St. • 343-3000

This is the official newspaper of the Capital Area Agency on Aging. It is published every other month and covers a wide range of news and information on services of interest to readers 60 and older in Richmond and seven surrounding counties. It has a circulation of about 38,000 copies.

Metro Business Monthly
111 N. Fourth St. • 649-6349

Published monthly by the *Richmond Times-Dispatch*, this business tabloid is mailed free of charge to companies throughout the Richmond metropolitan area. The *Times-Dispatch* business news department is responsible for news content. In addition to news, the publication contains advice for career advancement, how-to tips, and a variety of information

Richmond Parks and Recreation sponsors tubing trips for the public down the James River in August.

columns that deal with business developments and concerns.

Northside Magazine
2900 Hungary Rd., Ste. 103

Northside Magazine is published monthly in a tabloid newspaper format by Stone Arch Publications Inc. It's a general interest magazine as it relates to the region it serves: the metro area north of the James River, including Richmond and Hanover and Henrico counties. About 24,000 copies are delivered to homes in those areas during the first week of each month, free of charge. Another 10,000 copies are distributed around Richmond.

Punchline
2928 W. Cary St., Ste. B • 213-0416

Published biweekly, *Punchline* is Richmond's best alternative guide to local entertainment, complete with feature articles, a calendar of events, and cartoons. It's distributed every other Thursday to 250 locations, free of charge.

Richmond Music Journal
P.O. Box 14857, Richmond, VA 23221
• 278-9753
• rmjournal@mindspring.com

Richmond Music Journal keeps tabs on the Richmond area's music scene with reviews of local releases and local shows. Published in tabloid format and released the last Tuesday of each month to any of the local music stores or coffee houses, this free publication is quick to disappear. If you don't catch it in time, call for back issues or play it safe with your own subscription ($20 a year).

Richmond Parents' Monthly
1510 Willow Lawn Dr., Ste. 203 • 673-5203

Published monthly, the *Richmond Parents' Monthly* is a tabloid-size family newspaper that provides information on events, health and fun for school-age children. It has a circulation of more than 40,000 copies and is available free of charge at area Ukrop's, Toy "R" Us, Captain D's, Shoneys, and McDonald's. Subscriptions are available for $15 a year.

South of the James
2900 Hungary Rd., Ste. 103

This new magazine is a sister publication to *Northside Magazine* and is published monthly in a tabloid newspaper format by Stone Arch Publications Inc. *South of the James* a general interest magazine covering the metro area south of the James River, including Richmond and Chesterfield County. About 25,000 copies are delivered to homes on the first Thursday of each month, free of charge. Another 15,000 copies are distributed in those areas to Ukrop's, CVS, and various restaurants and bookstores.

Style Weekly
1118 W. Main St. • 358-0825

If there is an "in" publication in Richmond, this is it. *Style Weekly* used to call itself "The Cultural Guide To Richmond," and that's what it is, in the broadest sense of the word. In addition to thoroughly covering the arts and cultural scene, the weekly explores, analyzes and dissects all the things that make Richmond tick and sometimes the things that keep it from ticking. Its lively editorial content, classy display ads and classified personals appeal to an influential audience. A press run of 40,000 copies is parceled out every Tuesday to 250 free-distribution locations. They go fast. Avid readers of *Style Weekly* live in mortal fear they may miss a copy if they don't put priority on picking one up on the day of publication.

Virginia Capitol Connections
1001 E. Broad St., Ste. 225 • 643-5554

Virginia Capitol Connections is a quarterly nonpartisan publication focusing on Virginia issues and government. It is filled with articles, point-counterpoint features, interviews and political cartoons. Its subscription base is upwards to 4,000, which includes business leaders, associations, elected officials and lobbyists.

Virginia Episcopalian
110 W. Franklin St. • 643-8451

This monthly newspaper is published by the Episcopal Diocese of Virginia. It contains diocesan, national and international news and commentary. Circulation is about 28,000 copies.

Virginia Lawyers Weekly
106 N. Eighth St. • 783-0770

Published every Monday, this newspaper includes digests of court cases decided the previous week, and other news and commentary of interest to Virginia lawyers and law firms. The newspaper is mailed to more than 3,700 subscribers.

Magazines

Enterprise Virginia
10043 Midlothian Turnpike • 323-6368

Relatively new to the Richmond business magazine scene is *Enterprise Virginia,* a monthly magazine focused on business, technology and the community. Yearly subscriptions sell for $24.95, and individual issues cost $2.95 apiece at area bookstores and newsstands.

Richmond Magazine
2500 E. Parham Rd., Ste. 200 • 261-0034

This is Richmond's city magazine and features articles on the arts, entertainment, business, finance, health, local lifestyles and local personalities. Published monthly, *Richmond Magazine* has an annual "Best and Worst" issue, and an annual "Newcomers Edition" that provides a broad base of information on housing, jobs, healthcare, newcomers organizations, schools, other data and phone numbers of value to new residents. The magazine has about 160,000 readers, is privately owned and is available at about 700 distribution points or by subscription for $12 per year.

Virginia Business
411 E. Franklin St., Ste. 105 • 649-6999

Edited and published in Richmond, this

is Virginia's statewide business magazine. It is an influential and respected publication and has a monthly controlled circulation of more than 32,000 copies to business, professional and government leaders. The publisher is Media General Business Communications Inc.

New Virginia Review
1312 E. Cary St. • 782-1043

Richmond is home-base for a literary magazine, *New Virginia Review*. This magazine is published three times a year and features poetry, fiction and essays. It is described in more detail in our Arts chapter in the section called "Writer's Groups."

Television

Richmond has three network affiliates, two independent stations, the public broadcasting operations of Central Virginia Educational Television (CVET) and two cable companies. Local stations and their network affiliates are:

WTVR Channel 6 (CBS)
WRIC Channel 8 (ABC)
WWBT Channel 12 (NBC)
WCVE Channel 23 (PBS/Independent)
WCVW Channel 57 (PBS/Independent)
WRLH Channel 35 (Fox)
WUPV Channel 65 (UPN/Independent)

Cable Television Providers

MediaOne
Richmond: 918 N. Boulevard • 266-1900
Ashland, Hanover and Henrico service:
5401 Staples Mills Rd. • 266-1900

Formerly Continental Cablevision, MediaOne provides cable service to about 130,000 customers in Richmond and in Hanover, Henrico and Goochland counties. Its standard service package includes 45 channels in Goochland and the town of Ashland; 56 channels in the City of Richmond and Henrico County; and 40 channels in Hanover

County. It also offers a premium package and additional channels as well as a 37-channel, 24-hour, commercial-free digital cable radio service called Music Choice. Its pay-per-view services includes major sports events, movies and special events. Senior citizen or multiple-installation discounts may be available, so be sure to inquire.

Comcast Cablevision
6510 Iron Bridge Rd. • 743-1150

Comcast serves more than 62,000 customers in Chesterfield County and offers a 42-channel standard package. It also offers a 10-channel basic service that includes local broadcast channels, selected cable channels such as C-SPAN and the Prevue Channel. Premium channels including HBO, The Movie Channel, Cinemax, Showtime and the Disney Channel are available at additional cost. Pay-per-view channels also are available, as is an FM cable radio service. Nineteen new channels, including HBO 2 and 3, are now available in certain upgraded areas.

Radio Stations

The most popular spots on the radio dial among the area's 775,000 listeners are country station WKHK-95.3 FM; urban contemporary WCDX-92.1 FM; light favorites WTVR-98.1 FM; news-talk WRVA-1140 AM; and urban rock/new rock WRXL-102.1 FM. Morning favorites range from WKHK's "Catfish & Kelly" to WRVA's Tim Timberlake and John Harding.

The area has several news/talk/sports radio stations that offer locally and nationally produced call-in programming. Blanquita Cullum, named one of the nation's "25 Most Important Talk Show Hosts" by *Talkers* magazine, launched her conservative, syndicated show here at WLEE in 1993. She moved her home base in 1995 to a studio in Washington, D.C., but is still carried by WLEE. A popular call-in show on WRVA is hosted by Doug Wilder, former governor of Virginia.

Among the nationally syndicated morn-

INSIDERS' TIP

The multi-Emmy-winning newsmagazine *Virginia Currents* airs on Richmond's local PBS affiliate WCVE-TV Channel 23.

ing shows are the Charlotte, North Carolina-based, "John Boy and Billy: Big Show," on classic hits station WKLR (96.5 FM) and "The Ken Hamblin Show," weekdays on WLEE-AM.

Formats change, but this is the way they stood as this book went to press:

Adult Hits, Light Favorites
WTVR 1380 AM (big band/nostalgia)
WTVR 98.1 FM (light favorites)
WMXB 103.7 FM (modern adult contemporary)

Christian and Gospel
WGGM 820 AM (Christian country and programs, CNN news)
WGCV 1240 AM (gospel, Christian programs)
WPES 1430 AM (gospel, inspirational, USA news and sports)
WREJ 1540 AM (gospel)
WFTH 1590 AM (contemporary gospel, news)
WYFJ 100.1 FM (sacred music, AP news)
WDYL 105.7 FM (Christian music and programs, CNN news)

Country
WXGI 950 AM (country and bluegrass, NBC news and sports)
WKHK 95.3 FM (country music)

News, Talk, Sports
WRNL 910 AM (local sports, talk, Virginia News Network, Mutual News)
WVNZ 990 AM (local and national news)
WRVA 1140 AM (local and national news, talk, features, CBS)
WHCE 91.1 FM (educational news and music)

Oldies
WLEE 1320 AM ('50s and '60s)
WCLM 1450 AM (solid gold soul)
WVGO 104.7 FM ('50s, '60s and '70s)
WRCL 106.5 FM ('50s and '60s)

Public Radio
WCVE 88.9 FM (National Public Radio)

Rock — New and Classic
WKLR 96.5 FM (classic hits)
WRXL 102.1 FM (classic rock, new rock)

Urban Contemporary
WREJ 1540 AM (urban contemporary, Christian music, Virginia News Network)
WCDX 92.1 FM (urban contemporary)
WRVQ 94.5 FM (contemporary hit music)
WPLZ 99.3 FM (urban contemporary)
WSOJ 100.3 FM (adult/urban contemporary)
WSMJ 101.1 FM (new adult contemporary)
WKJS 104.7 FM (R&B)

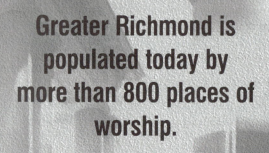

Greater Richmond is populated today by more than 800 places of worship.

Worship

Considered by many to be the single most important piece of legislation ever passed, the Virginia Statute for Religious Freedom was the first in the world to protect free expression of individual religious beliefs. Largely the work of Thomas Jefferson and James Madison, it became law on January 16, 1786, in the old Statehouse at the northeast corner of 14th and E. Cary streets. Subsequently it was the basis for the first article of the First Amendment to the Constitution, the Bill of Rights.

With this heritage, it should not be surprising then that Greater Richmond is populated today by more than 800 places of worship.

While the city's early roots were in the Anglican, Presbyterian and Baptist churches, the area today consists of a wide variety of religious traditions. The city's first Jewish congregation was organized in 1789 and was one of the first in the country. The metropolitan area is now the home of three sitting Christian bishops, five Islamic mosques, a Hindu temple and a Buddhist monastery. And the Richmond area is now seeing the establishment and growth of ethnic Christian congregations including those consisting of Vietnamese Catholics, Spanish Seventh-day Adventists, Chinese Baptists and Korean Presbyterians.

Most Richmonders of African lineage are Baptists. In the rich fabric of African-American Baptist history there probably has been no more colorful figure than the Rev. John Jasper who founded the Sixth Mount Zion Baptist Church on Duval Street. In his famous sermon, "De Sun Do Move," which is still reenacted at the church during Black History Month, he quoted verses from Genesis, Exodus and Revelation to prove the sun rotated around the earth. His theme came from Joshua's battle when Joshua asked the sun to stand still. If someone in the Bible asked the sun to stand still, it had to be moving, right? By the time he died in 1901 at age 89, Mr. Jasper had delivered the message 250 times across the South, including once before the General Assembly of Virginia.

For Christians who find themselves typically turned off by church or have grown tired of denominational politics, the Richmond area is seeing a rise in churches and missions unaffiliated with specific religious denominations. There are currently more than 50 such groups that meet anywhere from members' living rooms to various rented church spaces. The motto of these nondenominational churches seems to be "keep it simple," with an emphasis less on the trappings of "churchdom" and more on the worship of God and serving the community.

The religious scene in Richmond is so rich and varied that any attempt at a comprehensive list of options would only misrepresent the city's true opportunities. So we won't try to create any such list. It's an obvious suggestion, but the Yellow Pages under "Churches" is always a good source for at least narrowing down the search. Since finding a church is as intensely personal as finding a mate, perhaps you should employ the same approach: start by building a network of friends. See where they go. Or, of course, you could always use the old-fashioned drop-in method: see a church; drop in for a visit. Richmonders are known for their hospitality.

INSIDERS' TIP

Murals on building walls at 14th and Cary streets mark the site where Virginia's 1786 Statute of Religious Freedom was enacted. An interpretive monument and First Freedom Center on the site are planned by the Council for America's First Freedom, 643-1786.

Index of Advertisers

Index